Being and Becoming a Principal

Role Conceptions for Contemporary Principals and Assistant Principals

L. JOSEPH MATTHEWS

Brigham Young University

GARY M. CROW

The University of Utah

Boston • New York • San Francisco
Mexico City • Montreal • Toronto • London • Madrid • Munich • Paris
Hong Kong • Singapore • Tokyo • Cape Town • Sydney

Series Editor: Arnis E. Burvikovs
Series Editorial Assistant: Christine Lyons
Marketing Manager: Tara Whorf
Production Editor: Michael Granger
Editorial Production Service: Modern Graphics, Inc.
Composition Buyer: Linda Cox
Manufacturing Buyer: JoAnne Sweeney
Cover Administrator: Kristina Mose-Libon
Electronic Composition: Modern Graphics, Inc.

For related titles and support materials, visit our online catalog at www.ablongman.com.

Between the time Website information is gathered and then published, it is not unusual for some sites to have closed. Also, the transcription of URLs can result in unintended typographical errors. The publisher would appreciate notification where these errors occur so that they may be corrected in subsequent editions.

Library of Congress Cataloging-in-Publication Data

Matthews, L. Joseph, 1950-
    Being and becoming a principal : role conceptions for contemporary principals and assistant principals / L. Joseph Matthews, Gary M. Crow.
       p. cm.
    Includes bibliographical references and index.
    ISBN 0-321-08060-2
      1. School principals. 2. Educational leadership. I. Crow, Gary Monroe, 1947- II. Title.
LB2831.9.M36 2003
371.2′012—dc21

2002071063

Printed in the United States of America

10 9 8 7 6 5 4 3 2 1   07 06 05 04 03 02

Contents

10 *Becoming an Innovative Principal   259*

Preface

Changing student populations, rapidly expanding knowledge, increasing accountability requirements, and escalating expectations that schools provide more services—these are a few of the new conditions facing you as you consider entering a principalship. These demands require a different kind of principal than you may have seen. Interested?

The population of schools, especially the number of students of color, has changed and will continue to change dramatically. The explosion of knowledge and technology, together with a changing economy, demands new ways to think about learning for which many schools and faculty are unprepared. The failure of various societal institutions has placed new pressure on schools to provide a wider range of services to students. In the midst of these dramatic changes, schools and their leaders are required to demonstrate that "no child is being left behind" in terms of learning outcomes. While your predecessors may have been able to get by with 50–75% of the students learning, you will be expected to ensure that all students are learning.

Tough demands, complex decisions, and expanding duties! But these are challenging and exciting times to enter a principalship. You have the opportunity to provide profound leadership to make schools learning communities that contribute to a more equitable and quality society.

This book will help you bridge the gap from traditional notions of the principal's role to innovative conceptions that respond to these changing conditions and demands. The book describes the traditional understandings of the role and then proposes innovative conceptions that focus on change and instructional improvement. Learning is a major topic of this book—your own learning, the learning of the other professionals with whom you work, and especially the learning of all students in the school. Student learning and school reform require principals to reconceptualize their roles. Instead of the traditional textbook that focuses on the functions of the principalship, this book identifies role conceptions, that is, ways of imagining the role in order to perform it in innovative ways. We propose to re-imagine the role conceptions of the principalship to include the principal as learner, mentor, supervisor, leader, manager, politician, and advocate. These views of the principalship provide seven approaches to the changing societal demands and seven ways to focus on the learning of all students.

Because most graduate students in educational leadership courses will first become assistant principals, we focus the discussion on both principals and assistant principals.

However, we do this for another reason that is more significant. Being proactive toward learning for all students means that the principal cannot be the only source of leadership for learning. Assistant principals have a significant leadership role to play that is often ignored.

In addition to focusing on what principals and assistant principals need to be in order for schools to reform and for all students to learn, this book provides an opportunity for you to reflect on your own learning and preparation. Understanding the learning process as you enter your first principalship is a critical part of your own preparation and will help you imagine the role in new ways. Re-conceptualizing the role of principal is not something you do once, but in this changing society you will need to redefine your role constantly.

To facilitate your journey in being and becoming a principal and assistant principal, we have provided four resources within the chapters. First, most of the chapters include a vignette to focus attention on one of the seven ways of reconceptualizing the role. The vignettes vary in terms of gender and race of the principal or assistant principal, school level, and community context. The vignettes will help you to focus your attention on the specific role conception and on how that role can be performed. *Second, each chapter contains professional dilemmas that encourage you to consider the complexity of contemporary school contexts and leadership decisions.* Contemporary school leaders increasingly confront messy issues that require more than stock answers. These professional dilemmas will give you a taste of these issues and an opportunity to develop your own learning. *Third, at the end of each chapter, we provide sample activities such as self-reflective questions and activities, peer-reflective activities, and course assignments.* Being and becoming a principal may have its lonely moments, but your learning will be more significant if you include peers in your reflections and considerations. *Fourth, we provide web resources for both course and self-reflective learning.* Each chapter ends with a list of web-sites that you can access to enrich your learning. These include cases of school situations that encourage reflection, links to additional information from professional associations and other organizations that can support your work as a principal, and a variety of other resources. Finally, Websites are provided with an expanded set of resources and links to further your learning and to allow you to explore related areas.

You have taken an exciting early step in being and becoming a principal—a significant way to make a difference in student learning. We welcome you to this professional journey.

Acknowledgments

We wish to acknowledge several people who have been helpful in bringing this book to publication. We first acknowledge the contributions of our cooperative and hard working graduate assistants: Ava Nebeker, Raija Kemppainen, and especially Michael Owens. Your help in locating meaningful material and sources, editing early drafts, suggesting new ideas, and critiquing our ideas were very helpful in our writing. Michael Owens was extrememly helpful in tracking references and permissions and developing links for the Website for this book. His contributions certainly enriched the contents and usefulness of this book. We wish all of these graduate students the best as they pursue their new careers.

We also acknowledge the contribution of students in our classes who tried on the role conceptions and gave enlightening and meaningful comments.

William Greenfield, in a paper delivered at the Annual Conference of the American Educational Research Association in 1995, inspired the title for this book. We acknowledge not only our debt for the title but also for his significant contributions to understanding how principals learn their jobs.

We also acknowledge our reviewers, both inside and outside of our institutions: Cliff Mayes for his understanding of the historical and social contexts; Ellen Williams for her understanding of how all children learn; Steven Baugh for his political and leadership savvy; Katherine O'Donnell for her insightful approach to instructional supervision; Robert A. Peña, Arizona State University; Larry W. Hughes, University of Houston; Marva T. Dixon, Grand Prairie ISD and Texas Christian University; Nancy Nestor-Baker, University of Cincinnati; and Jackson Flanigan, Clemson University.

Finally, we acknowledge the support and cooperation of our families, especially for the hours this work took us away from them; for their patience with our temperamental whims; and for their inspiration in prodding us along with this work. To our wonderful wives, Sue and Judy: we love and appreciate you.

New Conceptions of the Principalship

1

Key Terms and Concepts

role conception

role conflict

role making

role taking

social justice

Introduction Most likely you have developed some idea of the role of a principal. After all, since you were a student in school, you have seen and known principals as the people in the school with power and authority, who often dished out discipline. As a teacher, you probably developed mixed perceptions of your principals that may have encompassed both respect and resentment. Perhaps you were even confused as to what your principal did all day. You may have dreaded the annual conference with your principal reviewing your evaluation. Perhaps you are a parent who has dealt with your own children's principals. You may have had to call your child's principal when a problem arose, or maybe you sat in the principal's office with your child. Perhaps you called the principal to "fix something," such as requesting a particular teacher or class for your child. You may have disagreed with some of the decisions of principals you have known. One of the authors decided to go into school administration at a time when, as a teacher, he was disappointed with a principal's decision making and decided that he should pursue school administration so that he would have a broader and more positive impact on young people's education.

Many players inside and outside of the school have different perceptions of and influences on the role. A new person coming into the principalship can be confused as to what is expected, what is needed, and what should be done. Considerable evidence indicates that the role has changed significantly over the past few decades (Beck & Murphy, 1993; Hallinger, 1992). Bredeson (1993) noted, "The traditional roles of principals and other educators in schools are changing and will continue to be reshaped, redefined and renegotiated as restructuring occurs" (p. 34). In fact, the principal's role that you have witnessed in the past may not be the one that you will eventually accept. Furthermore, much of the current debate on school reform and restructuring emphasizes that reform necessitates further reconceptualizing the principal's role (Crow, 1993; Crow, Hausman, & Scribner, 2002). The bottom line: The principalship has emerged as a vibrant and dynamic role, in many ways unique in its influence on students' education, but inherently important in establishing *social justice*—the value that focuses on helping the disadvantaged members of a community. One major example of the change is the emphasis on learning for *all* children.

When you begin your career as a principal or assistant principal, several factors will affect how you will practice the role. You bring with you experiences, knowledge, and basic assumptions that factor into your practicing the role. Other people in the school also will affect your work. Teachers will influence how you will perform the role. The district office also will outline policies and expectations. These factors all play into the role conception of the principal and assistant principal. *Role conception* is defined as the values and underlying assumptions that influence the way leadership is practiced in a school.

Sociologists describe role conception by using two perspectives, individual and social. As you begin your administrative position, either as a principal or an assistant principal, you carry with you to the position a certain amount of baggage, both good and bad. Individual baggage items include your personality, personal characteristics, experiences, education, training, and so forth. For example, your experiences as a teacher will play heavily in the way you will take on an administrative role. Were you a strict disciplinarian as a teacher? If so, chances are that enforcing the rules will be important for you as a principal. Were you actively involved in out-of-class activities? If you were, you probably will continue to have interest in those areas. Did you take on a specific teaching role such as reading specialist? Again, if you did, it could be likely that you will emphasize reading as a principal. Other personal characteristics also will factor into your being a principal. Are you a highly organized person who likes everything in its place? If so, then no doubt you will have an organized office and expect those around you to have the same. All these experiences and inclinations are part of the baggage that you bring to the principalship. Some of the baggage you may discard along the way, but you also will pick up a few other pieces to carry along with you.

From the social perspective, *role conception* has been defined as an image or a set of images of the profession held by members of the organization (Caplow, 1954; Van Mannen & Barley, 1984). In a school, these images usually are defined by teachers, students, parents, and community members and are identified as important for that person in that role. Although a concept of the principalship role exists in most people's minds, school communities and cultures define the role differently. For example, in some communities you will be strongly expected to be involved with community organizations such as Kiwanis or Rotary clubs. In some schools you will be expected to be highly involved with professional development. And in some school districts others will expect you to be a visible leader in promoting the district's goals, such as bond elections and reform efforts.

Roles are also constructed in the context in which they are performed. Principals have to act within these specific contexts. When you accept an appointment as a principal, you likely will accept a role that predates you. The role was established long before you signed the contract. Although you may come to the school with a certain role in mind, it is very likely that this role will be altered around the context that exists at the school. The process in which a principal accepts the role at a school that has been established within that context is referred to as *role taking* (Hart, 1993). Hall (1987) stated, "To function effectively in a new role, a person must develop a way of viewing himself or herself in that role—a subidentity" (p. 302).

This does not rule out entirely the principal's concept of the role. Over time and depending on the context, you can have influence as to what the role is or becomes. When as a new principal or assistant principal you apply knowledge, skills, and behaviors to the school and act in ways not previously expected of the role, then you assert a new role. This process is referred to as *role making* (Hart, 1993).

Both role taking and role making can occur when a principal comes to a new school. Seldom do principals have opportunities to create their roles without consideration of the expectations by people in other roles in the school. However, one principal can enter a school that has experienced previous problems and may have more influence on role making than another principal who comes to a successfully led school. The contexts of both the school and the individual determine how much role taking and role making take place.

Who helps define the role of the principal? A unique feature about the principalship role is that it has multiple influences, both internal and external. Internal sources of influence are teachers, students, secretaries, custodians, coaches, hall monitors, librarians, and about everyone else who works in the building. Some have been in the building for most of their careers and can have an especially strong influence on shaping the role. Most principals have encountered the statement, "This is not the way we have done things before." Such statements from those who have been around for some time help shape and influence the role and the expectations of the principal. Others, for example, new teachers, may have limited influence.

External sources of influence may include the superintendent, the school board as a whole and school board members individually, other administrators and coordinators in the district office, principals in other schools, parents of students, community members, and the media. Another unique aspect of the principalship role is its familiarity to so many. Virtually everyone has had some experience with the role of the principal either as a student or a parent. Although many external sources of influence do not fully understand the role, they definitely help shape the role. This influence can be a source of *role conflict*.

Role conflict exists if coexisting expectations conflict or if simultaneous demands cannot be met. For example, teachers may expect the principal to help with classroom instruction activities, while parents may expect the principal to be available in the office during school time. These coexisting expectations cause conflict because the principal is hard pressed to be in both places to satisfy both groups. Further, role conflict could exist within the principal if he or she wants to help teachers with instruction and also wants to be available to the parents and the public.

Understanding role conception is important in understanding the principalship. Several researchers and theorists contend that role conception plays an important part in the way individuals successfully enact their role. Researchers found that the meaning principals attach to their actions differs between those who are effective and those who are ineffective. Effective administrators have a broader vision of their actions and tasks, which includes values and beliefs that prioritize tasks, an understanding of how these actions and tasks fit into the school, and a determination of the ultimate purpose of their role—the promotion of student learning (Dwyer, Barnett, & Lee, 1987; Murphy, 2002; Scott, Ahadi, &

Krug, 1990). For example, principals can view disciplining a misbehaving student as either enforcing a punishment or educating the student as to natural consequences based on the student's actions.

In this book we emphasize broader role conceptions of principals and assistant principals rather than specific technical functions. In the past, principal preparation programs and textbooks often have emphasized learning certain functions or skills of the role. Some publications have finitely numerated these skills, such as twenty-one domains of the principalship or the top ten skills needed to be an effective principal. These functions and skills, such as decision making, communication, student management, and so on, are important aspects of the job, but they are also contingent on the context of the school culture. By emphasizing role conceptions, we hope to provide a stronger and broader link between the role and how it is practiced in the particular context of a school. In order to do this, however, we must first discuss leadership and how it applies to the principalship.

Principalship and Leadership

A major assumption in this book is that the principalship involves the leadership of learning. Such an assumption does not mean that all principal behaviors are leader behaviors or that all principals by virtue of their position are leaders. It does not mean, however, that we view the principal as a technician or bureaucrat—hired, for example, to purchase supplies and complete reports. Instead, we view the principal as a critical player in the attempt to give direction and focus to the school to bring about student learning.

The Definition of Leadership

The term *leadership* literally has hundreds of definitions. Although commonalties exist, there is not a universally accepted definition. In fact, there are several controversies around various definitions. For example, definitions of leadership in the military usually are quite different from those in religious organizations. Before we discuss a definition for educational leadership, we need to explore some of the misconceptions that presently exist and how these misconceptions affect the principal's role.

The first misconception is that leadership is *management*. We are not suggesting that management is less important or is less desirable than leadership; in fact, in Chapter 7 we discuss the vital importance of management. What we suggest is that leadership and management have common elements but are also quite different. Although management is very necessary, leaders do more than just manage. They help establish a shared vision and influence a school's culture to focus on learning for *all* students. Leaders probably will use management activities to influence others, such as scheduling the preparation period of a middle school team of teachers at the same time so that they can meet and plan together. Although scheduling is a management activity, it has leadership implications. Clearly, good leadership requires good management, yet management can exist without evidence of any real leadership. For example, if the principal schedules faculty meetings without any vision or goal in mind, then the activity is only a management task and involves no leadership. On the other hand, if the faculty meetings are organized around the vision of developing a learning environment for all students, then leadership is more apparent.

On occasion, policymakers, such as school board members and state legislators, expect more management activities from a principal or assistant principal than leadership activities. For instance, some districts have outlined discipline codes with zero-tolerance policies for certain misbehaviors. A zero-tolerance policy not only outlines the infraction but also will state the punishment or consequence of a violation that is applied in every case. Often such policies inhibit the leadership of the principal and the assistant principal by limiting judgment, which in turn limits the leadership capacity in the school.

A second common misconception held by many people is that leadership resides only in a particular person or position. Perhaps this conception began with the reign of kings and queens passing on the crown to their sons and daughters. When the prince or princess received the crown, he or she became the leader. However, holding such a position only gives authority and power but not necessarily leadership. Leadership consists of far more than the activities of one person or position, and it exists among many people in the organization. A formal position does not necessitate that leadership exist in any greater degree than it does with any other subordinate position. For example, leadership in a school is more likely to change and adapt because of the interrelationships among the administrators, faculty, and staff than because of the inspiration of one individual.

A third misconception about leadership is that it comes naturally and is something that a person has rather than develops. Many people believe that leadership is not learned. This misconception is associated with the so-called great man theory—certain individuals have qualities and traits that will produce good leaders. People who adhere to this misconception look at the qualities and traits of leaders such as Winston Churchill, Mahatma Gandhi, Mother Teresa, or Martin Luther King, Jr. and try to emulate their traits so that they too can be great leaders. Seldom do they recognize that these individuals became great leaders through their experiences. They did not just arrive at a leadership position as effective leaders. Likewise, this misconception implies that great leaders can survive and thrive under any environment. For example, this belief would hold that Winston Churchill would have been a great leader even if Great Britain were not involved in World War II. History, however, indicates that Churchill struggled as Prime Minister when the war was over. Churchill lost his office shortly after World War II ended. Leaders succeed in some environments but are unsuccessful in others. Perhaps you are aware of a principal or superintendent who was effective and popular in one setting and then moved to another setting and experienced difficulty.

Another slant on this misconception occurs when a new principal tries to emulate another principal's traits. A beginning principal may think that successful leadership traits can be imitated. Emulating another principal's traits, however, is seldom effective because of environmental factors, such as faculty, community, and district goals. This is especially true in emulating a noneducational leader. Leaders in corporate and military organizations usually are involved in different environments than school environments, and therefore, the leadership strategies may not be emulated effectively.

With these misconceptions in mind, we extend a definition of leadership that supersedes these misunderstandings and attempts to focus on essential elements of the leadership process. Rost (1991), after studying various definitions of leadership, finally created his own definition: "Leadership is an influence relationship among leaders and followers who intend real changes that reflect their shared purposes." (p. 102) We emphasize four key elements within Rost's definition:

1. Leadership involves influence.
2. It occurs among leaders and followers.
3. These people intend significant changes.
4. These changes reflect shared purposes toward creating a learning environment for *all* students.

Influence designates a relationship among people that is not passive or coercive. Western culture often has depicted leadership as something that someone does to someone else. However, in an influence relationship, leadership is reciprocal; that is, principals influence teachers, and teachers influence principals. Those participating in a leadership relationship use a variety of power resources to influence others. These power resources could include rewards, coercion, prestige, position, authority, and many others. We discuss these power resources and the implications that they have on the relationships among participants in Chapter 8.

According to Rost (1991), the people involved in leadership want significant changes. Leadership involves creating change, not necessarily maintaining the status quo, unless a good reason exists to do so. The changes are enduring and essential and improve key elements of the purpose of the school, including democratic schooling, school improvement, and social justice (Murphy, 2002). In addition, leaders do not dictate the changes, but the changes reflect purposes shared by both leaders and followers. Daft (1999) suggested that these changes are working toward an outcome that leaders and followers want, a desired future or shared purpose that motivates them toward this more preferable outcome. "Thus leadership involves the influence of people to bring about change toward a desirable future" (p. 5). Rost (1991) used the term *intend real change* (p. 113), suggesting that people are actively involved in the pursuit of change toward a desired future. Each individual takes a personal responsibility to achieve the intended change. In schools, leadership should not focus on any change but rather on change that is learner-centered.

Rost (1991) also suggested that leadership inherently involves followers. "Followers can become leaders and leaders can become followers in any one leadership relationship" (p. 109). Followers may be leaders for a while, especially when they have a certain expertise that is needed by the group. For instance, a principal may need the assistance of a teacher to help a newcomer implement cooperative learning. However, Rost pointed out that followers do not do followership; they do leadership. Both leaders and followers form one relationship that is leadership. They are in the leadership relationship together.

Followership is an area that has received some recent attention, but traditional leadership studies only skirted the area. Some evidence exists (see Kelley, 1988) that the qualities needed to be an effective leader are the same as those needed to be an effective follower. Kelley defined *effective* followers as having the social capacity to work well with others, the character to flourish without heroic status, the moral and psychological balance to pursue personal and corporate goals at no cost to either, and the desire to participate in a team effort for the accomplishment of some greater common purpose. Kelley (1992) identified three categories of skills and characteristics possessed by exemplary followers in formal organizations, which suggest that followers' have active roles. First, these followers prove their value to the organization. They accomplish this by how they perform their jobs, by being focused and committed to organizational goals, and by taking initiative to increase their value to the organization. Second, followers weave a web of relationships in the organization by working with teams, networks, and leaders. These relationships intensify their value to the organization and their work effectiveness. Third, exemplary followers exhibit a courageous conscience. They are willing and able to disagree with directions others have chosen if they feel that they are inappropriate. Exemplary followers actively attempt to persuade others at times to change course or direction.

Rost's (1991) definition suggests the need to conceive of leadership as the direct influence that an individual has on others and the facilitating of others' influence. In this book we discuss the role conceptions of the principalship in terms of these two types of leadership: direct and facilitative. Principals have both types of roles to play in contemporary schools. It is no longer sufficient to emphasize the direct influence that principals have. It is critical to understand that principals facilitate others' leadership, that is, they are leaders of leaders (Schlechty, 1990).

Learning about Leadership

Learning how to be an effective leader in an organization involves a complex set of factors. Many people and organizations have marketed a variety of materials on becoming a successful leader. Bookstores have a number of publications proclaiming how to be an effective leader. Leadership seminars, centers, consultants, and programs are available everywhere. If you want to learn the "how to" of leadership, you do not have to go far. The problem arises as to how you are going to determine the type of training that is effective and appropriate for public-sector organizations such as schools. If we adhere to Rost's (1991) definition of leadership, we must recognize that learning about leadership is quite complex and will involve most of our careers. In fact, most principals who are near the end of their careers will tell you that what they once thought important in leadership turned out to be less important.

Daft (1999) organized four stages of acquiring leadership competence (Figure 1.1). Most people start in the first stage, unconscious incompetence. In this stage, individuals do not have any competence in leadership, and they are unaware that they lack competence, probably because they have never tried to be a leader. They discover their incompetence and find that they need help to move ahead. By reading, observing, listening, and studying, they become conscious of what is required, moving into the second stage. In this stage, individuals become conscious of what they are required to do but are still personally incompetent. Daft likens this to swinging a golf club for the first time. You are trying

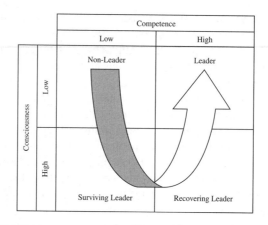

FIGURE 1.1   Stages of Leadership Competence.

Source: Adapted from Daft, R. L. (1999). *Leadership Theory and Practice.* Fort Worth, TX: Dryden Press.

to keep ten things in your mind as you attempt to hit the ball straight down the fairway—and as most golfers know, this seldom happens in the beginning.

   In the third stage, the individual's conscious awareness of the correct things to do gradually transforms into leadership competence. The person learns to visualize a desired future, influence others to engage in that future, and has the courage to take on real change for student learning. This is the stage when individuals receive positive feedback so that they are aware of how well they are doing. This competence sets up the transition into the fourth stage, where the leadership skills and behaviors become a part of the individual. These skills and behaviors occur naturally, and as Daft (1999) indicated, "You no longer have to consciously think about creating a vision; it emerges intuitively" (p. 24).

Principal Leadership in Practice

Principals do not develop their conceptions of leadership in a vacuum. The general society, other principals, the schools in which they work, and their own experiences influence the ways principals and assistant principals understand and develop their roles as leaders.

   Society in particular plays an important role. We see leaders everywhere. We watch C-SPAN and see our political leaders debating and speaking on issues. We go to the movies and see a "take charge" general leading his troops into battle. We listen to our chief executive officer (CEO) neighbor talk about the trends in her business. It is easy to see parallels between leaders in society and the types of leaders we think are needed in our schools. Consequently, many people believe that leaders in other organizations in our society have answers to leadership problems in our schools.

   We certainly can learn about leadership in, for example, the corporate world, but is it the type of leadership that we want to use in schools? Will it be an influence relationship among leaders and followers who intend real change (Rost, 1991)? The answer seems to be both yes and no. There is no doubt that school principals can learn leadership from other elements in society, but we have to be cautious and realize that schools are a quite different type of organization requiring a different kind of leadership—leadership for learning.

Principals also learn about leadership from other principals. You have spent countless hours observing other principals since you began kindergarten many years ago. You continued your observation as a student, then as a teacher, and perhaps as a parent. You will begin your career as a school administrator with a significant number and variety of leadership images. It is certainly a much longer exposure period than exists for most other professions. Thus it is not surprising that Greenfield (1977) found that veteran principals were the most significant influence on the socialization of new principals. This can be good and bad. For instance, veteran principals may contribute to the filtering process of what a newcomer will learn as a leader. The veteran may filter out more innovative and even radical images of what a principal should be in a modern setting, an area we discuss in Chapter 10. However, veteran principals also add wisdom. They have experiences that transcend generational gaps.

The school in which a principal and an assistant principal work also influences the kinds of leadership that can be learned and practiced. In the past when principals entered a new school, it was believed that they brought with them a toolbox of leadership traits and behaviors that could be applied to the new setting. However, considerable research (see Hart, 1993) suggested otherwise. Schools and the people in them act as socializing agents for both newcomers and veteran principals. Teachers, parents, and students express and reward the types of leadership qualities and images that fit the context and are acceptable.

Our specific view of leadership can be described in terms of two sources of leadership: person and system. If we think of the source of leadership as a person, we usually (but not always) think in terms of an individual in a position of authority. Individuals use various resources, such as rewards, punishments, expertise, tradition, and charisma, to achieve the goals of the organization. Others, who we call *followers*, look to and rely on this individual for guidance, direction, and interpretation. This view of leadership is the most common notion of the source of leadership found in both research and the practical literature. By far the largest attention to the principal's role uses this view of the principal as the school's leader responsible for developing a vision and persuading others to buy that vision.

Another way to think of the source of leadership is systemic (Ogawa & Bossert, 1995). In this view, leadership is the network of individuals and groups within an organization. These networks also use various resources, such as expertise, rewards, and punishments. Instead of leadership flowing from one individual, the leader, it flows within the organization from various sources. This view of the source of leadership has been used only recently in discussing the principal's role. In this view, the principal is one among many individuals who are involved in the leadership process. The network of relationships among principals, teachers, students, staff, parents, community members, district supervisors, and governmental entities is the source of vision, inspiration, direction, and persuasion.

Both these sources of leadership use various processes to achieve goals. To illustrate this point, we provide examples of a few processes and mechanisms that will be elaborated in the rest of the book. By far the most common process is leadership as social influence. Leadership is an influence relationship among leaders and followers in which a limited number of group members control and direct the group's activities. In more effective leadership, influence involves the persuasion, rather than coercion, of followers to follow the leaders' direction, vision, and so on. The direction, however, should be seen as mutually beneficial to both leaders and followers (Burns, 1978). In the principal literature, behaviors involving influence have received the most attention. Principals as leaders are viewed as performing various types of behaviors aimed at influencing others to agree with their view of the strategies for reaching goals. These behaviors have been described as anything from throwing their weight around to providing incentives for followers to try the innovations envisioned by the leader.

Another example of leadership processes involves such leadership behaviors as coaching, monitoring, problem solving, reflecting, and adapting. These leadership behaviors mediate between group actions and the group's performance (Fisher, 1986; Weick, 1978). The process of leadership in this view is one of sense making. "Leadership is a form of mediation that aids groups in constructing a collective structure which facilitates achieving goals and removing obstacles from their goal paths" (Barge, 1989). As groups encounter the external demands of their environments, they need leadership to help them make sense of these demands and of their responses to them. This sense making, or mediating, does not necessarily precede taking action. Groups frequently take action and then make sense of their actions. Leadership helps groups form a picture of their environments and of their responses. This view of the process of leadership has received little attention in the general literature or principal literature, but it has strengths for conceiving the principal's leadership role in a more innovative way. For example, principals spend a great deal of time on the job talking (Gronn, 1983). This talk sometimes is used to persuade others to follow some plan. More frequently, however, the talk is to help others understand external constraints, to help newcomers understand the rationale for certain school processes, to reflect on a problem and the organization's response to it, and to serve a variety of other purposes. Thus, rather than only to influence or persuade others, leadership in schools helps faculty, students, parents, and the community make sense of what happens in the school.

School administrators frequently experience this distinction in leadership processes in the seemingly contradictory advice to be decisive and adaptable. Principals and assistant principals have to be decisive; that is, they have to know what needs to be done and persuade people to follow their lead. Emergency situations, responses to governmental mandates, and decisive leadership in rapidly responding to student needs frequently are given as reasons for the need for administrators to use influence. These same administrators, however, are also required to have "a pulse on the school," to anticipate problems, and to interpret the school organization for others. Such demands require that the school administrator be adaptable to constantly changing conditions, such as demographics and social needs, and the complexity of schools.

To exclusively define school leadership as being decisive runs the risk of the administrator oversimplifying problems, organizational constraints, and responses. As we will discuss in Chapter 3, in schools in postindustrial society, such an oversimplification is dysfunctional, if not dangerous. Schools are highly complex organizations that are changing rapidly. Being decisive is only one requirement of contemporary school administration. Being adaptable is equally—if not more—important for today's school leaders.

Seven Role Conceptions

In discussing the principalship as an evolving role and as a leadership role for improving instruction, we will organize our discussion in terms of seven role conceptions that we believe most clearly and comprehensively define the roles of assistant principal and principal. We organize these roles around a model that illustrates the relationships of the roles to each other.

Principal as Learner

As Figure 1.2 indicates, fundamental to the conceptions of the principal's role that we identify and discuss in this book is the centrality of learning. The principal as learner is necessary and pivotal for an innovative understanding of the role. As we discuss in Chapter 3, as a leader in a school organization, you should hold learning as central because schools are above all else learning organizations. As Barth (1990) suggested, principals should be neither head managers nor head teachers but rather head learners in the school. Within the current context of administering schools in a period of community and media scrutiny, student achievement, and school improvement, you must be a constant and rigorous learner using various capacities and methods. The principal as learner involves being connected to the wider community of education, schooling, and leadership. The

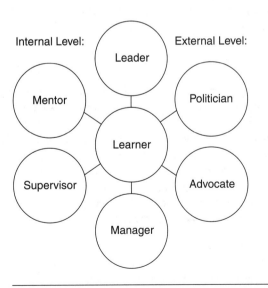

FIGURE 1.2   Principalship Role Conceptions

school leader needs to seek and create knowledge. This conception of learner provides the skills and dispositions to both influence school constituents and interpret the rapidly changing and complex school context for constituents. The principal as learner involves self-awareness, reflectivity, inquiry, and complexity that are essential for school leadership.

Principals not only must engage themselves in lifelong quests after knowledge but also need to model and instill this behavior in others. Principals and assistant principals play an important role in facilitating opportunities for the continued growth of faculty and staff through individual and professional development. Reform movements involving empowering teachers and developing teacher leadership encourage a systemic view of leadership in which administrators have an important role.

Principal as Leader

Leadership is intimately tied to learning in an innovative conception of the principal's role. Principals are not only learners themselves; they are also leaders of learning. This role necessitates examining the learning environment and influencing reform that brings about school improvement in learning. Leadership is also the vehicle for creating change and reform in schools. Principals and assistant principals create, maintain, and change a school culture; build a shared school vision; solve problems, make decisions, and interpret school decisions; and develop collaborative and teaming strategies.

In this book we conceive of learning and leading not just as several important activities in the school but as foundational to all other activities. What occurs both inside and outside the school must reflect the concern with teaching and learning. The other five conceptions flow from leadership and learning. These conceptions focus on both internal and external features of the school. Schools are not isolated institutions but organizations that are, of necessity, open to their larger environments. Principals are boundary spanners who negotiate both internal and external audiences and demands.

Principal as Mentor

On the internal side, principals are primarily responsible for the learning environment within the school. The two conceptions of principals as mentors and supervisors emphasize the internal responsibility that is focused on learning. As a mentor, the principal takes a central role in helping individuals, namely, teachers and students, to learn. The role of mentor is closely associated with the role of teacher and coach. The traditional concept of the principal separates the role of principal and the role of teacher. However, the newly conceptualized role renews an understanding that historically placed the role as a principal teacher. In addition, an important role is to instill the concept of mentoring in others, especially teachers as they mentor students and fellow teachers.

Principal as Supervisor

Inherent in the role of principal has been the task of supervision. The traditional conceptualization of this role often has placed the principal and assistant principal as middle managers. Teachers often perceive their administrators as evaluators of their teaching performance by coming into their classroom to observe two or three times a year, completing a personnel evaluation report, and forwarding it to the superintendent and school board. The newly conceptualized role requires more of the principal than this. Principals are expected to become instructional leaders who plan, develop, supervise, and assess instructional capacity and curriculum programs. These tasks involve both influencing faculty to improve their instruction and helping them make sense of external demands on school improvement and internal school cultures that encourage the improvement of instruction. The principal also empowers teachers and assistant principals to be instructional leaders. In this way, principals expand the instructional leadership systemically.

Principal as Manager

Traditional roles of principals emphasized the role of scientific management and often excluded the role of leadership. In contrast to these earlier conceptions of the principal's role, our framework views management as serving leadership and learning conceptions. Principals play an important managerial role in school reform especially as they deal with finance, facilities, programs, and activities. In many of these areas, the principal helps faculty and staff understand the connections among programs, activities, buildings, finances, and so on. The principal also enables others to manage efficiently. In a context of school reform, such as shared decision making and site-based management, the development of systems thinking and the acquisition of various managerial skills are critical for teacher leaders and other administrators. Management decisions of innovative principals focus on how to enable internal and external school constituents to contribute to a learning organization where all students and adults learn.

Principal as Politician

On the external side, as Figure 1.2 illustrates, principals span the external boundary by being politicians and advocates. In both cases, learning is fundamental, and leadership is critical. For many decades, school leadership and politics were artificially separated. However, politics is a necessary concept of the new role of the principal. Helping external constituents understand the school's mission and helping internal school constituents understand the external demands are important. Equally important to the role of principal as politician is the role that the principal plays as a facilitator and mediator of others to be politically astute through their involvement in parental and community arenas. Building community, mediating conflict, and fostering meaningful collaboration are important political roles of the principal that lead to improving student learning.

Principal as Advocate

Learning also involves advocacy. School populations have become increasingly heterogeneous, and learning must involve all students. Driven by social justice, access to knowledge, statutory regulations, and legal decisions, the school community has had to adapt to the diversity of ethnicity, disabilities, language acquisition, and gender and socio-economic issues. Some of these issues have lead to the creation of new programs to serve special populations. Likewise, some issues have caused increased tensions and stresses on teachers, students, and parents. The principal needs to serve as advocate for all children by helping other educators perform their roles equitably and by promoting social justice and access to education for all children.

Conclusion

As you read this book and engage in conversations with your professors and colleagues, reflect on how your own conception of the principalship is evolving. Your awareness of your own growth and development is important to becoming an innovative principal and assistant principal. Your learning is also fundamental in helping to make contemporary schools inviting and stimulating learning environments for both students and adults.

Activities

Self-Reflection Activities

1. Reflect on your own image of the principalship. What is the content of that image, and what sources influence that image?
2. Peruse the titles of leadership books in your local bookstore. What different conceptions of leadership did you find?

Peer Reflection Activities

1. Discuss with a colleague the principals you have both known. How did each principal balance leadership and management?
2. View the movies *Patton* and *Norma Rae*. Compare and contrast the conceptions of leadership found in these two movies.

Course Activities

1. Invite a second- or third-year principal and a veteran principal (someone who has had several principalships) to class. Interview the principals regarding changes they made when they first entered their current schools. Afterwards, discuss the degree of role taking and role making in each principal's experience.
2. Have class members ask their principal the following question: The principalship is like _____ ? Analyze the types of metaphors and what they suggest about different role conceptions.

Websites

- *http://www.nsdc.org/leadership.html*
  New NSDC Report Outlines National Strategy for Principals to Bolster Skills, "Report Calls Principals Crucial to School Improvement, Recommends Targeting Federal Funds to Strengthen Principal Leadership in Low-Income Schools."

- *http://www.ascd.org/readingroom/edupdate/2000/1may00.html*
  The Contemporary Principal: New Skills for a New Age, "Schools across the United States are on the lookout for strong leaders. This would be good news, except for one problem: There may not be enough strong leaders to go around."

- *http://www.edweek.org/sreports/special_reports_article.cfm?slug=leaders.htm*
  Leadership in Education, "Study after study shows that a crucial factor in determining whether schools—and school districts—succeed or fail is the quality and stability of their leadership,"

- *http://www.oise.utoronto.ca/~vsvede*
  School Leadership: A Profile Document. This site allows you to compare your present leadership practice with the ideal practice toward which you strive.

References

Barge, K. (1989). Leadership as medium: A leaderless group discussion model. *Communication Quarterly, 37*, 237–247.

Barth, R. S. (1990). *Improving Schools from Within: Teachers, Parents, and Principals Can Make a Difference.* San Franciso, CA: Jossey-Bass.

Beck, L. G. & Murphy, J. (1993). *Understanding the principalship: Metaphorical Themes, 1920s–1990s.* New York: Teachers College Press.

Bredeson, P. V. (1993). Letting go of outlived professional identities: A study of role transition and role strain for principals in restructured schools. *Educational Administration Quarterly, 29*(1), 34–68.

Burns, J. M. (1978). *Leadership.* New York: Harper and Row.

Caplow, T. (1954). *The sociology of work. New York: McGraw-Hill.*

Crow, G. M. (1993). Reconceptualizing the school administrator's role: Socialization at mid-career. *School Effectiveness and School Improvement, 4*(2), 131–152.

Crow, G. M., Hausman, C. S., & Scribner, J. P. (2002). Reshaping the role of the school principal. In J. Murphy (ed.), *The Leadership Challenge: Redefining Leadership for the 21st Century* (pp. 189–210). Chicago: National Society for the Study of Education.

Daft, R. L. (1999). *Leadership Theory and Practice.* Fort Worth, TX: Dryden Press.

Dwyer, D., Barnett, B., & Lee, G. (1987). The school principal: Scapegoat or the last great hope? In L. Sheive, and M. Schoenheit (Eds.). *Leadership: Examining the Elusive.* (pp. 30–46). Alexandria, VA: Association and Supervision and Curriculum Development.

Fisher, B. A. (1986). Leadership: When does the difference make a difference? In R. Hirokawa & M. Poole (Eds.). *Communication and group decision making* (pp. 197–215). Beverly Hills, CA: Sage.

Greenfield, W. D. (1977). Administrative candidacy: A process of new role learning, Part 1. *Journal of Educational Administration Quarterly 19*(2), 5–26.

Gronn, P. (1983). Talk as work: The accomplishment of school administration. *Administrative Science Quarterly 28*(1), 1–21.

Hall, D. T. (1987). Careers and socialization. *Journal of Management, 13*(2), 302–321.

Hallinger, P. (1992). The evolving role of American principals: From managerial to instructional to transformational leaders. *Journal of Educational Administration, 30*(3), 35–48.

Hart, A. W. (1993). *Principal Succession: Establishing Leadership in Schools.* Albany: State University of New York.

Kelley, R. E. (1988). In praise of followers. *Harvard Business Review* (November–December), 142–148.

Kelley, R. E. (1992). *The Power of Followership: How to Create Leaders People Want to Follow and Followers Who Lead Themselves.* New York: Doubleday.

Murphy, J. (2002). Reculturing the profession of educational leadership: New blueprints. In J. Murphy (Ed.), *The Leadership Challenge: Redefining Leadership for the 21st Century* (pp. 65–82). Chicago: National Society for the Study of Education.

Ogawa, R. T., & Bossert, S. T. (1995). Leadership as an organizational quality. *Educational Administration Quarterly, 31*(2), 224–243.

Rost, J. C. (1991). *Leadership in the Twenty-First Century.* New York: Praeger.

Schlechty, P. C. (1990). *Schools for the Twenty-First Century: Leadership Imperatives for Educational Reform.* San Francisco: Jossey-Bass.

Scott, C., Ahadi, S., & Krug, S. (1990). *An Experience-Sampling Approach to the Study of Principal Instructional Leadership II: A Comparison of Activities and Beliefs as Bases for Understanding Effective School Leadership.* Urbana-Champaign, IL: National Center for School Leadership, University of Illinois, College of Education.

Van Mannen, J. & Barley, S. (1984). Occupational communities: culture and control in organizations. In B. Staw and L. Cummings (Eds.). *Research in organizational behavior,* Vol. 6. (pp. 287–365). Greenwich, CT: JAI Press.

Weick, K. (1978). The spines of leaders. In M. McCall and M. Lombardo (Eds.). *Leadership, Where Else Can We Go?* (pp. 37–61). Durham, NC: Duke University Press.

Historical View of the Principal's Role

2

Key Terms and Concepts

AASA
ASCD
common school movement
ethical leadership
headmaster

in loco parentis
instructional leadership
moral leadership
NAESP
NASSP

normal schools
principal teacher
scientific management
theory movement

Introduction As a new principal, you will assume a historically important education role. This imprint of professional history is a powerful influence on your role, responsibilities, and practice as a principal or assistant principal. In this chapter we describe the various historical conceptions of the principal and assistant principal roles. This discussion is designed to demonstrate how administrators are in part influenced by the previous emphases of the role and how society has influenced the values and assumptions of the role. We identify and discuss contemporary demands, expectations, and challenges that influence how the roles of the principal and assistant principal are viewed.

American schools during the seventeenth and eighteenth centuries were mostly private or church institutions. Around 1800, the demand for public education in America began to grow. Thomas Jefferson was among the first to propose a system of free public elementary schools. Jefferson's theory of education grew out of his political ideals: "If a nation expects to be ignorant and free in a state of civilization, it expects what never was and never will be." Establishing and maintaining a system of public instruction at the state's expense was not the popular and accepted belief that it is today. Jefferson's proposal encountered the opposition of wealthy taxpayers who protested at being taxed to educate other people's children. Consequently, Jefferson's proposal was never adopted, but the seeds were sown. A few decades later, largely as a result of the work of Horace Mann in Massachusetts and Henry Barnard in Connecticut, the public school movement in America was launched, usually referred to as the *common school movement*. The common school movement became one of the most significant social crusades in American history.

Tyack and Hansot (1982) suggested that it takes some effort of historical imagination to reconstruct the context within which Americans of the mid-nineteenth century embarked on the ambitious and successful social movement to create a common school system:

> It is easy to forget that mid-nineteenth century America was four-fifths rural, had a minuscule government, possessed only a rudimentary industrial system composed mostly of small firms, and had only begun the bureaucratization that would later make a mature corporate society. . . . Yet this social movement produced by the end of the century more schooling for more people than in any other nation and resulted in patterns of education that were remarkably uniform in purpose, structure, and curriculum, despite the reality of local control in hundreds of thousands of separate communities (p. 17).

Origin of the Principalship

It has been said that the principalship was conceived in a halo of chalk dust. The precise origins of the principalship are not clearly recorded. We do know that the word *principal* appeared in Horace Mann's (1842) report to the Massachusetts School Board in 1841. We also know from such early writers as Pierce (1935) and Cubberley (1916) and more recent writers such as Campbell, Fleming, Newell, and Bennion (1987) and Beck and Murphy (1993) that the role of the principal emerged from the teaching ranks and that it was connected with teaching for several decades before it became a separate role. Campbell and colleagues reported that the administration of schools was hardly differentiated from teaching. Teachers in one-room schools throughout America simply performed the necessary administrative, clerical, and janitorial tasks associated with schooling. As schools grew, however, the complexity of these tasks increased, requiring a single person to assume responsibility for them. The person designated as the *principal teacher* continued to function in the classroom but also served as the head of the school (Pierce, 1935).

The Common School Teachers' Association addressed an inquiry to the Board of Education in Cincinnati in 1839 to determine the relative duties of principal teachers. The committee outlined what it deemed the chief responsibilities of the principal teacher, namely:

1. To function as the head of the school charged to his care
2. To regulate the classes and course of instruction of all the pupils, whether they occupied his room or the rooms of other teachers
3. To discover any defects in the school and apply remedies
4. To make defects known to the visitor or trustee of ward or district if he were unable to remedy conditions
5. To give necessary instruction to his assistants
6. To classify pupils
7. To safeguard school houses and furniture
8. To keep the school clean
9. To refrain from impairing the standing of assistants, especially in the eyes of their pupils
10. To require the cooperation of his assistants (Pierce, 1935).

When exactly the word *principal* changed from being an adjective to a noun is not clearly known. Pierce (1935) reported that the modern public school principalship had its beginnings in America's early high schools. These high schools were patterned after the private academies of the late eighteenth and early nineteenth centuries, which were designed after English and other western European schools. Some of the earliest descriptions of the work of school administrators can be found in the writing of the German Johann Sturm (1507–1589). In 1537, the magistrates of Strasburg, Germany, needed a rector to organize a local gymnasium, a secondary school for boys. They hired Johann Sturm, a classically trained renaissance scholar, to organize a curriculum, develop teaching methods, and hire and supervise teachers for approximately 600 male secondary school students. With this specific charge in mind, in 1538 Sturm published *The Best Mode for Opening Institutions of Learning.* In this particular work and in numerous other books, essays, and treatises published over the next forty-five years, we find such modern problems discussed as principles of education, school organization, educational values, teachers' salaries, relation of parent and school, entrance requirements, discipline and conduct of pupils, how to bring education within the reach of poor boys, class instruction against individual instruction, responsibility of the teacher, and the like (Ensign, 1923).

Johann Sturm was unique, however, and many of his ideas for organizing schools and the curriculum were not adopted to any significant degree across Europe until several centuries later.

In the English public schools we also find antecedents of the modern-day principalship. By the eighteenth century, the term *headmaster* was in common use, and the roles and responsibilities for these headmasters were focused primarily on discipline and supervision of student life of boys attending school away from home (Ensign, 1923). Hart and Bredeson (1996) speculated that this early role responsibility provides at least a partial explanation for the importance of discipline in the evolving role of principals codified in the legal principle of in *loco parentis,* which means "in place of the parent."

The early American school principal had responsibilities very similar to those of the headmaster of the English academies. He (the principal was invariably male) had a small number of teachers to supervise and only simple administrative duties to perform. A large share of his time was spent in teaching.

Origin of the Assistant Principal Role

The history of the assistant principal is also quite vague. Glanz (1994) suggested that the role might have emerged from two teacher supervisory roles. During the 1920s in larger school settings, the principal selected a special supervisor from among the teaching faculty to help less experienced teachers in subject matter mastery. Some of the larger schools, for example, had special supervisors in each of the major subject areas. Because this role came from the ranks of teachers, the special supervisor was most often female. These special supervisors had little independent authority and did not serve in an evaluative capacity. Another role emerged that Glanz referred to as a *general supervisor.* Male teachers more often filled this role to assist the principal in logistical operations of the school. Glanz believed that the general supervisor became the primary assistant to the principal. Because of the amount of authority given to the general supervisor, the special supervisor role disappeared in most schools in the 1930s. By the 1940s and 1950s, the literature more accurately reflected the relationship between the principal and the general supervisor by using the title *assistant principal.*

Kelly (1987) suggested that the assistant principal's role was developed originally to aid principals in meeting the increasing demands of the job. The role was not intended to change the structure of the principal's job but was meant to give the principal more time for instructional leadership by sharing the load. The assistant principal's part of the load was attending to administrative and management details—those activities that were essential but could be carried out by someone other than the principal.

In the 1970s, the literature began reflecting the assistant principal role as being a significant position in educational administration. The literature since the 1970s has used such metaphors describing the assistant principal as "subordinate to the principal," "parallel with the principal," "henchman," and "specialist." The more recent literature suggests an expanded and significant instructional role for principals, one that we acknowledge in this book (Hartzell, Williams, & Nelson, 1995). For our purposes here, we describe the assistant principal's role as a mirror image of the principal's role in that both usually function in a parallel fashion.

Women and Minorities in the Principalship

It is obvious to any observer that women and minorities are underrepresented in school administration and have been for most of history (Shakeshaft, 1999). Although both groups have occupied the classroom, few women and minorities have occupied the principal's office as compared with white males. Ortiz and Marshall (1988) reported that "women, especially minority women, but even minority men, continue to occupy the lowest positions in the administrative hierarchy, white males the higher and the more powerful positions" (p. 127). The National Center for Education Statistics (NCES) periodically studies the demographics of school principals in public and private schools. The results of the 1988-1989, 1990-1991, and 1993-1994 studies are given in Tables 2.1 and 2.2. Although the percentages of female and most minority principals have increased since 1988, the growth has

TABLE 2.1   Percentage of Public School Principals by Sex within School Level: 1987–1991, and 1993–1994

	Overall		Elementary		Secondary	
	Male	*Female*	*Male*	*Female*	*Male*	*Female*
1987–1988	75.4	24.5	69.9	30.1	90.6	9.4
1990–1991	70.0	30.0	63.5	36.5	89.0	11.0
1993–1994	65.4	34.5	58.9	41.1	86.2	13.8

Source: National Center for Education Statistics (1992, 1994, 1998).

TABLE 2.2   Percentage of Minorities as Principals in Public Schools: 1988–1989, 1990–1991, and 1993–1994

	White	*Black*	*Hispanic*	*Asian or Pacific Islander*	*American Indian or Alaskan Native*
1987–1988	88.6	8.6	3.19	0.557	1.050
1990–1991	85.9	8.6	3.93	0.671	0.887
1993–1994	84.2	10.1	4.11	0.779	0.792

Source: National Center for Education Statistics (1992, 1994, 1998).

been small. To understand the phenomenon behind the under-representation of women and minorities in educational administration, we look again at history.

An early woman pioneer in school leadership was Ella Flagg Young. A principal of two elementary schools in Chicago, she became superintendent of Chicago schools and later was elected as the first female president of the National Education Association (NEA). In 1909, she confidently predicted that women were destined to rule the schools in every city. Her comments reflected movements during the early part of the twentieth century that had been gaining momentum among women teachers in New York, Chicago, and other major cities. The women were protesting the domination of top administration and professional associations by males and the higher pay for male teachers. These early movements by women did account for some gains in the first decades of the twentieth century, but as schools became even larger and more bureaucratic, women "lost even their tenuous toehold on good jobs" in education (Tyack & Hansot, 1982, p. 181).

Kalvelage (1978) researched the early gains of women in educational administration and the subsequent demographic changes that occurred in midcentury. She reported that in 1928, 55 percent of elementary school principals were women (the highest year ever recorded). However, by the 1970s, the number of women as elementary school principals had declined drastically to about 20 percent. During the 1980s and 1990s, women slowly regained some principalship positions. By 1994, women comprised 41 percent of elementary school principalships but only 13.8 percent of secondary school principalships (National Center for Education Statistics, 1998).

What caused the decline of female elementary principals in mid-twentieth century? Kalvelage (1978) offered several suggestions. First, she proposed that since the early elementary principalship was both a teaching and an administrative position (principal teacher), females related to that role more than to the nonteaching principal role that became more prominent as the schools increased in size. Second, she suggested that as male-dominated school boards gained more authority, a more corporate model for schools prevailed, limiting the role of women in leadership positions—similar to the corporate world. Third, Kalvelage proposed that as the role became more specialized and university training became more of a requirement, the transition from being a teacher to being an administrator became more difficult for women because a university education was more

Ella Flagg Young

Born in Buffalo, New York, but reaching fame in Chicago, Ella Flagg Young was one of America's earliest female principals, Chicago's first woman superintendent and the first in a large city in America, and the National Education Association's first female president. She began her teaching career in Chicago at the tender age of seventeen in a classroom full of young roughneck students called "the cowboys"—young men who herded cattle on the outskirts of the city. After her husband died early in her marriage, she devoted the rest of her life to education, and the children of Chicago became her adopted family. She expected other educators to have the same devotion. As principal and superintendent, she frequently visited classrooms and observed teaching. On one particular occasion she was observing a fourth grade class when a student came in tardy. The teacher told the young girl to stand in a corner and then asked Ella Flagg Young, "What would you do with a little girl that came in tardy?" "Well," said Mrs. Young crisply, "I do not see that she has lost much" (Fenner & Fishburn, 1944).

For six years Mrs. Young was a professor in the Department of Pedagogy at the University of Chicago. As a colleague of John Dewey, her experience in education and his philosophy resulted in their coauthoring six monographs. She helped John Dewey translate his philosophical ideas into educational practice. Dewey said of her that she was the inspiration of many of his thoughts and conceptions about education. Dewey once wrote, "I would come to her with these abstract ideas of mine, and she would tell me what they meant."

accessible to men than to women. Tyack and Hansot (1982) also mentioned this problem for early women educators. They claimed that in graduate work in educational administration the professors were almost all men, and they recruited and sponsored males. Finally, Kalvelage also suggested that as court cases and legislation sought for equity, women "had lost even the dubious asset of being cheaper than men" (p. 18). All these factors combined to cause a gradual decline in the number of female elementary school principals that would not see a reversal until the late twentieth century.

Tyack and Hansot (1982) offered some additional insight into the cultural reasons that many women did not pursue or were not appointed to school leadership positions. According to these authors, women who wished to climb the normal ladder to become top administrators faced both external and internal barriers. The early advocates of employing women as teachers assumed that they would leave their work when married and that marriage was the goal of all proper women. In fact, in 1900, only 10 percent of female teachers were married, and in 1940, only 22 percent were. As Tyack and Hanson reported, "Not only did most women internalize these cultural norms, but official policies also barred married women from educational employment. . . . The situation grew worse during the depression, as thousands of districts passed new bans" (p. 191).

Compared with research on women, there is much less historical information available about minorities entering school leadership positions. With some ethnic groups, the rise and fall of numbers in school administration almost parallel those of women. For example, African Americans held more school leadership positions in the first half of the twentieth century than they did in the second half. One explanation given for this in the literature is the elimination of segregated schools during the 1950s and 1960s that resulted in fewer African Americans in the leadership hierarchy. Almost all segregated schools had African American administrators. When schools were integrated, few African Americans were appointed to leadership positions.

The first African American school administrators mentioned in history were those in the Quaker-sponsored institutions. At the turn of the twentieth century, Quaker Anna T. Jeanes endowed $1 million toward maintaining and assisting rural, community, and county schools for southern African Americans. The Jeanes supervisors, about 80 percent of whom were black women, concentrated on bringing the school and community together and raising the general standard of living. They trained teachers, developed curriculum, demonstrated teaching methods, and conducted professional development activities in child growth and development, in other words, duties that principals were doing in schools across America. Most of the Jeanes supervisors were in rural schools with small populations. As schools grew and more principals were hired, the Jeanes program became less important. Nevertheless, the program established black leadership in black schools in many areas of the south.

Representation of Latino/as and Native Americans in school leadership appears to be affected by cultural issues. Both groups historically have resented attempts by public schools to acculturate them to white Anglo-Saxon values and beliefs. DeJong (1990) reported that Native Americans are not adverse to Western education, but they see it as a way to acculturate rather than educate. Negative perceptions ingrained in culture have affected the career choices of many Latino/as and Native Americans.

Repeatedly, studies focusing on women and minorities in school administration raise the issue of *sponsorship*. Sponsorship is a major mechanism for recruiting and selecting school administrators. Veteran administrators sponsor potential candidates by encouraging them to enroll in university preparation programs and by providing visibility opportunities to promote their careers. Both women and people of color historically have been less likely than white males to be sponsored by other administrators to enter school leadership (Shakeshaft, 1987). As Ortiz (1982) noted, problems created by a lack of sponsorship are compounded by blockages to socialization. In this respect, both women and minorities who aspire to school leadership have not had a mentor in a position to sponsor them and therefore find it difficult to gain entry. In a previous work, we (Crow & Matthews, 1998) examined the importance of mentors and socialization in succeeding in school leadership. The sponsorship by those already in the career level has been a contributing factor for career advancement for newcomers. As you reflect on your choice to go into school leadership, most likely you also can identify someone in a leadership position who has formally or informally influenced your career decision.

Interacting Elements that Have Influenced the Principal's Role

The principal's role emerged from the teacher's role over a period of time and over various geographic areas. The present role in which you are most familiar is a product influenced by various interacting elements. In the following section we discuss four of these elements and how each has helped the principal's role emerge to its present concept.

Changing Social Demographics of Cities and Schools

An important factor in the early development of the principalship was the growth of cities, which caused school enrollment to grow rapidly, resulting in an increase in the number and size of schools. The early American high schools and elementary schools were relatively small. For example, Pierce (1935) reported the enrollment of the St. Louis High School in its first year (1853) as 72 pupils and the enrollment of the Chicago High School in its fourth year (1859) as 286 pupils. In the larger metropolitan centers, both elementary and secondary schools grew to considerable size, and their organization became more complex. The most rapid development of the principalship resulted from conditions and problems connected with urban schools. Between the American Civil War and the end of the nineteenth century, the growth of cities resulted in larger and more diverse school-age populations enrolled in larger and more complex schools. In 1890, approximately 2,500 high schools were serving over 200,000 students. By 1910, over 10,000 high schools were serving over 900,000 American students (National Center for Education Statistics, 1992).

Not only did population growth lead to more and larger schools, but also in urban areas higher concentrations of population encouraged the creation of school districts and the separation of elementary and high schools. These conditions lead to the practice of designating one of the instructors as the principal teacher, someone who had some authority over other faculty. In urban secondary schools with diverse student populations, principal teachers increasingly spent more time carrying out administrative responsibilities.

Coinciding with the changes in the cities, the character of the school population also changed dramatically, particularly at the high school level. Early in the twentieth century, a minority of the high school age group went to high school. By the end of the twentieth century, due in part to compulsory education laws, nearly all youth of high school age enrolled in high school, resulting in a much more diverse school population. The issue became more critical as many central cities deteriorated and impoverished people became concentrated within the inner cities. Changes in the school population required more work than any one principal teacher could handle adequately. Despite the desire to retain a role combining both teaching and administrative responsibilities, the sheer numbers of students and teachers and the time required for principal teachers to carry out major organizational and administrative reporting tasks in larger schools resulted in school boards relieving principal teachers of classroom teaching responsibilities.

Historically, larger school systems possessed several characteristics not commonly found in rural schools, and these assets gave urban schools some educational advantages. Larger student enrollments permitted greater specialization in instruction and more diversified curriculum. Social and cultural conditions of cities resulted in more emphasis on education, and a greater concentration of economic and cultural resources provided more material support for program development. Callahan (1962) reported that school districts in the largest cities, such as Boston, New York, and Chicago, became lighthouses for public education. Superintendents in these urban systems emerged as prototypes for educational management, and their behaviors were admired and adopted by many principals and superintendents throughout the United States. In a sense, these early occupants of the superintendent's office established an exemplary role not only for superintendents but also for principals throughout the country.

Academic Study and State Certification Requirements

Data concerning the academic qualifications of early principals are meager. Some of the early school leaders, notably in the eastern cities, were either ministers or men trained in theology. Little professional development for individuals in the principalship or for those who desired to go into the principalship took place prior to the end of the nineteenth century. However, little formal training took place for teachers either except those who were geographically connected with *normal schools,* which focused on teacher training. Those who occupied school principal posts relied on their common sense, innate abilities, and teaching experience to perform largely management-related tasks.

Tyack and Hansot (1982) reported that an 1890 survey of educational departments in twenty leading universities uncovered only two courses in educational administration. Starting in 1914, pressures to utilize management techniques to broaden the education of school executives forced Teachers College of Columbia to give more attention to business methods, finance, and efficiency techniques. By 1917, offerings in educational administration at Columbia increased from two to eight courses (Callahan, 1962). Culbertson (1988) noted that the 1950s saw a "leap toward an administrative science" (p. 14) in education. Culbertson also noted the high value placed on the development of professional preparation programs that emphasized "theory development and . . . the building of a 'science of administration'" (p. 16). This trend, referred to as the *theory movement,* applied theories and concepts from the social and behavioral sciences to problems of educational administration (Crowson & McPherson, 1987).

As the levels of academic and professional training of principals increased, so did the states' requirements in certifying principals. In fact, state requirements often stimulated the growth of university preparation programs. At first, certification of principals was not necessary because the only prerequisite was a teaching certificate. However, as university programs grew to include more administrative preparation, states followed with more requirements for administrative certification (Tyack & Hansot, 1982).

Kowalski and Reitzug (1993) reported that during the 1920s, certification of school administrators was advocated primarily for two reasons: (1) many superintendents of that period had not taken a single college course in school administration, and (2) certification was perceived as one avenue for achieving professionalization of the role of principals. Callahan (1962) stated that by 1932, nearly half the states had adopted certification standards for administrators. In the 1950s, all states required some form of administrative certificate, although the requirements for each state varied as to both university course work and teaching experience. Even today, certification requirements still vary among the states. As you prepare to become an administrator, you should check your state's certification requirements and determine if your preparation program meets those requirements.

Professional Associations

Another large event in the emergence of the modern principalship occurred when the NEA established the Department of Secondary School Principals in 1916, followed by the Department of Elementary School Principals in 1921. During this time, the NEA was an umbrella association for many groups of educators, including superintendents, teachers, professors, and educational researchers. The creation of the school administrative departments signaled official recognition of the position of principal by a national body of professional educators. The influence these departments had on shaping the role of the contemporary principal cannot be overestimated. By establishing these departments, more scientific research was conducted in the work, problems, and role of the principal. The departments stimulated the professional interests not only of individual principals but also of other principals' associations throughout the country. Research studies on the principal's role regarding significant aspects of the work appeared in professional journals and conferences.

During the 1960s and early 1970s, the NEA went through several stages of reorganization. The specialty divisions of the NEA, including those serving school administrators, disaffiliated themselves from the national organization. Several researchers (e.g., Kowalski & Reitzug, 1993; Tyack & Hansot, 1982) have claimed that the increased popularity of collective bargaining developed tensions among the specialty divisions. This dissatisfaction resulted in the formation of independent national organizations to serve the needs and interests of school administrators. Although many of these groups maintain a close working relationship with each other, they often compete for members. Superintendents tend to belong to the American Association of School Administrators (AASA), high school principals and assistants to the National Association of Secondary School Principals (NASSP), and elementary school principals and assistants to the National Association of Elementary School Principals (NAESP). Middle level administrators often choose either NASSP or NAESP or belong to both. Another association that principals often choose is the Association of Supervision and Curriculum Development (ASCD), which generally focuses on curriculum and instruction.

Since breaking away from NEA, both NAESP and NASSP have worked to improve the status and profession of the principalship. Both associations provide legal protection for members, conduct research, publish journals and newsletters, and provide development opportunities such as workshops and national conventions. These association activities and their state affiliates' activities have helped in establishing the principal's and assistant principal's role.

Practice of School Administrators

An important factor in the emergence of the principalship is the development of practice over time. Two interconnected areas, namely, management and supervision, helped establish the role of the principal as a separate and distinct responsibility from its roots in teaching. In the early history of the principalship, management and supervision were often associated. It was not until the mid-twentieth century that the two areas became distinct.

The growth of cities and schools was a contributing factor in the transfer of management and supervision from the superintendent to the principal. One of the main functions of early superintendents was to evaluate the schools. Pierce (1935) claimed that the problems in administration caused by increased population put so many demands on superintendents' time that they were unable to give personal attention to the management and supervision of local schools. The logical step was to turn local management of schools over to the principals.

An initial approach to educational administration was grounded in the scientific management and industrial efficiency tenets of Frederick W. Taylor. During the early years of the twentieth century, schools were under considerable pressure to produce results. America was becoming an industrial nation. It was perhaps inevitable that Frederick Taylor's philosophy of scientific industrial management would now be applied to the schools. The *scientific management* approach asserted that educational organizations, like commercial establishments, could be made business-like and efficient. Tasks and responsibilities could be defined carefully and planned fully to lead to maximum organizational productivity. Many people believed that educational administration could best be improved by the scientific application of managerial expertise. This included carefully planned schedules for work, the instructions for doing it, and the expected standards of performance (Morris, Crowson, Porter-Gehrie, & Hurwitz, 1984).

Industrial scientific management was a movement that perfectly reflected its time because it emphasized the critical importance of managerial officialdom. Ellwood P. Cubberley (1916) wrote a highly influential textbook for school leaders in which he emphasized the school administrator as organizer, executive, and supervisor of work. In fact, Cubberley suggested that the educational leader should exercise large powers, apply broad knowledge and larger insight to educational needs, and plan all policies even though "the details might be best kept to himself" (p. 15). The importance of the school administrator was not diminished by Cubberley's added advice to be honest and square, clean and temperate, honorable, and "able to look men straight in the eye" (p. 15). To Cubberley, so important was the role of the principal that he later wrote in 1923, "We are not likely to overestimate the importance of the office of school principal" (Cubberley, 1923, p. 28). He further summarized his belief with his often-quoted statement: "As is the principal, so is the school" (p. 15).

Another important factor in the emergence of the principalship was the freeing of principals from teaching duties so that they could supervise other classroom teachers. In dealing with the supervisory functions of the principal, the definition of the term *supervision* becomes important. A common definition is that supervision is the technique for improving teaching. However, distinguishing between supervisory and managerial activities of principals is usually quite difficult. A common distinction is that a principal manages things and supervises people. Although this statement may be too simplistic, it does draw attention to the two functions. For purposes of studying the emergence of the principalship, however, it is important to note that supervision may have related more to the early principal's management role of "inspector" than to the role of "mentor" as it is more commonly used today.

Pierce (1935) reported that supervisory activities were first exercised in public schools by visiting committees of laymen, usually consisting of the learned men of the town, namely, ministers and physicians. These committees visited the schools and determined the efficiency of instruction by examining the teachers. After boards of education were established, schools were inspected, pupils examined, and teacher's methods directed by official school committees. As the complexity of school organization increased, many of the supervisory functions developed by these committees were delegated to the principal.

Conceptual Frameworks Influencing the Principalship Role

As the principalship emerged, a distinct and important role in American education was created. Certain conceptual frameworks influenced how the role was played out. In this section we will discuss three of these frameworks, *moral* and *ethical leadership,* social and community leadership, and instructional leadership and how, in particular, these frameworks have influenced the seven roles that we discuss later in this book.

Moral and Ethical Leadership

Many of the first principals of schools were directly associated with the ministry, and many others were heavily influenced by the Christian (mostly Protestant) ideal. Cubberley (1923) noted "the great spiritual importance" (p. 561) of the principal's work and likened the principal to "the priest in the parish" (p. 26). Cubberley's own career story gives interesting insight to the influence of religion in education. Tyack and Hansot (1982) reported:

> When Ellwood P. Cubberley applied for the superintendency of schools in San Diego in 1896, the chairman of the school board was worried about his qualifications for the job. Cubberley had never had a course in education, but that was not the problem. He did not have a graduate degree, but that was not the problem either. The sticking point for the chairman was the question of Cubberley's piety, his religious orthodoxy, for he was a scientist who had written about geology and was known to be a believer in evolution. What was his view of religion, the chairman wanted to know, and what were the guarantees of his good character? Cubberley replied to the inquiry with a strong testimonial from his Indiana minister and his own affirmation that "I believe firmly in God and the principles of the Christian religion." He continued, "I am in the strongest sense a harmonizer of Religion and Science, there is no conflict in my mind between the two" (pp. 114–115).

The people in public school leadership in the early years of the twentieth century usually were individuals who worked hard, were thrifty, and maintained high moral values—influenced by strong Protestant principles. Many either had been clergymen or had intended to enter the ministry. In fact, many not only were leaders in the schools during the week but also took on teaching and leadership roles on Sunday. Religion provided an important criterion for selection to school leadership. Being Protestant and an active church member were important requirements for selection as a leader in the public school system.

During the middle to late nineteenth century, the Catholic Church opposed the common school movement because of its reliance on Protestant teachings, its use of the King James Bible, and the refusal to use public tax monies for Catholic schools (Tyack & Hansen, 1982). Because of these issues, many Catholic parents chose not to send their children to public schools. Many parishes developed their own schools, leading to the largest private educational system in America. Initially, these Catholic schools were mostly administered and staffed by the ecclesiastical sisters and brothers, as well as the priests of the congregations. The Second Vatican Council of the early 1960s changed the school personnel regulations. Although Catholic schools employed few laypersons in administration before the 1960s, since then, laypersons are the majority of Catholic principals, especially in elementary schools. The transition to laypersons in high school administration is also the trend but has proceeded much more slowly (Michaletz, 1984). Brubacher (1966) suggested that although well meaning and sympathetic to education, few priests were professionally trained and, therefore, lacked the pedagogical insight to supervise instruction and curriculum. Thus the transition to laypersons was important in the Catholic system to have schools staffed and administered by professional educators.

Public school principals and parochial school principals are more similar than different. Both emerged as efficiency-minded, thrifty, and highly moral school leaders. Beck and Murphy (1993) submitted that these character images combined to create "a picture of the principal as one whose role is linked to timeless truths and values" (p. 15). Cubberley (1923) also suggested that values are linked to the community:

> The principal must remember that he holds a particularly responsible position as a model in his community. . . . He must, in his dress, his manner, his speech, and his bearing, so conduct himself that he will easily win and hold the respect of teachers, pupils, and the community (p. 26).

The nature of the moral and ethical leadership provided by the principal has changed since the early part of the twentieth century, but many of the standards still exist. Each year principals are removed from office for failure to assume their leadership obligations or for breach of ethics or moral character. Recognizing the importance of ethics for school leaders, the AASA adopted a code of ethics in 1976 (updated in 1992), and this code was soon after adopted by the two principal associations, NAESP and NASSP (Figure 2.1).

In the last decades of the twentieth century, several writers revisited the moral and ethical aspects of leadership. Greenleaf (1970) proposed a powerful conceptual framework in suggesting that the leader begins by being a servant leader. Greenleaf maintained that "conscious choice brings one to aspire to lead" (p. 7). Burns (1978) differentiated between transactional and transformational leadership by suggesting that most leaders are transactional—exchanging one thing for another thing with followers. "Transforming leadership is a relationship of mutual stimulation and elevation that converts followers into leaders and leaders into moral agents" (p. 4). According to Burns, leadership is a process of morality because leaders and followers have shared motives and goals. Covey (1989) presented a conception of leadership that is centered on ethical principles. For Covey, principle-centered leadership is based on the reality that we cannot violate natural laws with impunity. Sergiovanni (1992) advocated that principals need to learn skills that ap-

The AASA Executive Committee adopted its current code of ethics in 1981. It represents a significant condensation of a version adopted in 1962. That code included a lengthy list of examples of appropriate and inappropriate conduct to provide specific direction to practitioners.

An educational administrator's professional behavior must conform to an ethical code. The code must be idealistic and at the same time practical so that it can apply reasonably to all educational administrators. The administrator acknowledges that the schools belong to the public they serve for the purpose of providing educational opportunities to all. However, the administrator assumes responsibility for providing professional leadership in the school and community. The responsibility requires the administrator to maintain standards of exemplary professional conduct. It must be recognized that the administrator's actions will be viewed and appraised by the community, professional associates, and students. To these ends, the administrator subscribes to the following statements of standards. The educational administrator:

- Makes the well-being of students the fundamental value of all decision making and actions, fulfills professional responsibilities with honesty and integrity, supports the principle of due process, and protects the civil and human rights of all individuals.
- Obeys local, state, and national laws and does not knowingly join or support organizations that advocate, directly or indirectly, the overthrow of the government.
- Implements the governing board of education's policies and administrative rules and regulations.
- Pursues appropriate measures to correct those laws, policies, and regulations that are not consistent with sound educational goals.
- Avoids using positions for personal gain through political, social, religious, economic, or other influences.
- Accepts academic degrees or professional certification only from duly accredited institutions.
- Maintains the standards and seeks to improve the effectiveness of the profession through research and continuing professional development.
- Honors all contracts until fulfillment, release, or dissolution mutually agreed on by all parties to contract.

FIGURE 2.1   AASA Statement of Ethics for School Administrators

proach moral leadership. He maintained that followers would be more receptive to leadership if the leader showed them that certain changes are the right thing to do.

Social and Community Leadership

In addition to being ethical leaders, principals of the twentieth century also have been expected to be social and community leaders. Cubberley (1923), writing on the principal, noted, "No other person in the community can so immediately mould [sic] its life and shape its ideals" (p. 36). He further commented that the principal "must remember to carry himself at all times as a gentleman of the world should and would" (p. 26).

Early twentieth-century writers on the principalship advised school leaders to develop positive community relationships. For example, Douglas (1932) recommended that the principal study the community as accurately as possible to determine its key people and organizations. "In every community there are men, women, and organizations that are outstandingly influential in determining community actions, attitudes, and actions. The principal must not neglect to know these people and to gain their confidence and their interest in his educational program" (p. 498). Cubberley (1923) claimed that community relations is one of the most important aspects of the work and that the community is, indeed, an asset to the school. A school leader "should know his community and be able to feel its pulse and express its wants, and the community should know him and believe in his integrity and honesty of purpose" (p. 153).

Concerns with community leadership of one type or another have been present in the literature in every decade of the twentieth century. During World War II, Gregg (1943) reported the need for the principal to be a leader in the community for the war effort: "Every leader . . . has not only the professional, but also the patriotic responsibility of an all out effort to make his school function in such a way that the nation and youth of his community will be served in the most effective way" (p. 7). Postwar America saw communities trying to rebuild themselves, often around their schools. Campbell and colleagues (1987) noted that the principal had an increased concern with community relations during this time that meant more involvement with parents and other community members. In 1973, Burden and Whitt suggested that principals relate not only to those within the school but also to persons in the community. Arguing that changing social situations force principals to extend the scope of leadership activities, they wrote:

> Community power is a coming reality. The previous view that the local school could remain aloof and isolated from those it was purported to serve is no longer a viable one. The changing concept of democracy that means all people are to be involved, not just those in power, places new responsibilities on the building administrator (p. xiii).

The last two decades of the twentieth century saw school leadership turn its attention to educating all children, no matter what their socioeconomic background or academic abilities. The principal became part of a social reconstruction of communities in which every person deserved an education with dignity and respect. At times, this social leadership role put the principal at odds with certain fundamentally conservative subcultures of the community. Consequently, being a strong social leader also required the principal to be a strong moral leader in the community and to take a position of what was right rather than what was popular or what had been done in the past. Beck and Murphy (1993) suggested that in the 1990s, "there [were] serious efforts developing to transform the principalship into an instrument of social justice" (p. 194).

To a modern observer, the community relations role of the principal might be associated with "playing politics." However, in the first half of the twentieth century, most educational leaders accepted the doctrine that politics should be separated from education. Playing politics often was associated with selfish and self-aggrandizing politicians and was meant to be more allied with policymaking than with social and community leadership. Kimbrough and Burkett (1990) speculated that politics in the early twentieth century took on a sleaziness that many political reformers wanted to keep out of government operations such as the public school system. As they put it, "No self-respecting educational leader would admit to engaging in . . . [politics]" (p. 90). However, during the last half of the twentieth century, politicians and educators collaborated on many issues of policy-making, and it would be difficult today for any school leader to claim that he or she is not engaged in some form of politics. Likewise, it would be difficult for any modern politician to have no agenda in education.

Not only did politics change, but communities did likewise, and with them so did the schools. These changes have made it difficult for school leaders to remain as close and responsive to their communities as they once were. Several modern reformers have suggested that community building and economic development are essential responsibilities for school principals and schools (Crowson, 2001). Proposals such as those offered by Theobold and Nachtigal (1995) aim to "redesign education for the purpose of recreating community—community that is ecologically sustainable" (p. 35). Sergiovanni (1996) saw community members responding to the substance of ideas, which implied that leadership builds a "shared followership . . . not on who to follow, but on what to follow" (p. 83). A school community, then, is a group of people who share common ideas about schooling and learning. The implications for school leaders are clear. Persons within the community need to be part of a group working toward the common good and sharing a set of values within the school. The school, as a community entity, needs to be part of a larger group that also has mutual values and goals (Drake & Roe, 1999). The continuing emphasis on social and community leadership is evident in a recent proposal for reforming the profession of educational leadership (Murphy, 2002). Two of the three pillars on which educational leadership should be based, according to Murphy, are democratic schooling and social justice.

Instructional Leadership

Instruction has always been a part of the role of the principal. Since its inception as a role separate from teaching, some responsibility has been assigned to the principal to influence teaching and learning in a school. At times and with some persons, the role of instructional leadership was submerged because other roles were more prominent, such as cleric, manager, and bureaucrat. Nevertheless, one of the reasons to free principals from their teaching assignments was to give them more time for instructional supervision. As good as the intentions of the normal schools were, many teachers never had the opportunity to attend them or did so only briefly. Consequently, much training remained to be done after the teachers entered into active service. In addition to helping teachers be better instructors, another condition evolved—the addition of new subjects in the curriculum. The dominant assumption was that the principal was in the best position to be the instructional leader and should be directly involved with teachers in improving instruction, creating a learning climate in the school, and facilitating development of the curriculum.

During the educational reform movements of the 1980s, the term used most to describe the principal's responsibilities with instruction and curriculum was *instructional leadership*. Greenfield (1987) noted that this term was used often as a slogan guiding the efforts of educational reformers. DeBevoise (1984) defined instructional leadership as "those actions that a principal takes, or delegates to others, to promote growth in student learning" (p. 15). Hallinger and Murphy (1987) noted that research on effective schools led to the expectation that principals in the 1980s were to play a more active role in instructional leadership. Their suggestion, however, was that instructional leadership was context-dependent rather than uniform in nature. Principals were to first understand the school environment, including teachers and students, and then diagnose what was appropriate instructional leadership.

This type of instructional leadership left out an important component—the role that teachers need to play as instructional leaders. As it became more apparent that principals could not correctly diagnose teaching and learning needs of teachers and students and that teachers, who were most involved in the learning process, understood their own and their student's needs, instructional leadership shifted from the principal as the sole leader to include teachers as instructional leaders. This shift then returned the principal's role to what it was originally—that of being an educator of educators, a leader of leaders. Furthermore, Barth (1990) recommended that principals not only be leaders of instructional leaders but also be leaders of learning. Not only are they to be well educated, but also they are expected to model and exemplify learning themselves. The focus on learner-centered leadership has been reignited by societal pressures of accountability and equity that emphasize learning for all students. This focus can be seen in Elementary Secondary Education Act (ESEA) 2001, professional association programs, and university preparation reforms (National Association of Elementary School Principals, 2001; Institute for Educational Leadership, 2000; Elmore, 2000). Likewise, the third pillar of Murphy's (2002) proposal for educational leadership reform was student learning.

Contemporary Conditions and Implications

The principalship has developed into a complex role—far more complex than it was originally conceived. Historically, the principal and assistant principal roles have been shaped by numerous social and cultural forces, and these roles continue to change as schools and society reshape them. Currently, there is an urgent and widespread demand to improve student performance and reform schools. The push for standards-based reform—and the pressure on schools to deliver in terms of academic performance—has raised the demands and pressures on principals and assistant principals and brought an unprecedented level of public scrutiny to their job performance. In some cases, principals' salaries and contracts now depend on gains in student achievement. Nor have the management functions traditionally associated with school leadership gone away—if anything, they have become more demanding. Charter schools, vouchers, decentralized governance, standardized testing, accountability, and youth social issues have provoked new pressures that no principal could have anticipated a decade ago when many entered the profession. In addition, other societal changes, including shifting demographics, the speed of communication, and the explosion of knowledge, are rapidly changing the look of and the demands on schools (Marx, 2000). Indeed, many worthy veterans have become disenchanted with the rapid changes and have considered or acted on early retirement. Whitaker (1995) interviewed principals to examine emotional exhaustion and depersonalization in their jobs. Four themes emerged that were related to these issues and that the respondents indicated might prompt them to leave the principalship:

1. *Increasing demands of the principalship.* Respondents cited accountability pressures, increased paperwork, time-management issues, and tensions related to restructuring.
2. *Lack of role clarity.* Respondents expressed frustration over the lack of clarity in new roles related to site-based management and shared decision making.
3. *Lack of recognition.* Principals perceived a need for more intrinsic and extrinsic rewards and recognition, especially from the district office.
4. *Decreasing autonomy.* Principals perceived that autonomy was slipping away because of collaborative decision making. Making decisions with staff, parents, and community members left principals feeling somewhat powerless and vulnerable (Whitaker, 1995, pp. 290–291).

Another study by the Education Research Society (2000) revealed an increasing shortage of administrative candidates for leadership positions in schools. The shortage was most acute at the secondary level and in urban settings. Although researchers (e.g., Bridgman, 1986) have reported shortages of school principals previously, the present shortage has caught many school officials without qualified candidates for administrative positions.

These reported shortages and the concern with recruiting sufficient numbers of qualified candidates have led to a focus on the attractions of the job. Pounder and Merrill (2001) found that potential candidates to the secondary school principalship identified two major attractions of the job: the desire to influence or improve education and the position's salary and benefits. However, these potential candidates identified time demands as the most unattractive aspect of the job, followed by the problems and dilemmas that come with the job.

The fact that school administration has been, and continues to be, a white male-dominated profession also obviously affects the way many potential principals and assistant principals perceive the roles. As might be expected, as students of color in the public schools become the majority, a higher demand will exist for principals of color.

Conclusion

In this chapter we have introduced the role of the principal and assistant principal and discussed how history has influenced the way you will practice that role. While many school administrators feel the sand shifting under their feet, the men and women who take on these roles of principal and assistant principal do so because they believe they can make a difference for children. Although ever-changing, these roles have proven their worth in the educational arena and in addressing various social needs.

The following vignette establishes an interesting situation regarding the role of one principal who was socialized differently from another principal who is now replacing him. In the chapters that follow we include other vignettes that introduce seven new role conceptions that contrast with the traditional role conceptions of the principalship. The first role conception that we introduce is the principal as learner, a role that is foundational to all the other role conceptions.

Vignette

Principal Ronald Montgomery's retirement open house attracted hundreds of people. It was to be expected, however, because anyone who had served as a principal for twenty-two years in the same building naturally would create a wide network of acquaintances. Besides, Principal Montgomery was well liked by the community. For most of his twenty-two years at Valleyview High School, it was the only school in the community. The community rallied around its high school, and Principal Montgomery became an icon in the community. As the valley grew, so did the need for another high school. Two years before his retirement, a new school was built, drawing on the new suburban housing developments for its population. Valleyview changed. Only half the size it used to be and serving part of the community that mostly housed lower-income families, Valleyview's demographics had changed rapidly. During the last two years, the high school lost most of its football and basketball games, could not field a marching band, and the community dismally attended the once-popular annual school musical. The state's standardized testing indicated, for the first time in school history, average scores below the fiftieth percentile. Although Principal Montgomery was given the choice to go to the new school, he chose instead to stay at Valleyview. However, not even he had predicted the changes that occurred in such a short time.

The "Blame Game" became part of the school culture. Those teachers remaining at Valleyview blamed the school board for drawing up unbalanced attendance area boundaries. Some of the teachers also were jealous that they had not been given the opportunity to transfer while other teachers had been "chosen" as the new faculty. The new school had fully equipped science labs, computers in every classroom, and athletic facilities that rivaled that of a small college. Parents blamed the newcomers for manipulating the board into building a showcase for their part of the community but leaving the old for the old.

Principal Montgomery had realized finally that new leadership was needed at Valleyview. He recognized that education had changed, that the community had changed, and that he and many others at Valleyview had not changed. The last two years had been extremely hard on his health, and the more he thought about what was needed at the school, the more he realized that his fire had long since been extinguished. It was time for new blood.

The retirement open house was a huge success—the only event that had tied the two communities together in the past two years. Coming through the reception line were present and former teachers, students, and parents. Civic dignitaries such as the mayor and several city council members were present. Also, standing in the line was Consuelos Gonzales, who had flown into town to attend the open house. She was the new blood—recently appointed as the principal of Valleyview High School. From out of town and out of state and a Latina, she knew that she had an uphill battle to gain community support. The open house would be a good start. Besides, she respected Mr. Montgomery for the many years of service he had given to the school. It was only right for her to be at his retirement open house. She knew she needed his support and help in the coming years. She also had been given a charge from the board to jump-start things at Valleyview—and the sooner the better.

Consuelos had been a principal for the past five years in a rural setting in a neighboring state. She had been recognized by the state affiliate of the Association of Supervision and Curriculum Development as the state's outstanding instructional leader for her innovative and comprehensive teacher development programs at her school. She understood the board's directive to give Valleyview a jump start, and she had great ideas. She also knew that the faculty and community were not as anxious or ready for these curricula and instructional changes. They were quite satisfied to continue with the same kind of leadership that Principal Montgomery used.

Activities

Self-Reflecting Activity

If you were Consuelos—in the vignette at the end of the chapter—what conceptual framework would you emphasize during your first few weeks as principal of Valleyview High School?

Peer Activity

Shadow an assistant principal for a day, and discuss the kinds of tasks performed with a colleague. Compare and contrast the tasks and speculate on what conceptual framework seems to be emphasized by these two administrators.

Course Activities

1. Interview a veteran principal who is near retirement. In what ways does this principal believe the role of principal has changed? Discuss with your classmates the specific purpose of the role as well as the tasks.
2. Role play Consuelos' first faculty meeting at Valleyview High. Considering the facts of the vignette, what should she emphasize?

References

Barth, R. S. (1990). *Improving Schools from Within: Teachers, Parents, and Principals Can Make the Difference.* San Francisco: Jossey-Bass.

Beck, L. G., & Murphy, J. (1993). *Understanding the Principalship: Metaphorical Themes, 1920s–1990s.* New York: Teachers College Press.

Bridgman, A. (1986). Better elementary leaders called for. *Education Week,* February 19, 1986.

Brubacher, J. S. (1966). *A History of the Problems of Education.* New York: McGraw-Hill.

Burden, L., & Whitt, R. L. (1973). *The Community School Principal: New Horizons.* Midland, MI: Pendell.

Burns, J. M. (1978). *Leadership*. New York: Harper and Row.

Callahan, R. (1962). *Education and the Cult of Efficiency*. Chicago: University of Chicago Press.

Campbell, R. F., Fleming, R., Newell, L. J., & Bennion, J. W. (1987). *A History of Thought and Practice in Educational Administration*. New York: Teachers College Press.

Covey, S. R. (1989). *The Seven Habits of Highly Effective People: Restoring the Character Ethic*. New York: Simon and Schuster.

Crow, G. M., & Matthews, L. J. (1998). *Finding One's Way: How Mentoring Can Lead to Dynamic Leadership*. Thousand Oaks, CA: Corwin Press.

Crowson, R. L. (2001). *Community Development and School Reform*. Oxford, England: Elsevier.

Crowson, R. L. & McPherson, R. B. (1987). The legacy of the theory movement: Learning from the new tradition. In J. Murphy and P. Hallinger (Eds.), *Approaches to Administrative Training in Education* (pp. 45–66). Albany, NY: State University of New York Press.

Cubberley, E. P. (1916). *Public School Administration*. Boston: Houghton Mifflin.

Cubberley, E. P. (1923). *The Principal and His School*. Boston: Houghton Mifflin.

Culbertson, J. A. (1988). A century's quest for a knowledge base. In N. J. Boyan (ed.), *Handbook of Research on Educational Administration*. New York: Longmans.

DeBevoise, W. (1984). Synthesis of research on the principal as instructional leader. *Educational Leadership 41*(5), 14–20.

DeJong, D. H. (1990). Friend or foe? Education and the American Indian. Unpublished M.A. thesis, University of Arizona.

Douglas, H. R. (1932). *Organization and Administration of Secondary Schools*. Boston: Ginn & Co.

Drake, T. L., & Roe, W. H. (1999). *The Principalship* (5th ed.). Upper Saddle River, NJ: Merrill.

Education Research Society (2000). *The Principal Keystone of a High-Achieving School: Attracting and Keeping the Leaders We Need*. Arlington, VA: Education Research Society.

Elmore, R. F. (2000). Building a new structure for school leadership. *American Educator 23*(4), 6–13.

Ensign, F. C. (1923). Evolution of the high school principalship. *School Review* (March), 179–190.

Fenner, M. S., & Fishburn, E. C. (1944). *Pioneer American Educators*. Washington, D.C.: Hugh Birch-Horace Mann Fund, National Education Association.

Glanz, J. (1994). Where did the assistant principalship begin? Where is it headed? *NASSP Bulletin* (October).

Greenfield, W. (1987). Moral imagination and interpersonal competence: Antecedents to instructional leadership. In W. Greenfield (Ed.), *Instructional Leadership: Concepts, Issues, and Controversies* (pp. 56–75). Newton, MA: Allyn and Bacon.

Greenleaf, R. (1970). *The Servant as Leader*. Indianapolis: The Robert K. Greenleaf Center.

Gregg, R. T. (1943). The principal and his school in wartime. *Bulletin of the National Association of Secondary School Principals 27*(112), 7–19.

Hallinger, P., & Murphy, J. (1987). Instructional leadership in the school context. In W. Greenfield (Ed.), *Instructional Leadership: Concepts, Issues, and Controversies* (pp. 179–203). Newton, MA: Allyn and Bacon.

Hart, A. W., & Bredeson, P. V. (1996). *The Principalship: A Theory of Professional Learning and Practice*. New York: McGraw-Hill.

Hartzell, G. N., Williams, R. C., & Nelson, K. T. (1995). *New Voices in the Field: The Work Lives of First-Year Assistant Principals*. Thousand Oaks, CA: Corwin Press.

Institute for Educational Leadership (2000). *Leadership for Student Learning: Reinventing the Principalship*. Washington, D.C.: Institute for Educational Leadership, Task Force on the Principalship.

Kalvelage, J. (1978). *The Decline in Female Elementary Principals since 1928: Riddles and Clues*. Eugene, OR: University of Oregon.

Kelly, G. (1987). The assistant principalship as a training ground for the principalship. *NASSP 7*(501), 13–20.

Kimbrough, R. B., & Burkett, C. W. (1990). *The Principalship: Concepts and Practices*. Boston: Allyn and Bacon.

Kowalski, T. J., & Reitzug, U. C. (1993). *Contemporary School Administration: An Introduction*. New York: Longmans.

Mann, H. (1842). *Fifth Annual Report of the Secretary of the Board*. Boston: Dutton and Wentworth, State Printers.

Marx, G. (2000). *Ten Trends: Educating Children for a Profoundly Different Future.* Arlington, VA: Educational Research Service.

Michaletz, J. E. (1984). The preparation and training of the catholic school administrator. In J. J. Lane (Ed.), *The Making of a Principal* (pp. 116–128). Springfield, IL: Charles C. Thomas.

Morris, V. C., Crowson, R. L., Porter-Gehrie, C., & Hurwitz, J., E. (1984). *Principals in Action: The Reality of Managing Schools.* Columbus, OH: Charles E. Merrill.

Murphy, J. (2002). Reculturing the profession of educational leadership: New blueprints. In J. Murphy (Ed.), *The Leadership Challenge: Redefining Leadership for the 21st Century* (pp. 65–82). Chicago: National Society for the Study of Education.

National Association of Elementary School Principals (2001). *Leading Learning Communities: Standards for What Principals Should Know and Be Able to Do.* Alexandria, VA: NAESP.

National Center for Education Statistics (1992). *The Digest of Education Statistics 1992: Schools and Staffing Survey, 1987–1988.* Washington, D.C.: U.S. Department of Education, National Center for Education Statistics.

National Center for Education Statistics (1994). *The Digest of Education Statistics 1994: Schools and Staffing Survey, 1990–1991.* Washington, D.C.: U.S. Department of Education, National Center for Education Statistics.

National Center for Education Statistics (1998). *The Digest of Education Statistics 1998: Schools and Staffing Survey, 1993–1994.* Washington, D.C.: U.S. Department of Education, National Center for Education Statistics.

Ortiz, F. I. (1982). *Career Patterns in Education: Women, Men, and Minorities in Public School Administration.* New York: Praeger.

Ortiz, F. I., & Marshall, C. (1988). Women in educational administration. In N. J. Boyan (Ed.), *Handbook of Research on Educational Administration.* New York: Longmans.

Pierce, P. R. (1935). *The Origin and Development of the Public School Principalship.* Chicago: University of Chicago Press.

Pounder, D. G., & Merrill, R. J. (2001). Job desirability of the high school principalship: A job choice theory perspective. *Educational Administration Quarterly 37*(1): 27–57.

Sergiovanni, T. J. (1992). *Moral Leadership: Getting to the Heart of School Improvement.* San Francisco: Jossey-Bass.

Sergiovanni, T. J. (1996). *Leadership for the Schoolhouse: How Is It Different? Why Is It Important?* San Francisco: Jossey-Bass.

Shakeshaft, C. (1987). *Women in Educational Administration.* Newbury Park, CA: Sage.

Shakeshaft, C. (1999). The struggle to create a more gender-inclusive profession. In J. Murphy & K. Louis (Eds.), *Handbook of Research on Educational Administration* (2d ed., pp. 99–118). San Francisco: Jossey-Bass.

Theobold, P., & Nachtigal, P. (1995). Culture, community, and the promise of rural education. *Phi Delta Kappan 77*(October), 35.

Tyack, D., & Hansot, E. (1982). *Managers of Virtue: Public School Leadership in America, 1820–1980.* Boston: Basic Books.

Whitaker, K. S. (1995). Principal burnout: Implications for professional development. *Journal of Personnel Evaluation in Education 9,* 287–296.

The Principal as Learner

3

Key Terms and Concepts

complexity
constructivist conception of
   learning
double-loop learning
inquiry

learning organization
organizational learning
praxis
professional learning
   community

reflectivity
self-awareness
single-loop learning
traditional conception of
   learning

Vignette

Nancy Lowenstein became the principal of East Jersey Elementary School during a changing time. Not only had the previous principal retired after twenty-five years in the school, but also the district recently had redrawn the school boundaries to include a part of the community that was predominately African American, and a new superintendent, Marcia Downing, had been hired last year. When Dr. Downing and Nancy had their first meeting after the board appointed Nancy, Dr. Downing made it clear that she wanted some changes at East Jersey.

Until this year, East Jersey Elementary School had been the center for a homogeneous segment of the district that included primarily Caucasian parents from evangelical Protestant backgrounds. The parents trusted the former principal and the largely veteran teacher group to maintain their values, nurture their children, and keep controversy out of the schools. The former principal, Don Martin, had grown up in the community and was revered as a father figure not only to the community but also to the teachers. The teachers appreciated the way Don buffered them from distractions and left them alone in their classrooms. Over time, Don had developed the practice of making all school-wide decisions, which he claimed protected the teachers' instructional time. The teachers did not seem to mind this practice and developed a dependency on Don to tell them what they absolutely needed to know and trusted Don to make the big decisions.

In their first meeting, Dr. Downing and Nancy discussed the upcoming school boundary changes that would be made at the beginning of Nancy's first year as principal of East Jersey. They also discussed Dr. Downing's vision of creating learning communities within the schools so that teachers, parents, students, administrators, and other community members would all contribute toward a shared vision of student learning. Nancy was excited about working with the East Jersey school community in creating their own learning community. In her administrative internship in a different district, Nancy had worked with a mentor principal who had been successful in helping his school to think of itself as a professional community where there was collaboration among teachers, where teaching practices were open to parents and other teachers, and where the focus was on developing shared values concerning student learning.

As she began her new job, Nancy made a point of meeting individually with the teachers and finding out something about their learning styles. The teachers for the most part were warm and inviting to Nancy. She also held an open house for all parents and teachers, expressing her openness to the entire school community and inviting everyone to discuss any concerns with her. The year began with few problems, and Nancy was amazed at how easily the students from the new part of the community adjusted to the school.

Early in the school year, Nancy met with the faculty to discuss the idea of developing a learning community. She distributed readings from Peter Senge and others and encouraged teachers to discuss with each other how they might include parents and others in developing a learning organization at East Jersey and specifically how to focus on the particular needs of the newest students.

At the next meeting, which Nancy had set aside to focus on the learning organization idea, teachers were quiet. When Nancy asked them what they thought of the ideas in the readings and how they might apply to East Jersey, one veteran teacher replied that this would take too much time away from their classrooms and important instructional activities. Nancy countered that she believed a learning organization would benefit each classroom's learning environment and provided some examples from her own administrative internship experience. A few of the newer teachers were familiar with the concept of a learning organization and said they were interested in talking more about how to implement such an idea at the school. The veteran teachers, however, for the most part were either silent or politely opposed to the idea. The meeting ended with Nancy setting up a discussion group for all those interested in the idea to read more material and discuss ways to implement a learning organization at East Jersey.

As the year progressed, the small discussion group became more and more excited about creating a learning organization at East Jersey. The group met regularly, attended conferences, and developed a partnership with a local university to conduct action research in their classrooms. Many of the action research projects focused on how to respond to specific learning needs of the new students who had been transferred to the school. Nancy found resources for the group, including travel money for conferences and substitutes to facilitate meetings and observations. Most veteran teachers, however, remained skeptical of the idea.

By midyear, several of the veteran teachers were coming to Nancy frequently with discipline problems, primarily with the new students. They said the new students could not keep up with other students and were disruptive in class; they also said that the parents were unresponsive when the teachers called them to discuss student problems. When Nancy observed these teachers' classrooms, she frequently found they were using mostly direct instruction with few individualized approaches. In some cases, the teachers expressed resentment of the newer students. When Nancy conferred with the teachers, she found their typical response was to blame the students and their parents. She also heard rumors that these veteran teachers resented the attention being paid to the newer teachers who were in the discussion group focused on learning organizations. Some of the rumors reflected feelings of mistrust toward Nancy, suggesting that she was giving more resources to these teachers and perhaps even placing more students with behavior problems in the veteran teachers' classes.

Toward the end of the year, a group of veteran teachers asked to meet with Nancy. Although polite, they expressed deep frustration in what they perceived "these new children and their parents have done to our school." Nancy tried to be sensitive to their frustrations. When she suggested that they look at the students' previous school experience, test scores, and learning styles and reflect on what the teachers could do, one teacher's frustration boiled over. "It's the principal's job to get these kids out of our rooms so we can teach. Are you going to help us or not?" Nancy became more and more frustrated as each teacher pushed her to remove the disruptive students from their classrooms. She ended the meeting without expressing her frustration.

That evening as she discussed the meeting with her good friend and mentor, Sue Bennett, she finally expressed her frustration that the teachers were unwilling to consider their own behavior and how that might be contributing to student disruptions. After giving Nancy time to vent, Sue encouraged her to do what she wanted the teachers to do, reflect on her own behavior as a learner. Sue asked her what information she had about the teachers' styles and experiences, and she encouraged Nancy to consider what kinds of professional development resources she might find for these teachers.

Introduction

Introduction Nancy Lowenstein's experience as a new principal illustrates a primary area for conceptualizing the principalship—the principal as learner. It may seem surprising to you that in an organization that focuses on learning, the role conception of principal as learner has received attention only recently. As we discussed in Chapter 2, the scientific management focus on school administration until recently has received the greatest attention. However, as Nancy and countless other new principals have discovered, the managerial focus of the principalship provides a limited conception of the role.

We begin with the principal as learner because it sets the stage for all the other role conceptions you will read about in this book. Understanding the principal's and assistant principal's roles as mentor, supervisor, leader, manager, politician, and advocate is based on the primary role of the principal/assistant principal as learner and as facilitator of learning. As we will do in subsequent chapters, we examine the role conception in two major ways: the principal as learner and as facilitator of others' learning. As Nancy hopefully realized, if she wants teachers to be learners, she must practice learning techniques herself.

The principal as learner sets the stage for understanding the rest of the role primarily because of the nature of what schools do and what school environments should be. First, the central task and techniques (core technology) of schools are teaching and learning. Nothing distinguishes schools from other organizations more than teaching and learning. The "bottom line" for schools is not generating money or products. This unique quality of schools has created numerous debates and conflicts among educators and others in society, especially those in business. Although good business practices have a place in school operations, they are secondary to the primary purpose of schools as contributing to the learning of students, their families, and other adults.

Emphasizing the primacy of learning leads to understanding schools as learning organizations and communities. If the core technology of an organization is to generate a product, then the organization can be seen more as a factory than as a community. As we will discuss later, learning is not an individual event but occurs within a social context—within a community. Although it may be possible to generate a product with individuals performing separate and isolated activities, the very nature of learning involves community.

Beginning with the principal as a learner and a facilitator of learning has implications for the other role conceptions. When we discuss the principal as mentor and supervisor, we do so with the understanding that these are focused on the principal's relationship with individual teachers as learners and with classrooms within the larger learning community. When we focus on the principal as leader, we emphasize the principal as a leader of learners within a school improvement setting. When we discuss the principal as manager, we set this view within a school improvement context and the principal's role in managing the resources and facilities that enable learning to occur for *all* students. When we discuss the principal as politician, we understand learning as the basis for power and the importance of providing equal opportunities for students, parents, teachers, and community members to share this powerful resource. Finally, in the chapter on principal as advocate, the foundation of our discussion is the right of *all* students to learn and to have access to learning.

In this chapter we organize our discussion of the principal's role as learner in three ways. First, we briefly discuss the meaning of learning, examining the traditional model of learning and more recent conceptual and empirical understandings of the meaning of learning. Second, we describe the principal as learner. In this section we will discuss the importance of continual learning for work roles in the twenty-first century and various components of the principal's and assistant principal's roles as learners, including self-awareness, inquiry, reflectivity, and complexity. As we discuss these components, we identify practical ways you can develop skills in these areas. In the third section of the chapter we focus on the principal as facilitator of learning. Here we discuss recent work on schools as learning organizations and professional learning communities and how you as a principal or assistant principal are key in helping create these learning environments.

Learning: Transmission versus Construction

The Traditional Conception of Learning

The traditional understanding of learning is tied to the industrial-age notion of organizations and schools. If we see schools as machines, we tend to see learning as machine-like, emphasizing worksheets and drills. Although recent developments in cognitive science suggest a different way to define learning (which we will discuss later in this section), schools typically reflect a more *traditional conception of learning*. The traditional conception of learning is in terms of its purpose, direction, and nature.

The traditional image focuses on the purpose of learning as transmission of skills, facts, knowledge, truth, and culture. The assumption, held over from the industrial age, is that learning involves transmitting the storehouse of facts and knowledge. Such an assumption ignores the dynamic nature of knowledge as constantly changing. This traditional view holds that it is the responsibility of the school to transmit the previous generation's values, knowledge, and cultural norms to the next generation. Schools have a valid role in transmitting values and norms to the new generation. However, to a certain extent, each generation negotiates and constructs its own values, norms, and knowledge.

Second, the traditional view assumes that learning occurs in one direction—from the teacher to the student. Peter Senge and colleagues (2000) suggested that this traditional conception of learning is based on the assumptions that children are defective and that the school's job is to fix them. "The deficit perspective assumes that something is broken and needs to be fixed. It is a reasonable way to think about machines, because machines cannot fix themselves. But it is a poor fit for living systems like children, which grow and evolve of their own accord" (p. 37). Senge and colleagues also suggested two other assumptions about learning that seem to flow from this unidirectional notion of learning. First, this view assumes that learning takes place in the classroom, not in the world. If the direction of learning is one way, then learning originates only with teachers in classrooms. Obviously, however, students and adults learn outside the school in their daily routines, conversations, and experiences. Second, Senge and colleagues argued that the industrial-age notion of learning has led us to view the school as being run by specialists whose chief aim is to maintain control. If the child is inherently defective, then control becomes a major issue. As Senge and colleagues suggested, there is nothing wrong with control, but the issue is the agent of control. In the industrial model, machines are controlled by their operators, but living systems learn to control themselves.

The third component of the traditional view of learning is that learning is individualistic, uniform, occurs in the head, and is based on knowledge as fragmented. One of the major views of learning is that it occurs individualistically. Senge and colleagues (2000) used the two basic actions of walking and talking, which seem totally individualistic, as examples of the limitations of this view. Young children hear others talking and watch others walking, running, and skipping. Their learning to walk and talk is actually learning to join the community of walkers and talkers. In this way, learning is collective rather than individualistic. Individuals also do not learn in the same way. Howard Gardner's (1983) work on multiple intelligences has emphasized that the linguistic and mathematical ways of knowing, which are emphasized in schools, are by no means the only ways of knowing. Research on learning styles suggests that individuals learn in different ways.

The nature of learning embedded in the traditional view also considers learning as only occurring in the head. Senge and colleagues (2000) suggested that the prevailing Western understanding divorces reason from perception, motion, or emotion. However, recent studies suggest otherwise. Senge and colleagues gave examples, such as riding a bike or recalling a telephone number by the action of dialing it, and suggested that these illustrate how much of what we know is involved not just in our heads but in our bodies.

The traditional conception of learning is based on a view of knowledge as fragmented. Schools teach subjects in discrete units, for example, American literature, language arts, world history, biology, and algebra. Yet the majority of learning that is necessary to live, work, and solve problems involves the integration of knowledge.

The traditional view of learning emphasizes the transmission of separate facts, values, and norms; the sole reliance on the teacher (or some other "expert") and the classroom as the source of learning; and an individualistic, uniform, mental, and discrete perspective on learning. As we have noted, many of these assumptions are not supported by recent cognitive research and fit only in an industrial-age model of schooling.

The Constructivist Conception of Learning

The conception of learning that we emphasize in this chapter and in this book is referred to in the literature as *constructivist*. We do not assume that this is the only valid perspective on learning, but we believe that it fits the notion of learning that occurs in an educational community that we want to emphasize in our discussion of the principal as learner. You will take or have taken courses in curriculum and instruction that elaborate more detail than this chapter can cover on how learning occurs. This section, however, will provide a brief overview to ground our discussion of the principal's role as learner.

The *constructivist conception of learning* has a notable history that includes such distinguished writers as Dewey, Piaget, Bruner, and Vygotsky. Each of these authors contributed important ideas to the development of constructivism. According to Walker and Lambert (1995), Dewey set the stage for constructivism by emphasizing that students needed to make meaning of their own learning based on individual and collective experiences. Piaget emphasized that knowledge is an ongoing process of continual construction and reorganization rather than some static operation. Bruner emphasized the learner as a constructor of knowledge and prior experience as deepening the learning experience. Vygotsky emphasized context as critical to understanding learning and the process of building on prior knowledge to create knowledge (scaffolding). In this case, knowledge and intelligence are socially constructed.

Prawat and Peterson (1999) identified two types of social constructivism: teleological and symbolic. These two types have implications for classroom and school-wide learning. First, the teleological view of constructivism is oriented toward results and "assumes that participation in goal-directed action is what binds the group together and provides the impetus for group 'social construction'" (p. 214). The apprenticeship model of learning is most closely identified with this type of social constructivism. In the classroom, this model would be applied when students learn by creating some product that will be used by others. In a school-wide application, this model can be seen in the opening vignette where the group of interested teachers at East Jersey focused on improving the school context for new students. In this application, Nancy Lowenstein acted as an intermediary "to facilitate deliberation that results in the establishment of a common goal or outcome" (p. 220).

The second type of constructivism, symbolic, is oriented toward the use of language and "assumes that creating meaning is what the group is all about—the development and testing out of new ways of looking at the world" (Prawat & Peterson, 1999, p. 214). Prawat and Peterson, in their discussion of the application of this type of constructivism, used Peter Elbow's (1986) two types of processes that a community goes through when testing new ideas. Methodological doubt encourages members to hold ideas at bay and to adopt a wait-and-see attitude. In contrast, methodological belief involves being open to new perceptions or formulations. People have to set aside their doubts momentarily and allow themselves to experience the full force of an unfamiliar or threatening idea. "It's like brainstorming, but here the listeners don't shut up, they help you find the fruitful implications in your suggestion. Such practice in looking at things differently in a supportive setting helps us learn to produce more and better ideas. Also, when trying to explore an idea, there is a peculiar fertility that comes from moving back and forth between doubting it and believing it" (Elbow, 1986, p. 288).

This constructivist understanding of learning can have a significant impact on how teachers teach and how schools become learning environments. "Teachers who understand, in a deep and profound way, a powerful idea behind much of the current discourse on learning and teaching—the notion that children literally construct their own knowledge, drawing on whatever resources, past or present, are available—not only think differently about student learning, they also view teaching and even disciplinary knowledge in a new light" (Prawat & Peterson, 1999, p. 220). This notion of groups constructing their own knowledge is a powerful way to think about school-level learning as well as classroom learning. At a school level, this model of constructivism moves away from restructuring to "reculturing" (Fullan, 1993), for example, teachers changing the way they think about teaching and learning.

Three major components of constructivism are emphasized in the literature and in our understanding of learning used in this book. We have chosen to refer to them as the three *C*'s: capacity, community, and criticality. First, learning involves the capacity of the learner to draw on prior experience. This emphasis contradicts the deficit model of the traditional view of learning. Instead of assuming that students at the classroom level and teachers at the school level are deficit in their knowledge, we assume the opposite. Both students and teachers bring with them knowledge based on prior learning and experience. They actively use this experience to construct new knowledge. The traditional deficit view has so contaminated our instructional approaches as educators that we forget not only that others bring capacity to the learning process but also that new learning occurs by building on this prior knowledge. In this sense, learning "reshapes classroom interaction from student as passive listener and teacher as source of knowledge, to learning as an interactive process entered into by both students and teachers" (Walker & Lambert, 1995, p. 15). As new administrators, your own learning works in the same way. You bring previous experience as a student, teacher, and learner that provides the scaffolding (Vygotsky, 1986) to construct new learning as an administrator. Reflecting on your previous experience can help you understand your own processes of learning.

The second component of constructivism is community. As we have noted, Vygotsky's (1986) major contribution to the development of constructivism was his emphasis on the collective nature of learning. Learning occurs in a social context that is cultural and historical. Rather than the individualistic quality of learning emphasized in the traditional view, social constructivism assumes a community of learners. One of your primary roles as a new administrator is to facilitate this community of learners. As teachers come together to make meaning of their collective experiences as learners and teachers, new learning develops. In the vignette that began this chapter, Nancy's proposal to develop a learning community can be seen not only as an innovative tool but also as a necessity for enabling the school and its constituents to grow professionally.

Third, social constructivism emphasizes critical reflection. In contemporary social contexts, such as schools, students, teachers, administrators, and parents encounter an avalanche of information. Often this information comes with no interpretative tools or evaluation. In the business field, some writers have estimated that the duration of innovations has shortened from a decade to less than a year (Micklethwhait & Wooldridge, 1996). The tendency in education is to cycle through fads about every three years. Such an uncritical acceptance of new ideas produces headaches for teachers in finding time for yet another new idea, for administrators in encouraging teachers to be innovative, and for the public in viewing the school's innovations as credible. As a new administrator, part of your role is to help teachers and parents as members of a learning community critically reflect on new ideas in such a way that learning is not mere assimilation of these ideas but the construction of meaning that acknowledges the tensions and contradictions of collective life in a community.

The definition of learning that we use in this book is based on constructivism and emphasizes the active capacity of all learners to construct new knowledge, the necessity of a community for the development of learning, and the importance of critical reflection in this learning process. In our discussion of learning, it should be obvious that these three components apply to the learning of teachers and administrators as well as students. In the next brief section we identify some of the major elements that are specific to adult learning.

Principles of Adult Learning

"All individuals have the potential to continually learn and grow. Adults, like children, bring their prior experiences, beliefs, and perceptions to their work with new experiences to construct knowledge and meaning" (Walker & Lambert, 1995, p. 26). Until a few years ago, this understanding of adult learning was not accepted or understood by the general public or psychologists. Many people assumed that once an individual completed puberty, no more development was possible or necessary. This assumption, fortunately, has been debunked. Now we know that, except in the case of those with certain rare diseases, there are no organic reasons why all adults cannot continue to learn. (See Oja & Reiman, 1998, for an excellent summary of adult conceptual development theories as they apply to teacher development and supervision.)

Although the components of constructivism that we identified in the last section apply to all learning, there are some differences between adult and child learning that are important to identify. One major difference that is especially relevant to our discussion of adult learning in schools is that adults are able to combine reflection and action, what Freire (1970) called *praxis*. They are able to consider the assumptions and values behind their actions and evaluate those actions. This quality is critical for building learning communities, such as schools, in which teachers and administrators reflect on their practice in ways to improve it.

Brookfield (1986) identified six principles that are critical to facilitating adult learning:

1. Participation in learning is voluntary; intimidation or coercion has no place in motivating adult participation.

2. Effective practice is characterized by respect among participants for each other's self-worth.

3. Facilitation is collaborative, with learners and facilitators sharing responsibility for setting objectives and evaluating learning.

4. *Praxis* is at the heart of effective facilitation, with learners and facilitators involved in a continual cycle of collaborative activity and reflection on activity.

5. Facilitation aims to foster in adults a spirit of critical reflection. Educational encounters should assist adults to question many aspects of their personal, occupational, and political lives.

6. The aim of facilitation is the nurturing of self-directed, empowered adults who will function as proactive individuals (cited in Glickman, Gordon, & Ross-Gordon, 1998, pp. 55–56).

Principal as Learner

As Chapter 2 emphasized, the principal's role has had a checkered history in terms of instruction. With beginnings as "principal teachers," principals moved quickly into a scientific management role that all but ignored teaching and learning, except as they affected efficiency. More recently, the literature on the principalship and numerous school reforms has emphasized an instructional leadership role, in which principals are expected to focus on teaching and learning and facilitate the learning community of the school. However, few writers have emphasized the principal as a learner.

The traditional role of principal seems to view teaching and learning as something that other professionals do, with the principal only facilitating resources for these professionals. In order for principals to be instructional leaders and facilitators of learning communities, they first must be active learners themselves.

In this section we will identify and discuss several components of the principal's role as a learner. However, before moving to this discussion, we begin with a discussion of the importance of learning for work in contemporary society and for schools that must address the issues of this contemporary society.

Importance of Learning in a Postindustrial Society

Numerous writers have noted that we are in a new era. This change is frequently contrasted with the industrial age and is referred to as *postindustrial society* (Bell, 1973). Hage and Powers (1992) claimed that there is ample evidence that we live in a new society. They identified the various institutional failures that are currently evident, including the increasing divorce rate and number of teenage pregnancies and other failures of older institutional forms. They also pointed to new institutional forms that are developing, including changes in the workplace, for example, experimentation, relaxed job descriptions, and a de-emphasis on status differences.

One primary reason for this societal change is the rapid explosion of knowledge that confronts almost all occupations. "The proportion of occupational categories that are knowledge intensive is expanding rapidly, while the number of less knowledge-intensive occupational categories is on the decline" (Hage & Powers, 1992, p. 38). This knowledge explosion confronts organizations such as schools with the need to change outdated forms of work that were developed during the industrial age.

Hage and Powers (1992) characterized the major features of work during the industrial age as emphasizing rationality, which leads to such work arrangements as standardization of procedures, deemphasis on human agency, limited interaction with other workers, and a focus on efficiency and quantity of work as assessment criteria. These arrangements were used to increase certainty and decrease ambiguity in the workplace.

Because schools are fashioned primarily after a factory model originating in the industrial age, these work arrangements are reflected in the work occurring in schools (Crow, Hausman, & Scribner, 2002). Standardization of procedures is evident in the reliance on policies for decisions of administrators and teachers. The policy manual has become the bible for most administrators. New administrators are admonished to check district and school policies in order to avoid lawsuits, grievances, and other complaints. Zero-tolerance policies that thwart educator discretion are good examples of attempts to decrease autonomy and reduce uncertainty. Various curriculum models also limit discretion among teachers. These models attempt to "teacher-proof" the curriculum by eliminating the judgment of the teacher.

Schools in their typical architectural and working structures reduce the contact among teachers. The "egg crate" school, where teachers teach alone with a group of students, emphasizes the limited contact among adults in the school. Mohrman and Cohen (1995) noted that those relationships that do exist among workers in an industrial-age work arrangement tend to be mediated by the boss. When teachers get together professionally to collaborate on school-wide issues, this collaboration tends to be initiated by the principal.

Teacher assessment has a long history of being based on the criteria of efficiency rather than innovation (Callahan, 1962) and quantity of content covered. In addition to these criteria, teacher assessment also tends to emphasize individual evaluations.

In the postindustrial society, Hage and Powers (1992) argued that new work arrangements are being developed. As we will see, learning becomes a significant necessity of these work arrangements.

Instead of the emphasis on increasing rationality and decreasing ambiguity found in industrial-age work arrangements, Hage and Powers (1992) claimed that in postindustrial society, complexity is emphasized. This complexity derives its importance from the rapid expansion of knowledge facing most occupations. These authors identified specific elements of work arrangements that reflect this complexity, including the need for customized response, greater emphasis on human agency, assessment based on innovation and creativity and reflecting a collective orientation, and a greater ability to search for information. Instead of searching the policy manual for solutions to problems, administrators may find the computer and the Internet to be their primary resources in the postindustrial society. The ability to know where to gather appropriate information in a timely way becomes more important than knowing the rules.

Various authors also have pointed to the increasing diversity and globalization of postindustrial work settings (Friedman, 1999). Schools are not exempt from these forces. The number of students of color is consistently increasing. By the year 2050, what have been called "minority children" will be closer to the majority. In many communities a highly diverse student body is already a reality. Economic realities, as well as Internet capabilities, make students global citizens in a context where information and knowledge are nonnationalistic.

Hage and Powers (1992) also claimed that one of the most important characteristics of work in postindustrial society will be the continuing need for workers to redefine their roles. Instead of a description that clearly and permanently defines a job, current and future jobs will be dynamic, and individuals will hold a variety of roles in their jobs. This book assumes that as a new principal or assistant principal, you will encounter some or all of these postindustrial realities. Instead of only viewing the principal's role as, for example, the instructional leader, you will need to be able to view your role from multiple standpoints and acknowledge that the nature of society and schools will require the ongoing ability to redefine your role. Such ability necessitates your continual learning and the learning of the teachers, students, and parents for whom you facilitate learning (Chapman, 1996).

As a principal in a society where knowledge forms the basis of the economy, you must be a learner and must facilitate the learning of others. In the rest of this section we identify four components of the principal as learner that reflect postindustrial reality: *self-awareness, inquiry, reflectivity,* and *complexity.*

Four Components of Principal as Learner

Self-awareness.   The scientific management and industrial-age conception of administration emphasized technical skills and intellectual capacity. Although these continue to be important, another set of skills is necessary for contemporary leaders. Daniel Goleman (1995) popularized the notion of *emotional intelligence* and emphasized its importance for leaders. Goleman defined emotional intelligence as "a different way of being smart. It includes knowing what your feelings are and using your feelings to make good decisions in life. It's being able to manage distressing moods well and control impulses. It's being motivated and remaining hopeful and optimistic when you have setbacks in working towards goals. It's empathy; knowing what the people around you are feeling. And it's social skill—getting along well with other people, managing emotions in relationships, being able to persuade or lead others" (quoted in O'Neil, 1996).

Goleman (1998) argued that when technical skills, IQ, and emotional intelligence are calculated as ingredients of exceptional performance, emotional intelligence is twice as important as the other two. Educators have long realized that interpersonal skills can make or break a principal (Davis, 1998). Schools in postindustrial society, with multiple roles, more diverse populations, and the need for rapid, customized responses, are likely to be places where conflict is present (Hage & Powers, 1992). As a principal or assistant principal, you will need good interpersonal skills in general and self-awareness in particular to respond to these highly conflictual situations. (See Chapter 6 for more discussion on conflict management.)

Goleman (1995) identified five components of emotional intelligence: self-awareness, self-regulation, motivation, empathy, and social skill. The first three involve self-management skills, whereas the last two involve working with others. In this section we focus on self-awareness as the most critical emotional skill related to the principal as learner.

Self-awareness involves "having a deep understanding of one's emotions, strengths, weaknesses, needs, and drives" (Goleman, 1998, pp. 95–96). Goleman explained that emotional intelligence is controlled by a part of the brain—the limbic system—that is very different from the part of the brain where analytical and technical abilities are controlled. Learning in the limbic system is more likely to occur through such processes as motivation, extended practice, and feedback. Goleman told the story of a Wall Street executive who intimidated his employees. The executive was interested in improving his empathy. He was amazed to find that not only his coworkers but also his family felt intimidated by him and often hesitated to deliver bad news for fear of his wrath. The executive hired a coach to help him become more aware of his behavior and took a trip to a foreign country where he did not speak the language to better understand his reactions to the unfamiliar. Over time, with feedback from his colleagues and coach, he was able to improve his understanding of himself and eventually of how people perceived him.

Goleman (1998) emphasized that emotional intelligence components such as self-awareness can be improved. Instead of the traditional assumption that principals' interpersonal skills are set before they enter the occupation, Goleman argued that these critical skills could be developed. As principals in a postindustrial society, you must focus on your own self-management skills, such as self-awareness, to lead schools.

One way to consider your own self-awareness is with a device known as a *Johari window* (Luft, 1970). Imagine a window with four panes (Figure 3.1). The first pane, referred to as the *public self*, involves your behaviors known by you and others. The second pane, the *blind self*, includes your behaviors that are known by others but unknown by you. For example, you may unintentionally behave in an aloof fashion, which is apparent to teachers but not to you as the principal or assistant principal. The third pane, known as the *private self*, involves your behaviors that are known by you but unknown by others. For example, the principal who in new situations "masks his or her unsureness by being extroverted in greeting others. Only the supervisor knows that this behavior is covering up insecurity" (Glickman, Gordon, & Ross-Gordon, 1998, p. 126). The fourth pane, the *unknown self*, includes your behaviors that are unknown by both you and others. The Johari window device emphasizes the need to be aware of your private and public behaviors as much as possible and to understand how they affect others. Sensitivity to how others perceive you provides a basis for understanding and developing your own self-awareness.

Inquiry. A second component of the principal as learner involves developing skills as an inquirer. Again, if you want to lead others to learn, you must be a learner yourself. The ability to be an inquirer has become essential for principals and assistant principals in understanding the school, making sense of such data as test scores, and using information to

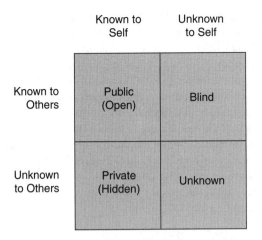

FIGURE 3.1   The Johari window.

make decisions. *Data-driven decision making* has become part of the vocabulary of principals and district administrators and involves the intentional collection and use of information to guide decision making. With recent accountability trends, principals can no longer depend on others to analyze data and interpret them to school faculty and the community. Frequently, principals discover that interest groups with a particular axe to grind misuse data in ways that reflect poorly on the school. Understanding data and being able to interpret them are critical skills for you as a principal or assistant principal.

There are at least four components to the principal as inquirer worth emphasizing. First, principals and assistant principals, to be good inquirers, must be able to define the problem. Sometimes administrators focus on problem solving without first understanding the real problem (problem finding) (McPherson, Crowson, & Pitner, 1986). Are there not enough problems without finding more? Problem finding is the inquiry skill of being able to identify the problem that needs to be solved rather than the problem as assumed or presented by others. Most veteran principals can tell you stories of solving what they presumed to be the problem, for example, a playground conflict or an "unmotivated" teacher, only to realize that this was not the real problem. In addition to a waste of time and energy, identifying the wrong problem can create new problems. Identifying credible sources of information, looking for patterns, and understanding history are among the many skills that principals and assistant principals need in problem finding.

Once a problem is identified, principals need skills in collecting information. There are two broad types of methods for collecting information as an inquirer: quantitative and qualitative. Quantitative methods, for example, surveys or checklists, focus on finding out the frequency of occurrence of an event or problem, such as how many times a teacher is absent or how often a student gets into trouble. Qualitative methods, for example, interviews, answer the question of why something happened or the meaning of a conversation. For example, what does a teacher mean when she says that a student is lazy? What does a student mean when he refuses a teacher's directive? Both types of methods are important for collecting information, but they have different purposes and will provide different information. Knowing how often something occurs will tell you whether it is an exception or a pattern, but it probably will not help you know why it occurs. On the other hand, knowing that a student refuses to obey a directive because of a disruption at home gives you insight about the reasons for this behavior but not whether it is typical.

Principals most often use two specific inquiry tools, talking to others and observing events. Talking to others is the most common administrative practice. The work of principals and assistant principals is essentially talk (Gronn, 1983). Principals collect information by talking to teachers, secretaries, custodians, students, cafeteria workers, parents, community members, and other administrators. The value of this talk for inquiry is related to several factors, including trust and rapport with these individuals, knowing what questions to ask, and listening actively to what others are saying.

The second most common method for inquiry is observing events. Knowing what to observe, when to observe, and how often to observe is critical to an inquirer. In Chapter 4 we will mention observation as a key element in the role of principal as supervisor, but observation also occurs in other areas of decision making, for example, resolving conflicts and identifying school-improvement strategies. Principals as learners develop an acuity that permits them to quickly and accurately size up situations without jumping to unwarranted conclusions.

Collecting information, through talking, observing, or any other means, is only part of inquiry. Principals must know how to make sense of their communications, observations, or of other forms of data, for example, test scores. Information does not appear already interpreted. Placing this information in the school context, identifying possible explanations and consequences, acknowledging the limitations and assumptions of the information, and considering plans of action are all part of the inquiry process. Frequently, principals are faced with community groups that have taken uninterpreted data, such as test scores, and drawn faulty interpretations. Knowing how to interpret data for yourself is a critical role for you as a learner and as a facilitator of others' learning.

Finally, inquiry must not remain in the head of the observer or listener. It must be reported to the appropriate stakeholders. It may mean reporting to teachers and parents who need the information to make decisions. If the information stays in the head of the principal, it cannot provide the needed input for school improvement and data-driven decision making.

Reflectivity.   The third component of the principal as learner involves the practice of reflectivity. Reflection is not a new idea; Dewey discussed it years ago as an integral part of the educational process. More recently, Donald Schon (1983) acknowledged its importance to practitioners. Senge and colleagues (2000) described reflection as part of the cycle of change. "People learn in cycles, moving naturally between action and reflection, between activity and repose. These cycles represent the way we improve what we do" (p. 93).

In discussing reflection, Argyris and Schon (1974) made a distinction between single-loop learning and double-loop learning. This distinction is useful in understanding how you can be more effective in your reflection. *Single-loop learning* is "observing our previous action, reflecting on what we have done, using that observation to decide how to change our next action, and applying that decision to another action. . . ." (Senge et al.,

2000, p. 93). Single-loop learning is the typical way to use reflection, that is, simply thinking about whether our previous action worked or not. Obviously, this type of reflection is more effective than not reflecting at all on our actions. However, a more effective form of reflection is found in Argyris & Schon's concept of *double-loop learning*. In this type of learning, the principal extends the reflection to include time to consider why we make choices, that is, our assumptions and values. "You reconsider the tasks you've set for yourself and you try to understand the ways that your own choices (both conscious and unconscious choices) may contribute to the frustration you feel or the effectiveness of your organization" (Senge et al., 2000, p. 95).

Senge and colleagues (2000) identified a cycle of learning that includes the double-loop use of reflection. This cycle includes the following parts:

1. *Observing.* Here the principal asks: "How well did it go? What were we thinking? When we made a mistake, what assumptions or attitudes might have helped lead us there?"
2. *Reflecting.* In this type of reflection, the principal contemplates the implications of what is observed and draws conclusions from them.
3. *Deciding.* The principal ponders the next action.
4. *Doing.* The principal "performs a task with as much experimental frame of mind as possible." (p. 95)

According to Senge and colleagues, what makes this process double-loop learning is what happens during the reflecting stage. They argued that three processes take place in this type of reflection that are different from the simple single-loop reflection. First, we reconsider our assumptions that got us to this place. Second, we reconnect by using new approaches and perspectives that are different from our usual sources of information. Third, we reframe or use new guiding ideas and consider whether they will stretch our capabilities. This type of reflection is more effective because it forces us to look deeper—by examining our assumptions—and look broader—by venturing outside our usual sources of information.

This method is not the most common approach to administrative learning. More typically we tend to stay within the box, never questioning our assumptions nor venturing beyond our "tried and true" sources of information. Senge and colleagues (2000) described a school district that decided that student tracking was not working effectively. The faculty observed that students in some tracks were not achieving minimal standards; they reflected on the fact that the bright kids got the most effective teachers and the other kids got the rest of the teachers. However, because they had always tracked, they never considered eliminating tracking. The faculty of the district did not question their assumptions about tracking itself. This example illustrates the nature and limitations of single-loop learning.

Dress codes and school uniform policies as methods for fighting gang activity are other examples of single-loop learning. They often are the result of reflections on and responses to gang activities in the school that never question assumptions about the reason for gangs. Typically, creating dress codes that outlaw certain types of clothing that are associated with gangs usually results in the gangs changing their clothing patterns.

Another way to improve your reflective skills is to use the distinction made by Argyris and Schon (1974) between espoused theories and theories in use. These authors identified the importance that theories play in our thinking and learning. These theories are not the abstract type typically discussed in graduate classes but rather are the assumptions that lie behind our everyday practices. Espoused theories involve the conscious and easily changeable assumptions that we make about our actions. Theories in use, on the other hand, are deeper, frequently difficult to articulate, and more difficult to change. Osterman and Kottkamp (1993) illustrated the discrepancies between espoused theories and theories in use: "A school administrator may espouse the concept of collaborative management and not recognize autocratic aspects of his or her own behavior. A teacher may read the effective schools research and agree wholeheartedly on the importance of high expectations for all students and not see the inconsistency in having very high expectations for students perceived to be bright and having 'adjusted' expectations for students with learning or behavioral problems" (p. 12). Osterman and Kottkamp argued that these discrepancies could only be addressed when individuals reflect on their habitual behavioral patterns, their assumptions, and the impact of what they do.

Responding to the demands of a postindustrial society will require you to be a learner that reflects in such a way that your assumptions are questioned and information is used from a wide variety of new sources. This reflectivity is not a luxury of professors but a necessity for administrators.

Complexity.   In our discussion of the nature of work in postindustrial society we noted that the primary feature is its emphasis on complexity. As a principal or assistant principal who is a learner, you must develop skills that allow you and others to respond to complexity in the school context and environment.

Karl Weick (1978), an organizational psychologist, proposed a somewhat surprising suggestion that leaders need to be docile. Counter-intuitive to the typical prescription that leaders should be directive and firm, Weick's proposal is built on the idea that leaders who are more flexible are more capable of reflecting and addressing complex environments. Weick used the example of the contour gauge, which allows one to trace an outline of an object, to illustrate this flexibility. The more teeth in the contour gauge, the more specific the tracing will be. A contour gauge with fewer and larger teeth will provide only a very rough estimate of the object, whereas a contour gauge with more and smaller teeth—thus providing more flexibility in tracing the object—will provide more detail of the object. Principals who are able to use multiple sources of information to understand what is happening in their schools and communities are more effective in responding to complex situations than principals who rigidly hold to one "reliable" source of information.

Weick (1978) argued that leaders act as mediums for their organizations, describing and explaining the world that workers experience. A leader whose picture is more believable because it describes more of what employees experience is more likely to be followed. "The leader continually reveals novel aspects of the situation, and it is this novelty that gives him power. People rely on the leader's pictures because he gets more accurate and more diverse or more suggestive pictures than do any of the followers" (p. 47). The ability to reflect and express the diversity and therefore the complexity of your environment increases your effectiveness in leading others. In a postindustrial society where standardization is less possible or desirable, a principal who can learn to deal with the complexity of schools by providing diverse images of what schools can do will be a more effective leader. "The more medium-like a leader is, the more images he should be able to invent and make available to his followers. And to the extent that those followers thrive on seeing themselves engaged in interesting activities housed in interesting worlds, this leader should be influential" (p. 50).

Weick (1995) provided useful guidelines for principals in dealing with complexity. Based on his research on how firefighters deal with the complexity of dangerous situations, Weick made connections between educational administration and fighting fires (not a far-fetched connection). He identified five suggestions that can facilitate principals being learners who respond to complexity:

1. Effective firefighting (principaling) occurs when people appreciate the complexity of small events and mobilize complex systems to make sense of and manage them.
2. Effective firefighting (principaling) occurs when people know what they don't know and simultaneously trust and mistrust their past experience.
3. Effective firefighting (principaling) occurs when people have a model for the origin of rogue events.
4. Effective firefighting (principaling) occurs when people strive to manage issues rather than to solve problems.
5. Effective firefighting (principaling) occurs when people improvise after first putting into place a system of lookouts, communication, escape routes, and safety zones.

These suggestions are different from the standard operating procedures and administrative folklore of the past era, in which routinization was emphasized. In a postindustrial age, the ability to learn in a complex environment is essential for the principal.

In addition to Weick's suggestions for the principal as learner in a complex setting, Bolman and Deal (1991) offered useful ways to consider this component of learning. They identified four frames for understanding organizations that can be useful to you as a principal and learner in using multiple perspectives to increase your ability to deal with complexity. These four frames are structural, human resource, political, and symbolic. The *structural* frame focuses on goals, roles, and structures. The *human resource* frame emphasizes the individuals who inhabit organizations—their feelings, needs, and motivations. The *political* frame draws attention to power in organizations and how individuals and groups struggle for power. Finally, the *symbolic* frame views organizations as cultures with stories, heroes, and myths. No one of these frames provides a complete picture of the school. Instead, Bolman and Deal encouraged the development of multiple frames that enable us to see and act on the complexity of the school. "Frames are both windows on the world and lenses that bring the world into focus. Frames filter out some things while allowing others to pass through easily. Frames help us to order experience and decide what actions to take" (p. 11). Ignoring the complexity of schools and assuming that there is one way of looking at schools is similar to "managers who master the hammer and expect all problems to be nails" (p. 11). However, learning to use multiple perspectives that enhance the view of the school's complexity enables you to be a learner who is more effective not only in your own learning but also in facilitating and improving the learning of others.

We have identified four components of the principal as learner: self-awareness, inquiry, reflectivity, and complexity. Certainly, there is more about learning that could be presented. However, given the principal's complex role in a changing society where learning is central, these four components constitute critical skills that you as a new principal or assistant principal will need to develop. If you have developed commitment, sensitivity, and expertise in your own learning, you will be in a much better position to facilitate the learning of others.

Principal as Facilitator of Learning

In the vignette that began this chapter, Nancy Lowenstein attempted to make learning an organization-wide effort and priority. Nancy's emphasis reflects one of the most discussed areas of reform in both the educational and business literatures. Instead of focusing on the principal as instructional leader working alone, this emphasis views the entire school and its community as learners. The principal's role becomes one of facilitating the learning of others.

In this section we will examine two ways of looking at schools using the learning theme: as learning organizations and as professional learning communities. Sergiovanni (1994) identified the two metaphors of organization and community that shape our thinking about schools. Although these two metaphors can overlap, and in fact, writers focusing on learning organizations and professional learning community often connect the two, these two images reflect unique understandings of the principal's role in facilitating the learning of others.

Schools as Learning Organizations

Many of the concepts we discussed earlier in this chapter regarding the nature of learning have been applied to organizations as well as individuals. Schools where *organizational learning* is emphasized and is an integral part of the practice are referred to as *learning organizations*. Frequently these terms, *organizational learning* and *learning organization*, are used interchangeably. "Organizational learning is a concept used to describe certain types of activity that take place in an organization, while the learning organization refers to a particular type of organization in and of itself. . . . A learning organization is one which is good at organizational learning" (Tsang, 1997, p. 74).

Although we will begin with organizational learning and then turn to schools as learning organizations, it might be helpful to begin with Peter Senge's core ideas about learning in organizations (Senge et al., 2000). Senge and colleagues are best known as the popularizers of the notion of organizational learning, a concept first credited to Karl Weick (1969). Senge and colleagues identified three core ideas that are foundational for our understanding of schools as learning organizations. First, "every organization is a product of how its members think and interact" (p. 19). The kinds of difficulties that schools, like all organizations, face are rooted in the way people in schools think and work together. This usually means the assumptions and values underneath our actions that influence and sometimes limit the way we think about what is possible. The second core idea is that "learning is connection" (p. 20). This idea reflects our earlier discussion of the nature of learning as a social process. The third core idea is that "learning is driven by vision" (p. 21). There must be some relevant purpose for learning. Senge and colleagues used the example of bike riding, which children learn to do because they want to play with their friends. Learning that results in school change is also guided by purpose. These three core ideas create a way of thinking about schools as learning organizations.

As educators, we usually think of learning as intentional; that is, we are consciously intending to acquire new knowledge (Huber, 1991). However, it does not take us long to realize that much of what individuals and organizations learn is unintentional, even accidental. For example, a student makes an off-handed remark that helps us understand how much learning occurs outside the classroom.

Learning, both individual and organizational, may not result in immediate improvements in performance. Individuals and organizations "can incorrectly learn, and they can correctly learn that which is incorrect" (Huber, 1991, p. 89). Huber argued that an individual or organization "learns if, through its processing of information, the range of its potential behaviors is changed" (p. 89). Learning provides us with alternatives for both thinking about our practice and actually practicing.

Huber (1991) identified four aspects of organizational learning: knowledge acquisition, information distribution, information interpretation, and organizational memory. Organizations acquire knowledge by what they inherit from the environment before their conception; what they experience through a variety of processes, such as self-appraisal and experimenting; what they learn vicariously from other organizations; what they acquire from new members; and what they search for in the external environment. Schools that are open to this type of organizational learning are sensitive to what other schools are doing, what their new members have to offer, and what information their communities possess.

In addition to acquiring knowledge, organizations must examine how the information found in the organization is distributed. What individuals or groups have useful knowledge that needs to be distributed more widely? Do organizational leaders hoard valuable information that prevents organizational members from actively participating in learning?

However, organizational learning involves more than acquiring knowledge and distributing information. It also involves interpreting the information or giving that information meaning as individuals and groups make sense of the information. What kinds of cognitive maps, interpretive schemes, or mental models do individuals use to make sense of information? Are all these mental models valued, or are some models considered "right" while others are disregarded or ridiculed?

Organizational learning also involves the process whereby organizations store their knowledge. What happens in the organization when the few people who possess the oral tradition or history of the organization leave or retire?

These four sets of processes suggest that organizational learning is an ongoing, dynamic process involving everyone in the organization. In the opening vignette, Nancy Lowenstein found that teachers at East Jersey Elementary School had reduced their organizational learning in part by relying on the former principal to make all the decisions.

Practices such as those of this former principal reduce the knowledge acquired, restrict the distribution of information, limit the interpretation of information to one person, and run the risk of a short organizational memory. These practices short-circuit the organizational learning capacity of the organization.

Another way to think of the nature of organizational learning is the five disciplines identified by Senge and colleagues (2000). According to these authors, these five dimensions form the foundation of organizational learning. First, personal mastery involves "the practice of articulating a coherent image of your personal vision—the results you most want to create in your life—alongside a realistic assessment of the current reality of your life today" (p.7). Although this discipline is what individuals do, they can be supported by their schools, "where people have time to reflect on their vision, by establishing an organizational commitment to the truth wherever possible, and by avoiding taking a position (explicit or implicit) about what other people (including children) should want or how they should view the world" (p. 60).

Shared vision, Senge and colleagues' (2000) second discipline, involves "the set of tools and techniques for bringing all of these disparate aspirations into alignment around the things people have in common—in this case, their connection to the school" (p. 72). Once individuals have identified their visions for the future and the current reality, organizations bring those visions together toward some common purpose. Frequently, teachers like those at East Jersey Elementary School expect the principal's vision to be the vision of the school. Yet, if organizational learning is to occur, there must be a collective purpose.

Third, organizational learning involves surfacing the mental models that we use to understand and learn. Mental models are typically below the surface, off our radar screens, in terms of our understanding of what we know and how we know it. Senge and colleagues (2000) pointed out that these mental models are the reason why two people can look at the same event and interpret it differently. Frequently, our mental models are built on our feelings that "our beliefs are *the* truth; the truth is obvious; our beliefs are based on real data; the data we select are the real data" (p. 68). Once we understand how inference works, we can ask each other the following questions:

1. What are the observable data behind that statement?
2. Does everyone agree on what the data are?
3. Can you run me through your reasoning?
4. How did we get from that data to these abstract assumptions? (p. 70).

The fourth discipline, according to Senge and colleagues (2000), is team learning. This discipline is reflected in current attempts, most notably in middle schools, to develop teacher teams that involve individuals coming together to combine their ideas and energies toward some common purpose. "Team learning is based on the concept of alignment—as distinct from agreement . . . [and] has the connotation of arranging a group of scattered elements so they function as a whole, by orienting them all to a common awareness of each other, their purpose, and their current reality" (p. 74). Team learning occurs primarily through dialogue—team members exchanging ideas. "In the process of dialogue, we pay attention not only to the words but to the spaces between the words; not only to the result of an action but to its timing; not only to the things people say but to the timbre and tones of their voices" (p. 75).

The final discipline of organizational learning is systems thinking, in which "people learn to better understand interdependency and change and thereby are able to deal more effectively with the forces that shape the consequences of their actions" (Senge et al., 2000, p. 8). Instead of seeing events in the school as isolated occurrences, individuals consider the ways other parts of the school interact to influence the events, for example, how reward systems and communication systems at East Jersey Elementary School may discourage teachers from trying innovative ideas.

Senge and colleagues (2000) argued that organizational learning in schools occurs at three nested levels: classroom, school, and community. These five disciplines must be applied to all three of these levels as students, teachers, staff, administrators, parents, and community members engage in organizational learning.

If organizational learning is what learning organizations do, what are the characteristics of learning organizations? Chapman (1996) used the characteristics of learning organizations identified by David Steward. According to Steward, learning organizations

1. Invest in their own future through the education and training of all their people.
2. Create opportunities for and encourage all their people in all their functions as employees, members, professionals, or students of the organization; as ambassadors of the organization to its customers, clients, audiences, and suppliers; as citizens of the wider society in which the organization exists; and as human beings with the need to realize their own capabilities.
3. Share their vision and sense of mission with their people and stimulate them to challenge it, to change it, and to contribute to it.
4. Integrate work and learning and inspire all their people to seek quality, excellence, and continuous improvement in both.
5. Mobilize all their human talent by putting the emphasis on learning and planning their education and training activities accordingly.
6. Empower all their people to broaden their horizons in harmony with their preferred learning styles.
7. Apply up-to-date open and distance delivery technologies appropriately to create broader and more varied learning opportunities.
8. Respond proactively to the wider needs of the environment and the society in which they operate and encourage their people to do likewise.
9. Learn and relearn constantly in order to remain innovative, inventive, invigorating, and in business (pp. 45–46).

Hargreaves (1995) acknowledged that organizational learning can benefit schools by being a source of learning. "It helps people to see problems as things to be solved, not as occasions for blame; to value the different and even dissident voices of more marginal members of the organization; and to sort out the wheat from the chaff of policy demands. Collaborative cultures turn individual learning into shared learning" (p. 19).

However, Hargreaves (1995) argued that not all ideas about organizational learning from the corporate sector are relevant to schools:

> For example, the commitment to continuous improvement can easily degenerate into interminable improvement, where no one values heritage and such vital ingredients of schooling as tradition, continuity, and consolidation. In such settings, only incurable change addicts prosper. Some teachers are habitual explorers, voracious readers, enthusiastic conference-goers, and willing committee and task force volunteers. Others, especially teachers in mid-to-late career, prefer to cultivate their own gardens, making small changes with their own classes where they know their efforts will make a difference (p. 19).

Principal/Assistant Principal's Role in Facilitating Learning Organizations.   The learning organization image of schools is a powerful one for contemporary schools that want to reform learning and teaching. In this image, principals and assistant principals perform a profound role in facilitating the learning organization of schools. However, this role is different from the traditional role. Charlotte Roberts (Senge et al., 2000) described this traditional role as the "principal-do-right image" and identified four elements:

1. A good leader gains and remains in control at all times. Take a stand and hold that position. No one else will defend the children (or policy, teacher, or curriculum) as well as you will.
2. A good leader "wins" all confrontations, regardless of the party with whom she or he is sparring—child, parent, teacher, administrator, board member, politician. Winning isn't always possible, so be able to recast the exchange as learning, planning or negotiating.
3. Negative feelings expressed by the principal indicate loss of control and maybe incompetence.
4. Being rational is a sign of being educated—it's that simple. An educator, after all, develops the minds of our young people. To not appear rational is to appear incompetent (pp. 412–413).

Roberts identified a more appropriate role for the principal based on learning organization principles. This type of principal will have four major competencies: engagement, systems thinking, leading learning, and self-awareness. Engagement involves the capability to recognize "messy" issues. Heifetz (1994) suggested that the principal asks questions in order to step back and diagnose the nature of the crisis and the attitudes of people involved; reflect on the levels of tension, stress, and learning in the community; and identify the places to intervene.

Another competency for principals is systems thinking. This competencey involves helping the faculty "recognize the hidden dynamics of complex systems and to find leverage" (Senge et al., 2000, p. 415).

The principal also models learning. Instead of an authority-centered approach to all problems, the principal models a learner-centered approach, which means that the principal is willing to accept uncertainty. "Leaders expect themselves and others to be uncertain, inquiring, expectant of surprise, and perhaps a bit joyful about confronting the unknown" (Senge et al., 2000, p. 417). This approach reflects the suggestion by Weick (1978), discussed earlier in this chapter, that docile leaders, who remain flexible, may be more effective than the traditionally decisive, firm leader.

Roberts (Senge et al., 2000) also advised that principals need self-awareness, a competency we identified earlier. This self-awareness requires taking time away to reflect and to engage others in helping this awareness to develop. For the same reason that principals need time for their own self-awareness, they need to facilitate the self-awareness of others in the learning organization.

Hart and Bredeson (1996) applied three leadership roles identified by Senge and colleagues to the principalship: designer, teacher, and steward. The principal as designer is in contrast to the typical engineer or director conception of the role. As a designer, the principal facilitates the learning organization by helping to formulate and nurture the mutual purposes of the school, develop policies and structures that translate this vision into reality, and institutionalize self-renewing learning processes so that they are norms and not surprises.

As a teacher, the principal acts as a coach or facilitator to "help students, teachers, and other staff understand the mental models and basic assumptions about teaching and learning in particular schools and communities. . . . Principals bring attention to the realities of school life at three distinct levels—individual events, patterns of individual behavior, and systemic structures—and help others understand the relationships among the three" (Hart & Bredeson, 1996, p. 137). One of the ways principals act as teachers to facilitate the school as a learning organization is to caution school constituencies of the trap of passing fads. There is a tendency in schools, partly because of funding structures, to choose a new fad about every three years. Such a process runs counter to the kind of critical inquiry process that schools as learning organizations need. "Nothing is more witchdoctorish than the suggestion that one magic potion will cure all ills" (Micklethwhait & Wooldridge, 1996, p. 324).

The third role that Hart and Bredeson (1996) identified from Senge and colleagues is the principal as steward. "Principals as 'servant leaders' are stewards for the people they lead and for the larger purposes and mission of the school" (p. 138). These principals remind teachers and other school constituents of the mission of the school and strive constantly for what is best for the children and their families.

The principal's role in facilitating the school as a learning organization occurs at all three levels: classroom, school, and community. In Chapters 4 and 5 we will focus on the principal's role in facilitating learning in the classroom as a mentor and supervisor. The principal as facilitator of the school as a learning organization has both internal and external roles to play. The internal role requires the principal to model the learner-centered approaches to teachers and students, helping them to understand their own visions, develop shared visions, acknowledge their mental models, develop their skills in team learning, and think systemically (Senge et al., 2000). As you, as a new principal or assistant principal, "get involved in organizational learning at your school, you become even more of a fulcrum point—not just a supervisor of teachers, but a 'lead teacher and lead learner,' and steward of the learning process as a whole" (Senge et al., 2000, p. 15).

The external role is no less significant. Schools are not isolated learning organizations but exist within a larger learning community that includes parents and extended families, the district office, community institutions, the media, and government entities. Understanding the systemic quality of learning organizations and communicating that to school constituents are vital and profound responsibilities for you as a new principal or assistant principal. A specific way that principals and assistant principals can facilitate the learning organization by encouraging teachers and others to become learners involves action research. In the vignette that began this chapter, the small discussion group that Nancy established to examine learning organizations conducted action research to investigate how to improve the learning of the new students in the school.

Action research is a technique or collection of techniques that focuses inquiry on some problem of practice or attempts to make change. Although it uses many of the techniques of academic research, action research is more narrowly focused on practice and is conducted by educators working alone or in groups with other educators, including professors within the context of the school. The process typically involves the steps of identifying a problem area, collecting and organizing data, interpreting data, acting based on the data, and reflecting. Action research can focus on a single classroom issue, a collective of classrooms with a common issue, a school-wide issue, or a district-wide issue (Ferrance, 2000).

Some school reform strategies use action research as a central component of their approach. For example, in the accelerated learning model (Levin, 1987), administrators, teachers, and parents develop processes of inquiry to investigate solutions to common problems and ways to implement change. The principal not only can facilitate action research on the part of teachers but also can be an active participant in the process in ways that benefit the principal's own leadership and learning.

Before moving to the next image of schools, we want to emphasize the specific role that assistant principals can play in facilitating schools as learning organizations. As we mentioned earlier, the traditional role of assistant principal has tended to ignore instructional leadership and focus, sometimes entirely, on student management. A more innovative conception of the role of assistant principal as learner and facilitator of learning broadens the role to emphasize instructional leadership. The assistant principal can join with the principal in providing instructional focus and a concern with learning throughout the organization.

The assistant principal, however, can make a distinctive contribution to the school as a learning organization. Assistant principals, because of their potentially extensive understanding of individual students in the school, can provide a sensitive and profound advocacy role for students as learners. Assistant principals often see students in a more holistic way than some teachers do. They see how learning is related to physical, emotional, and social aspects of the students' lives and how creating a learning community must take into consideration these elements. This sensitivity can help other educators avoid the illusion that learning occurs only in the classroom.

Assistant principals also can facilitate the school as a learning organization through their familiarity with outside school agencies, such as social services, mental health, and other community organizations, that can be resources in broadening the school's influence. In addition to promoting and improving learning beyond the classroom, assistant principals can help other educators think systemically about how learning occurs.

Schools as Professional Learning Communities

The second image of schools that provides a conception of the principal's role in facilitating learning is the school as a *professional learning community*. Sergiovanni (1994) contrasted the two metaphors of organization and community and encouraged greater use of community as a way to think about schools. The organization metaphor emphasizes management structures and procedures. Schools are described in terms of department or grade levels, job descriptions, and curriculum plans. A major part of the administrator's role in this image of schools is control. Administrators must convince others that they are in control, and they do this by using rules and regulations. In contrast, the community metaphor emphasizes commitment rather than contracts. "Communities are socially organized around relationships and the felt interdependencies that nurture them. Instead of being tied together and tied to purposes by bartering arrangements, this social structure bonds people together in special ways and binds them to concepts, images, and values that comprise a shared idea structure. This bonding and binding are the defining characteristics of schools as communities" (Sergiovanni, 1994, p. 217).

Westheimer (1999) identified five characteristics of community found in the literature. First, communities can be identified by the shared beliefs held by their members. Second, the high level of interaction and participation among members is a feature of community. Identity and commitment result from this high level of interaction. Third, members of communities exhibit a great deal of interdependence that results in reciprocity and mutual need. Fourth, in addition to this interdependence, community members share a concern for individual and minority views. Finally, meaningful relationships are present in community based on common purpose. Although variations in these characteristics may be found in any actual community, these components are critical to the existence and maintenance of community.

Several researchers have identified characteristics of professional learning communities, but we will use those found in the research of Bryk, Cambron, and Louis (1999). These authors defined professional communities as schools where "interaction among teachers is frequent and teachers' actions are governed by shared norms focused on the practice and improvement of teaching and learning" (p. 753).

Bryk, Camburn, and Louis (1999) identified three core practices of a professional community. First, teachers in these communities engage in reflective dialogue with their colleagues about their instructional practices and student learning. This reflective dialogue occurs frequently and in various places in the school, including the cafeteria, the hall, and the teachers' lounge (Little, 1982). Second, these communities are recognized by the deprivatization of practice. Instead of confining teaching practices behind the classroom door, they are brought to light by teachers regularly observing each other's practices. Deprivatization of practice also involves joint problem solving as a typical rather than exceptional activity. Teachers become advisors, mentors, and specialists for each other. Third, professional communities are known for their peer collaboration, in which teachers engage in actual shared work in school-wide problem solving and decision making.

These three practices, reflective dialogue, deprivatization of practice, and peer collaboration, are supported by two other components (Bryk, Cambron, & Louis, 1999). Teachers and administrators in these professional learning communities share norms that are focused on student learning. Thus dialogue, practice, and collaboration focus specifically on student learning and are reflected in shared norms. In addition, these professional learning community practices are supported by socialization structures that reinforce the shared norms around student learning, especially for new teachers.

However, are all professional learning communities the same? In a study of two California middle schools where teachers and administrators were explicit about their commitment to fostering teacher professional communities, Westheimer (1999) found two general patterns of community in the two schools, named Brandeis and Mills.

> Brandeis's professional community emphasizes teachers' individual autonomy, rights, and responsibilities to colleagues. . . . Mills's is driven by a strong collective mission and collective values. Whereas Brandeis's mission is broad minded and liberal in its notion of the individual separate from the community, Mills's is specific-minded and communal in its notion of the individual in relation to the community. Brandeis's teachers seek support from one another, Mills's seek solidarity (p. 86).

Westheimer labeled these two types of professional communities "liberal" and "collective." The practices in these communities vary in terms of what they talk about, how leadership positions are filled, and how they deal with disagreements. In the liberal community, Brandeis, teachers talk primarily about pedagogy and practices, whereas in the collective community, Mills, teachers talk about philosophy and principles. Furthermore, at Brandeis, leadership positions are hierarchically appointed, but at Mills leadership positions are determined more by abilities than by ascribed titles. Disagreements at Brandeis are handled primarily in private conversations, not in public forums, whereas at Mills disagreements are handled in collective discussions.

In a study of Chicago elementary schools, Bryk, Cambron, and Louis (1999) found that professional learning communities could exist in a variety of school contexts regardless of student composition factors such as race and socioeconomic status (SES). Three organizational conditions, however, facilitate these communities. First, professional learning communities thrive best in smaller elementary schools of less than 350 students rather than in larger schools. The authors suggested that smaller schools make reflective dialogue, deprivatization of practice, and collaboration more possible. Smaller schools also reinforce social trust, which is the second organizational condition that facilitates professional learning communities. In fact, social trust is probably the strongest facilitator of these communities. "When teachers trust and respect each other, a powerful social resource is available for supporting the collaboration, reflective dialogue, and deprivatization characteristics of a professional community" (p. 767). When trust among colleagues is absent, it is unlikely that people will have extended meaningful conversations, expose their practices, and form cooperative relationships. The third organizational condition is principal leadership.

Principal/Assistant Principal's Role in Facilitating Professional Learning Communities.

Bryk, Cambron, and Louis (1999) described the importance of principal leadership for building professional learning communities. A debate in the literature, however, exists regarding whether the most effective leadership style is directive or facilitative. Regardless of the style, principals play a key role, according to these authors, in creating a normative climate that reinforces the practices of professional learning communities. The results of the Chicago study found that

> The elements of professional community are supported by principals who are in regular contact with their faculty, even to the extent of visiting teachers' classrooms on a regular basis. The elements of professional community were also more prevalent when principals were viewed as having more inclusive facilitative styles. These results suggest that principals' regular involvement with faculty members is important, but that involvement that goes beyond regular contact, that encourages teachers to be involved, to innovate, and to take risks, may be particularly supportive of professional community (p. 768).

The role of the principal as supervisor, working directly with individual teachers, will be the subject of the next chapter.

Scribner and colleagues (1999), in a study of three rural schools, identified principal leadership practices that fostered or impeded the development and maintenance of professional learning communities. At the Northridge School, the principal's leadership focused on building trust among the school's faculty and staff and in so doing helped create a sense of common purpose. This leadership was reflected in the principal's trust in the faculty's ability to lead, and in turn, the faculty's trust in the principal grew out of the principal's commitment to both teachers and students.

The principal of the Cedarbrook School took a more hands-off approach that negatively affected the professional learning community. He approached school improvement by abdicating responsibility to a group of teacher leaders. In refusing to use his position as a "bully pulpit" to engender support for improvement, this principal impeded the development of professional community.

In the third school, Westwood, the principal's espoused values failed to match his practice. Although cordial and professional in his treatment of faculty and staff, this principal tended to choose the same leadership group for all improvement efforts and thus weakened the chances of the faculty as a whole for developing decision-making expertise. Limiting the wider opportunities for shared leadership impeded the development of a professional learning community at Westwood.

Both the studies of Bryk, Camburn, and Louis (1999) and Scribner and colleagues (1999) clearly asserted that the principal's facilitative role in creating a sense of social trust among faculty is critical for developing professional learning communities. Trusting faculty enough to share leadership is a potent resource for encouraging reflective dialogue, deprivatization of practice, and collaboration.

The principal's facilitative role is an active rather than passive role. Research findings continue to promote the notion that the principal plays a powerful role in facilitating both learning organizations and professional learning communities.

Conclusion

Nancy Lowenstein, in the opening vignette, attempted as a new principal to create a professional learning community at East Jersey Elementary School. The faculty met Nancy's attempt with both excitement and reluctance. Her focus on learning is illustrative of what we believe is the fundamental role conception for principals and assistant principals who are moving beyond the traditional managerial role to an innovative leadership for learning role. Principals and assistant principals as learners have a profound role to play in their own learning and in facilitating the learning of others. We have identified specific ways you, as a new principal or assistant principal, can enrich your own learning as you respond to the complexity of postindustrial schools and work roles. We also have described how you can facilitate a professional learning community committed to teaching and learning for all students.

The emphasis on the principal as learner in this chapter is foundational to the other six role conceptions we believe characterize innovative principals and assistant principals for postindustrial schools. In the next two chapters we focus on how this emphasis is implemented at the internal school level. Chapter 4 describes a role for principals that is rarely identified—principal as mentor—but which is important for creating learning environments in classrooms so that all students and teachers can learn.

Activities

Self-Directed Activities

1. If you were Nancy's mentor in the opening vignette, what other suggestions would you provide to help Nancy respond to the veteran teachers' reluctance to be part of a learning organization?
2. Reflect on how your previous experience provides "scaffolding" for your current preparation to be a school leader.
3. Identify examples of school policies that are responses to single-loop learning and double-loop learning.
4. Using the five disciplines of Senge and colleagues, assess the organizational learning of a recent reform effort in your school.

Peer Activities

1. Compare the traditional and constructivist views of learning in terms of your and your peers' experiences as students in high school classes.
2. With a valued and sensitive peer, try the Johari window activity in this chapter. Identify, as much as possible, behaviors that fit into each pane.

3. Discuss a principal you both know who has the image described by Charlotte Roberts as "principal-do-right." How do teachers and other school constituents respond to this principal's approach? How do you think the image affects school change?
4. Identify and interview one or two assistant principals who are reputed to have developed an instructional leadership image of their role. What do these assistant principals do to facilitate the learning of others in the school?

Course Activities

1. Select one of the cases in the on-line *UCEA Journal of Cases in Educational Leadership* (*www.ucea.org/cases*). Reflect on the inquiry skills used in the class to analyze this case. For example, what different methods do class members use to define the problem or collect information to address the case?
2. Using this case or another, discuss how single-loop learning and double-loop learning would differ in analyzing the case.
3. Using Bolman and Deal's (1991) frames, analyze the preceding case or a new case. What strengths and weaknesses do you find for each frame?
4. Analyze the characteristics of a school reputed to be a professional learning community. The class might be divided into small action research groups to investigate each of the five characteristics of professional learning communities identified by Bryk, Cambron, and Louis (1999).

Websites

The *Journal of Cases in Educational Leadership (JCEL)* is an electronic publication of the University Council for Educational Administration in cooperation with the University of Utah. The *JCEL* publishes in electronic format peer-reviewed cases appropriate for use in programs that prepare educational leaders. The University Council for Education Administration sponsors this journal in an ongoing effort to improve administrative preparation. The following articles can be found on the Web site by looking at the past-issues link (*http://www.ucea.org/cases/past.html*). We also encourage you to visit the site regularly to view current issues of the journal.

■ *http://www.ucea.org/cases/*
  Cases from the Journal of Cases in Educational Leadership.
  Bradshaw, L. K. (1999). Opportunities for instructional leadership at Rolling Ridge Middle School. *Journal of Cases in Educational Leadership* 2(3).
  Smith, B., & Louis, K. S. (1999). Changes at Big Mountain High School. *Journal of Cases in Educational Leadership* 2(1).

■ *http://www.ed.gov*
  U.S. Department of Education. This Web site offers several resources for principals and assistant principals to help make sure children start school ready, learn to read, and succeed in school.

■ *http://www.ed.gov/pubs/TeachersGuide/*
  The New Teacher's Guide to the U.S. Department of Education. This guide, provided by the De-

partment of Education, includes information about voluntary national tests in reading and math, about raising academic standards, and about various offices of education.

- *http://www.mdk12.org/process/leading/p_indicators.html*
  Indicators for Effective Principal Leadership in Improving Student Achievement. The performance indicators are intended to provide clarity about the skills, beliefs, and knowledge a principal needs be effective.

- *(http://www.middleweb.com/ash.html)*
  The Principal as Chief Learning Officer: The New Work of Formative Leadership. Creating an organizational culture and infrastructure that supports leadership possibilities for everyone requires a new set of leadership skills.

References

Argyris, C., & Schon, D. A. (1974). *Theory in Practice: Increasing Professional Effectiveness.* San Francisco: Jossey-Bass.

Bell, D. (1973). *The Coming of Post-Industrial Society.* New York: Basic Books.

Bolman, L. G., & Deal, T. E. (1991). *Reframing Organizations.* San Francisco: Jossey-Bass.

Brookfield, S. (1986). *Understanding and Facilitating Adult Learning.* San Francisco, CA: Jossey-Bass.

Bryk, A., Camburn, E., & Louis, K. S. (1999). Professional community in Chicago elementary schools: Facilitating factors and organizational consequences. *Educational Administration Quarterly 35*(Suppl.), 751–781.

Callahan, R. (1962). *Education and the Cult of Efficiency: A Study of the Social Forces That Have Shaped the Administration of the Public Schools.* Chicago: University of Chicago Press.

Chapman, J. (1996). A new agenda for a new society. In K. Leithwood, J. Chapman, D. Corson, P. Hallinger, & A. Hart (Eds.), *International Handbook of Educational Leadership and Administration* (pp. 27–59). Boston: Kluwer.

Crow, G. M., Hausman, C. S., & Scribner, J. P. (2002). Reshaping the role of the school principal. In J. Murphy (Ed.), *The Leadership Challenge: Redefining Leadership for the 21st Century* (pp. 189–210). Chicago: National Society for the Study of Education.

Davis, S. (1998). Superintendents' perspectives on the involuntary departure of public school principals: The most frequent reasons why principals lose their jobs. *Educational Administration Quarterly 34*(1), 58–90.

Elbow, P. (1986). *Embracing Contraries: Explorations in Learning and Teaching.* Oxford, UK: Oxford University Press.

Ferrance, E. (2000). *Action Research.* Providence, RI: Northeast and Islands Regional Educational Laboratory at Brown University.

Freire, P. (1970). *Pedagogy of the Oppressed.* New York: Herder and Herder.

Friedman, T. L. (1999). *The Lexus and the Olive Tree.* New York: Farrar Straus Giroux.

Fullan, M. (1993). *Change Forces: Probing the Depths of Educational Reform.* London: Falmer Press.

Gardner, H. (1983). *Frames of Mind.* New York: Basic Books.

Glickman, C. D., Gordon, S. P., & Ross-Gordon, J. M. (1998). *Supervision of Instruction: A Developmental Approach.* Boston: Allyn and Bacon.

Goleman, D. (1995). *Emotional Intelligence.* New York: Bantam Books.

Goleman, D. (1998). What makes a leader? *Harvard Business Review 76*(6), 93–102.

Gronn, P. (1983). Talk as the work: The accomplishment of school administration. *Administrative Science Quarterly 28*(1), 1–21.

Hage, J., & Powers, C. H. (1992). *Post-Industrial Lives: Roles and Relationships in the 21st Century.* Newbury Park, CA: Sage.

Hargreaves, A. (1995). Renewal in the age of paradox. *Educational Leadership 52*(7), 14–19.

Hart, A. W., & Bredeson, P. V. (1996). *The Principalship: A Theory of Professional Learning and Practice.* New York: McGraw-Hill.

Heifetz, R. (1994). *Leadership Without Easy Answers.* Cambridge, MA: Harvard University Press.

Huber, G. P. (1991). Organizational learning: The contributing processes and the literature. *Organization Science 2*(1), 88–115.

Levin, H. M. (1987). New schools for the disadvantaged. *Teacher Education Quarterly 14*(4), 60–83.

Little, J. W. (1982). Norms of collegiality and experimentation: Workplace conditions of school success. *American Educational Research Journal 19*(3), 325–340.

Luft, J. (1970). *Group Processes: An Introduction to Group Dynamics.* New York: National Press.

McPherson, R. B., Crowson, R. L., & Pitner, N. (1986). *Managing Uncertainty.* Columbus, OH: Charles E. Merrill.

Micklethwhait, J., & Wooldridge, A. (1996). *The Witch Doctors: Making Sense of the Management Gurus.* New York: Times Books.

Mohrman, S. A., & Cohen, S. G. (1995). When people get out of the box: New relationships, new systems. In A. Howard (Ed.), *The Changing Nature Of Work* (pp. 365–410). San Francisco: Jossey-Bass.

Oja, S. N., & Reiman, A. J. (1998). Supervision for teacher development across the career span . In G. R. Firth & E. F. Pajak (Eds.), *Handbook of Research on School Supervision* (pp. 463–487). New York: Simon & Schuster McMillan.

O'Neill, J. (1996). On emotional intelligence: A conversation with Daniel Goleman. *Educational Leadership, 54,* 6–11.

Osterman, K. F., & Kottkamp, R. B. (1993). *Reflective Practice for Educators: Improving Schooling Through Professional Development.* Newbury Park, CA: Corwin Press.

Prawat, R. S., & Peterson, P. L. (1999). Social constructivist views of learning. In J. Murphy & K. S. Louis (Eds.), *Handbook of Research on Educational Administration* (pp. 203–226). San Francisco: Jossey-Bass.

Schon, D. A. (1983). *The Reflective Practitioner: How Professionals Think in Action.* San Francisco, CA: Jossey-Bass.

Scribner, J. P., Cockrell, K. S., Cockrell, D. H., & Valentine, J. W. (1999). Creating professional communities in schools through organizational learning: An evaluation of a school improvement process. *Educational Administration Quarterly 35*(1), 130–160.

Senge, P., Cambron-McCabe, N., Lucas, T., Smith, B., Dutton, J., & Kleiner, A. (2000). *Schools That Learn: A Fifth Discipline Fieldbook for Educators, Parents, and Everyone Who Cares about Education.* New York: Doubleday.

Sergiovanni, T. J. (1994). Organizations or communities? Changing the metaphor changes the theory. *Educational Administration Quarterly 30*(2), 214–226.

Tsang, E. W. K. (1997). Organizational learning and the learning organization: A dichotomy between descriptive and prescriptive research. *Human Relations 50*(1), 73–90.

Vygotsky, L. (1986). *Thought and Language* (A. Kozulin, trans.). Cambridge, MA: MIT Press.

Walker, D., & Lambert, L. (1995). Learning and leading theory: A century in the making. In L. Lambert, D. Walker, D. P. Zimmerman, J. E. Cooper, M. D. Lambert, M. E. Gardner, & P. J. F. Slack (Eds.), *The Constructivist Leader* (pp. 1–27). New York: Teachers College Press.

Weick, K. (1969). *The Social Psychology of Organizing.* Reading, MA: Addison-Wesley.

Weick, K. (1978). The spines of leaders. In M. W. McCall, Jr., & M. M. Lombardo (Eds.), *Leadership: Where Else Can We Go?* (pp. 37–61). Durham, NC: Duke University Press.

Weick, K. (1995). *Fighting fires in educational administration,* Paper presented at the University Council for Educational Administration, Salt Lake City, UT, October 25.

Westheimer, J. (1999). Communities and consequences: An inquiry into ideology and practice in teachers' professional work. *Educational Administration Quarterly 35*(1), 71–105.

The Principal as Mentor

4

Key Terms and Concepts

career development function
    of mentoring
marginal teachers
mentor

peer mentors
primary mentor
professional development
    function of mentoring

psychosocial development
    function of mentoring
reflective mentoring
secondary mentor

Vignette

Felicia Martinez had been the assistant principal of Mark Twain Middle School for the past two years. She and her principal, Latonya Jefferson, began their careers at Mark Twain at the same time. Both knew each other from the time when Latonya had been assistant principal at the school where Felicia taught. When Felicia was selected as assistant principal, Latonya made it clear that she wanted the assistant principal to be a partner in the leadership team and an instructional leader. Some bumpy roads had emerged during the past two years, especially in convincing the faculty that the assistant principal's role involved more than student management. Additionally, Felicia's age was a factor of contention. Some teachers felt that, at twenty-six years old, Felicia did not have sufficient teaching experience to help them with curricular and instructional issues.

Last year Felicia and Latonya worked with the faculty in developing a school-wide mentoring program where volunteer veteran teachers and the two administrators were matched with new teachers. Felicia was matched with Gloria Ayres, a forty-five-year-old new teacher who had come to teaching after staying home until her children were in junior high school.

Felicia and Gloria had met once to discuss the mentoring arrangement. They agreed to meet every two weeks to discuss any issues on which Gloria felt she needed help. Their first two meetings went fine, with Felicia mostly giving Gloria information about school procedures. After the second meeting, Felicia made a routine observation in Gloria's room. She expected to find some classroom management concerns, as she had found during the early weeks with other new teachers. What she found surprised her. Gloria's sixth grade classroom was extremely orderly and quiet. In fact, students made no sounds—no questions, no comments, no responses. As she watched, these new middle school students seemed afraid to make a sound. Gloria's style was extremely stern and teacher-directed.

At their third mentoring meeting, Felicia discussed her observation with Gloria and asked her about her teaching style. Gloria responded that she knew what middle school students were like because she was a parent and that they needed strict discipline. She said other teachers also had told her to begin firm and then she could lighten up.

Felicia could tell that when they began to discuss Gloria's teaching style, Gloria became more guarded in her comments and seemed to dismiss Felicia's suggestions for creating an open environment for learning. Felicia had the distinct feeling that while Gloria appreciated Felicia's help on procedural matters, she was more suspicious of her help on instruction and classroom management. Felicia felt the age difference and realized that the mentoring program was more complicated than she first imagined.

Introduction
The traditional model of school administration includes roles that differ from paternalistic guidance to autocratic direction to *laissez-faire* indifference. Some administrators attempt to support teachers and others by smothering them with guidance. This approach frequently creates dependency relationships in which the teacher, for example, is dependent on the administrator for resources, ideas, and support. Although this approach in the short run reduces the teacher's isolation and frustration, such paternalistic dependence reduces the teacher's long-term professional growth and learning. Autocratic direction may give the new teacher strategies to reduce survival anxiety, but it also decreases the teacher's opportunities for professional growth. The *laissez-faire* approach leaves the guidance of new and veteran teachers to chance, hoping that someone else will come along to mentor and support the teacher. These traditional approaches are ineffective because they ignore either the importance of professional growth or the way that learning occurs in new and veteran teachers.

The innovative school administrator—both principal and assistant principal—plays a critical role for teachers and for school reform. This role does not involve telling teachers what to do or ignoring their needs but rather mentoring and creating an environment where mentoring is encouraged and supported. In addition, mentoring provides the innovative principal with a strategy for school improvement that involves creating the kind of learning environment we discussed in Chapter 3. Felicia's experience illustrates a more innovative conception of principals as mentors. It also, however, illustrates some of the difficulties inherent in this role conception. In this chapter we discuss the research, theory, and practice of mentoring and identify how the principal's and assistant principal's roles can include a mentoring conception. Mentoring as a form of professional learning could have been discussed in Chapter 5 on the principal as supervisor. We have chosen, however, to give this role conception its own chapter. Mentoring has received considerable attention in the current literature, but much of that literature assumes that principals have only an indirect role to play. We believe that principals and assistant principals have a direct and significant role in mentoring that deserves special attention, especially as a way to create a professional learning community that contributes to improving student learning.

Our treatment of the principal's role as mentor begins with an introduction to the literature on mentoring, focusing on the expanding nature of mentoring; the roles, participants, content, and processes of mentoring; and the benefits and pitfalls of mentoring. In the second part of this chapter we focus on the principal's role at the internal level by mentoring new and veteran teachers and students. In the third part we discuss how principals contribute to systemic mentoring by facilitating an environment that encourages mentoring relationships to improve student learning.

Introduction to Mentoring

In Homer's *Odyssey,* Odysseus requests a friend, named Mentor, to guide his son, Telemachus, while Odysseus is away on a twenty-year-long trip. Thus began the use of the word *mentor* to identify the process of guiding one person by another. Although the idea of mentoring has been around for years, more recently it has gained attention in the business and education literatures. Businesses have created formal mentoring programs to guide and support newcomers to facilitate their successful entry and performance. In education, mentoring has become a popular strategy for supporting the entry of new teachers. However, much of the literature on mentoring has been atheoretical and non-empirical (Crow & Matthews, 1998). Frequently, educators assume that mentoring is an effective strategy for inducting new teachers and thus ignore its pitfalls.

The Nature of Mentoring

In the traditional view, mentoring has been understood as an expert guiding a novice in what is typically a one-to-one relationship.

> A mentor acts as a coach, much like in athletics, advising and teaching the political nuts and bolts, giving feedback, and rehearsing strategies. He or she provides you with exposure, visibility, and sponsorship, helping to open doors to promotions and seeing that you get assignments that will get you noticed. And mentors take the blame for your mistakes, acting as protectors until you're established enough to shoulder criticism on your own (McPartland, 1985, p. 8).

This traditional definition of mentoring assumes that the mentor has all the knowledge, skills, and attitudes needed by the novice and that the transfer of this knowledge is one-way communication from the mentor to the novice.

Some writers have expanded the notion of mentoring in at least two ways: its nature and its sphere. Gehrke (1988), for example, argued that the traditional definition of mentoring focuses on the transfer of knowledge and sponsorship. Instead of the market economy view of mentoring, where knowledge and skills are exchanged, she proposed an understanding of mentoring, at its most personal level, as "gift giving." She also suggested that what is given is an awakening. The mentor as "door opener, information giver, supporter; [is] no doubt important. . . . The greatest gift the mentor offers is a new and whole way of seeing things. . . . It is a way of thinking and living that is given" (p. 192). Gehrke's understanding of mentoring moves beyond simply giving the technical secrets of the work role to the newcomer to imparting a new way of conceiving the role. Such an awakening reduces the typical shortcoming of mentoring as perpetuating the status quo and opens possibilities for learning and innovation. However, as Felicia discovered in the opening vignette, moving beyond the technical procedural aspects to imparting a new way to conceive of teaching may not be accepted readily by the teacher.

Recent literature on mentoring also involves expanding who mentors are and the nature of their relationship with protégés. Mullen and Cox (1997) and Mullen and Kealy (1999) proposed a co-mentoring model:

> The best way to teach a new skill is to create a collaborative whose members share a common purpose yet bring different abilities and levels of understanding to the group. Co-mentoring names a process of supportive assistance that is provided by several connected individuals who reconstruct traditional mentoring relationships in nonhierarchical ways (Mullen & Kealy, 1999, pp. 38–39).

This approach highlights mentoring as an evolving relationship among mentors and protégés.

> Mentoring as a lifelong process is not about being "shadowed" throughout life by one's protégé or about shadowing one's mentor indefinitely. Instead, it is a process of learning and growing that brings people closer together at times, and further away at other times in different contexts for learning. . . . The needs of mentors and protégés change over time (Mullen & Kealy, 1999, p. 44).

This change in the understanding of mentoring also suggests that individuals can have multiple mentors. Kram (1986), a leading researcher and theorist in the mentoring field, discussed the relationship constellation in which mentoring exists. Individuals find support from a number of groups, including family, peers, superiors, and subordinates. As they develop, individuals' needs change, and the place where they find support to meet those needs is likely to change as well. Understanding the relationship constellation would enable organizations to "create avenues for employers to build such relationships through job design and various human resource management practices. Then as individuals feel unsupported or exposed to considerable stress, they could consider how their relationship constellations could be modified to provide critical developmental functions" (p.173).

The nature of mentoring that is reflected in recent literature is one in which mentoring occurs with a variety of individuals, throughout life, and need not be unidirectional. This expanded nature of mentoring offers principals a more dynamic mentor model. Instead of being the parent figure, smothering the new teacher with directives on how to conduct the job, the principal and assistant principal mentor and facilitate an environment that supports mentoring so that individuals at all career stages are mentors and are mentored. Such an understanding of mentoring has the possibility of creating environments for professional learning that are not dependency-based but are lifelong and systemic. Likewise, this expanded understanding offers the principal and assistant principal an effective strategy for supporting organizational learning that focuses on teaching and learning.

Mentoring Roles and Functions

Odell (1990b) characterized the roles that mentors play as trusted guide (Homer), teacher (Levinson et al., 1978), sponsor (Schein, 1978), challenger (Daloz, 1983), and confidant (Gehrke & Kay, 1984). More recently, Gardiner, Grogan, and Enomoto (2000) identified nine metaphors that describe the types of interactions mentors have with protégés:

- Boss or superior
- Advisor
- Teacher
- Guide
- Parent
- Spiritual or philosophical guru
- Gatekeeper
- Public role model
- Friend or peer

These metaphors suggest the wide variety of roles and relationships that are possible in mentoring. Some are more likely than others to occur in school settings and in principal-teacher relationships.

Although these roles have different qualities, there are three functions that are included in these different roles: *professional, psychosocial,* and *career.* Kram (1985, 1986) defined two of these functions. *Career development functions* refer to "those aspects of a relationship that enhance learning the ropes and preparing for advancement in an organization" (p. 161). She includes in this category sponsorship, coaching, protection, exposure, and challenging work (p. 162). *Psychosocial development functions* refer to "those aspects of a relationship that enhance a sense of competence, clarity of identity, and effectiveness in a professional role" (pp. 161–162). These functions include role modeling, counseling acceptance and confirmation, and friendship.

Although Kram (1986) included both career development and professional development in the career development function category, we believe that career development in education is different from that in business and other occupations and should be separated from the more technical aspects of learning the role (Crow & Matthews, 1998). Thus we identify three roles that administrators as mentors play in schools. First, the professional development role of mentors refers to helping others learn the knowledge, skills, behaviors, and values inherent in an educational role. Second, the psychosocial development role of administrators as mentors focuses on personal and emotional well-being, as well as role expectation, conflict, and clarification. Finally, the *career development function* of mentors includes issues of career satisfaction, career awareness, and career advancement.

In light of our previous discussion of the expanded nature of mentoring, we do not assume that as principal or assistant principal you will necessarily mentor individuals in the school in all three areas. Mentoring literature suggests two types of mentors: *primary mentors* and *secondary mentors* (Phillips-Jones, 1982). Primary mentors have characteristics such as altruism, unselfishness, and caring and are less common than secondary mentors. They also tend to play more of the three roles identified earlier. Secondary mentors play a more limited role and are likely to be part of an exchange relationship in which mentoring benefits both mentor and protégé. Principals and assistant principals may be primary or secondary mentors, or they may contribute to mentoring by facilitating the development of school cultures where others become the primary and secondary mentors.

Participants of Mentoring

In a traditional model of school administration, principals are the mentors, and teachers are the protégés. Or perhaps veteran teachers are the mentors, and new teachers are the protégés. The expanded notions of mentoring described earlier suggest a broader and more inclusive set of participants.

In the comentoring view (Mullen & Cox, 1998; Mullen & Kealy, 1999), mentors are likely to be a diverse group who play different roles in the school. Principals and assistant principals, such as Felicia in the opening vignette, of course, should be mentors. But they also can be mentored. A new principal or a principal new to a particular school frequently may participate in a mentoring relationship with veteran teachers or staff members who help the principal learn the role and discover how to fit into the organizational culture and context.

Teachers, both new and veteran, can and should act as mentors and protégés. Although it might seem unusual to think of a new, barely surviving teacher as a mentor, this individual does not come to the school as a blank slate. New teachers come with skills, knowledge, insights, and beliefs that can be beneficial to the learning environment of a school. Although veteran teachers frequently are seen as mentors, they also need the professional, psychosocial, and career support that mentoring can provide.

In addition to experience and position, gender is a relevant consideration in mentoring. Ample research, both in business and in education, has demonstrated the tendency for men to be more likely to have mentors than women (Rowe, 1981; Nicholson, 1996). Although this may be changing, it is extremely important for principals and assistant principals to recognize that both men and women need mentoring and are potential mentors and to facilitate a school environment in which mentoring is a resource for all.

In a school environment where all individuals—new and veteran, teacher and administrator—are seen as both mentors and mentored, collegiality and innovation are more likely. This expanded understanding makes mentoring a significant and effective strategy for creating professional learning communities.

Content of Mentoring

The content of mentoring is reflected in the three functions we identified earlier: professional, psychosocial, and career development. Mentoring in the professional development area includes knowledge, skills, behaviors, and values. For example, new teachers need mentoring in such areas as knowledge of student differences, school procedures, and curriculum sequencing. They also need mentoring in such skill areas as classroom management. Behaviors in areas such as curriculum selection, instructional decisions, and disciplinary strategies are an important part of the mentoring contribution. In the opening vignette, Felicia's mentoring of Gloria reflects a focus on professional development. However, mentoring also involves helping new teachers develop values that are central to the school's vision, such as innovation and collaboration. For veteran teachers, one of the most important components of mentoring content is helping these teachers develop new ways to conceive of their roles (Gehrke, 1988).

As the research and theory on adult development mature, we realize that personal and professional roles overlap and that individuals' self-esteem affects their professional abilities. Kohn and Schooler's (1978) and Schooler's (1989) research on the reciprocal relationship between intellectual flexibility and job complexity demonstrated that personal characteristics interact with job and role characteristics. In addition, the psychological and social qualities of teaching and other roles in the school demand attention to psychosocial development. Role conflict and role ambiguity also have resulted from the increasingly complex responsibilities that educators have and that are inherent in postindustrial society (see Chapter 3). These issues have psychosocial implications for mentoring.

The career development function of mentoring includes such content as networking, career awareness, and procedures for advancement. Obviously, career mentoring will vary depending on the needs and career stage of the protégé. Principals frequently view the teacher's career within the confines of a classroom or even the school. However, career development requires expanding this notion to recognize the teacher as a professional whose growth includes awareness of career opportunities and networking possibilities.

Another view of the content of mentoring is in terms of two types of learning: technical and cultural (Greenfield, 1985).

> Technical aspects include learning "how things are done," that is, the instrumental knowledge and skills necessary to perform the job. Cultural aspects include learning "how things are done around here," that is, the expressive norms, values, and beliefs of a school culture (Crow & Matthews, 1998, p. 13).

Learning "how things are done" without learning "how they are done around here" can be problematic for new faculty members and ineffective for instructional improvement. Thus mentoring must include both technical and cultural learning.

Processes of Mentoring

McIntyre and Hagger (1996), in their research on mentoring in British schools, suggested three types of processes involved in mentoring. The first and most basic level of mentoring is a personal relationship "where a relative novice is supported by a more experienced peer in coming to terms with a new role" (p. 147). The second process is "active guidance, teaching, and challenging of the protégé by the mentor, who accordingly needs to claim some expertise, wisdom and authority" (p. 147). The final process is more organizational and involves "management and implementation of a planned curriculum tailored of course to the needs of the individual, and including collaboration with other contributors in one's own and other institutions" (p.147). Whether or not you agree with these authors' view of the nature of mentoring, the processes they identified seem to be common to most mentoring arrangements.

The personal relationship and active guidance are fundamental to the process of mentoring. Dembele (1996) argued that intentionality is a critical component of what mentors do. He referred to the mentor as an "educational companion" who is constantly asking what does the protégé need in this context at this time to meet these demands. The specific content of mentoring, whether it be professional, psychosocial, or career development, must be viewed with the intention of how will this help meet the needs of the protégé within a learning and reform context.

The third process identified by McIntyre and Hagger (1996) involved an organizational or systemic quality to mentoring. Instead of understanding the processes of mentoring strictly from a one-on-one personal relationship, mentoring should be seen in a more systemic light. Whether one refers to this as "circles and chains of relationships" (Mullen & Cox, 1997; Mullen & Kealy, 1999) or "relationship constellations" (Kram, 1986), mentoring processes take on a more communal spirit. Principals and assistant principals play a significant role in facilitating a school culture that supports these mentoring processes and encourages the use of mentoring to improve teaching and learning.

Benefits and Pitfalls of Mentoring

Principals who are considering mentoring as an instructional improvement strategy should recognize that it has both benefits and pitfalls. In this section we will examine the benefits for protégés, mentors, and others, as well as the pitfalls of mentoring.

Benefits.   Research on mentoring benefits suggests that this socialization strategy has advantages for newcomers that reflect the different functions of mentoring: professional, psychosocial, and career development. Mentoring can facilitate the socialization of newcomers into the organization (Clawson, 1980; Berlew & Hall, 1966). By helping newcomers learn the knowledge, skills, and dispositions of the role, mentoring can expose newcomers to new ideas (Torrance, 1984) and provide challenging opportunities. Mentoring also has benefits in light of its psychosocial function. For example, it can increase an individual's confidence and competence as they acquire new skills and attempt risk-taking experiences. Mentoring can benefit career development of teachers and administrators. It provides visibility for candidates to those who make promotion decisions and can help shield newcomers from situations that may damage their careers.

Mentoring also benefits the mentor. Daresh and Playko (1993) found that mentoring helps renew the enthusiasm of the mentor. Megginson and Clutterbuck (1995) suggested that mentoring can provide new insights to veterans. Mentors also can benefit by becoming more reflective and critical of their own intuitive processes and by developing networks for ideas and opportunities for promotion. The mentoring relationship also can develop into long-lasting and meaningful friendships. Some mentors find that mentoring allows them to regain the satisfaction they felt in becoming a teacher (Crow & Matthews, 1998). An additional benefit of mentoring lies in its role in fostering leadership development for the mentor teachers. Ganser, Marchione, and Fleischmann (1999) reported that many mentor teachers in their study eventually assumed more formal leadership positions.

Mentoring can benefit larger school and district organizations. Researchers have noted that mentoring can reduce turnover and burnout leading to attrition (Dalton, Thompson, & Price, 1977; Kram, 1985). Data from several studies have indicated that mentoring actually increases the rate of retention of beginning teachers. For example, Odell and Ferraro (1992) studied 160 teachers four years after their mentored year and concluded that approximately 96 percent of those teachers located were still teaching. They asserted, "Teacher mentoring may reduce the early attrition of beginning teachers" (p. 200). District administrators also can benefit from mentoring by learning who the promising candidates for administrative and teaching positions are (Nash & Treffinger, 1993).

Although mentoring has obvious benefits for individual teachers—both novices and mentors—the primary reason for mentoring in schools is to improve teaching and learning. Daresh and Playko (1993) argued that mentoring could energize school leaders and encourage a community of learning within the school. We have found no research that demonstrates a direct relationship between mentoring and student achievement. Mentoring, however, can contribute to a school culture that emphasizes collegiality and innovation, features found in effective schools (Little, 1982; Fullan, 1999).

Pitfalls. Mentoring has potential pitfalls to which the principal must be sensitive. Mentoring simply can perpetuate the status quo and discourage innovation (Hart, 1991, 1993; Crow & Matthews, 1998). Hay (1995) noted that mentoring could encourage cloning, where mentors attempt to replicate themselves in the conduct of protégés.

Sometimes mentors have personal agendas that are dysfunctional for the protégé (Muse, Wasden, & Thomas, 1988). For example, mentors may use the honor of being a mentor to gain visibility for themselves or may create a dependency relationship in which the newcomer is forced to rely on the mentor for answers (Daresh & Playko, 1993). Moreover, a major pitfall that principals and assistant principals must acknowledge and avoid is the potential for using mentoring in a power-abusive way. Manipulating and coercing teachers to support the principal's agenda is a dangerous and unethical use of mentoring. For example, Felicia, in the opening vignette, needs to be sensitive to Gloria's potential feeling of being coerced into changing her classroom management philosophy.

Mentoring also runs the risk of restricting decision making, classroom management, or problem solving perspectives. In so doing, new teachers and administrators may come to believe that there is only one way to establish discipline, one type of instructional approach, or one way to work with parents.

As a principal or assistant principal using mentoring as a reform strategy and as a way to facilitate a learning environment, you must be aware not only of the benefits but also of the pitfalls. Such awareness permits you and the community of learners in the school to create an environment that diminishes the restrictive, dysfunctional, and conservative elements of mentoring and increases the expanding, innovative, and functional benefits of mentoring.

Having this understanding of mentoring, we now turn to how principals and assistant principals can include mentoring as a reform strategy to improve teaching and learning. This section discusses the principal's direct involvement as a mentor and as a facilitator of mentoring in a school-wide professional learning context. The principal's role in mentoring and facilitating mentoring focuses on three categories: new teachers, veteran teachers, and students.

The Principal's Role in Mentoring

Mentoring New Teachers

The support and development of a new teacher are highly moral acts of leadership that every administrator should take seriously. The principal's role in a person's life and career is a substantial responsibility. Although hiring and placement of new teachers are extremely important, the leadership role in supporting and developing new teachers is even more important. Unfortunately, this responsibility is too often neglected or abdicated by principals. The prevailing thought concerning new teachers is that if they come from a reputable teacher education program, then they have the needed skills and behaviors for teaching. In realty, new teachers do not emerge from their college or university preparation as fully developed professionals. They vary greatly in the skills and life experiences that they bring to the classroom. Newly prepared teachers need administrative support and help with the types of assignments, the nature of the school's norms and values, and their development in making the transition from novice to experienced professional. Such support and development fall heavily on principals, who must be both mentors themselves and facilitators of mentoring by veteran teachers.

The principal's and assistant principal's roles in mentoring new teachers are far more complex than the way that most administrators were mentored when they were beginning teachers. Because most administrators began teaching with limited mentoring from their administrators, they often do not know what or how to mentor or they simply abdicate the role of mentoring to others. Traditional mentoring programs often relegate the principal to organizing the program and ignore responsibility for directly mentoring teachers.

Although new teachers may feel more comfortable with peer mentors than with their administrators, principals cannot relinquish this important role. Peer mentor programs are an important part of the new teacher's induction, but principals should be highly and personally involved in all aspects of the induction and mentoring process—much more than just assigning a good peer mentor to coach and assist a new teacher. Teachers cite more visible signs of support from the administration as their greatest need during their first year (Deal & Chatman, 1989). New teachers may appreciate the help they receive from their peers, but they expect assistance from their administrators. After all, it was most likely the administrators who were involved in their hiring and also with whom they have some allegiance and relationship. Earlier in this chapter we discussed primary and secondary roles in mentoring. A primary mentor is one who mentors in almost all aspects of a person's development, namely, professional, psychosocial, and career. Principals and assistant principals should ensure that all new teachers have primary mentors. The principal, assistant principal, or veteran teachers may act as primary mentors. Many will serve as secondary mentors, who mentor in some aspects of the new teacher's development but not as extensively as primary mentors. As a new generation of school leaders emerges, principals and assistant principals need to understand their important mentoring role. The principal's and assistant principal's role in the professional development of new teachers is twofold. First, school leaders must see themselves as mentors, and second, they must facilitate the mentoring process in the induction program. In the following subsections we discuss the process and content of the principal's role in mentoring and facilitating mentoring.

Mentoring New Teachers in Professional Development

As a new teacher, one of the authors remembers well the first time he turned his lesson plans into the principal, a weekly task asked of all new teachers. No instructions or lesson designs were added to the directive other than to have the lesson plan book into the principal's office before leaving on Friday afternoons. He was taught in college to have a lesson plan that included objectives, anticipatory sets, learning activities, and student assessment. He began working on the lesson plans for each of his six classes late on Friday afternoon. Well into the evening, he was still not finished. Furthermore, he could not figure out how to write his whole lesson plan outline into the small squares of the plan book that was to be turned in. Frustrated and tired, he finally stapled his completed lesson plans to the plan book and put them in the principal's box. The next Monday morning he received his lesson plans back with an attached note from the principal that simply stated, "These plans are very complete, but all I am interested in is what you are doing in each of your classes and when you are doing it. Please abbreviate and turn back into me."

More frustrated than ever, he finally went to his department chair and asked for help. She kindly explained what the principal expected and what he needed to do. It became obvious that the detailed lesson plans he had learned in his college class were not an expected norm in this school. Although he continued to put considerable time into lesson planning, the Friday afternoon plan book exercise was a lot simpler and quicker after that first week's experience.

Many new teachers have similar experiences that can be frustrating, time-consuming, and even embarrassing. Although principals and peer mentors cannot be expected to mentor new teachers in every aspect of their job, they need to be aware of the continuing plight of beginning teachers and their professional development. We identify two goals of mentoring new teachers in professional development. The first goal is to improve performance in all aspects of teaching, including the classroom environment, instructional practices, planning and preparation, and professional responsibilities. The objective with this goal is, of course, to improve student learning. The second goal in mentoring new teachers in professional development is to transmit the culture of the district, school, and community. Too often beginning teachers are not aware of the cultural aspects of the school and the district. New teachers rarely learn the history, lore, or values of a particular school or district. If anything, they are oriented to policies, procedures, and plan books rather than to philosophy and pedagogy. Typically, a new teacher learns the ropes in isolation through trial and error. As discussed earlier in this chapter, cultural aspects include learning "how things are done around here, that is, the expressive norms, values, and beliefs of a particular school culture" (Crow & Matthews, 1998, p. 13).

Content.   Compared with other professional organizations, the importance of bringing new people into valued practices of a school is too often left to chance. Consequently, teachers often fumble their way through their first years. Deal and Chatman (1989) concluded that unlike employees of other organizations, teachers learn to cope as islands without the support of colleagues or a community that lets them know what is valued or expected. New teachers are not drawn into a shared system of meaning. Whatever meaning they construct is often done alone and with students in an individual classroom. New teachers bring their previous experience into this process of constructing meaning. In the vignette at the beginning of this chapter, Gloria's parenting experience influenced her perception of how early adolescents should behave and how she should respond to them.

Glickman (1990) contended, "In most professions, the challenge of the job increases over time as one acquires experience and expertise. In teaching, we have had it reversed. Typically, the most challenging situation a teacher experienced was in his or her first year" (p. vii). This process of inverse beginner responsibilities is expanded in Glickman's (1985) work, "The Supervisor's Challenge":

> Administrators often place the most difficult and lowest achieving students with the new teacher. . . . The message to beginning teachers is, "Welcome to teaching. Let's see if you can make it." . . . If new teachers do make it, they pass their initiation rites onto the next group of beginners (pp. 38–39).

Usually, the problems about which new teachers complain and the discouragement that they express have little to do with their command of the subjects they teach. Most of them have been successful in their college course work and their teacher training experiences, so they are more than ready to handle the subject matter requirements of the job. However, all this knowledge is of little use if new teachers have not yet learned how to establish instructional techniques for their classrooms. Beginning teacher needs, as defined by Veenman (1984) in his meta-analysis of 83 studies, are instructional and pedagogical skills that require support from others in the school. Veenman ranks the following as the most frequently stated problems of beginning teachers:

- Managing student behavior
- Motivating students
- Dealing with individual differences
- Assessing students' work
- Relating with parents
- Organizing class work
- Dealing with insufficient materials and supplies
- Dealing with the problems of individual students

Linda Darling-Hammond (1984) reported similar results. She found that new teachers are pressured by class size and diversity, management considerations, failure to master subject content, and the inability to assimilate into the culture of the school environment. She also reported that overwhelming and time-consuming non-teaching responsibilities and lack of support from school building leadership negatively affected teachers' professional development.

Beginning teachers have substantial needs in understanding important aspects of pedagogy, relationships, and school culture. School leaders cannot assume that these aspects should be left for new teachers to learn as they can. However, the principal and assistant principal's responsibility also extends to how this content is best given to the new teacher.

Process.　　Anne Sullivan mentored Helen Keller in important content areas such as communication skills, but it was through Anne Sullivan's process of mentoring that Helen Keller became a nationally recognized spokesperson for those with disabilities. Likewise, famous artists, musicians, writers, athletes, and performers have learned certain important skills, but it is through mentoring and coaching that they learned to excel. Even Olympic champions, who can outperform their own coaches, have a constant mentor who guides, directs, and motivates them. Given the importance of teaching, it is only logical that teachers also need mentoring and coaching in their professional development—especially from their leaders.

Mentors always should be aware that a few weeks or months earlier, the new teachers probably were students in college, fulfilling roles quite different from the ones they now fulfill. Although new teachers do not come to their first year without any knowledge or expertise, mentors, especially early in the beginning teacher's career, may have to tell the new teacher what things need to be done, how those things are done, and how those things are done in a particular school. Caution should be given, however, in that the learning style of most adults does not fit well with being told what to do, especially in a culture that encourages learning by doing. When information giving is necessary, a show-and-tell approach is usually more beneficial.

Tomlinson (1995) recommended that the mentor consider suggesting specific possibilities to the new teacher. Beyond directly telling the new teacher how to do something, a principal may instead offer suggestions. For example, the principal may inform the new teacher about reporting student progress to parents and then suggest various approaches to communicating with parents that have been effective with parents in that particular community. The principal and the new teacher can later discuss the approaches and reflect on what worked best.

An important aspect of a teacher's induction is solving and resolving problems and conflicts. Tomlinson (1995) suggested that when mentors perceive problems in some aspect of a new teacher's work or teaching style, they should "alert, explain, and challenge" (p. 187) the new teacher. The mentor alerts the teacher to the perceived problem, explains the problem, and then challenges the teacher to try new approaches. Likewise, a principal coaches new teachers to handle potentially damaging situations and conflicts that may occur in the future. Together the principal and teacher consider problems that may occur and reflect on possible ways for the new teacher to either solve the problem or seek help to solve the problem.

At times, the principal may protect the new teacher from certain situations because the novice may not yet have the necessary skills. An example may be the principal who shields the beginning teacher in responding to an angry and irrational parent. Shielding novices may be essential, but Kram (1985) warned that a mentor's decision to intervene and to provide protection is critical in that it enhances or interferes with the new teacher's learning experience. Although a beginning teacher can learn a great deal from problematic situations, certain incidents can be devastating to a beginner's morale and may even interfere with future career goals. Likewise, a new teacher may need to experience problematic situations to gain insightful solutions for future encounters. Herewith lies an important decision for the principal: to shield and protect the beginner or to allow the natural course of events to unfold. In either situation, principals need to be close at hand, mentoring and coaching the new teacher so that problem-solving skills are being learned.

Reflective Mentoring

One method for helping new teachers become better problem solvers and decision makers is a process of reflective mentoring. *Reflective mentoring* is a method in which the mentor guides the protégé through a mindful analysis of present, past, and future decision making and problem solving. Schön (1983) identified this process as mentoring "in-action, on-action, and for-action." Because teaching is a matter of decision making, reflective mentoring is a method of improving decision making. Mentors facilitate reflection by conferencing with the teacher in an active, open-minded exploration of the teacher's perspectives.

Conferencing is an important reflective mentoring activity. Sitting with the new teacher in a conference, the principal may ask about certain aspects of the teacher's instructional approach, discipline methods, or pedagogical philosophies. The postobservation conference is one type of conference between the principal and the teacher (discussed in Chapter 5). However, conferences with new teachers should not be limited to formal conferences following a classroom observation. Establishing both formal and informal times for conferencing can bring rewarding, and sometimes surprising, results. As an illustration, Ava, an assistant principal, was informally meeting with Bryan, a young, new teacher, reflecting on his first days in the school. It became apparent to Ava that Bryan did not know that she was the assistant principal. Although the two had been introduced and had been together at the orientation, Bryan was overwhelmed with meeting so many people that he had confused Ava with another teacher. When Bryan realized who Ava was, he also was surprised that she had come by his classroom to talk with him regarding his students. Ava created a mentoring moment by her availability to visit Bryan and engage in an

Professional Dilemma 4.1

Should the principal inform the new teacher about all parental criticism? Parents often will call the principal to complain about a new teacher's approach to instruction and discipline. Should a principal relay all complaints to the new teacher, or should certain complaints be put aside until the new teacher is better adjusted to teaching and the school culture? Likewise, should criticism that is not constructive or helpful ever be shared with teachers?

informal conference. Consequently, they were able to reflect on other issues regarding Bryan's assimilation to the school.

Reflective mentoring does not just occur. The mentor has to help make it happen. In previous work (Crow & Matthews, 1998), we gave the following guidelines to help mentors make the reflective conference more effective:

1. *Engage in active listening.* Use good verbal cues that show good listening, such as leaning forward, making eye contact, and paraphrasing.
2. *Refrain from judgment and offering too much advice.* Allow the new teacher to reflect on options rather than simply suggesting your own opinions.
3. *Ask insightful questions.* Consider the circumstances and then frame questions around those conditions. These circumstances may change in another situation or setting. Ask the teacher to consider those other situations.
4. *Brainstorm alternative approaches.*

Reflective mentoring also helps to avoid the potential mentoring pitfall of restricting perspectives. By asking the new teacher insightful questions that help him or her to understand what happened in the classroom, the mentoring helps broaden the alternative approaches that new teachers are able to consider.

Part of the adventure in a new setting is listening to stories from the past. Stories play a significant role in integrating a newcomer into a culture. They are useful tools for mentors to use to share important events, rites, and legends. However, to be most effective, storytelling should be combined with reflection. Leaving the new teacher with the story without reflection can lead to misunderstanding and confusion. Stories provide an excellent means for engaging in a reflective conference on the meaning of roles, norms, beliefs, values, and basic assumptions in the school culture.

Helping new teachers develop professionally involves planning, commitment, and time. Although socializing new teachers involves many methods, mentoring is one method that cannot be replaced adequately by any other process. Mentoring new teachers involves improving the beginning teacher's performance and understanding of role in all aspects of the school, including the school and classroom environment, instructional practices, planning and preparation, and professional responsibilities. Always the objectives are to increase student learning and success in school and to increase teacher professional learning.

Mentoring New Teachers in Psychosocial Development

Most aspiring principals have either taught or been associated with teaching and can identify easily with the feelings of loneliness, frustration, fear, and bewilderment that new teachers face. Several researchers have suggested that a lack of self-esteem is strongly related to burnout, which, has a direct causal relationship with the teacher attrition rate. Brighton (1999) identified the need for psychological support aimed at building the new teacher's sense of self and ability to handle stress. She defined this support as a form of therapeutic guidance and ranked it as more important than instructional-related support.

New teachers bring with them the developmental needs that any adult has. Frequently these needs affect the resources that new teachers have available in responding to the self-esteem and confidence issues of the early months of teaching. In Chapter 3 we identified the important adult development considerations that principals and assistant principals must understand in their roles as learner and facilitator of learning. Nowhere is this understanding more important than in mentoring new teachers.

The mentoring goal in psychosocial development involves offering assistance, support, and perhaps counseling for new teachers in understanding their role in the district, in the school, and in balancing their private and professional lives. Brighton (1999) highlighted the need for psychosocial development when he reported that a gap emerges between new teachers' expectations and the realities of the job.

Novice teachers are optimists, certain that they can change the world and the children in their charge. Many young people enter the field of education for the same reasons that others join the Peace Corps or other service organizations. They see their mission as shaping the lives and minds of children. Once these idealistic teachers enter their classrooms, they often are discouraged that the work is so challenging, the children so needy, and the expectations so high. New teachers do not leave because of the difficulty but feel disheartened that the reality is so different from their expectations (Brighton, 1999, pp. 198–199).

Content.   The preservice training experience for new teachers does not seem to contain many elements of psychosocial development. Although most new teachers have had some type of student teaching practicum, these experiences vary greatly from one institution to another. As Brighton (1999) reported, student teaching experience is sometimes misleading because the cooperating teacher and the student teacher share job responsibilities, which do not usually occur in real teaching situations. Additionally, the student teaching experience typically begins after the cooperating teacher has established classroom climate, rapport with parents, and behavior and work expectations. The cooperating teacher supervises closely so that he or she is able to rescue the student teacher from lessons gone awry. Brighton concluded that student teachers are easily lulled into believing that these elements will be the same in their future classrooms. Therefore, when new teachers realize that their real jobs differ from their student teaching experiences, they can encounter anxiety and frustration.

From whatever sources, anxieties and frustrations can emerge easily for beginning teachers and can contribute to their psychosocial development. The current literature provides several themes that principals should consider in the mentoring content of new teachers. Beginning teachers reported some degree of stress or anxiety with the following:

1. *Conflict with administrative policies and practices* (Rosenholtz, 1985). This is an area that may not be limited to new teachers.
2. *Student misbehavior* (Rosenholtz, 1985). This is a fairly common problem with new teachers.
3. *Overwhelming workload with insufficient preparation time* (Rosenholtz, 1985). This is often linked with too many preparations and out-of-class responsibilities.

4. *Changes in administrators* (Bowers & Eberhart, 1988). These usually affect teachers after they have been hired by one administrator but teach with yet another administrator.

5. *Grade-level changes* (Bowers & Eberhart, 1988). These affect new teachers and second- and third-year teachers who have taught at one grade level and then are assigned to a new grade level.

6. *Lack of parental support* (Brighton, 1999). Some parents communicate reticence about dealing with new teachers, fearing that they are largely unorganized, inexperienced, and unable to control student behavior.

7. *The expectations and scope of the job* (Brighton, 1999). A disparity exists between new teacher's original perceptions and the realities of the job.

8. *Feelings of isolation in their classrooms* (Darling-Hammond, 1983; Brighton, 1999). Teachers are usually the only adult in a room full of children during the instructional day, a cultural norm rooted from the one-room school era.

A significant factor that appears in the literature dealing with new teachers' psychosocial development is the cultural context of the school and the community. Schools with diverse populations pose differing factors in the psychosocial development of new teachers. For example, California schools are populated with the most diverse student population in the world. Of the more than 4.9 million students attending California's public schools, one-third come from homes where languages other than English are spoken (Bartell & Birch, 1993). Providing a quality education for all children in such an environment can be difficult for experienced teachers, but the task often can be overwhelming for novices. Ingersoll and Alsalam (1997) indicated that teacher turnover rates are higher in public schools where half or more of the students receive free or reduced-price lunches. Teachers in these schools often perceive a lack of respect from parents in part due to the parents' own negative childhood experiences within the schools.

Process. A strong mentoring program is an essential element in the socialization of new teachers adjusting to their roles. Certain elements in the mentoring process should be considered for purposes of psychosocial development. Brighton (1999) suggested that administrators should provide teachers with tiered expectations—a gradual induction into the profession—for responsibilities involving class assignments, outside duties, and committee work. Within each tier, principals and assistant principals should be offering guidance and support. New teachers often are shocked to realize that they have more duties, more challenging classes, and more committee expectations than their more experienced peers. The added expectations beyond regular teaching duties are often the straws that break the backs of new teachers. Gradually assigning responsibilities and duties can be a gentle way of inducting new teachers. They will be more prepared, and subsequently more successful, if they are presented with new challenges in small, incremental steps.

Storytelling is a favorite activity for educators and an important mentoring tool. When mentors tell stories, they share information about how they handled similar situations in their teaching experience. New teachers may feel that they are the first to experience the role conflicts that emerge and that other teachers have been immune to such conflicts. It is through listening and reflecting on stories from mentors that new teachers develop a sense of meaning and understanding of their role (Crow & Matthews, 1998).

Mentoring New Teachers in Career Development

Nearly 30 percent of teachers leave in the first five years, and the exodus is even greater in certain school districts. Research also indicates that the most talented new educators are often the most likely to leave (Gonzales & Sosa, 1993). In 1988, a Metropolitan Life study indicated that teachers of color were leaving the teaching profession in disproportionately greater numbers than their white counterparts (Harris, 1988). In addition, the teaching career is unique among professions in that it is unstaged in its reward system (Lortie, 1975). Although various writers have identified career development stages, such as stages of concern, survival, mastery, and impact (Fuller, 1969)—these stages do not reflect the reward system. Although most school systems have a salary structure based on experience and education, additional responsibility or merit promotion are not considered for career development. However, a few districts such as Denver, Colorado, and Cincinnati, Ohio, have tried performance-based salary systems with positive results. New teachers typically enter with the same responsibilities as veteran teachers and do not expect promotions. This presents a significant issue for the principal and assistant principal in mentoring the new teacher in career development.

The mentoring goals in career development are both systemic and individual. A system goal would be to increase the retention of promising new teachers and to help them establish life-long, productive careers in education. An individual goal would be to mentor new teachers in establishing a positive role conception for a satisfying and promising career.

Content.   The content in career development involves mentoring new teachers as to the responsibilities and opportunities of teaching as a career and profession. Most states have instituted professional development requirements that are necessary for re-licensure. Although a new teacher may have trouble seeing this as relevant, the principal is responsible for making sure that all teachers see the need and advantage of continuing learning that supports career development.

Perhaps one of the toughest realizations for both teachers and principals is the fact that not all individuals are suited for teaching. Teaching may not be the glamorous position that many think it is. In fact, some new teachers soon realize that unmotivated learners, disruptive students, and burned-out colleagues replace the dream they once held.

Furthermore, marginality cannot be accepted in teaching. Accountability is more than a catchword in present-day schools. Teacher accountability is the focus of many reform efforts both inside the education community and among policymakers on the outside. Because marginality in veteran teachers is a major concern for administrators, mentoring beginning teachers becomes even more important. New teachers need to be mentored by their principal in helping them understand tenure laws, orderly dismissal policies, evaluation systems, accountability initiatives, and classroom supervision technique.

Process. The principal's role in mentoring new teachers involves three processes. The first process is establishing career goals, that is, creating a vision of what the new teacher wants to become. Too often new teachers are overwhelmed by so much of the newness that exists around them that they can easily forget their own goals and vision. Their engagement in surviving the present does not allow a vision for the future. The principal should support beginning teachers by helping them establish realistic goals and by challenging them to work toward fulfilling their vision.

The second process is celebrating the new teacher's accomplishments. Celebrations can be an important mentoring opportunity for career development. Too often new teachers are not recognized for their performance or achievement when they reach certain milestones in their careers. Isolation among educators probably contributes to this lack of celebration. Through celebrations, principals provide meaningful mentoring in career development that enhances role identity by giving new teachers assurance, validity, and recognition—which also enhances their psychosocial development. Celebrations promote continued positive behavior in instructional methods. If beginning teachers receive recognition for their behaviors through celebrations, they often repeat those behaviors.

Celebrations involve both private and public activities. Private celebrations could be the administrative team having lunch with the new teacher or stopping by the teacher's classroom to give a simple gift such as a candy bar. A private celebration can be a validating gesture for the new teacher. Public celebrations could involve an announcement at a faculty meeting or an article in the school newsletter.

The third important mentoring process in career development involves counseling new teachers to continue in their development or, perhaps, to leave teaching. Although great care always should be given before counseling a person out of his or her chosen career, nevertheless, an unhappy teacher or a person unsuited for the profession should be given guidance in finding the right career.

Counseling new teachers who show promise involves challenging them to attend workshops and conferences, to read professional journals and books, to participate in teacher associations, and to attend faculty and staff socials and activities. New teachers are socialized into the profession as they participate in these types of activities. They also develop networks of relationships with others who may be valuable assets to their professional career growth.

Networking can be an important mentoring tool for the retention of teachers. Through relationship building, a person can find personal satisfaction in a job. The principal needs to introduce the new teacher, through formal and informal ways, to the school community.

The Principal as Facilitator of Mentoring for New Teachers

Although principals and assistant principals serve as mentors for new teachers, the induction process would be woefully incomplete if it did not include mentoring by other teachers. *Peer mentors* are veteran teachers who serve as primary and secondary mentors for beginning teachers. In response to the needs of beginning teachers, peer mentoring programs have become increasingly common. These programs are sponsored by a variety of organizations, including individual schools and school districts, consortia of schools, state departments of education, and colleges and universities (Gold, 1996).

Many states and districts have written policies outlining a mentoring program for beginning teachers. For example, the Utah Legislature in 1990 passed a law (Educator Evaluation, 1990) requiring all principals to assign "consulting educators" (mentors) to beginning teachers. Policies such as these, however, may not always receive the results that policymakers intended. The current movement in peer mentoring began in the mid-1980s. Feiman-Nemser and colleagues (1999) reported that before 1980 only one state had mandated a beginning teacher mentoring program. The U.S. Department of Education in 1996 reported that peer mentoring programs are likely to expand substantially due to a large influx of beginning teachers entering the profession (U.S. Department of Education, 1996). It is reasonable to presume that most American districts and schools either have or will have new teacher mentoring programs.

Beyond its part in providing beginning teachers with a more humane and professionally sound induction into teaching, peer mentoring makes a desirable professional activity for veteran teachers and reflects the expanded nature of mentoring recommended in the co-mentoring models (Mullen & Kealy, 1999). Experienced teachers gain insight into their own teaching by sharing and reflecting as they mentor novices. Mentoring encourages them to be reflective about their own beliefs about teaching, students, learning, and their careers. Ganser (1996) found in his studies that veteran teachers frequently characterized working closely with beginning teachers as a source of fresh, new, cutting-edge ideas about curriculum and teaching. Mentors often characterized what they learned from new teachers as more immediately accessible and useful in their work than much of what they learned through graduate courses or traditional inservice activities and workshops. Ganser found several cases where a mentor and a beginning teacher simultaneously implemented innovative strategies in both their classes.

The principal's role and responsibility with peer mentoring programs have not always been clearly defined. In some districts, the peer mentoring program exists outside the principal's responsibilities, a system that appears to be incongruent with strong principal instructional leadership. The principal's role should be that of primary facilitator in developing the peer mentoring program. The principal's responsibility in developing the mentoring program involves selecting, matching, training, and supporting: selecting veteran teachers to serve as peer mentors, matching them with the new teachers, training them to be mentors, and supporting them with resources to have effective mentoring relationships.

Selecting and Matching Teachers to Be Mentors: Two Perspectives

Principals should consider two perspectives in selecting teachers as mentors and then matching those mentors with beginning teachers. The first perspective is the approach in which the principal helps establish and maintain a collegial and supportive environment that promotes peer mentoring and in which beginning teachers have several mentors, both primary and secondary. This approach reflects the expanded nature of mentoring proposed by the co-mentoring model (Mullen & Kealy, 1999) and the presence of a relationship constellation in which individuals can rely on a variety of mentors in the school (Kram, 1986). In this approach, the principal is the facilitative leader who brings together new and veteran teachers to help create a professional learning community within the faculty. The entire faculty helps the novices as they encounter the newness of the school's culture and classroom challenges. This is a type of learning community that takes time to develop, and as each year passes, the culture becomes stronger in its professional collegiality. It is not a culture that is developed easily in all settings. A learning community of this nature requires constant and consistent nurturing. It can be time-consuming, disappointing, and frustrating. However, the results can be immense, as we suggested in Chapter 3. As this type of culture is in transition, the principal should consider a more formal approach that a second perspective can offer.

With the second perspective, the principal selects veteran teachers who are willing and qualified to mentor and then matches them with novice teachers for at least a year—perhaps longer. This approach is more programmatic and usually can be established sooner than the first perspective, depending on the existing culture of the school. Not surprisingly, achieving this kind of mentoring program does not happen by magic. It requires planning and special effort by the school principal. As described earlier in this chapter, mentoring is a specialized and complex role. To assume that all veteran teachers can be effective mentors, even if they are outstanding teachers, is not realistic. Furthermore, many veteran teachers may not want to be mentors because mentoring requires a considerable amount of time and energy. Those teachers who principals may want to serve as mentors are usually very active professionally, and the demands of mentoring may require them to be freed from other activities.

Professional Dilemma 4.2

Should a good veteran teacher be considered to be a mentor? Some veteran teachers might be great teachers with children but lack the relationship skills to be a good mentor with adults. As a principal, should you pursue helping the outstanding veteran teacher become a good mentor or just move on to other teachers who show more promise as mentors?

The first step for principals in the mentor selection process is to consider those teachers in the faculty who would be qualified, available, and willing to serve as mentors. Principals should consider several issues in mentor selection. The first consideration was recommended by Odell (1990a) who suggested that, when possible, the mentor and the novice should teach the same grade level or academic area so that the new teacher can get help with specific questions about curriculum and subject matter. A second consideration is how much teaching experience a mentor should have. Doyle (1988) reported that it takes at least five years for a novice to master the demands of teaching. Likewise, it takes several years for an individual to fully understand the school and community culture. A third consideration is the quality of teaching and the quality of the individual as an employee and team player within the organization. Fourth, the principal has to determine if personalities are compatible and relationships can be established between the veteran teacher and the beginner. Finally, consideration needs to be given as to the mentor and beginning teacher's gender, age, ethnicity, personality, and other contributing factors that play into the relationship. In the opening vignette, Felicia's age was problematic for some teachers in her school. Although this does not mean that newer teachers or administrators cannot mentor more experienced educators effectively, age may influence the mentoring relationship and should be considered carefully in mentor selection. Race also is an important consideration. Gardiner, Grogan, and Enomoto (2000) studied African American and Latin American women who were participating in a mentoring program. These women of color reported that race was more of an obstacle than gender in receiving adequate mentoring.

The West Des Moines Community School District established qualifications, knowledge areas, and skills that mentor teachers should have. These are shown in Figure 4.1.

Job summary: Provide expertise and ongoing support and professional growth opportunities to enhance the skills and effectiveness of beginning teachers.

   Qualifications:
   ____Ability to model effective teaching strategies
   ____Ability to work in a collaborative manner
   ____Ability to maintain confidentiality
   ____Ability to manage time effectively

   Knowledge:
   ____Knowledge of research-based effective teaching strategies
   ____Knowledge of instructional effectiveness

   Demonstrated skills:
   ____Professional competence
   ____Effective verbal and nonverbal communication
   ____Interpersonal skills of caring, kindness, and understanding

   Experience:
   ____Subject and/or grade-level experience
   ____Three or more years of successful teaching experience

   Responsibilities:
   ____Attend training as required
   ____Provide expertise and ongoing support
   ____Visit new teachers' classrooms and provide feedback

FIGURE 4.1.   West Des Moines Community School District job description for a mentor teacher.

Mentor Training

You should not assume that good or even outstanding teachers will be successful mentors without any special training and support. Several studies (Veenman, 1984; Bey & Holmes, 1990, 1992; Ganser, 1996; Feiman-Nemser, et al., 1999) supported the unique role of mentoring that warrants special preparation. These studies indicated that the unique training for prospective mentors includes both knowledge and skills. Mentor training in the knowledge component includes four parts:

1. Information about teacher career development and the predictable problems of beginning teachers
2. An understanding of the profession of teaching itself, including the induction of beginning teachers and schools as work places with site-specific cultures
3. Information about adult development and adult learning
4. Information about mentoring beginning teachers, including typical mentoring roles and activities

Mentor training for specific skill building includes

1. Reflective conferencing and story telling
2. Problem-solving strategies (e.g., defining a problem, collecting information, determining and implementing a strategy, and assessing the outcomes)
3. Helping teachers formulate short- and long-term professional goals
4. Methods of observing teaching and conducting a reflective conference

Providing Support for Peer Mentoring

At the heart of effective mentoring is the time that beginning teachers and their mentors spend together. Ganser and colleagues (1996) reported that new teachers were generally less interested in extrinsic rewards than in being provided with at least some time released from other obligations to engage in mentoring activities. Peer mentors and beginning teachers need time to discuss experiences and to engage in collaborative problem solving and goal setting. Observing a beginning teacher and then conferencing with that teacher as a reflective activity require time for both the mentor and the protégé.

What peer mentoring reasonably can be expected to accomplish is related to the amount of time available for mentoring. The principal and assistant principal can overload teachers in the number of preparations, types of courses, schedule, duty assignments, and "floating" or "carting" among several classrooms. Principals have to consider these elements in a new teacher's responsibilities so that the mentoring process can be positive. Lightening the load of new teachers allows them the time and the energy to be effective recipients of mentoring.

Feiman-Nemser and colleagues (1999) claimed that if administrators took new teachers seriously as learners, they would not expect them to do the same job or have the same skills as experienced teachers. Rather, they would adjust their expectations for success and effectiveness to fit the teachers' stage and structure assignments to allow time for observation, collaborative problem solving, and reflection. A high school in the San Francisco Bay Area developed an induction program for new teachers that reduced the new teacher's load considerably and allowed for mentoring to take place. New teachers are assigned only half the normal teaching load. They have one subject preparation and repeat the courses they teach. During the other half of the day, new teachers receive mentoring from both an assigned peer mentor and the principal or assistant principal. They have opportunities to visit experienced teachers' classes, visit other schools, attend workshops and conferences, and consult with district personnel. The administrators and faculty of this school are committed to the development of beginning teachers. Although the challenges faced by first-year teachers make the case for such an induction program, the sad reality is that in most schools new teachers are expected to perform equal to that of experienced teachers.

Schlechty (1984) recommended that beginning teachers be afforded the opportunity to develop a sense of being members of an important group that shares an ordeal and to understand that others are experiencing the same stressful period. Cohort groups of beginning teachers might reduce isolation among novice teachers and foster their professional growth. Carter and Richardson (1989) suggested that networking among beginning teachers should allow them to develop understandings of teaching and that in some instances it may be necessary to include beginning teachers from several schools to achieve a functional cohort group.

Mentoring Veteran Teachers

The mid-career stage of teaching varies for each teacher. Many veteran teachers have fallen into a survival mode. Others may be less concerned with survival but continue to seek recognition in their work and lives. Often teachers have changed grade levels or have been assigned other subjects to teach to rejuvenate their careers. Some veteran teachers have remained in the same school for most of their careers and have found a sense of pride in being part of the school history and culture. A few of these teachers find it difficult to change their teaching styles and want schools and students to remain the way they think they were in the past.

Kram (1986) reported that many individuals in mid-career are no longer establishing competence and defining an occupational identity. Instead, they are adjusting self-images and realizing they are no longer novices. They question their own competence in relation to peers and new teachers. For those who are satisfied with their accomplishments, it may be a time of shifting creative energies away from advancement concerns to interests about leisure time and family commitments. Alternately, for those who are dissatisfied with their accomplishments, it may be a time of self-doubt and a sense of urgency as they realize that life is half over and their careers have been determined (Crow & Matthews, 1998). For these different types of veteran teachers, mentoring as an "awakening" to a new way of seeing things can be a powerful learning resource for improving their teaching (Gehrke, 1988).

A typical assumption by many educators—including administrators—is that most veteran teachers have been involved in teaching for a number of years and do not need mentors. Effective principals recognize the importance of continued mentoring of teachers in mid-career. Research clearly links student achievement with teacher quality. Although many reform efforts have failed to recognize the importance of teachers, effective principals have not. In fact, several studies have indicated that effective schools have principals who emphasize quality teaching in those schools (e.g., Edmunds, 1979).

Many strategies for mentoring teachers in mid-career are similar to those used in mentoring new teachers. For example, veteran teachers have continued needs in professional, psychosocial, and career development. One important strategy in mentoring veteran teachers involves principal visibility. As a principal's visibility increases, so do mentoring opportunities. Principals in isolation seldom have the opportunities to be active mentors of veteran teachers. Studies have indicated that strong positive relationships exist between principals' visibility and teacher commitment (Sheppard, 1996) and teacher motivation (Blase & Blase, 1998). Teachers and students notice when principals are actively involved in instructional improvement. Relationships are developed more easily, and mentoring opportunities occur more often.

Several studies (e.g., Blase & Blase, 1994) have indicated that veteran teachers respond well to individual praise and compliments. Criticism, although sometimes needed, often results in a negative effect on the mentoring process. Criticism seldom promotes positive behaviors in others, whereas individual praise actually can enhance positive behaviors to be repeated. A study by Blase and Kirby (2000) indicated that praise is most effective when it deals with professional performance (such as a specific teaching strategy) rather than with appearances (dress or hairstyle).

Perhaps one of the most challenging aspects of being a principal is dealing with veteran marginal teachers. *Marginal teachers* are those who exhibit a range of problems, including limited teaching skills, ineffective communication, unproductive student achievement, and neglect of or indifference to professional responsibilities. The challenge for school administrators is to work with these teachers in ways that will return them to the ranks of effective educators. Principals are responsible to help marginal teachers make the improvements that are needed for the benefit of the children and for the reputation of the school and profession. Supervising marginality in teaching is discussed in Chapter 5; however, mentoring should be the first strategy in helping these teachers become better educators. The literature on helping marginal teachers offers several suggestions for principals:

1. *Modeling.* The principal should model effective leadership skills and professionalism and demonstrate by word and action that maintaining productive learning opportunities for students is a top priority (Blank, Kershaw, and Sparks, 1999).
2. *Information giving.* Principals need to have a working knowledge and be able to advise others as to state tenure laws and district policies and procedures that relate to teacher performance and employment.
3. *Conferencing.* Principals need to help the teacher become aware of the problem early. Helping a teacher correct small problems is easier than unraveling crises.
4. *Supporting.* The psychosocial problems of teachers can affect their professional roles. Principals can support teachers who need assistance with personal problems by offering suggestions as to resources, remediation, and counseling.

The Principal as Facilitator of Mentoring of Veteran Teachers

Much of the discussion of the principal as facilitator of mentoring new teachers can be applied to the principal's and assistant principal's roles in creating a professional learning environment that supports mentoring. For example, the importance of time to meet and the significance of training are pertinent to system-wide mentoring for all teachers. In fact, it is highly unlikely that a positive and healthy environment that supports mentoring of new teachers will exist separately from the larger school context that supports mentoring of veteran teachers.

One of the most important things that principals do to facilitate mentoring for veteran teachers is to emphasize its relevance to the school by paying attention to mentoring. Principals who talk about mentoring, encourage mentoring for instructional improvement, and acknowledge the role of mentoring in their own development send a strong message about its importance for all teachers in the school.

Another important contribution that principals and assistant principals make to facilitating mentoring of veteran teachers is to develop and support relationship constellations (Kram, 1986) in which teachers can find mentors to help with different aspects of their professional, psychosocial, and career development. Sometimes the principal's and assistant principal's actions are as simple as making teachers aware of what other teachers are doing—their innovations, experiments, and successes. This awareness encourages teachers to talk frequently with each other about instructional improvement—a significant component of effective schools (Little, 1982) and professional learning communities (Bryk, Cambron, & Louis, 1999). This awareness of what other teachers are doing also facilitates peer mentor pairing. The more teachers know what other teachers are doing in their classes, the more information they have for choosing a mentor and developing a peer mentor relationship.

In Chapter 3 we discussed various components of the principal's role as learner and facilitator of learning. Certainly these components apply to facilitating an environment for mentoring all teachers. One component, however, stands out in its importance for facilitating mentoring. As principals and assistant principals, you should recognize your own mentoring needs, participate in peer mentoring, and communicate the importance of mentoring as a central feature of the school's professional learning community.

Principal as Mentor of Students

The principal's greatest responsibility in mentoring is with teachers and improving the instructional and educational environment. However, principals are also teachers and thus interact and influence students. Principals and assistant principals find many opportunities to mentor students, such as correcting behavior problems, using their talents, achieving better academic results, and fulfilling leadership roles.

Research has indicated that leadership development starts early in a child's life. Gardner (1987) concluded that the skills critical for effective leadership, including the capacity to understand and interact with others, develop early. In another study, Garrod

(1988) found that these skills begin to form before five years of age. He also found few differences between those adolescents identified as student leaders and those not identified as such. Garrod concluded that it is not possible to predict exceptional leadership performance in adolescents. Van Linden and Fertman (1998) supported this assertion and concluded that all teenagers have the potential to lead.

Employers are more interested in adolescents who are leaders. For many employers, this initially equates with being at work on time, doing the job, and not causing problems. Over time, though, employers assess youths' leadership in the workplace in the form of taking on more responsibility and showing concern about the quality of the work being done. Van Linden and Fertman (1998) warned that leadership in the workplace could be confused with the concepts of management and supervision. "These can be particularly overwhelming notions for adolescents, and their fear of 'bossing' can keep them from exploring their leadership potential" (p. 7). It makes sense that teenagers may be reluctant to lead or to take on formal leadership positions if they believe it is associated with "bossing." However, the basic premise of student leadership is a set of skills and attitudes that can be learned and practiced and that all students can develop these skills and attitudes (van Linden & Fertman, 1998).

School is the place where students begin to learn how to behave in groups outside their family and to see leadership in action. Students learn a lot about leadership from their teachers and principals. Most students associate teachers and principals with authority and leadership. In many cases, unfortunately, the principal is someone a student wants to avoid, perceiving principals as people who make decisions about the school and the students. If principals are going to serve as mentors for students, then these young people must get to know them and not shy away from them.

The principal's opportunity to mentor students to develop leadership skills can occur in many settings and situations. Principals and assistant principals often have opportunities to mentor students in understanding correct social behaviors, which may include skills in decision making, communication, and relationship building. Mentoring leadership behavior in students is usually much easier in positive situations than in negative ones. When students excel or do something extraordinary, it is easy to encourage and support their efforts. If their effort to use leadership skills has a less than positive outcome, it is difficult for school leaders to see the benefit. However, it might be in those settings and situations that the principal provides the most beneficial mentoring. For example, a visiting accreditation team asked a middle school student about certain aspects of the school. The principal was mortified when the student told them about those things that bothered him the most, namely, smoking in the restrooms, dirty restrooms, and litter in the halls. This was not what the principal wanted the accreditation team to hear. The student understood the principal's reaction to mean that he really did not want his opinion. The student left the meeting feeling that the principal did not find these issues important and that his leadership was not regarded as meaningful.

Perhaps the most important message you can give to students at any age is that you believe that they can be valuable leaders and can influence what happens inside and outside their school.

Conclusion

In the opening vignette, Felicia and Latonya attempted to develop a school-wide mentoring program for new teachers using themselves and veteran teachers as mentors. Although difficulties arose, persistence in creating such an environment will help develop the learning community that they desire. Your understanding of mentoring is an important aspect in developing a learning community and in improving instruction. However, mentoring does not happen without careful planning, preparation, training, and organization. Your understanding of both the process and the content of mentoring is important in your developing a mentoring program in a school. Furthermore, your own participation in mentoring will indicate to others the importance you place on mentoring.

In our model described in Chapter 1, two role conceptions focus on the internal context of the principalship, mentoring and supervision. In Chapter 5 we discuss the principal as supervisor.

Activities

Self-Directed Activities

1. Describe a primary mentor and a secondary mentor in your career. What were the differences in your primary and secondary mentors?
2. Do you know of new teachers who quit? How might a mentoring program have helped them?
3. Who are the teacher mentors in your school? What are their characteristics? What are the characteristics of effective teacher mentors?

Peer Activities

1. With a colleague, identify the different professional, psychological, and career functions that your own mentors have played. Were there times or settings in which different functions were more important for you?
2. Compare your mentoring experiences as new teachers in terms of the benefits and pitfalls.
3. Discuss with your colleague the two professional dilemmas in this chapter regarding whether the principal should inform the new teacher about all parental criticisms and whether a good veteran teacher should be a mentor.

Course Activities

1. Have each class member identify the characteristics of her or his mentor. What are the similarities and differences for men and women mentors and for mentors at different career stages?

2. As a class, develop a formal mentoring plan for a specific school. Be sure to include purpose, participants, content, and processes and to cover the three functions of mentoring.

3. Use the opening vignette as the basis for a class role play of a mentoring conference between Felicia and Gloria. Reflect on how age may affect the mentoring relationship. Also identify possible approaches Felicia might take to make the mentoring relationship more effective and nurturing.

Websites

■ *http://www.ucea.org/cases/*
Cases from the Journal of Cases in Educational Leadership.
Fossey, R., Angelle, P. S., & McCoy, M. H. (2001). Burnout: Steve Watson's first year as an inner city teacher. *Journal of Cases in Educational Leadership* 4(2).

■ *http://www.nsdc.org/library/jsd/denmark214.html*
The Mettle of a Mentor: What It Takes to Make this Relationship Work for All. It's vital to the profession to provide professional development for experienced teachers, and mentoring is one way of doing just that.

■ *http://www.middleweb.com/msdiaries02/MSDiary*
New Teachers Making a Smooth Transition—With Plenty of Help. A middle school principal relates the benefits of effective mentoring.

■ *http://www.ascd.org/readingroom/edlead/9905/rowley.html*
The Good Mentor. As formal mentoring programs gain popularity, the need for identifying and preparing good mentors grows.

References

Bartel, C. A., & Birch, L. W. (1993). *An Examination of the Preparation, Induction, and Professional Growth of School Administrators for California.* Sacramento: Commission on Teacher Credentialing.

Bey, T. M., & Holmes, C. T. (1990). *Mentoring: Developing Successful New Teachers.* Reston, VA: Association of Teacher Educators.

Bey, T. M., & Holmes, C. T. (1992). *Mentoring: Contemporary Principles and Issues.* Reston, VA: Association of Teacher Educators.

Berlew, D. E., &. Hall, D.T. (1966). The socialization of managers: Effects of expectations on performances. *Administrative Science Quarterly 11,* 207–223.

Blank, M. A., Kershaw, C., & Sparks, B. S. (1999). How to supervise the marginal teacher. *NASSP Tips for Principals* (January 1999).

Blase, J., & Blase, J. (1994). *Empowering Teachers: What Successful Teachers Do.* Thousand Oaks, CA: Corwin Press.

Blase, J., & Blase, J. (1998). *Handbook of Instructional Leadership: How Really Good Principals Promote Teaching and Learning.* Thousand Oaks, CA.: Corwin Press.

Blase, J., & Kirby, P. C. (2000). *Bringing Out the Best in Teachers: What Effective Principals Do* (2d ed.). Thousand Oaks, CA: Corwin Press.

Bowers, G. R., & Eberhart, N. (1988). Mentoring and the entry year program. *Theory into Practice 27*(3), 226–230.

Brighton, C. M. (1999). Keeping good teachers: Lessons from novices. In M. Scherer (Ed.), *A Better Beginning: Supporting and Mentoring New Teachers* (pp. 197–201). Alexandria, VA: Association for Supervision and Curriculum Development.

Bryk, A., Camburn, E., & Louis, K. S. (1999). Professional community in Chicago elementary schools: Facilitating factors and organizational consequences. *Educational Administration Quarterly 35*(Suppl.), 751–781.

Carter, K., & Richardson, V. (1989). A curriculum for an initial year of teaching program. *Elementary School Journal 89*, 405–419.

Clawson, J. G. (1980). Mentoring in managerial careers. In C. B. Deer (Ed.), *Work, Family, and the Career.* New York, Praeger.

Crow, G. M., & Matthews, L. J. (1998). *Finding One's Way: How Mentoring Can Lead to Dynamic Leadership.* Thousand Oaks, CA: Corwin Press.

Daloz, L. A. (1983). Mentors: Teachers who make a difference. *Change 5*(6), 24–27.

Dalton, G. W., Thompson, P. H., and Price, R. L. (1977). The four stages of professional careers: A new look at performance by professionals. *Organizational Dynamics 6*, 19–42.

Daresh, J. C. and Playko, M. A. (1993). *Leaders Helping Leaders: A Practical Guide to Administrative Mentoring.* New York: Scholastic.

Darling-Hammond, L. (1983). Teacher evaluation in the organizational context: A review of the literature. *Review of Educational Research 53*(3), 285–328.

Darling-Hammond, L. (1984). Taking the measure of excellence: The case against basing teacher evaluation on student test scores. *American Educator: The Professional Journal of the American Federation of Teachers 8*(3), 26–29, 46.

Deal, T. E., & Chatman, R. M. (1989). Learning the ropes alone: Socializing new teachers. *Action in Teacher Education 11*(1), 21–29.

Dembele, M. (1996). *Mentors and Mentoring: Frames for Action, Ways of Acting, and Consequences for Novice Teachers' Learning (Professional Development),* Ph.D. Dissertation, Michigan State University.

Doyle, W. (1988). *Learning to teach: Directions from the current research base.* Paper presented at the Meeting of the Association of Teacher Educators, San Diego, CA.

Educator Evaluation, Utah Code, Subsection 53A-10-108 (1990).

Edmunds, R. (1979). Effective schools for the urban poor. *Educational Leadership 37*(12), 15–24.

Feiman-Nemser, S., Carver, C., Schwille, S., & Yusko, B. (1999). Beyond support: Taking new teachers seriously as learners. In M. Scherer (ed.), *A Better Beginning: Supporting and Mentoring New Teachers* (pp. 3–12). Alexandria, VA: Association for Supervision and Curriculum Development.

Fullan, M. (1999). *Change Forces: The Sequel.* Philadelphia: Falmer Press.

Fuller, F. F. (1969). Concerns of teachers: A developmental conceptualization. *American Educational Research Journal 6*(2): 207–266.

Ganser, T. (1996). Preparing mentors of beginning teachers: An overview for staff developers. *Journal of Staff Development. 17*(4), 8–11.

Ganser, T., Marchione, M. J., & Fleischmann, A. K. (1999). Baltimore takes mentoring to the next level. In M. Scherer (ed.), *A Better Beginning: Supporting and Mentoring New Teachers* (pp. 69–76). Alexandria, VA: Association for Supervision and Curriculum Development.

Gardiner, M. E., Grogan, M., & Enomoto, E. (2000). *Coloring Outside the Lines: Mentoring Women into School Leadership.* Albany, NY: SUNY Press.

Gardner, J. W. (1987). *Leadership Development: Leadership Papers.* Washington: Independent Sector.

Garrod, A. (1988). Psychological skills of adolescent leaders. Unpublished manuscript, Dartmouth College, Hanover, NH.

Gehrke, N. (1988) Toward a definition of mentoring. *Theory into Practice 27*(3), 190–194.

Gehrke, N. J. and Kay, R. S. (1984). The socialization of beginning teachers through mentor-protege relationships. *Journal of Teacher Education 35*(3), 21–24.

Glickman, C. D. (1985). The supervisor's challenge: Changing the work environment. *Educational Leadership 42*(4), 38–40.

Glickman, C. D. (1990). Preface. In T. M. Bey, & C. T. Holmes (Eds.), *On Mentoring: Developing Successful Teachers.* Reston, VA: Virginia Association of Teacher Educators.

Gold, Y. (1996). Beginning teacher support: Attrition, mentoring and induction. In J. Sikula, T. J. Buttery, & E. Guyton (Eds.), *Handbook on Research on Teacher Education.* New York: Macmillan.

Gonzales, F., & Sosa, A. S. (1993). How do we keep teachers in our classrooms? The TNT response. *IDRA Newsletter 1*(March), 6–9.

Harris, L. A. (1988). *The Metropolitan Life Survey: The American Teacher 1988: Strengthening the Relationship Between Teachers and Students.* New York: Metropolitan Life Insurance Co.

Hart, A. W. (1991). Leader succession and socialization: A synthesis. *Review of Educational Research, 61*(4), 451–474.

Hart, A. W. (1993). Principal succession: Establishing leadership in schools. Albany, NY: State University of New York Press.

Hay, J. (1995). *Transformational Mentoring: Creating Developmental Alliances for Changing Organizational Cultures.* London: McGraw-Hill.

Ingersoll, R. M., & Alsalam, N. (1997). *Teacher Professionalization and Teacher Commitment: A Multilevel Analysis. Statistical Analysis Report* (0 16 048975 x NCES 97 069). Washington D.C.: National Center for Education Statistics U.S. Department of Education.

Kohn, M. L. & Schooler, C. (1978). The reciprocal effects of the substantive complexity of work and intellectual flexibility: A longitudinal assessment. *American Journal of Sociology 84*, 24–52

Kram, K. E. (1985). *Mentoring at Work.* Glenview, IL: Scott, Foresman.

Kram, K. E. (1986). Mentoring in the workplace. In D. T. Hall (Ed.), *Career Development in Organizations* (pp. 160–210). San Francisco: Jossey-Bass.

Levinson, D. J., Darrow, C. N., Klein, E. B., Levinson, M. H., & McKee, B. (1978). *Seasons of a Man's Life.* New York: Ballantine Books.

Little, J. W. (1982). Norms of collegiality and experimentation: Workplace conditions of school success. *American Educational Research Journal 19*, 325–340.

Lortie, D. C. (1975). *Schoolteacher: A Sociological Study.* Chicago: University of Chicago Press.

McIntyre, D., & Hagger, H. (1996). Mentoring: Challenges for the future. In D. M. and H. Hagger (Eds.), *Mentors in Schools: Developing the Profession of Teaching.* London: David Fulton.

McPartland, C. (1985). The myth of the mentor. *Campus Voice 2*(1), 8–11.

Megginson, D., & Clutterbuck, D. (1995). *Mentoring in Action.* London: Kogan Page.

Mullen, C. A., & Cox, M. D. (1997). Breaking the circle of one through mentorship. In C. A. Mullen, M.D. Cox, C.K. Boettcher, & D.S. Adoue (Ed.), *Breaking the Circle of One: Redefining Mentorship in the Lives and Writings of Educators* (pp. xv–xxiii). New York, Peter Lang.

Mullen, C. A., & Kealy, W. A. (1999). Breaking the circle of one: Developing professional cohorts to address challenges of mentoring for teacher educators. *Teacher Educators Journal 9*(1), 35–50.

Muse, I. D., Wasden, F. D., & Thomas, G. J. (1988). *The Mentor Principal: A Handbook.* Provo, UT: Brigham Young University.

Nash, D., & Treffinger, D. (1993). *The Mentor: A Step-By-Step Guide to Creating an Effective Mentor Program in Your School.* Waco, TX: Prufrock.

Nicholson, P. (1996). *Gender, Power and Organization: A Psychological Perspective.* London: Routledge.

Odell, S. J. (1990a). *Mentor Teacher Programs.* Washington: National Education Association.

Odell, S. J. (1990b). Support of new teachers. In T. M. Bey, & C.T. Holmes (Eds.), *Mentoring: Developing Successful New Teachers* (pp. 3-23). Reston, VA: Virginia Association of Teacher Educators.

Odell, S. J., & Ferraro, D. P. (1992). Teacher mentoring and teacher retention. *Journal of Teacher Education, 43*(3), 200–204.

Phillips-Jones, L. (1982). *Mentors and Protégés.* New York: Arbor House.

Rosenholtz, S. J. (1985). Political myths about education reform: Lessons from research in teaching. *Phi Delta Kappa 66*, 349–355.

Rowe, M. (1981). Building mentorship frameworks as part of an effective equal opportunity ecology. In J. Farley (Ed.), *Sex Discrimination in Higher Education: Strategies for Equality* (pp. 23–87). Ithaca, NY: Cornell University Press.

Schein, E. H. (1978). *Career Dynamics: Matching Individual and Organizational Needs.* Reading, MA: Addison-Wesley.

Schlechty, P. (1984). *Restructuring the teaching occupation: A proposal.* Paper presented at the American Educational Research Association, Washington, D.C. November.

Schon, D. A. (1983). *The Reflective Practitioner: How Professionals Think in Action.* New York: Basic Books.

Schooler, C. (1989). *A sociological perspective in intellectual development.* Paper presented at the Biennial Meeting of the Society for Research in Child Development (ERIC ED 308 932). Kansas City, MO, April 27–30, 1989.

Sheppard, B. (1996). Exploring the transformational nature of instructional leadership. *Alberta Journal of Educational Research 42*(4), 325–344.

Tomlinson, P. (1995). *Understanding Mentoring: Reflective Strategies for School-Based Teacher Preparation.* Buckingham, UK: Open University Press.

Torrance, E. P. (1984). *Mentor Relationships: How They Aid Creative Achievement, Endure, Change, and Die.* Buffalo, NY: Bearly.

U.S. Department of Education (1996). *A Back to School Special: The Baby Boom Echo;* available at *http://www.ed/gov/nces/bbecho.*

van Linden, J. A., & Fertman, C. I. (1998). *Youth Leadership: A Guide to Understanding Leadership Development in Adolescents.* San Francisco: Jossey-Bass.

Veenman, S. (1984). Perceived problems of beginning teachers. *Review of Educational Research 54,* 143–178.

Principal as Supervisor

5

Key Terms and Concepts

administrative evaluation
evaluation

formative supervision
instructional capacity

summative evaluation
supervision

Vignette

Bill Payne sat in his office at the end of the day before the December holiday reflecting on his first semester as a new principal. He was appointed principal of Mt. Ares Elementary School fresh out of graduate school. Bill had been a fourth grade teacher who was well known in the district for his innovative teaching style and his mentoring of new teachers. He was excited when he was appointed principal not only because of his desire to be a principal but also because Mt. Ares was known as one of the district's best schools. The teachers at Mt. Ares were considered among the most innovative in the district, and parents hounded district administrators to get their children into the school.

Last year several of the veteran teachers retired, and Bill was faced with more new teachers than the school had had in some time. He looked forward to working with these new teachers but knew that with his new administrative responsibilities this would be a hectic year.

After his appointment, Bill developed a plan for working with the new teachers. He wanted to observe and conference with these teachers, but he knew that he needed help from the veteran teachers in order to provide effective mentoring and supervision for these new teachers.

Soon after the school year began, Bill approached Frances Kilgore, one of the most respected teachers in the school, to discuss his plan for professional development of the new teachers. He talked to Frances about the need for the new teachers to have veteran peers who would observe them in their classrooms, allow the new teachers to observe the veterans, and provide regular feedback. He promised that he would get substitutes for the teachers and even offered to substitute himself whenever possible.

The reaction from Frances was shocking to Bill. Essentially, she said that the reason the veteran teachers at Mt. Ares were respected by the community was that they limited their "extracurricular activities" and focused on the children and their own class-rooms. She said that she also believed that new teachers needed to spend some time struggling and working out their own style. When Bill pointed out the statistics that one-third of new teachers leave teaching by their third year, Frances replied, "Well, maybe that's the way to weed out the bad teachers." Frances also told Bill that she could see no incentive for herself in spending all that time working with new teachers. "How will that benefit me or my students?"

When Bill left the conversation with Frances, he thought maybe Frances was the exception. In the next few weeks, however, as he spoke with other veteran teachers at Mt. Ares, it became clear that Frances' views were the norm, not the exception.

As he sat in his office pondering the semester, Bill felt good about most things that had happened. He had made a good impression on the parents and teachers, and the district office felt that he had made a nice transition to administration. However, Bill was not satisfied with what was happening with new teachers. As much as he tried to spend time in their classrooms and conference with them, he simply could not provide the kind of supervisory support that most of these new teachers needed.

Introduction

Bill Payne's concerns call attention to a role for principals and assistant principals that results from the roles we have discussed in the preceding two chapters: learner and mentor. These roles come together in the role of supervisor. Although not as much attention has focused on the principal as learner and mentor, a great deal of literature, both popular and academic, discusses supervision.

The educational administration literature has a love-hate relationship with the word *supervision*. On one hand, the instructional leadership literature emphasizes the principal's role as supervisor, observing and working with teachers to improve instruction. On the other hand, educators have criticized the word *supervision*, referring to it at times as "snoopervision." Some have even suggested that principals and assistant principals, because of their hierarchical positions, cannot supervise or at least cannot be both supervisor and evaluator.

School administrators have had a similarly contradictory perception of supervision. Principals claim that instructional leadership activities such as supervision are extremely important and should receive high priority in their practice (Doud & Keller, 1998). Yet studies repeatedly demonstrate that principals and assistant principals spend less time on supervision than on managerial concerns. In a case study of a rural high school principal, business consumed 58 percent of the principal's time, compared with 6 percent spent on supervision (Hill, 1993).

In this chapter we discuss a conception of the principal's and assistant principal's role as supervisor that attempts to refocus attention on the importance of *supervision* but defines the role in both direct and facilitative ways. We begin with a discussion of the traditional role of principal as supervisor before moving to our discussion of a new conception. Like previous chapters, our discussion of the principal as supervisor includes both the direct ways principals and assistant principals act as supervisors and the more indirect but critical way principals and assistant principals can facilitate a culture of supervision within the school. This chapter is not intended to replace a course or textbook on the foundations and techniques of supervision. Rather, we hope this chapter introduces you, as a new and aspiring assistant principal or principal, to a new way to think about how you can contribute to the professional learning community of the school. Thus our focus is not on techniques but on conceptions of the role.

Before beginning our examination of the traditional conception of the supervisor role, two points need to be clarified. First, as we noted previously, the term *supervision* typically connotes inspection. The word suggests hierarchical and perhaps autocratic techniques. We struggled with whether we should use a different word to label this principal role. However, *supervision* is part of the administrative vocabulary. We have decided to redefine the word rather than replace it. As we discuss the traditional role and the innovative conception of the role, this redefining will become clearer.

Second, *supervision* and *evaluation* frequently are used synonymously in practice. We maintain that there needs to be a separation between the formal and typically summative process of evaluation and the more formative process of supervision. However, unlike some writers, we argue that both these functions can be performed by principals and assistant principals and, in fact, should complement each other. Although we spend the majority of space in this chapter on the formative process of working with teachers to improve practice, we believe that much of this material is useful for the summative process of evaluating teachers.

Traditional Role of Principal as Supervisor

The traditional conception of the role of supervisor is chiseled into the minds of most new administrators. Because most principals and assistant principals were teachers and remember principal "visits" to their classrooms, new administrators come to the principalship with a traditional view of supervision. However, this conception did not appear overnight. There is a history to the role of principal as supervisor.

Historical Overview of the Supervisor's Role

As we noted in Chapter 2, the principal's role began as a teacher and moved to a hierarchical position in part responsible for monitoring the behavior of both students and teachers. Luehe (1989) described this early role as an inspection role, in which the principal's responsibility as supervisor was to weed out weak teachers and ensure school boards that standards were being upheld. With the advent of scientific management, the role took on additional elements. Luehe emphasized the attention to added administrative and managerial tasks involving checking to make sure that the teacher's behavior contributed to improved student performance. Monitoring test results became a function of supervision. According to Luehe, a third shift in the role came as a result of a human relations focus. The early human relations advocates, although still interested in increasing productivity, focused on faculty and staff morale. More contemporary approaches advocate supervision as building collegial relationships among teachers to support school improvement and student learning. This supervisory role involves exchanging ideas, working with teachers to identify instructional problems, serving as a resource person, and assisting in bringing about change where appropriate.

Beach and Reinhartz (2000) charted similar changes in the way supervision has been conceived. They began with the colonial period, when the focus was on inspection, and subsequent expansion and growth periods of the late 1800s, when state and local authorities monitored curriculum and instruction. The early 1900s saw the scientific and professionalization periods, when supervisors became efficiency experts or educational specialists. During the progressive period, supervision became less focused on monitoring than on providing assistance to teachers to improve instruction. During the late 1950s and 1960s, more attention was paid to curriculum development. These authors argued that during the 1970s the focus was more clinical, helping teachers to diagnose teaching and learning problems. Finally, the 1980s and 1990s brought the instructional leadership era, when supervisors were responsible for coaching teachers in the context of reform. Figure 5.1 charts these changes in supervisory practice.

Blase and Blase (1998) argued that although there has been considerable disagreement on the appropriate approaches to supervision over the last 140 years, there has been little change in practice. "The practice of supervision has often been one of inspection, oversight, and judgment" (p. 8).

Elements of the Traditional Role of Principal as Supervisor

Blase and Blases' (1998) criticism of the practice of supervision suggested that the traditional role of supervision needs examination and change. In the following description of the traditional role of principal as supervisor, we have relied on Reitzug's (1997) discussion of the various components of the conception of principal as supervisor. He based his discussion on a careful examination of ten of the most frequently used supervisory texts between 1985 and 1995. The discussion identified elements based on the views of the principal, the teacher, teaching, and the process of supervision.

According to Reitzug (1997), texts "primarily portrayed the principal as expert and superior, the teacher as deficient and voiceless, teaching as fixed technology, and supervision as a discrete intervention" (p. 326). In this traditional view, principals, because of their hierarchical position, are assumed to be the experts in student learning and instruction. Reitzug argued that this image weakens the role of both teachers and principals. First, it devalues the practical knowledge that teachers have developed in their work. Second, it burdens the principal with having to possess all knowledge in regard to student learning and instruction. Third, it reduces the value of collaborative inquiry.

This traditional view of the principal as supervisor also assumes that the teacher is deficient. Instead of focusing on teaching and learning as a continuing process of improvement, the images found by Reitzug (1997) focused on finding and correcting errors. The images assume "that it is the supervisor/principal's judgment that counts; that the teacher may have an opinion is barely recognized. Finally, the images imply that the principal is the agent of improved instruction, not the teacher" (p. 333).

This traditional conception also assumes that teaching is a "fixed technology," a view that is incongruent with contemporary research on the nature of teaching. Several researchers on teaching (Stodolsky, 1988; Darling-Hammond, Wise, & Klein, 1995) and a few on supervision (Nelson & Sassi, 2000) have pointed to the finding that good teaching techniques can vary with the situation or the subject. For example, direct instruction,

Time Period/Theme	Supervisory Role	Supervisory Focus
1600–1865 (the colonial period), early beginnings	Authoritarian and autocratic committees	Inspecting to maintain conformity to lay standards
1865–1910 (the state and national period), expansion and growth	State and local administrators and managers of schools, students, and curriculum	Overseeing of state and local curriculum and instruction
1910–1920 (the scientific and organizational period), science applied to learning and organizations	Efficiency experts and scientific managers	Implementing standardization and regimentation of curriculum and instruction
1920–1935 (the professionalization and bureaucratic period), becoming a profession	Career managers and educational specialists (bureaucrats)	Monitoring progress of teachers and students toward educational goals
1935–1955 (the progressive and cooperative period), changing the way schools are viewed	Facilitators and counselors	Providing direct assistance to teachers in improving instruction
1955–1970 (the curriculum-development and change-oriented period)	Curriculum specialists and writers	Assisting teachers in developing curriculum and implementing instructional change
1970–1980 (the clinical and accountable period), dealing with differences	Clinicians and analytical observers	Helping individual teachers be more effective and accountable by analyzing the teaching-learning process
1980–1995 (the entrepreneurial and reform period), the reform influence of business	Instructional leaders and managers	Coaching teachers in the fine points of effective instruction while reconfiguring the school organization
Supervision and the future: what's next?	Multitalented and collaborative partners	Creating schools as learning organizations through professional development

Source: From Beach, D., & Reinhartz, J. (2000). *Supervisor Leadership: Focus on Instruction.* Boston: Allyn & Bacon.

FIGURE 5.1   Charting the Changes in Supervisory Practice

which is sometimes used as the major form of teaching for all subjects, is only appropriate for about 40 percent of teaching (Rosenshine, 1986).

Finally, the traditional role assumes that supervision consists of a discrete intervention, for example, an observation or evaluative conference. Such an image ignores the value and need for continuing learning and a school-wide culture of learning. Reitzug

(1997) pointed out that this traditional conception includes only the teacher as needing growth. Instead of a conception of the school as a professional learning community (Bryk, Cambron, & Louis, 1999) or as a community of inquiry (Smyth, 1997), this traditional image focuses attention only on teachers as learners.

The traditional image also assumes that the principal's role consists solely of directly supervising teachers rather than facilitating supervision through others. In the traditional conception, everything flows from the principal. However, this limits the instructional capacity of the school and thwarts the development of a professional learning community.

Traditional Supervisory Role of the Assistant Principal

In addition to the previously identified components of a traditional role of the supervisor, assistant principals encounter other factors that are part of a traditional role. First, the assistant principal's role has come to reflect a noninstructional orientation that primarily emphasizes student management, defined as crowd control or policing disruptive students. Some assistant principals are hired specifically for these functions and are expected to take on this role rather than to make or mold a more innovative role. They find that the informal expectations for them to handle the student management function are so strong that little time is left for any instructional leadership role and that the student management role is usually not seen as a component of instructional leadership. Although job descriptions may include instructional leadership elements, the actual practice of the assistant principals tends to de-emphasize any supervisory contribution.

Second, when assistant principals are expected to take a supervisory role, it frequently emphasizes the inspection function we discussed previously. In this traditional role, the assistant principal becomes essentially an informant who extends the inspection arm of the principal to check up on teachers. Clearly, such an inspection/informant role decreases the assistant principal's credibility with teachers to be a resource for instructional reflection and improvement and a collaborative partner in a community of learners.

In the next two sections we focus on what we believe is a conception of the principal's and assistant principal's roles that takes seriously the role of supervisor but redefines that role in a more effective and facilitative way—the type of role Bill Payne tried to implement in the opening vignette. In the following section we focus on what principals can do and be in a direct way as supervisors. In the subsequent section we focus on how principals can facilitate supervision throughout the school.

The Principal's Role in Direct Supervision: An Innovative Conception

In Chapter 3 we discussed the critical role of principal as learner and facilitator of learning. The principal's supervisory role, which we will describe in the remainder of this chapter, fits within this context of a community of learners. The contrast we make with the traditional inspection role of the principal emphasizes supervision as a learning process rather than as a monitoring process. In Chapter 3 we discussed the principal's role in creating a school-wide culture of learning, and in Chapter 4 we discussed the importance of mentoring as a learning tool. In this chapter we focus on the principal's role at the internal level of the classroom. In this section we begin with a brief overview of this innovative role conception and then move to a discussion of three major functions of the principal's role, including recruiting and selecting capable educators, promoting educator growth, and evaluating educational results.

If supervision is a learning process rather than a monitoring process, what does this mean for your role as a principal? In Reitzug's (1997) terms, it means that principals are partners in "collaborative inquiry" around teaching and learning. Frequently, however, the argument for collaborative inquiry fails to specify what the principal's direct role is in addition to a facilitative role. We argue that principals have a direct role to play in supervision in addition to facilitating a school-wide culture of collaborative inquiry.

This direct role involves building *instructional capacity,* the capability of schools to enhance student learning based on internal and external resources. If, as we have emphasized in Chapter 3, principals and assistant principals are responsible for helping the school become a professional learning community, one component of that role is the learning that occurs with teachers and students. The central focus of schools is teaching and learning. One of the most important ways principals and assistant principals contribute to this focus is to ensure that the school has the capability for teaching and learning to occur. Although instructional capacity involves a variety of concerns, including fiscal and physical management, community support, and resources, one of the central features of instructional capacity is what happens when students and teachers come together.

In order for this to occur, we identify three major functions of the principal's role in building instructional capacity: recruiting and selecting capable educators, promoting educator professional growth, and evaluating educational results. All three are direct and vital roles that principals play in building instructional capacity.

Recruiting and Selecting Capable and Committed Educators

Among the most important roles that you will play as a principal is securing capable and committed educators for the school. There is no way to build instructional capacity without finding teachers who are able, effective educators for students. Although most new principals do not have the opportunity to recruit and select all teachers for a school, the appointment of each teacher sends an important message to students, parents, district administrators, and other teachers of your view of a capable and committed educator.

Districts vary in terms of the role that principals can play in recruiting and selecting teachers. Most districts involve the principal significantly in this process, even to the point of allowing the principal or a school committee to make the final recommendation to the school board. Some districts have a site-based management process in which this final recommendation ultimately is left to a school committee composed of principal, teachers, parents, and occasionally students. A few districts make teacher selection decisions at a centralized level, essentially leaving out school-level input. This approach ignores the fact that the selection process significantly influences an educator's credibility. If administrators, fellow teachers, parents, and community members are left out of the recruitment and selection process, the teacher often will be seen as an outsider and will face an uphill battle for acceptance. Being an effective teacher involves supportive relationships with other educators, parents, and students.

Recruiting teachers is as important as selecting teachers and often is overlooked. Except in times of critical teacher shortages, the typical practice of some principals is to "wait and see" who the district office sends to be interviewed or who applies. This approach seldom results in finding the cream of the crop. A more proactive recruitment approach involves the principal keeping in close and continuing contact with university teacher educators, professional association representatives, and administrative colleagues to know who and where the best teachers are. Word travels fast about the best, conducive environments for teaching and the schools with the greatest instructional capacity. Word also travels fast about which schools lack the instructional capacity to foster teacher growth and student learning.

Although recruiting a teacher who is presently teaching in another school is sometimes seen as unprofessional, principals can employ certain recruiting tactics that are not offensive. For example, one high school principal recruited a band instructor simply by announcing the position opening at a state music festival. An elementary school principal told the Parent Teacher Association (PTA) about openings for the next year, and one parent told a neighbor teacher who became interested in the opening.

Selecting teachers is also a critical part of your role as a principal, even if the final selection is not yours. Three major criteria are critical in the selection process: fit, expertise, and diversity. Selecting teachers who fit the school's culture is critical. Although fit is a traditional concern of teacher selection, a more innovative supervisory role for principals involves recruiting and selecting teachers who have similar values and norms that contribute specifically to a professional learning community. These norms and values involve characteristics of a professional community that we have discussed in Chapter 3: collaboration, de-privatized practice, shared values, and reflection (Bryk, Cambron, & Louis, 1999). Selecting teachers who are willing to collaborate, reflect, open up their teaching to other educators, and share similar values of teaching and learning is a critical role for principals in building instructional capacity. No doubt there are other considerations of fit, for example, teaching philosophy, but these are usually less critical if the teacher is collaborative, reflective, open to critique, and values learning.

When considering expertise, criteria become more difficult to identify succinctly. There has been considerable research on effective teaching. However, the clear finding is that what is effective must be defined in terms of the goals (Glickman, Gordon, & Ross-Gordon, 1998). Effective teaching in a school where the goals are the development of a learning community is different from effective teaching in a school where higher achievement test scores are the only goal. Sergiovanni and Starratt (1998) identified characteristics of teachers who would be recruited by a learning community. These teachers

- Are committed to the principle that all children can succeed at learning and will do all in their power to bring that about.

- Are convinced that significant learning is achieved only by the active engagement of the learner in the production or performance of multiple expressions of authentic understanding.
- Are committed to collaborating with other teachers in the school to build a flexible, responsive, and dynamic learning environment that engages every student.
- Know the content of the academic disciplines they are teaching as well as the methodologies of inquiry of these disciplines.
- Know the components of the meta-curriculum—the aspects of higher-order thinking and the major conceptual frameworks, models, and methodologies of the disciplines—and can recognize productions and performances that authenticate learners' reflective proficiency in the meta-curriculum.
- Have executive control of a wide variety of instructional protocols and strategies for opening up the curriculum for youngsters.
- Can design a variety of learning activities for individuals as well as groups that will maximize autonomous, active involvement with the material.
- Continually monitor students' work through dialogue and action research so as to assess whether an individual student is experiencing difficulties, to discover what the source of those difficulties are, and to respond in ways that will facilitate mastery of the learning tasks.
- Are committed to working with parents as partners in supporting the learning tasks in which their children are engaged.
- Can evaluate, in both formative and summative procedures, a variety of assessment performances and portfolios.
- Can construct, in collaboration with parents, administrators, and the school board, the school's learning environment whenever necessary (pp. 103–104).

The third criterion that principals must address in recruiting and selecting capable educators is diversity. In light of the changing demographics of contemporary schools and the increased heterogeneity projected for the future, school faculty and staff members need to reflect the ethnic diversity of the students. Although school boards may differ in terms of controversial issues such as using quotas to diversify the faculty, there should be no disagreement that students, both majority and minority, need the opportunities inherent in an ethnically diverse teaching force.

In addition to recruiting ethnically diverse faculty, principals must recruit and select educators who represent different points of view. Here lies a dilemma for the principal. As we have noted previously, teachers need to share the values with the school's culture. However, if everyone thinks the same, shares the same philosophy of teaching, and graduates from the same university teaching program, innovation is likely to be thwarted. The fundamental values of reflection, collaboration, and shared values do not mean that there is one best way to teach or interact with students. *Contrived collegiality* (Hargreaves, 1990) and *groupthink,* in which everyone uses the same process for reaching the same decisions, are not conducive to the development of a professional learning community. Principals need to actively recruit and select educators who value openness, collaboration, reflection, and inquiry and who are not afraid to disagree with other educators, including the principal.

Professional Dilemma 5.1

As a principal, do you select a teacher who matches the culture or one who contributes to the diversity of points of view? What situational factors contribute to the decision?

Although recruiting and selecting may have been a responsibility of the principal, an innovative conception of the role means that principals and assistant principals will perform these functions in a new way. Primarily, this innovative conception of the role of principal means that principals and assistant principals will be proactive in their recruitment, will consider characteristics that contribute to the school as a professional learning community, will focus on teaching and learning within this context of collaborative inquiry, and will encourage diversity.

Promoting Educator Growth

The primary concern in building instructional capacity involves the role of the principal and assistant principal in promoting educator growth. That role involves fostering teacher practical knowledge, encouraging reflection, and offering expertise in a climate of mutual inquiry. These three components represent an innovative role for you as a principal or assistant principal in contributing to teacher growth and student learning.

First, the principal fosters teachers' practical knowledge (Sternberg & Wagner, 1986). Teachers are not blank tablets waiting for principals to write strategies for improvement. They have more potential understanding of classroom culture, student learning styles, and in most cases curricula than the principal. The principal's role is to value this practical knowledge and help teachers articulate it and use it to solve instructional problems and create more responsive learning environments. Obviously, the degree of practical knowledge will vary depending on the teacher's career stage and experience.

Second, the principal encourages reflection. The purpose of supervisory practices, such as post-observation conferences, is not simply to list the teacher's strengths and weaknesses. Rather, fundamentally the conference is to provide an opportunity for reflection within an accepting context. In addition, the principal's role is to encourage reflection on teaching and learning throughout the school and throughout the teacher's career. Reflection is an ongoing process, not a once-a-year event.

Third, the principal offers expertise in a climate of inquiry. Being an expert and sharing expertise are positive characteristics unless the principal and/or teacher assumes that only the principal possesses expertise. Opening the principal's own practice to inquiry and critique not only encourages teachers to do likewise but also sends a powerful message to the school that inquiry is valued by all. The principal also shares expertise by identifying and using alternative perspectives for the critique of practice.

In this subsection we will continue the examination of the role of principal as supervisor in promoting educator growth by organizing our comments along the lines of Reitzug's (1997) analysis: conception of teacher, view of teaching, conception of the supervisor, and conception of supervision.

Conception of the Teacher.   The first component of an innovative role of the principal in promoting educator growth is a view of the teacher as a professional with practical knowledge or the potential for developing this knowledge. As Reitzug (1997) pointed out, research has demonstrated the presence of widespread knowledge acquired by teachers through their daily involvement in defining and shaping the problems of practice (Lieberman & Miller, 1991). Viewing the teacher as a learning professional means that the teacher may have more understanding of the classroom culture, more knowledge of the curricula, and greater sensitivity to student needs and learning styles than the principal or assistant principal. Admittedly, new teachers and some veteran teachers may not yet have developed these characteristics or are incompetent (Bridges, 1986; Roberts, 2000), but the existence of incompetence or inexperience in a few teachers does not necessitate viewing teachers generally as incompetent or inexperienced. Discovering doctors who are callous or lack knowledge regarding particular diseases should not result in a view that all doctors are quacks. Why should teachers be considered otherwise?

Part of being a professional is being a self-directed learner. The teacher is responsible for reflecting on and improving teaching and learning in the classroom. In a professional learning community, this learning is also collaborative. The principal promotes educator growth by having confidence in and encouraging the learning capacity of the teacher.

The principal's understanding of the teacher's role also acknowledges teacher differences and development. Glickman and colleagues (1998) developmental approach to supervision is based on the recognition that teachers differ and the need for supervisory approaches varies depending on these differences. A number of models of adult and teacher development identify teacher differences with regard to concerns (Fuller, 1969), conceptual level (Hunt, 1966), moral development (Gilligan, 1982; Kohlberg & Armon, 1984), and life-cycle development (Erikson, 1963). For example, Fuller's concerns model identified the stages of concern that teachers face in their careers: survival, mastery of tasks, and impact. This model suggests that not only are teachers professionals but also that, like all adults, they vary in terms of their development. As Tracy (1998) pointed out, this variation in development means that the supervisory focus is not predetermined; the teacher rather than the supervisor or some external criteria decides on the focus.

View of Teaching.   Reitzug (1997) argued that the traditional view of supervision holds that teaching is a "fixed technology." In fact, research demonstrates that teaching is a highly complex, context-specific, interactive activity (Cochran-Smith & Lytle, 1992). Instead of viewing teaching as a set of generic principles that occurs similarly in all contexts regardless of demographics, goals, values, and so on, a principal should view teaching as a dynamic, complex process.

Regardless of whether teaching is seen as art (Eisner, 1985), science (Hunter, 1984), or some combination of both, it needs to be viewed as a complex and dynamic activity. It is complex because it involves discretion and judgment rather than routines. It is dynamic because it necessitates responses to students who are constantly changing in their maturity, development, interests, and commitment.

As pointed out in Chapter 3, work roles in the twenty-first century will move from an emphasis on rationality to an emphasis on complexity (Hage & Powers, 1992). Work defined by routines and standardization of practice will give way to work that emphasizes human agency and the continuing process of information search. This type of work also will emphasize customization and innovation rather than efficiency and volume of work. After decades of trying to "teacher-proof" the curriculum, administrators and teachers must look at teaching as a complex and dynamic process.

Teaching is also complex because of the increasing demand that teachers interact with multiple agencies and professionals (Crowson, 2001). Instead of isolated classroom activities with occasional interactions with parents, many teachers interact daily with professionals, such as counselors, special educators, mental health and social service agency personnel, and law enforcement officers. In order to provide more comprehensive responses to the needs of students, teaching has become more complex in the variety and number of professionals who are interacting. Encouraging the professional growth of teachers, then, requires acknowledging this more complex form.

Conception of Supervisor.   The third component of Reitzug's (1997) view of supervision is a new conception of the supervisor. Instead of the principal being the sole repository of expertise and the author of change, the teacher becomes the agent of improved instruction. The supervisor's role becomes one of facilitating the teacher's agency within a context of mutual, collaborative inquiry.

Revising the role of supervisor means considering anew the notion of professional authority and control. Instead of the principal having supervisory authority by virtue of position and having absolute control of the supervisory process, an innovative role of supervisor acknowledges a more functional authority and variation in control of the supervisory process. Tracy (1998) presented categories of supervisory approaches that reflect different notions of authority. In the case of *clinical supervision,* principals have functional authority based on experience and insight rather than expertise. In this case, they partner with teachers to identify goals, problems, and alternative courses of action. In *collegial supervision,* the role of the supervisor is to provide resources and help for teachers. In *self-directed supervision,* professional authority resides with the teachers who work alone on their professional development. *Informal supervision* includes encounters that are more casual and authority that is more functional. Finally, in the inquiry model, instructional problems are co-researched.

In their developmental supervision approach, Glickman and colleagues (1998) argued that authority and control depend on the developmental level of the teacher. In a *directive approach,* where the teacher's development is at a low, more conceptually concrete level, the principal as supervisor takes more control. The authority resides with the principal. In a *non-directive approach,* where the teacher's development is at a high, more conceptually abstract level, the teacher takes the control and possesses the authority. In a *collaborative approach,* principal and teacher share authority and control.

In addition to issues of authority and control, the role of the supervisor raises concerns about the relationship between teachers and principals. This relationship is critical in the everyday work life of schools. Principals frequently are concerned that supervisory activities can threaten this relationship. Several research studies have examined this relationship in the context of supervisory practice. Bulach, Bothe, and Michael (1999) surveyed over 200 graduate students to examine their view as teachers of their principals' supervisory behaviors. Two interesting findings resulted. Teachers with more experience were more likely to rate their principal's supervisory behavior as lower in terms of trust behavior. These authors suggested that one possible explanation for this is that "principals could be using the same authoritarian leadership style with experienced and better prepared teachers as well as beginning and bachelor degree teachers" (p. 10). These authors also found that elementary school teachers were more likely to rate their principals' supervisory behavior as more caring and trustworthy than were secondary school teachers. Elementary school teachers also were more likely to see their principals as more capable in curriculum and instruction areas.

Some principals assume that teachers do not want them involved in supervision. However, Gordon, Stockard, and Williford (1992) found that teachers want their principals knowledgeable of and involved with the instructional program. Other principals may not believe that their supervision is effective. Sheppard (1996) found a strong and positive relationship between principals' instructional leadership behaviors and teacher commitment, professional involvement, and innovation. The kinds of principal behaviors related to these teacher practices included supervising and evaluating instruction, providing incentives, and maintaining high visibility. The most influential behavior for both elementary and secondary school teachers was the principal's behavior in promoting professional development.

Probably the most important characteristic of the role of principal and assistant principal as supervisor relates to mutual inquiry. The conception of supervisor that we encourage is one in which principals and assistant principals are participants in the community of learners. In this regard, they open their own practice to critique and inquiry.

Part of acknowledging the principal and assistant principal as participants in the community of inquirers is an acknowledgement that principals, like teachers, continue to develop in their roles. Crehan and Grimmett (1989) examined the relationship between teachers' conceptual level and principals' conceptual level and concluded that although a teacher's conceptual level may be critical to the success of the supervisory conference, the principal's conceptual level may be key to its failure. When the principal's conceptual level was low, there was a tendency for the focus of the conference to get deflected to other issues. These findings suggest that the principal's own conceptual growth is an important component of supervisory practice. Very little research has been conducted on principals' conceptual development, yet it seems critical to the success of supervisory practice.

Although it should be obvious by this point, we believe that assistant principals have an important role to play as supervisors. The traditional role of assistant principal has tended to ignore the instructional leadership role and force the assistant principal into a role-taking orientation. However, a more innovative role places a strong emphasis on the assistant principal as an instructional leader with a supervisory function. Glickman and colleagues (1998) and Peters (1989) maintained that good supervision requires time, and thus the assistant principal needs to be involved in observing and conferencing with teachers. This innovative role conception encourages assistant principals to focus on role making, in which they mold the role to a more instructional leadership orientation.

Conception of Supervision. Reitzug (1997) argued that the traditional conception of supervision involves a discrete intervention, usually an observation and a conference. However, an innovative conception views supervision as a sustained, integrated, and ongoing process in which professional development is seen as involving all educators, including the principal, and continuing throughout the career. Based on Smyth's (1997) notion of communities of inquiry, Reitzug viewed supervision as providing an environment in which it is safe to make mistakes, try new ideas, and risk failure. This learning environment also involves greater autonomy, opportunities for professional conversation, and alternative frameworks for thinking about teaching and learning.

Tracy (1998) identified a set of assumptions of future models of supervision that seem especially relevant to an innovative conception of supervision. These assumptions include

1. The school is a community of life-long learners.
2. Persons are capable of taking responsibility for their own growth, of being self-directed and self-supervising, when the proper resources and support mechanisms are available.
3. Adult learners have their own unique needs that are distinct from those of children.
4. To improve the performance of any one individual, we must consider the total organizational environment in which that person works.
5. People learn best and are motivated by collaborating with others (p. 105).

This conception of supervision that encourages a community of learning and inquiry also involves a broader and more varied view of supervisory activities. Claudet and Ellett (1999) suggested that supervision involves both micro- and macro-level events. Traditionally, supervision has included only "isolated microevents," where the principal observed the teacher and conducted a conference. However, supervision activities in schools should be much broader.

Supervisory activities engaged in by school personnel can include, but are not limited to, such things as involvement of teachers and administrators (and sometimes instructional supervisors) on instructional and curricular improvement teams and committees, supervision of intern teachers by tenured teachers, formal and informal peer or colleague supervisory activities, and individual and/or group (collaborative) planning of inservice efforts and staff development activities (p. 318).

In addition, activities that are more casual, such as informal hall conversations or ongoing memos around instructional issues, are supervisory in nature. We will return to these larger macro-level supervisory events in the last section of this chapter. However, it is useful to realize that the conception of supervision recommended in this chapter involves the principal and assistant principal in a broad and varied set of activities that go beyond the "discrete interventions" of observing and conferencing.

Another way to conceive of supervision has been introduced by Blase and Blase (1998) in their study of what good instructional leaders do. These authors proposed that the conception of supervision of good principals involves three major components, which they refer to as the "TiGeR model." First, good principals *talk* with teachers. This involves activities such as observing, conferring, building trust, and maintaining visibility. Second, good principals promote teacher *growth* by providing resources and time, giving feedback, providing professional development, and supporting practice of new skills, risk taking, and innovation. Third, good principals foster teacher *reflection*. In order to do this, these principals engage in such activities as developing teachers' reflection skills; modeling and developing teachers' critical study (action research) skills; becoming inquiry-oriented; using data to question, evaluate, and critique teaching and learning; and extending autonomy to teachers. Their conception of supervision is based on findings regarding the differences between effective and ineffective principals. Effective principals are visible but do not interrupt or abandon teachers. Effective principals praise rather than criticize. And effective principals extend autonomy rather than maintain control (p. 18).

An innovative conception of supervision involves more sustained professional development and a broader assortment of activities than the traditional conception. Principals and assistant principals who mold their roles in this more innovative way will see supervision as an ongoing process rather than a once-a-year event. They will be actively engaged in activities that keep teaching and learning at the forefront of attention. And they will be involved in mutual inquiry, which means that they will model by subjecting their own practice to scrutiny.

Evaluating Educational Results

The third component of an innovative role for the principal as supervisor involves evaluating educational results. In Chapter 3 we discussed one aspect of this component in the school-wide context, that is, assessment. In this subsection we will focus on evaluating instructional capacity in the classroom.

> Too often teacher evaluation means the rating, grading, and classifying of teachers using some locally standardized instrument as a yardstick. Generally the instrument lists traits of teachers assumed to be important, such as "The teacher has a pleasant voice," and certain tasks of teaching considered critical, such as "The teacher plans well" (Sergiovanni & Starratt, 1998, p. 219).

The traditional conception of evaluating teachers that Sergiovanni and Starratt (1998) characterized also sometimes includes an annual observation followed by a conference with the teacher. In some districts, new teachers are evaluated more often during their probation period, and veteran teachers are evaluated less often and sometimes rarely. State and/or local policies and procedures usually prescribe the evaluation process.

This evaluation process is typically held to two types of standards (Webb, Montello, & Norton, 1994). *Technical standards* involve validity, reliability, and utility. *Legal standards* involve substantive due process concerns that relate to the objectivity of criteria, standards, evidence, and results and procedural due process issues that relate to the fairness of the process.

The typical evaluation process involves *summative evaluations* rather than formative ones. This process may involve comparison of the teacher with others (norm-referenced) or with some established standard (criterion-referenced) (Sperry, Pounder, & Drew, 1992).

This traditional conception of evaluation relies on several assumptions that Sergiovanni and Starratt (1998) called into question and cautioned supervisors to be wary of. The first assumption is that "there is a clear set of criteria or standards understood and accepted by all with which a teacher's performance can be evaluated" (p. 303). As we pointed out in an earlier section, the research suggests that there is no one set of teacher behaviors that is appropriate in every context. The second assumption is that "sporadic, unannounced classroom visits, with no prior conversations and no subsequent discussion, are a legitimate and acceptable way to assess teacher performance" (p. 303). Some principals believe that if they and the teacher plan the classroom visit, the teacher may be able to "stage" an atypical lesson. In addition to a conception of the role that emphasizes inspection, this belief assumes that what the principal observes in an unannounced visit is a fair sample and that the principal knows what the teacher intended by the lesson. The third assumption identified by Sergiovanni and Starratt is that "student achievement of course objectives is the only way to evaluate teacher performance" (p. 304). Two difficulties inherent in this assumption are that we know how to measure student achievement in a holistic sense and that student achievement is totally controlled by what the teacher does. Finally, Sergiovanni and Starratt argued that the summative evaluation frequently assumes that the "evaluation of teacher performance should deal only with observable classroom behaviors" (p. 304). If the principal assumes that counting, for example, the types of questions the teacher asks or how many times the teacher calls on boys versus girls, is the only measure of teacher performance, this ignores the content that the teacher teaches.

These assumptions do not mean that evaluation is neither unimportant nor impossible for the principal. Rather, they suggest that if the principal evaluates teaching with these assumptions in mind and assumes that the evaluation is a completely objective assessment of the teacher, the result may be an incomplete picture of the classroom instruction and perhaps a legally indefensible position.

We propose that evaluation can be an important role for principals in assessing the instructional capacity of the school. An innovative conception of evaluation involves creating an environment that helps teachers and other staff in the school, including principals and assistant principals, to assess the instructional strengths and needs of the classroom. This conception of evaluation begins with the recognition that the teacher is a partner in evaluation. Instead of evaluation targeting the teacher's deficiencies, the purpose becomes one of assessing the classroom's instructional capacity, which includes not only what the teacher does but what students do, what the principal provides, what resources parents and others provide, and so on.

In developing this innovative conception, it may be helpful to distinguish types of evaluation and to understand the difference between evaluation and supervision. Sergiovanni and Starrat (1998) identified three types of evaluation: supervisory formative evaluation, supervisory summative evaluation, and administrative evaluation. Supervisory formative evaluation is designed to provide ongoing reflective professional growth and is the process we discussed in the preceding subsection. We would in fact label this as *formative supervision* and the other two as *summative evaluation* and *administrative evaluation*. The point of supervisory formative evaluation, from our perspective, is not evaluation in the usual sense of the term but rather professional growth. No attempt is being made to provide a summative judgment of the teaching or the teacher.

Supervisory summative evaluation, on the other hand, is designed to provide an assessment of performance. Although the typical gatherer of this information is the administrator in the context of some district or state requirement, we believe that teachers should be partners both in its process and in its product.

The typical tool used in this type of evaluation is an observation checklist completed by the principal to rate the teacher. However, numerous other tools provide multiple sources of information and thus perspectives on classroom instruction, for example, portfolios, client surveys, student performance data, self-evaluations, and peer evaluations. These last two tools are used rarely but offer valuable sources that could enrich the information provided on instructional capacity in the classroom and could encourage teachers to become collaborative partners in the evaluation process. If the purpose is to move beyond simply giving a judgment of the teacher's deficiencies to providing a richer assessment of the classroom's instructional capacity, these multiple sources could be very useful.

One principal described how he and the teachers redesigned the evaluation process to make it more useful to teachers (Rooney, 1993). The process included a peer evaluation model in which teachers observed each other's classrooms and conducted postobservation conferences with the principal present, which satisfied the district's conferencing requirement. However, the principal's role was nonevaluative during the conference. Instead, the principal asked questions of the teachers to help them reflect on and assess the classroom learning. The final annual conference continued to be between the principal and the teacher, but the potency of that conference was strengthened by the previous peer evaluations.

The third type of evaluation mentioned by Sergiovanni and Starratt (1998) is administrative evaluation. This type must be clearly distinguished from the other two in purpose. *Administrative evaluation* occurs when there is some quality control issue or problem, for example, an incompetent teacher. It is also used to make tenure, promotion, or dismissal decisions. The process is formal and must be consistently administered in legally defensible ways.

This type of evaluation, obviously, is not the most comfortable for administrators. However, the principal often is legally responsible for making recommendations in this type of evaluation. Bridges (1986), in his research on incompetent teachers, identified four responses of principals: to avoid, to compromise, to confront, and to tolerate. Roberts (2000) found that principals were most likely to say that they confronted incompetent teachers and were next likely to say that they compromised. She also found that there were a variety of factors including union pressure, contracts, and time that principals said influenced the response they made to incompetent teachers.

Some educators have argued that the principal cannot both supervise and evaluate because the two processes are contradictory; one is for professional growth, and one is for quality control. We believe that it is important for the principal and assistant principal to do both because to limit the principal's role to evaluation removes the principal from a substantive instructional leadership role. There are, undoubtedly, problems inherent in the principal performing both supervision and evaluation, for example, diminished rapport with teachers who realize that the person encouraging their professional growth is also the one who will provide the summative assessment.

In order for the principal and assistant principal to do both supervision and evaluation, they and the teachers must clearly distinguish these roles and when they are being performed. The different purposes and processes of supervision and evaluation must be clearly articulated and acknowledged. The principal and teacher must understand why and how administrative evaluation is conducted and distinguish it from supervision and summative evaluation.

In this section we have identified a direct role for the principal and assistant principal as supervisor. We have defined this role in terms of three areas: recruiting and selecting capable educators, promoting educator growth, and evaluating educational results. All three of these areas contribute to building instructional capacity in the classroom. In the next section we focus our understanding of the principal's role as facilitator of supervision.

The Principal's Role as Facilitator of Supervision

As principals or assistant principals, you can extend the instructional capacity of the classroom by facilitating the involvement of the entire school in the supervisory process. In the opening vignette, this facilitative role is what Robert attempted to implement with the veteran teachers providing supervisory help to new teachers. As Robert's experience pointed out, this facilitative role is not always welcomed but is, nevertheless, a critical, innovative role for principals and assistant principals to play. This facilitative supervision role fits into the previously discussed role of the principal as learner in facilitating the learning community of the school. It also fits with the preceding chapter on mentoring as the principal facilitates the mentoring of peers. In this section we will discuss why the facilitative role in supervision is critical. We also will develop a conception of the role of principal as facilitator of supervision.

Why Supervision Should Be Shared

Facilitating supervision in the school-wide learning community is critical both to your own work as principal and to the work of the faculty. First, the increased complexity of the principal's role (Crow, Hausman, & Scribner, 2002) and the resulting time demands necessitate that building instructional capacity in the school must be the responsibility of others in addition to the principal. Various writers in the supervision literature (e.g., Glickman and colleagues, 1998) pointed out that the specific requirements of conducting intensive supervision defined as professional growth requires significant time. These authors, in fact, estimated that an average principal could directly supervise (based on the developmental supervision model) approximately ten teachers per year. Because most schools are larger than this, it is obvious that others in addition to the principal, for example, the assistant principal, must be involved in supervision.

The second reason for sharing supervision is reflected in the innovative role we proposed in the preceding section. The principal should not be considered the sole expert on supervisory knowledge or skills. If we assume that there are multiple experts, the principal may not always be the appropriate person to work with a particular teacher. Other educators may have more appropriate expertise because of their experience, perspective, subject matter, or training. For example, because teaching expertise is related to content (subject matter) as well as pedagogy, a teacher may be the most relevant supervisor (Nelson & Sassi, 2000).

Third, sharing supervision with others in the school communicates the important message that professional growth is valued in the school community. When the principal or assistant principal does all the direct supervision in the school, other faculty find it easy to assume that this is not a value of the school's culture but an administrative preference. Professional growth needs to be viewed as a school-wide responsibility, not an administrative duty.

In addition to promoting professional growth as a value in the school community, sharing supervision can contribute to other features of the school culture. Ebmeier (1999) found that collaborative supervision by peers contributed to increased teacher desire for collaboration and commitment to teaching. Ebmeier also found that sharing supervision made teachers more involved in decision making about their classroom activities, supported classroom innovation, supported collaboration among teachers, increased the clarity of school goals, provided feedback on classroom performance, and provided opportunities to observe the practice of other teachers. All these behaviors are elements of a professional learning community.

Finally, sharing supervision contributes not only to the teachers who are the focus of problem solving or professional growth but also to the veteran teachers and administrators who work with them. Sharing supervision contributes to the professional growth of all faculty who are involved in the process, thus enriching the instructional capacity of the school.

Elements of the Principal's Role as Facilitator of Supervision

In this subsection we will identify several elements that constitute an innovative role for the principal as facilitator of supervision. We do not assume that these constitute all the activities you will engage in and responsibilities you will have as a principal or assistant principal in facilitating supervision, but we provide them as examples to stimulate your conversation and development of the innovative role. In the preceding section on the principal's direct role in supervision, we identified three major areas: recruiting and selecting educators, promoting educator growth, and evaluating education results. We return to these three areas and will focus primarily on the second area.

Recruiting and Selecting Capable and Committed Educators. Although the traditional role involves the principal alone in recruitment and selection processes, we suggest that a more innovative role is one in which the principal facilitates the involvement of the entire school in this important function. This involvement can include the use of faculty in helping to design the job. Teachers have a wealth of expertise in understanding what responsibilities and qualities are needed in a new appointment. Furthermore, including teachers and other school constituents in this process builds an awareness of school-wide needs. One of the traditional reasons for the principal being involved in the recruitment and selection process is that principals have a school-wide perspective that enables them to understand the gaps in faculty or staff strengths that need to be filled to build or maintain school instructional capacity. Involving others in this process increases the awareness of those strengths and gaps among school constituents.

Two difficulties of involving others in recruitment and selection are the schedule of the school year and teacher availability. In order to solve these problems, principals may need to work with district administrators to secure compensation for teachers to stay late or come in during the summer months to interview teacher candidates.

Facilitating the involvement of teachers and other school constituents in recruiting and selecting is also valuable in building instructional capacity. Taking advantage of teacher networks increases the chances of recruiting a large and rich pool of candidates. As we mentioned earlier in this chapter, taking a "wait and see" attitude is counterproductive for locating the best teachers.

More and more principals are developing strategies for including the entire school in the selection process, including teachers, support staff, parents, and in some cases students. Group interviews, role playing, observations of teaching, and other simulations, as well as screening applications, can involve a wide array of school constituents and enrich the perspectives for selection. In order for this to be done appropriately, the principal must help those involved in the recruitment and selection process to be aware of good interviewing techniques, district policies, and legal parameters (Webb et al., 1994).

Promoting Educator Growth.   Various supervisory models, including peer supervision, collaborative supervision, mentoring, and cognitive coaching, take advantage of veteran teachers in the process of stimulating and promoting educator growth. In Chapter 4 we discussed the value and process of mentoring and the principal's role in facilitating mentoring by others. In this subsection we will discuss how principals facilitate supervision by others in ways that promote educator growth.

Earlier we discussed Claudet and Ellett's (1999) distinction of micro- and macro-level supervisory events. This distinction is especially useful in understanding the kinds

Professional Dilemma 5.2

Who should help in the teacher selection process? In a middle school social studies department, a teaching opening occurred that created a difference of opinion between the school's principal and the department chair. The social studies department in the school was well known as being the most social group in the school. The teachers had their own Friday afternoon parties and frequent out-of-school activities, and they often went to the local NBA games together. The department chair wanted to select a teacher who fit the department's social circle. The principal wanted someone who believed in the middle school philosophy and had experience in teaching early adolescents. Although the principal wanted input from the department, it was obvious that department members were looking for different attributes than the administration. To solve the problem, the principal asked other teachers from the school to help with the selection. This proved to be quite successful in that other teachers looked for more of a school culture fit than a department clone.

of activities that principals do in promoting educator growth as an organizational and an individual phenomenon. Although micro-level events such as individual principal-teacher supervisory conferences are important, macro-level events are also critical. These can include department and grade-level faculty curriculum planning projects, group planning of various professional development activities, joint participation in supervisory meetings, and planning activities. By developing these opportunities and providing the time and other resources necessary for them to be successful, principals facilitate the school-wide promotion of educator growth.

At times, the principal's facilitating role involves providing resources such as time, training, and other supports for teachers to work with each other in promoting professional growth. This includes providing time for teachers to observe each other, visit classrooms and other schools, meet in conferences, and enjoy other opportunities to promote growth. Principals secure substitutes or cover teacher classes themselves in order to provide the opportunities for peer supervision to occur.

Another resource that principals provide and by so doing facilitate the involvement of others in promoting growth is training. Providing opportunities to attend local, regional, and national conferences not only inspires, builds supervisory skills, and encourages networking but also provides incentives for veteran teachers to take on the additional responsibilities of peer supervision.

Although these resources are important for successful school-wide involvement in promoting educator growth, even more important is the supportive relationship that principals demonstrate with teachers and other staff. In order for teachers to accept the help of other teachers, for novice teachers to respect veteran teachers' views, and for veteran teachers to look to each other for help in their professional growth, there must be trust in the school. Social trust is a critical element in promoting professional growth and enriching instructional capacity in the school (Smylie & Hart, 1999). Hoy, Tarter, and Witkoskie (1992) found that a supportive relationship between principal and teachers influenced collegiality among teachers and trust in the principal, which in turn influenced a school-wide trust in colleagues. This collegial trust then leads to school effectiveness.

Part of growing professionally involves making teaching practices public. Doing so requires trust not only between the principal and teacher but also among teachers. Principals can go a long way toward facilitating the involvement of others in supervision by the supportive relationship that is demonstrated by respecting teachers' practical knowledge, providing needed resources, keeping confidences, and emphasizing the power of a school-wide culture of learning and growth.

Another element of the principal's role in facilitating supervision by promoting educator growth involves who serves as supervisor. Tracy (1998) described future models of supervision as including

> . . . teams of professionals rather than the traditional supervisor-teacher dyad. Members of a team will have different expertise, yet they will function as equals. A single supervisor, which is common in the traditional models, will not have sufficient knowledge or skills to support this new paradigm. A range of people will, therefore, be needed. The majority of these persons will probably be peers rather than individuals designated with some formal supervisory title (p. 105).

Yet, with this move to a broader representation of people as supervisors, the principal has a critical facilitative role to play in making sure this happens. The principal facilitates this broader view by providing training and resources to these new supervisors.

Evaluating Educational Results.   The third element in building instructional capacity is evaluating educational results. As we mentioned before, this evaluation means assessing the entire instructional program of the classroom, including student performance, teacher performance, and resources. Typically, evaluation involves only the assessment of teacher performance. There is ample evidence of teacher reluctance to engage in peer evaluations. The egalitarian norm in which teachers avoid comparisons among themselves discourages experimentation with peer evaluation. Yet one critical feature of a profession is evaluation by peers.

In most districts, principals retain the legal responsibility for evaluating teachers. We propose an argument for peer evaluation and for the principal's role in facilitating evaluation by colleagues. If we define evaluation in terms of assessing the instructional capacity of the classroom, as we did earlier in this chapter, peers play a vital role in helping each other make this assessment. Because of their expertise in the classroom and the rapport that hopefully exists in a culture that supports professional growth, teachers are in an excellent position to help their colleagues assess the various components of instructional capacity in the classroom.

Teachers, along with administrators, need to develop skills in data-driven decision making. Although we discussed some of the elements of assessment in Chapter 3, for example, qualitative and quantitative methods, these tools of data-driven decision making are critical for evaluating instructional capacity in classrooms. Principals and assistant principals can help teachers understand how to use quantitative techniques not only to measure student achievement but also to assess student growth and areas for additional instructional emphasis. Enlisting district and university personnel to help teachers develop quantitative and qualitative tools to measure specific classroom instructional processes and outcomes is an important facilitative role for principals. Such a role enhances teachers' abilities to diagnose instructional problems, assess growth, and evaluate practices and contributes to an environment of mutual inquiry.

Principals can facilitate peer evaluation by providing time, training, support, and trust. In the same way that these resources are necessary for promoting educator growth, they are important for facilitating peer evaluation. Teachers need time to observe and talk with each other. They need training in how to assess instructional capacity and use a variety of information sources. They need encouragement from the principal to make the process effective and to continue when the result is not always positive. Finally, they need the respect and trust of the principal that such an evaluation results in a more effective learning environment for students and adults.

Conclusion

Bill Payne, the new principal in the opening vignette, discovered what we emphasize in all the role conceptions we discuss in this book, that is, that although principals have a direct role to play in supervision, they cannot succeed alone. Supervision, like the other roles, requires the principal to facilitate supervision by others. In this chapter we have described an innovative way to think about supervision that moves beyond the inspection role, which devalues the expertise of teachers, to a collaborative role, which builds instructional capacity. This innovative role involves the three activities of recruiting and selecting capable and committed educators, promoting educator growth, and evaluating educational results.

In the next chapter we move beyond the internal roles that principals and assistant principals play in classrooms and schools to begin our consideration of the larger leadership role that principals play both internally and externally. If learning is the foundation for all the role conceptions, leadership is the glue that integrates the role.

Activities

Self-Directed Activities

1. Reflect on the ways that supervision is still inspection in your teaching experience.
2. Interview an assistant principal in terms of his or her experience in attempting to provide supervision to teachers.
3. Reflect on your answer to the professional dilemma presented earlier regarding selecting teachers who match the school culture versus opting for diversity.

Peer Activities

1. Compare and contrast the positive and negative characteristics of the ways that you and a colleague have been supervised.
2. With your colleague, develop and critique a plan for involving teachers, parents, and students in the recruitment and selection process.
3. Brainstorm ideas for Bill Payne in the opening vignette to encourage veteran teachers to contribute their efforts toward the supervision of new teachers.

Course Activities

1. Invite a principal reputed to be an effective instructional leader to visit your class. Interview the principal in terms of the mechanisms used to recruit and select teachers.
2. Conduct a small research study on teachers' responses to their principals' supervisory styles. Examine the relationship between teaching experience and perceptions of supervisory style.
3. As a class, design a process for peer evaluation. What would the principal's role be in implementing this? Consider such issues as district support, legal and union considerations, and trust building.

Websites

■ *http://www.ucea.org/cases/*
  Cases from the Journal of Cases in Educational Leadership
  Anfara, V. A., Endy, C., Kester, C., Mumford, A., & Rothman, H. (1999). Will the lemons continue to dance? Hard times in Westlake School District. *Journal of Cases in Educational Leadership* 2(1).
  Bruner, D. & Livingston, M. (2002). Out of the mouths of babes. Journal of Cases in *Educational Leadership* 5(1).
  Covrig, D. (2001). Get rid of incompetent teachers, any way you can. *Journal of Cases in Educational Leadership* 4(2).
  Zepeda, S. J. (2001). At odds: Can supervision and evaluation co-exist? *Journal of Cases in Educational Leadership* 4(1).

References

Beach, D., & Reinhartz, J. (2000). *Supervisory Leadership.* Boston: Allyn and Bacon.

Blase, J., & Blase, J. (1998). *Handbook of Instructional Leadership: How Really Good Principals Promote Teaching and Learning.* Thousand Oaks, CA: Corwin Press.

Blase, J., & Blase., J. (1999). Principals' instructional leadership and teacher development: Teachers' perspectives. *Educational Administration Quarterly* 35(3), 349–378.

Bridges, E. M. (1986). *The Incompetent Teacher.* Philadelphia: Falmer Press.

Bulach, C., Bothe, D., & Michael, P. (1999). *Supervisory behaviors that affect school climate.* Paper presented at the American Educational Research Association, Montreal, Canada, April 19–23.

Bryk, A., Camburn, E., & Louis, K. S. (1999). Professional community in Chicago elementary schools: Facilitating factors and organizational consequences. *Educational Administration Quarterly* 35(Suppl.), 751–781.

Claudet, J. G., & Ellett, C. D. (1999). Conceptualization and measurement of supervision as a school organization climate construct. *Journal of Curriculum and Supervision 14*(4), 318–351.

Cochran-Smith, M. & Lytle, S. L. (1992). *Inside/Outside: Teacher Research and Knowledge.* New York: Teachers College Press.

Crehan, E. P., & Grimmett, P. P. (1989). *Teachers' perspective on dyadic supervisory interaction.* Paper presented at the American Educational Research Association, San Francisco, March 27–31.

Crow, G. M., Hausman, C., & Scribner, J. (2002). Reshaping the principal's role. In J. Murphy (Ed.), *The Leadership Challenge: Redefining Leadership for the 21st Century* (pp. 189–210). Chicago: National Society for the Study of Education.

Crowson, R. L. (2001). *Community Development and School Reform.* Oxford, England: Elsevier.

Darling-Hammond, L., Wise, A. E., & Klein, S. P. (1995). *A License to Teach: Building a Profession for 21st Century Schools.* Boulder, CO: Westview Press.

Doud, J. L., & Keller, E. P. (1998). The K-8 principal in 1998. *Principal 78*(1), 5–6.

Ebmeier, H. (1999). The impact of peer and principal collaborative supervision on teachers' trust, commitment, desire for collaboration, and efficacy. *Journal of Curriculum and Supervision 14*(4), 351–378.

Eisner, E. W. (1985). *The Educational Imagination: On the Design and Evaluation of School Programs* (2nd ed.). New York: Macmillan.

Erikson, E. H. (1963). *Childhood and Society* (2nd ed.). New York: Norton.

Fuller, F. (1969). Concerns of teachers: A developmental conceptualization. *American Educational Research Journal 6*(2), 207–266.

Gilligan, C. (1982). *In a Different Voice.* Cambridge, MA: Harvard University Press.

Glickman, C. D., Gordon, S. P., & Ross-Gordon, J. V. (1998). *Supervision of Instruction: A Developmental Approach* (4th ed.). Boston: Allyn and Bacon.

Gordon, B. G., Stockard, J. W. J., & Williford, H. (1992). The principal's role as school leader. *Educational Research Quarterly 15*(4), 29–38.

Hage, J., & Powers, C. H. (1992). *Post-Industrial Lives: Roles and Relationships in the 21st Century.* Newbury Park, CA: Sage.

Hargreaves, A. (1990). *Contrived Collegiality: The Micropolitics of Teacher Collaboration.* Toronto, Canada: Ontario Institute for Studies in Education.

Hill, D. A. (1993). The realities of the principalship. Unpublished certificate of advanced study, Castleton State College, Vermont.

Hoy, W. K., Tarter, C. J., & Witkoskie, L. (1992). Faculty trust in colleagues: Linking the principal with school effectiveness. *Journal of Research and Development in Education 26*(1), 38–45.

Hunt, D. E. (1966). A conceptual systems change model and its application to education. In O. J. Harvey (Ed.), *Experience, Structure, and Adaptability* (pp. 277–302). New York: Springer-Verlag.

Hunter, M. (1984). Knowing, teaching, and supervision. In P. Hosford (Ed.), *Using What We Know about Teaching.* Alexandria, VA: Association for Supervision and Curriculum Development.

Kohlberg, L., & Armon, C. (1984). Three types of stage models used in the study of adult development. In M. Commons, F.A. Richards, and C. A. Armon (Eds.), *Beyond Formal Operations: Late Adolescent and Adult Cognitive Development.* New York: Praeger.

Lieberman, A., & Miller, L. (1991). *Staff Development for Education in '90s: New Demands, New Realities, New Perspectives.* New York: Teachers College Press.

Luehe, B. (1989). *The Principal and Supervision.* Bloomington, IN: Phi Delta Kappan Educational Foundation.

Murphy, J. (2002). Reculturing the profession of educational leadership: New blueprints. In J. Murphy (Ed.) *The educational leadership challenge: Redefining leadership for the 21st century.* Chicago: National Society for the Study of Education.

Nelson, B. S., & Sassi, A. (2000). Shifting approaches to supervision: The case of mathematics supervision. *Educational Administration Quarterly 36*(4), 553–584.

Peters, D. A. (1989). How to get the most from teacher observations: Tips for principals from NASSP. *Tips for Principals 3.*

Reitzug, U. C. (1997). Images of principal instructional leadership: From supervision to collaborative inquiry. *Journal of Curriculum and Supervision 12*(4), 324–343.

Roberts, R. (2000). Principals' responses to perceived teacher incompetence. Unpublished Ed.D. dissertation, University of Utah, Salt Lake City, UT.

Rooney, J. (1993). Teacher evaluation: No more "super" vision. *Educational Leadership 51*(2), 43–44.

Rosenshine, B. V. (1986). A synthesis of research on explicit teaching. *Educational Leadership 43*(7), 60–69.

Sergiovanni, T. J., & Starratt, R. J. (1998). *Supervision: A Redefinition* (6th ed.). New York: McGraw-Hill.

Sheppard, B. (1996). Exploring the transformational nature of instructional leadership. *Alberta Journal of Educational Research 42*(4), 325–344.

Smylie, M. A., & Hart, A. W. (1999). School leadership for teacher learning and change: A human and social capital development perspective. In J. Murphy & K. S. Louis (Eds.), *Handbook of Research on Educational Administration* (2nd ed., pp. 421–442). San Francisco: Jossey-Bass.

Smyth, J. (1997). Is supervision more than the surveillance of instruction? In J. Glanz & R. F. Neville (Eds.), *Educational Supervision: Perspectives, Issues, and Controversies* (pp. 286–295). Norwood, MA: Christopher-Gordon.

Sperry, D. J., Pounder, D. G., & Drew, C. J. (1992). Educator evaluation and the law: A case study of common statutory problems. *Education Law Quarterly 1,* 415–429.

Sternberg, R. J., & Wagner, R. K. (1986). *Practical Intelligence: Nature and Origins of Competence in the Everyday World.* Cambridge, England: Cambridge University Press.

Stodolsky, S. (1988). *The Subject Matters: Classroom Activity in Math and Social Studies.* Chicago: University of Chicago Press.

Tracy, S. J. (1998). Models and approaches. In G. R. Firth & E. F. Pajak (Eds.) *Handbook of Research on School Supervision* (pp. 463–487). New York: Simon & Schuster McMillan.

Webb, L. D., Montello, P. A., & Norton, M. S. (1994). *Human Resources Administration: Personnel Issues and Needs in Education* (2nd ed.). New York: Macmillan.

6

Principal as Leader

Key Terms and Concepts

attribution theory
collective vision
consideration (person
orientation)

contingency theories
initiating structure (task
orientation)
personal vision

stewardship theory
transactional leadership
transformational leadership

Vignette

"I love teaching in this school," stated Louise as she visited with her principal in his office. "I think we are doing some great things. The teams that we organized a few years back have really brought us together as a faculty. I think we have made some significant changes for the good. However, I know that I have said this before, but I want to say it again. We are too much like a mini-high school. In fact, the high school drives our curricula." Robert sat listening to Louise as he had done with the entire faculty during the end of the school year goal reviews. He had established these informal chats with the teachers and staff at the end of each school year since he became principal five years ago. Louise was his last teacher, and school was ending in two weeks. No teacher had expressed any great concern about Franklin D. Roosevelt Junior High School, in fact, everyone had expressed positive comments. Robert knew that he had a stable and dedicated faculty.

Louise continued with her conversation, "I recently visited Lakeside Middle School over in Vernon. They have changed their junior high into a middle school concept. It has some interesting implications, and maybe we ought to consider some of their ideas." Robert pondered this for a few moments and then responded, "You know, I would be interested in that. Perhaps, we could get a team together and do some investigating about the middle school concept."

Louise left the meeting feeling positive. It was refreshing, indeed, for her to be able to talk to her principal so informally. She appreciated how he listened to her ideas and had not wanted to implant his own philosophies on her. When she had visited Lakeside Middle School, it was not to understand the middle school concept, but it was to attend a meeting of the local Phi Delta Kappa (PDK) chapter. The speaker for the breakfast meeting was a university professor who addressed the issue of the needs of early adolescents. She was followed by Lakeside's principal, who talked about how the school faculty had used the middle school model to better serve their students.

Louise had left the PDK meeting impressed but had been too busy to think about the middle school concept. She had always wanted to learn more about middle schools but had never taken the opportunity. Now with the invitation from her principal to investigate it further, she started reflecting on changing Roosevelt Junior High School to a middle school.

A month later, school out of session and her summer vacation going quite well, Louise happened to meet Robert at a movie theater. After some casual conversation, Robert suggested that they get together during the summer and explore the middle school concept. Robert asked her to think of others who might be interested. Louise had no idea who else might be interested in the middle school concept but did think of four teachers who were innovative and open to new thinking. The next day, she e-mailed Robert with her suggestions. In the meantime, Robert decided to do some investigating on the Web and searched for some sites on middle schools. He was surprised to find so much information on the middle school concept. He explored the National Middle School Association site and was delighted to find some useful information. He printed several research summaries and made copies for Louise and other interested teachers.

Robert and Louise invited the four teachers to a luncheon to explore the idea of middle schools. As they met, one teacher asked if Roosevelt Junior High School was going to adopt a middle school model. His brother had told him about the school where he was teaching that had changed to a middle school. His brother's experience was that the faculty felt that the curriculum was watered down and that the students were just meant to feel good and not learn anything. The teacher reminded Robert that Roosevelt Junior High had emphasized high academic standards for a long time and that he was not interested in changing that. Robert acknowledged the teacher's comments and confirmed his own allegiance to high standards. Robert also suggested that the team not think about adoption quite yet until they had done some studying and reflecting on the concept. He then suggested that they read the materials he and Louise had put together and meet again. They all thought that was a good idea and arranged to meet in two weeks.

Robert kept the team reading new materials for the next month and then suggested that they invite a few middle school educators from other schools in the area to visit with them. As the summer ended, the team had put together an impressive portfolio of information regarding the middle school philosophy. They decided to organize a retreat in August before school began and share their information with the faculty. They would then explore the faculty's interest in pursuing the change to a middle school. The team's plan was to develop five important components of middle schools and suggest that the faculty adopt one for the next school year. A new team could be developed to study the components and suggest the order of implementation if, indeed, the faculty chose to pursue it.

Louise had not been as excited for school to begin since her first year of teaching. She continued to explore the various components of middle schools and was convinced that this was a positive move for Roosevelt. She hoped other teachers would feel the same.

In August, Robert talked to his area superintendent and the district curriculum director. They gave their approval to continue exploring the idea. Robert then went to the newly elected parent representatives and suggested some readings for them. He was encouraged at the reception of the district office and the parent committee. Although the middle school concept was still far from being implemented, he knew that some major hurdles had already been crossed.

Introduction   In this chapter we explore the concept of leadership, in particular principal leadership—an obvious role for the 21st-century principal but a rather new role conception in the history of principals. Robert, Louise, and other teachers showed leadership by planning and implementing a change at Roosevelt Junior High School. Although they went about the changes in a systematic and systemic manner, not all school reform movements will ever go this smoothly. Our reason to introduce this chapter with a positive vignette is to attempt to show that change can happen, improvement can take place, and reform is an expected part of the principal's leadership role. In fact, by the definition we use, leadership means change, and if a principal is not looking at instructional improvement efforts, then the role of leader is not taking place.

Leadership is a broad area and cannot be covered adequately in one chapter. Most principal preparation programs have leadership courses that are separate from the principalship course. Our attempt in this chapter is to discuss some leadership concepts and in particular the principal's and assistant principal's roles as leaders and facilitators of leadership. We first explore the nature of leadership and its purposes. This is followed by a brief exploration of research on leadership. Then we discuss the purpose of principal leadership. We then introduce a model of school reform that includes discussions on culture, vision, and leadership tools, including communication and collaboration. As in other chapters, we conclude by exploring how the principal can facilitate leadership among others.

The Nature of Principal Leadership

As we discussed in Chapter 2, the origin of the principalship and its practice have not always emphasized a leadership role. The early responsibilities of principals had little to do with leadership and more to do with unlocking the doors and managing the daily routines. Indeed, the managerial function of the principalship rather than any leadership qualities has received most of the attention (Beck & Murphy, 1993). Principals were assumed to be more like business executives, using good management and social science research to run schools effectively and efficiently. The topic of leadership has grown in importance for contemporary principals and assistant principals because of three sources of leadership: external sources, internal sources, and the principal as his or her own source of leadership (Crow, Matthews, & McCleary, 1996).

Leadership from External Sources

As a new principal or assistant principal, you will quickly discover that many individuals and groups outside the school practice leadership. In the opening vignette, Robert recognized the importance of district office administrators and the Parent-Teacher Association (PTA) as sources of external leadership that influenced Roosevelt Junior High School.

Likewise, as a principal, you will need to recognize those external sources that influence your school. To help you understand these external sources, we have categorized them into three areas: other administrators, policymakers, and constituents.

Other administrators in the school system, in particular the superintendent, personnel director, curriculum directors, and other school principals, exercise leadership by influencing the district vision, rewarding particular administrative practices, and setting the direction for policies and procedures. "Schools are nested in districts and therefore are both nurtured and constrained by them" (Crow, Matthews, & McCleary, 1996, p. 3). In the vignette, Robert's attempt to investigate the middle school philosophy was influenced by the willingness of his district administrators and by the other school administrators who had converted to a middle school model. For example, Lakeside Middle School principal and faculty served as the catalyst for Robert and the Roosevelt faculty to implement the middle school concept.

Policymakers, such as school boards, also offer leadership that can affect the school. In particular, school boards and state legislatures establish policies that guide schools in what they can and cannot do. Odden (1995) claimed that in the late 1980s state governments started taking a stronger leadership role in education. These policymakers focused public attention on particular features of school effectiveness by directing the financial resources for specific areas, such as statewide testing. Likewise, policymakers such as school boards and state legislatures receive widespread media attention. When the media reports on the proceedings from these groups, they also increase the attention of the public to the issues.

Similar to government policymakers are high school state activities associations. Although schools voluntarily join these associations, they can greatly influence the schools' activity and academic programs. For example, a high school's alignment with an athletic conference will determine the school's travel for competitions. These travel arrangements can affect the academic programs if they require students to be out of class to participate. This is especially an issue in rural school settings, where traveling long distances is necessary to have an interscholastic activity program.

The school's constituencies also exercise leadership that affects the school. School constituencies consist of such individuals and groups as parents, business people, religious groups, media personnel, and community agencies. For example, parents influence schools in such areas as curriculum offerings, teacher and principal selection, library books, and textbooks. Parents now more than ever are choosing the schools their children attend and the teachers they will have. These decisions affect the leadership of the principal. For example, in considering the opening vignette, what if several parents protested Roosevelt Junior High School's move to a middle school concept? Or what if many parents chose to take their children out of the school and enroll them elsewhere? The principal and faculty would have to consider these parental decisions, which would affect the planning and implementation of the middle school concept. Chances are that if many parents were against the middle school concept, the plan would have to be abandoned.

Principals and assistant principals work within a context in which leadership is exercised by various external sources. These sources are often strong enough and vocal enough to make it clear that school administrators are not the only leaders in the school. As a principal or assistant principal, you need to recognize these external leadership sources, listen to them, and when needed, attempt to influence them for the benefit of student learning. A principal juggling different balls in the air illustrates external sources of leadership—it only takes a glance away from the juggling act to miss catching one of the balls.

Leadership from Internal Sources

Within a school, several individuals and groups play leadership roles. Many recent reform efforts such as site-based management and shared decision making have emphasized stronger leadership roles for teachers and others in the school. Teachers can be particularly influential, as in the opening vignette when Louise was the catalyst in getting the middle school concept introduced at Roosevelt. The teacher team that the principal organized also was influential in the middle school movement and in influencing others to consider the model.

Two other roles within the school deserve mentioning as strong influences on leadership, namely, secretaries and custodians. In subtle but powerful ways, these two roles can affect the decision making of school leaders. For example, a secretary often screens the communication that goes into and out of the principal's office. A school secretary also can be a keeper of the cultural history of the school, often knowing more about the school and its community than many others in the building. Similarly, the school custodians influence leadership by their contact and visibility with teachers, students, visitors, and others in the building. Not only are custodians and secretaries often the first to meet parents and visitors to the school, but also their influence on leadership is seen in how they communicate the school's vision to others. As a principal, do not overlook their valuable input.

Although students always have influenced leadership in the school, their presence in leadership roles is greater now than ever. Many school boards have student representation. Most site councils include student participation. Student councils are no longer limited to secondary schools but are integral parts of elementary schools. Student groups other than the elected student councils also are influential. For example, some student groups have become more aggressive in their demands, such as gay and lesbian, ethnic, feminist, and environmentalist groups. For an interesting case study on a gay and straight club's influence on a high school, see McCreary (2001).

Principals must acknowledge and work with these internal groups to carry the vision of the school forward. Otherwise, principal leadership will be ineffective as an influence in any substantial improvement efforts. School leadership is a more potent source for improvement efforts if the leadership of others is developed and empowered.

Principal Leadership

The leadership of principals and assistant principals is influenced not only by external and internal sources but also by their own leadership practice, style, and development. Knowing how to influence and develop leadership capacity in others is a significant and important endeavor. For example, Robert at Roosevelt Junior High School recognized the limitations of his formal position of principal and instead used his influence to develop leadership capacity in Louise and other teachers. By distributing leadership among others, he was able to gain faculty ownership of the middle school concept.

As we have discussed throughout this book, the assistant principal plays a significant role in schools. Although we believe that the role should be reconceptualized in many school settings, assistant principals in any school do more than just student management and campus supervision. The principal's leadership is incomplete without the assistant principal's participation. As a team member, contributor, counselor, advisor, mentor, and soul mate, assistant principals significantly influence the leadership in the school.

As you go through your preparation program and as you read about, discuss, and observe leadership, you will develop new ways of seeing your role as a leader. By reflecting on your own style and on the influences and constraints that affect your leadership capacity, you will begin to develop a relevant and realistic role (Crow, Matthews, & McCleary, 1996) of school leader.

Leadership Literature

When you walk into a bookstore, you probably have noticed the volumes of leadership and management books that are on the shelves. Many are meant to be self-help and motivating books. Often these popular books take on a cookbook style of sharing recipes that have worked for the author. With the vast amount of literature that exists on leadership, it is important to determine what will be of most help to you as you begin your career as a principal or assistant principal. In this subsection we have created three categories in which to organize leadership literature in an attempt to help you understand the kinds of literature that are available.

The first category of leadership literature we call the *popular literature*, or what often can be found easily in bookstores. This category of literature can include books and popular magazines that occasionally print leadership-related articles. Popular literature is generally not peer reviewed before its publication and usually is distributed to a large general audience.

The second category includes literature from professional associations. This type of literature is usually available through educational leadership associations, such as the Association of Supervision and Curriculum Development (ASCD), the National Association of Elementary School Principals (NAESP), and the National Association of Secondary School Principals (NASSP). These publications are available in most libraries, especially university-associated libraries, but these books and journals often are not peer reviewed but are selected by an editorial board or staff based on the topic's relevance and applicability. You may have to have membership in the association to receive its literature, but most associations will offer their literature to nonmembers.

The third category includes scholarly works. This type of literature is available in most university and college libraries and is becoming increasingly available on the Internet. Most of this literature is found in scholarly journals and books that are reviewed by peers. Because of the peer review, authors are especially careful with their research design and data interpretation so that errors are not published unwittingly. However, just because it is reviewed by peers does not make the literature accurate, only that it is more likely to have been closely reviewed for research errors.

These three categories are not absolutes, and some works will have characteristics in more than one category; for example, professional associations publish research studies that are relevant to practitioners. Remember that there is a considerable amount of leadership literature, and you need to be aware of the kinds of literature that exist and the relevance of the work. Effective leadership does not involve quick fixes, so be cautious as you read popular literature that involves an easy solution. Likewise, some leadership literature offers a "how to" approach that may be effective in some organizations but not in others. It is especially important for you to realize that many leadership books and articles are written from perspectives other than for public-sector organizations such as schools. This type of leadership literature may be more effective for business or corporate organizations.

Research on Leadership

Just as many authors have written about leadership, many researchers have studied it, especially in the last sixty years. In this section our attempt is not to provide an exhaustive review of the leadership literature but to offer a description of how this research relates to the leadership role of principals and assistant principals. We organize the discussion around six major approaches in the literature: trait, behavior, contingency (situational), relationship, leadership as an organizational quality, and moral leadership.

Trait Approaches

Early efforts to understand leader effectiveness focused on personal traits. Research in the 20th century examined leaders (almost always male) who had achieved a level of greatness and hence became known as the *great man theory*. Fundamental to this theory was the idea that some people were born with qualities and traits that made them natural leaders. The research sought to identify those traits that leaders possessed that distinguished them from people who were not leaders. However, these attempts to identify and measure leadership traits were unsuccessful primarily because of the lack of any evidence that such qualities guaranteed effectiveness. Many critics of this approach such as Yukl (1994) found only a weak relationship between personal traits and leader success. Blackmore (1991) labeled the great man theory as the search for the "fantasy figure or philosopher-king" (p. 101) and critiqued its overreliance on masculine imagery and valorization of hierarchical and elitist relationships. Watkins (1986) believed that trait theories ignore the relationship between leaders and followers and separate the world into leaders and non-leaders.

Regardless of the lack of evidence for trait theories, many people, including educators, still use the approach. For example, many who hire school principals do so based on certain personal qualities that they have witnessed that made other principals effective. Likewise, many principals hire teachers based on certain qualities that they possess.

Recently, interest in personal qualities of leaders has been resurrected as psychologists and social scientists have continued to study leadership in social settings. Research conducted by Kirkpatrick and Locke (1991) indicated that some traits are essential to

Professional Dilemma 6.1

One assistant principal candidate had tried for several years to attain a position. The problem: He was a big man and did not fit the usual high school assistant principal mold. Weighing in at 340 pounds, he was a highly successful and popular teacher but could not get beyond an interview for an administrative position. Most of the principals who had interviewed him were concerned that the position was to taxing for an obese man. Should obesity be considered as a criterion for an assistant principal who has responsibilities to supervise high school campuses? Although this candidate was a successful teacher, does his physical appearance and physical abilities determine how effective he will be as an assistant principal?

effective leadership if practiced in combination with other factors. Three of the traits deemed essential are self-confidence, honesty, and drive. These leadership traits are hard to argue against, especially in the context of social settings such as schools. However, there are examples of people deemed as good leaders who did not possess these personal traits. Consider Abraham Lincoln, who many claimed did not have high self-confidence, or Adolf Hitler, who was anything but an honest leader. Nevertheless, traits such as self-confidence, honesty, and drive have great value for leaders, especially in combination with other behavioral and situational factors.

Behavior Approaches

Behavior theories appeared after the trait theories proved inadequate. Instead of looking at what leaders are, social scientists began looking at what they do, especially because behaviors can be learned more readily than traits, enabling leadership to be accessible to more people.

The first studies on leadership behaviors were conducted at Iowa State University (Lewin & Lippet, 1938). These experiments indicated that individuals reacted differently to an autocratic leadership style than to a democratic leadership style. The groups with autocratic leaders performed effectively as long as the leader was present to supervise them. However, feelings of hostility arose frequently. Participative techniques used by the democratic leaders helped groups perform well even when the leader was not present. Daft (1999) suggested that these characteristics of democratic leadership may explain in part why empowerment is a popular trend in organizations today.

Another set of studies on leader behavior was conducted at Ohio State University. Narrowing a list of nearly 2,000 leader behaviors into a written instrument, researchers developed the Leader Behavior Description Questionnaire (LBDQ). Hundreds of employees, including many educators, responded to behavior examples according to the degree to which their leaders engaged in the various behaviors. The analysis of ratings resulted in two categories of leader behavior types named *consideration (person orientation)* and *initiating structure (task orientation)*. Thousands of research articles and dissertations, many of them concerning the principalship, have used the LBDQ.

Although many leadership behaviors fall along a continuum comprising person and task orientation, these behavior categories are independent of one another. A leader can display a degree of both behaviors. For example, a principal can be high in task orientation and low in people consideration or high in both areas. In the opening vignette it could be said that Robert was high in both task orientation and people skills.

Simultaneous studies at the University of Michigan (Katz, Maccoby, & Morse, 1950; Likert, 1961) took a different approach by analyzing the behaviors of effective and ineffective leaders. The effectiveness of leaders was determined by productivity of the subordinate group. Similar to the Ohio State study, the Michigan study identified two types of leadership behavior: job-centered and employee-centered. Unlike the consideration and task structure defined by the Ohio State studies, Michigan researchers considered job-centered and employee-centered to be distinct styles in opposition to each other.

At the University of Texas, Blake and Mouton (1978) plotted leadership on a grid with concern for people on a vertical scale and concern for production on a horizontal scale. Blake and Mouton offered some interesting titles to the leadership styles when the two criteria were plotted on this grid. For example, high concern for people and low concern for production were labeled "country-club management." "Impoverished management" was the absence of concern both for people and for production. Blake and Mouton considered the most effective style as "team management," where both people and production were regarded highly.

Daft (1999) suggested that the research into behavior approaches raises certain questions for students of leadership. The first question is whether the two dimensions (people orientation or task orientation) are the most important leadership behaviors. Daft suggested that these two behaviors are important because the findings are based on *empirical research*; that is, researchers went into the field to study leaders across a variety of settings. While these are not the only important behaviors, they certainly require attention.

Daft's (1999) second question concerns whether people orientation and task orientation exist together in the same leader and, if so, how. Blake and Mouton's (1978) study argued that both were present when people work with or through others to accomplish an activity. Some researchers argue that "high-high" leaders alternate the type of behavior from one to the other, showing concern one time and task initiation another time. Another approach claims that effective "high-high" leaders encompass both behaviors simultaneously in a fundamentally different way than people who behave in one way or the other (Fleishman & Harris, 1962). A high task-oriented and low relationship-oriented principal might set difficult goals and pressure teachers to improve student achievement. A high relationship-oriented and low task-oriented principal might deemphasize test scores and seek improvement by building positive relationships with teachers. In contrast, the "high-high" leaders seem to have a knack for displaying concern for both people and production.

A third question suggested by Daft (1999), and one that leads into the next leadership research approach, is whether "high-high" leadership styles are situational; that is, does the behavior tend to be effective in every situation? Likewise, does it mean that the behavior succeeds only in certain situations? Daft reported that leadership with concern for people tended to be related to higher employee satisfaction and fewer personnel problems across a wide variety of situations. Likewise, task-oriented behavior was associated with higher productivity across a large number of situations.

The last question raised by Daft (1999) concerns whether people actually can change themselves into leaders high on people and/or task orientation. The original behavior studies at Ohio State, Michigan, and Texas assumed that leadership behavior could be learned. This does not mean that it will always be practiced effectively. Consequently, studies emerged as to what leader behaviors should be used in certain situations. These studies form a group of research investigations known as *situational* or *contingency theories*.

Contingency Approaches

While leader behaviors were still studied, the central focus of contingency research was the situations or contingencies in which leadership occurred. Daft (1999) suggested that *contingency* means that one thing depends on other things, and "for a leader to be effective there must be an appropriate fit between the leader's behavior and the conditions in the situation. A leadership style that works in one situation may not work in another situation. There is not one best way of leadership" (pp. 93–94).

Consider the opening vignette to this chapter. Several situational variables such as task, structure, teachers' commitment and abilities, resources, and external factors such as the district office and parental commitment contributed to the successful implementation of the middle school model. In particular, the maturity and cohesiveness of the teachers and the principal played an extremely important role.

Contingency theories try to match the various styles of leadership to the appropriate situations. Among the various studies were the path-goal theory by House (1974), Fiedler's (1967) contingency model, Vroom and Jago's (1988) contingency model, and Hersey and Blanchard's (1977) situational leadership model.

The movement from the leader's personal traits and behaviors to situations or contingencies acknowledged two important factors in the leadership research. First, situational leadership models recognized that others in the organization (we will use the term *followers*) matter. Follower characteristics, primarily those inherent in the organizational or group context (e.g., experience, training, and effort) influence leadership effectiveness. The second contribution made by the contingency theories was that leadership could be developed (and thus be more effective) by understanding the situations in the environment. Both of these contributions added to the understanding of leadership and influenced more research, especially on the relationships that developed among the participants in the leadership relationship.

Leadership as a Relationship

Theorists who emphasized leadership as a relationship believed that trait, behavior, and contingency theories oversimplified the relationship between leaders and followers. This approach studied the influence that followers have on leaders and why leaders have more influence over some followers than others. These theorists argued that leaders do not uniformly broadcast a trait such as self-confidence and have it received equally by each person in the organization.

Leadership as a relationship grew out of social science literature that emphasized power and influence. The approach identified the types of power that leaders used to influence followers. For example, French and Raven (1959) identified five sources of power: reward, coercion, legitimate, expert, and referent (personal). We discuss sources of power and influence further in Chapter 8. Although informative as these sources of power and influence are on leadership, this literature ignored the reciprocal nature of the relationship among leaders and followers.

The development of the dyadic approach is based on four stages. The first stage is the awareness of a relationship between a leader and each subordinate rather than between a leader and a group of subordinates. The second stage examines specific attributes of the exchange between leader and subordinate. The third stage explores whether leaders could intentionally develop partnerships with each subordinate, and the fourth stage expanded the view of dyads to include larger systems and networks (Daft, 1999). A good example of research that used a reciprocal understanding of the leader-follower relationship is Blase's (1989, 1991) work on the tactics used by teachers to influence principals. These tactics varied depending on whether principals were open or closed in their approach to teachers. Currently, the dyadic approach has not received a lot of research to substantiate the theory. Nevertheless, the theory does suggest an important leadership concept, especially for school organizations. Principals and assistant principals need to build networks wherein a large number of people can influence each other. This relationship approach brought attention to yet another level of research and theorizing, that of leadership as an organizational feature.

Leadership as an Organizational Feature

Moving beyond defining leadership as particular roles, leadership as an organizational quality focused on the social interaction among roles in the organization. This perspective had roots in the work of several organizational theorists, including Barnard (1948), Thompson (1967), Tannenbaum (1962), and Katz and Kahn (1966, 1978). However, Ogawa and Bossert (1995) more recently described leadership as an organizational quality in schools from an institutional theory view. Instead of the traditional emphasis on leadership to accomplish organizational goals, their approach focused on leadership to make the organization legitimate and credible in the eyes of its constituents. Their argument extends beyond the obvious by suggesting that leadership flows through the networks of roles that comprise organizations. The currency of leadership lies in personal resources of people. Leadership shapes the system that produces patterns of interaction and the meanings that other participants attach to organizational events.

This perspective is particularly useful in understanding the principal's role by broadening the understanding of leadership beyond one role or position and acknowledging the interaction among roles (Crow, Matthews, & McCleary, 1996). Ogawa and Bossert (1995) also suggested that principal leadership roles are changing because of reforms that emphasize empowering teachers and others associated with the organization. Similarly, discussions on the development of professional learning communities and the shared responsibility that characterize these communities reflect the change in principal leadership.

Moral Leadership

The leadership approaches we have examined so far in this chapter are nonevaluative; that is, the perspectives could be used to describe both effective and ineffective leaders in good and poor organizations. Many theorists have developed a leadership approach that is based on moral authority. For example, Sergiovanni (1992) and Johnson (1990) wrote that morally based leadership is meaningful because it taps what is important to people and what motivates them.

Most of the literature on moral leadership implies the development of followers into leaders, thereby developing their potential rather than using the leadership position to control others. This type of moral leadership began with Burns's (1978) concept of *transformational leadership*, in which "leaders and followers raise one another to higher levels of morality and motivation" (p. 20). Burns contrasted transformational leadership with transactional leadership. *Transactional leadership* involves an exchange process between leaders and followers. The leader recognizes specific follower desires and provides resources that meet those desires in exchange for the follower's loyalty and goal attainment. Leadership is a series of transactions to achieve specific goals. Because transactional leadership involves commitment to follow the rules, transactional leaders often maintain stability within the organization rather than promote change (Daft, 1999). On the other hand, transformational leadership is based on personal values, beliefs, and qualities of the leader rather than on an exchange process.

Another moral leadership approach that supports the belief that leaders are to empower others is *stewardship theory*. Block (1993) argued that traditional views of leadership were based on patriarchy and self-interest and maintained by command and control—hence breeding dependency. Stewardship is grounded in service and is supported by commitment and empowerment. Block suggested that stewardship is the belief that leaders are accountable to others as well as to the organization. He provided four principles in a stewardship framework:

1. *Reorient toward a partnership assumption.* Leaders and followers are jointly accountable for outcomes.
2. *Localize decisions and power to those closest to the work and the customer.* Decision making should be at the point where the work gets done.
3. *Recognize and reward the value of labor.* The reward system ties everyone to the success of the organization.
4. *Expect core work teams to build the organization.* Teams define goals, create a nurturing environment, and respond to a changing environment.

Sergiovanni (1992) believed that the concept of stewardship was attractive to principals. He suggested that stewardship embraced all internal and external members of the school as community and argued against the premise that the good leader is one who gets his or her subordinates to do something. Sergiovanni suggested that shifting emphasis from leader behavior to establishing meaning can help schools recapture leadership as a powerful force for school improvement.

Servant leadership takes stewardship one step further. Servant leadership transcends self-interest to serve the needs of others, helps others grow and develop, and provides opportunity for others. The fulfillment of others is the servant leader's principal aim. Greenleaf (1970) proposed that leaders can operate from the basic precepts of servant leadership, such as the principal encouraging teachers to participate in a master's degree program or engaging the faculty in a shared vision.

Moral leadership also produces an interest in the cultural side of leadership, as outlined by Schein (1992). Whereas most leadership has focused on the technical side, be it task-oriented or person-oriented, this approach focuses on the values, beliefs, and assumptions of work—how values and beliefs are formed, how they affect the quality of life and work in schools, and how they are modified. Leadership from this perspective examines what principals do to build and maintain a school culture that reinforces the values, norms, and beliefs and to add meaning to the educational work that goes beyond mere accomplishment of tasks (Crow, Matthews, & McCleary, 1996).

How Useful Is Research on Leadership?

Scholars and practitioners have argued for decades about the practical uses of leadership research. Many studies involved groups that were not representative of leaders in certain fields or categories. For example, the early studies were conducted with mostly male subjects who had had military experience in World War II or the Korean War. Obviously, the results from these studies may not be the same as findings from an occupation such as nursing or teaching. Also, some studies only reported results from American business organizations that often were going through declining budgets, layoffs, and union threats. Leadership in the public sector is likely to be different from that in the private sector. Some people argue that leading an organization of professionals such as teachers is quite different from leading a factory of union workers. Likewise, some studies looked only at certain kinds of success, such as a financial profit or followers' satisfaction.

Some researchers (e.g., Pfeffer, 1978) also claimed that other researchers were only seeing leadership because they expected to see it. Proponents of *attribution theory* argued that if, for example, researchers observed a business turnaround and there was no other obvious cause, the turnaround was attributed to leadership. Alternatively, if the researchers were looking for certain traits or behaviors, they would find them although the traits and behaviors may not have contributed to the leadership outcome.

Regardless of the various critics of leadership study, the research has contributed to a greater understanding of leadership and the literature base. Because of the scholarly research on leadership, we know more about what has proven effective in certain environments. However, there is still considerable understanding about leadership that we do not possess.

The Purpose of Principal Leadership

Could schools operate efficiently without principals? If a head teacher managed the resources and other incidentals, would not that be enough for schools? To argue for the value of principal leadership requires adding a purpose to the role of principal as leader. In this section we discuss that purpose and present a model that depicts the ingredients of establishing principal leadership.

To understand the purpose of principal leadership, let us review the definition of leadership that we presented in Chapter 1. We proposed that a definition of leadership that is useful in studying principal leadership was given by Rost (1991) when, after studying many definitions, he defined leadership as "an influence relationship among leaders and followers who intend real changes that reflect their mutual purposes" (p. 102). With this definition serving as our foundation, we suggest that the purpose of principal leadership involves the intention to significantly change and reform schools in substantive ways to improve teaching and learning for *all* students.

Defining Significant School Change and Reform

Three important points about the purpose of leadership are evident from Rost's (1991) definition. First, leaders and followers intend real change, and they see change as a continuing process rather than a one-time reform effort. These changes involve not just the leader's goals for change but also the goals for both leaders and followers. Indeed, if this purpose is only the leader's, no leadership exists. Both leaders and followers must acknowledge the need for improvement in teaching and learning for *all* students.

Second, real change in schools is change that is substantial. Cuban (1988) suggested labeling the difference between superficial and substantial change as *first-order* and *second-order changes*. First-order changes only seek to make current practices more effective. No new practices are adopted. Teachers and students perform their duties in much the same way as they have done in the past. Examples of first-order changes may be a new attendance policy where the expectation is still held that students are to be in school, but the consequences of nonattendance are stiffer. Second-order changes entail a shift in values, beliefs, and practices. Underlying assumptions are challenged. School goals, mission, vision, and roles shift. Teachers become leaders and take responsibility in the school's decision-making process. Students are not just recipients of learning but take an active role in constructing their learning. Teachers and administrators are not satisfied with some or even most students learning but are committed to *all* students learning. Second-order changes are significant and have a lasting impact on the school's culture. Leadership for school improvement involves changing the school culture so that leaders and followers are willing to consider substantive second-order changes.

Third, leadership for change focuses on the mutual purposes of leaders and followers. Rost (1991) maintained that this mutuality is forged in the noncoercive influence relationship. As principals, teachers, students, and parents work together, they forge shared purposes about changes that will positively affect teaching and learning. The content of mutual purposes should reflect what many reformers (including Barth, 1990; Louis & Murphy, 1994; Murphy, 1994; Sergiovanni, 1992) repeat as the main theme in school reform: Teaching and learning is at the heart of school change. The mutual purposes of leaders and followers should be located in classroom instruction and learning. Teachers, principals, parents, and students come together to forge a shared purpose for improving classroom instruction. As principal or assistant principal, the most critical purpose of your leadership will be to create a school culture in which adults and children grow together in developing a learning community that shares a mutual purpose to improve student learning.

We believe that principal leadership involves three factors that interact with each other to create improvement in teaching and learning. These leadership factors include

- Understanding school culture to be able to create, maintain, and change that culture
- Developing a personal vision that is to be incorporated into a shared vision among the learning community
- Using leadership tools such as communication and collaboration to implement the shared vision in the school to improve teaching and learning for all students

In the following subsections we will discuss these three areas as principal and assistant principal leadership. Then we will discuss them as components of the principal's facilitating role.

Understanding School Culture

The first factor for principal leadership in improving teaching and learning is understanding the school's culture. One of the challenges you will face as a new school leader is to view the school's organization in a holistic way. Teachers view the school through a lens that often is confined to their own classrooms. The challenge for school leaders is to open that lens to a broader view of the whole organization. This wide-angle view helps create an understanding of the school's culture and how that culture affects the values, beliefs, and attitudes that exist.

Defining School Culture.

Before recent reform efforts, school culture had not been an area that had been considered in school reform. Studying culture in schools is relatively new and somewhat ambiguous. Suggesting that the field of education lacked a clear and consistent definition of school culture, Stolp (1994) reported that the term came to education from the corporate world with the idea that it would provide direction for a more efficient and stable learning environment. Deal and Peterson (1999) noted, "Of the many different conceptions of culture, none is universally accepted as the one best definition" (p. 3). Several writers have suggested definitions of culture such as the way we do things around here (Bower, 1996), the shared beliefs and values that closely knit a community together (Deal & Kennedy, 1982), a pattern of basic assumptions (Schein, 1992), and a complex web of traditions and rituals (Deal & Peterson, 1999).

Based on Schein's (1992) work, we believe that culture is best defined as a blend of several elements:

- Historical and current artifacts (including behavior norms, traditions, and myths)
- Commonly held values and beliefs among internal and external participants in the organization

- Basic assumptions that provide the underlying basis for actions, values, and beliefs by the participants

Some educators have simplified the understanding of culture by referring to certain isolated aspects as school culture. For example, some educators mistakenly use such terms as *school environment, climate, community,* or *school spirit* as synonymous with culture. In addition, school culture has been referred to as the history of the school or the traditions that have been established. School culture consists of much more than any one of those elements. It is a combination of many aspects that teachers, principals, students, parents, and community members construct to make sense of the school's organization and features. The veteran teachers, staff members, community members, and administrators translate and interpret the school's culture for newcomers as the way to do things in the school. Veteran teachers, staff members, parents, and administrators pass along the culture to newcomers in various ways, both formally and informally. Beginning-of-the-year orientations, faculty meetings, and professional development are examples of more formal approaches to passing along culture. Hallway conversations, faculty lounge discussions, and veteran storytelling are examples of informal approaches.

Artifacts are characteristics of an organization's activities. School cultural artifacts include such things as celebrations, rituals, stories, heroes, and language. Artifacts also include jargon and metaphors that help describe the school. For example, a historical artifact of an old three-storied elementary school is that it grows and nurtures community leaders. On a hallway wall in the school is a "Hall of Fame" with pictures of prominent alumni who have served as leaders. The school has many alumni who have become civic leaders, including a governor, senator, three mayors, a lunar mission astronaut, and several collegiate and professional athletes. The metaphor of growing and nurturing leaders was displayed prominently and communicated in and out of school. Artifacts can be a part of history that are no longer used, or they can be myths that serve to explain a practice or a belief. Many myths have no historical foundation but are passed along and often embellished.

Beliefs and values that are commonly held by most members of the school community also add to its culture. Values and beliefs provide reasons people behave as they do. Successful school improvement will depend a great deal on how well leaders understand the values and beliefs of those involved in the school. Because the beliefs and values of people in the school shape that school's culture, the effect of school culture on school improvement is significant. Many innovations are not put into practice because they conflict with deeply held beliefs and values of those involved.

Likewise, basic assumptions provide the underlying basis for people's actions, beliefs, and values. For example, some teachers may assume that students from high socioeconomic backgrounds can learn quickly and others cannot. They then act on those assumptions by their teaching methods with those students. These assumptions can permeate the entire school and affects its culture. Daft (1999) claimed that most assumptions generally start as expressed values but that over time they become more deeply embedded and less open to question. Members take these assumptions for granted and often are not even aware that they guide their behavior, language, and patterns of social interaction.

Some theorists (Daft, 1999; Schein, 1992) have suggested that culture consists of different levels of understanding. The first level consists of visible elements such as a manner of dress, office organization, or ceremonies. These elements are things that people easily see, hear, and observe by being around members of the school. For example, in the opening vignette, Louise visited the Lakeside Middle School and observed certain elements of the middle school philosophy that impressed her.

At a deeper level of culture are the expressed values and beliefs that are not necessarily observable but can be discerned by how people explain and justify what they do. These are values that members of the school hold at a conscious level. For example, Richard met with each teacher at the end of the school year. These teachers knew that the school had a collaborative and open atmosphere in which they could easily discuss ideas with their principal. Some elements of culture are so deeply embedded that members may not be consciously aware of them. These basic underlying assumptions are the deepest essence of the school's culture. At Roosevelt Junior High School, these assumptions might include teachers knowing they can be innovative in their instructional approaches and that they can receive support from each other and their principal.

Several researchers have compiled some impressive evidence on school culture. Certain school cultures correlate strongly with increased student achievement and motivation, as well as with teacher productivity and morale. Fullan's (1999) studies on school change efforts identified the school culture as critical to the successful improvement of teaching and learning. In addition, a five-year study by Newmann and colleagues (1996) concluded that to have success, both new structures and professional culture are needed. The researchers found that school success thrived in cultures with a focus on student learning, high expectations, and support for innovation. Deal and Peterson (1990) claimed that a school's culture encouraged learning and progress by fostering a climate of purposeful change and support for risk taking and experimentation. School culture also correlates with teachers' attitudes toward their work. Cheng (1993) found that stronger school cultures had more motivated teachers. Lortie's (1975) classic study of teachers also found that culture helped teachers overcome the uncertainty of their work.

School culture also has a certain staying power. This stability can promote school change, or it can inhibit it. The tenacity of school culture is often seen with principals who make a difference while they are at a school, but their vision is more their own than the organization's. Therefore, soon after the principal leaves, the school reverts to its old culture. Essentially, the vision dies with the leader. Commitment is short term, and the culture is not altered significantly. If this trend continues with other principals, teachers often will become tenacious in their reluctance to change.

Understanding a School's Existing Culture

Principals who are interested in school reform and improvement need to first understand the existing culture. How do principals read and understand the school's culture? Deal and Peterson (1999) suggested that principals and assistant principals should be both historians and anthropological sleuths in understanding their school's culture. In fulfilling these roles, they recommended several questions that would give principals a way to understand school culture:

- How long has the school existed?
- Why was it built, and who were the first inhabitants?
- Who had a major influence on the school's direction?
- What critical incidents occurred in the past, and how were they resolved, if at all?
- What were the preceding principals, teachers, and students like?
- What does the school's architecture convey? How is space arranged and used?
- What subcultures exist inside and outside the school?
- Who are the recognized (and unrecognized) heroes and villains of the school?
- What do people say (and think) when asked what the school stands for? What would they miss if they left?
- What events are assigned special importance?
- How is conflict typically defined? How is it handled?
- What are the key ceremonies and stories of the school?
- What do people wish for? Are there patterns to their individual dreams? (pp. 17–19)

Perhaps nothing is more important as you enter a school as a principal or assistant principal for the first time than to take the time to understand the school's culture. All other efforts will be contingent on your understanding of what already exists. We now turn our discussion to principal leadership in what Schein (1992) argued distinguishes the leadership role, that is, creating, maintaining, and changing culture.

Principal Leadership in Creating, Maintaining, and Changing Culture

Creating School Culture.   Only a few principals have the opportunity to create a new culture. More than likely, you will inherit a culture that has developed over several years. However, you still can play a major role in maintaining and changing a school's culture. With the new models that are emerging in education, such as charter, magnet, and alternative schools, you may even be part of creating a school's culture. In these cases, the types of teachers and students recruited, the particular features of school life to which you pay attention, and the ways you react to crises help to create an organizational culture.

Schein (1992) identified two sets of mechanisms that leaders use to embed culture. The first set, "primary embedding mechanisms," includes the following:

- What leaders pay attention to, measure, and control on a regular basis
- How leaders react to critical incidents and organizational crises
- Observed criteria by which leaders allocate scarce resources
- Deliberate role modeling, teaching, and coaching
- Observed criteria by which leaders allocate rewards and status
- Observed criteria by which leaders recruit, select, promote, retire, and excommunicate organizational members (p. 231)

Principals in new schools, such as charter schools or redesigned schools, create culture by the activities and behavior to which they attend. If resources are distributed in ways that emphasize one subject or grade level over another, these actions and their underlying values become part of the culture.

As the culture of new organizations begins to develop, a second set of mechanisms acts as culture reinforcers:

- Organizational design and structure
- Organizational systems and procedures
- Organizational rites and rituals
- Design of physical space, facades, and buildings
- Stories, legends, and myths about people and events
- Formal statements of organizational philosophy, values, and creed (Schein, 1992, p. 245)

In creating school culture, principals can use artifacts to embed and transmit the values, beliefs, and basic underlying assumptions. For example, the dress code, the physical layout of the school, the language used to describe school activities, and the behavioral expectations of teachers and students create and reinforce values and beliefs about how things are done at this school.

Maintaining School Culture. Often teachers, students, and parents expect the principal to maintain an existing culture of the school, especially if it has been perceived as successful in solving the school's internal and external problems. The role of maintaining culture involves three audiences: internal veterans, internal newcomers, and external constituents. As principal, you would hope to influence veteran teachers and staff members to "keep the faith," that is, to abide by the norms of the school's culture. Principals often do this by using ceremonies, stories, and rituals that reinforce the values, beliefs, and basic assumptions of the culture.

Newcomers to the school present a special challenge for leaders in maintaining culture. Newcomers may bring with them new ideas and different backgrounds. Often new teachers are recent graduates of university programs and hold to more idealistic philosophies. Because of these different values, beliefs, and assumptions, they can be either a positive or a negative threat to the existing culture. As principal or assistant principal, your role is to help recruit and hire new teachers and staff members who already possess some of the school's values and beliefs and then provide a socializing process to the newcomers about the prevailing norms, values, beliefs, and assumptions of the school's culture. A major complaint of new teachers is their difficulty in uncovering the secrets of how things are done in the school (Crow, Matthews, & McCleary, 1996).

Even in the midst of helping new teachers learn to survive, principals can socialize newcomers by what principals attend to, how they deal with crises, what kinds of behavior they reward, and how they respond to failure. Peters and Waterman (1982) argued that the leader's response to failure is as important as his or her response to success in building an innovative culture. If new teachers see attempts at innovation punished if they are unsuccessful, these new teachers are less likely to try them (Crow, Matthews, & Mc-Cleary, 1996).

The third audience to which leaders must attend in maintaining the culture is external constituents—those individuals outside the organization who are connected to it. Your role is to communicate the norms, values, beliefs, and assumptions of the school's culture to these individuals and groups. You will want to ensure their understanding of the school's culture and to enlist their support in the school's mission and vision. At the same time, you will have to be sensitive to the concerns of the external constituents. School cultures cannot remain vibrant if they only emphasize the values and beliefs of faculty and staff members and ignore the concerns of the community. Because of this, principals must be actively involved in their communities, being sensitive to the ways communities are changing and to the views that external constituents have about the school's values and how well schools are doing in their academic and activity programs.

To illustrate the importance of the principal's sensitivity to the needs of the community, consider this unpleasant incident. Several years ago, a hazing incident occurred among high school students in a small rural community. This particular hazing incident was only one in a long chain of similar incidents at the high school over several years. In fact, it could be considered part of the school's culture because it had become a ritual, even though the school's administrators and faculty did not support the ritual. One high school boy was particularly offended by the incident and attempted to protest to the principal. Unable to gain an audience with the principal, the boy and his parents wrote a letter to the editor of the local newspaper. Other news media became interested in the story and sought an interview with the principal. The principal, for whatever reason, turned down the opportunity for an interview, and the media published the story without hearing both sides of the issue. Many observers of this situation thought that if the principal had responded in a timely and sensitive manner to the student, parents, and the media, he could have saved the school from embarrassment.

Changing School Culture.   At times, principal leadership also involves changing culture. The two major reasons for changing a school's culture reflect the two primary organizational problems, namely, external adaptation and internal integration (Parson, 1951). When environmental demands on the school change and the school's culture is out of step with these demands, cultural change is necessary. The external environment that confronts schools today provides good examples. This environment has undergone fundamental changes. First, diversity and changing demographics of student populations have created challenges and opportunities for schools. Second, technology and the knowledge explosion have troubling consequences for traditional curriculum-based programs. Third, new school structures and organizations such as charter schools and increased choice have made schools more competitive than they have ever been. Fourth, the reform and standards movement by policymakers and other public entities has placed greater scrutiny and focus on school improvement efforts. All these external environmental factors, and others that you will no doubt experience, place a challenge on a school's culture. As a school leader, you will need to help coordinate change in the school's culture to reflect these external environmental forces.

Oakdale Elementary School is a good example of external adaptation problems that require cultural change. The school at one time served the children of professors and other professionals in a suburban college town. The private college in the town was built around the turn of the 20th century, and the buildings were in disrepair. The governing board of the college did not have finances to upgrade the facilities and was forced to close the college and sell the campus to a medical instrument manufacturing firm. As the professionals moved out of Oakdale Elementary School boundaries, blue-collar workers moved in. The school's population went through a dramatic change. Rather than changing to meet the educational needs of the new community, the teachers and principal stood on their past accomplishments and blamed the students' lack of achievement on their families. The once positive culture of the school soon became very negative.

Changing school culture also becomes necessary when internal integration breaks down, such as when faculty morale becomes low (Crow, Matthews, & McCleary, 1996). At times, groups within a school can hold differing and opposing values and beliefs. This type of situation can occur when a group of newcomers enters a school where a group of veterans has remained close. The two groups may hold different instructional and curricular beliefs and thus lack a sense of community or shared vision. In an instance such as this, the principal must use influence to reinforce the current set of values that are working and support cultural change where it is needed.

The Dark Side of Culture.   The benefits of culture are obvious. Culture represents an effective way of holding an organization together and providing a purpose for those involved. However, there is a dark side of culture that also can develop. Some cultures become so strong that they become rigid and backward in accepting new adaptations. Weick (1985) suggested "a coherent statement of who we are makes it harder for us to become something else" (p. 385). Schools such as Oakdale Elementary have developed toxic cultures. The people in the schools have lost sight of positive values and beliefs and hold onto negative assumptions about students and parents. They shift blame away from instructional practices to other factors, thus avoiding the necessity to improve. Deal and Peterson (1999) characterized such toxicity in schools as having the following elements:

- *The school becomes focused on negative values.* The values work better for adults than for students, and the focus is on outcomes that are less important, such as athletic achievements.
- *The school becomes fragmented.* Meaning is derived from subculture membership, antistudent sentiments, or life outside work. The fragmentation decreases the sense of a shared purpose. Little cooperation or collaboration takes place among the faculty.
- *The school becomes almost exclusively destructive.* Faculty and administrators often dislike their clientele and foster negative mind sets about their students.
- *The school becomes spiritually fractured.* People in the school display anomie and unreflective mindlessness.

In the section dealing with facilitating others in understanding and developing culture, we will further explore actions that principals can take that will help make change of culture possible.

The school's culture plays an important role in school improvement efforts. Although no school culture is totally free of some toxicity, and likewise, no school culture is totally toxic, school improvement efforts start with understanding the culture that exists and then reinforcing the valuable aspects, revitalizing the aspects that have slipped away, and changing the toxic aspects that need it.

We suggest that as a principal or assistant principal you carefully consider the school's existing culture before embarking on any reform efforts. After you understand the culture, you may then want to decide what parts of the culture need to change and what parts need to be enhanced. It will be here that you will want to develop your own personal vision and help the school develop a shared vision, topics we discuss in the next subsection.

Creating a Collective Vision

Vision works in a number of important ways. An effective vision provides a link between the present and the future, serves to energize and motivate people, provides meaning for their work, and sets a standard of excellence in the organization (Daft, 1999). Vision is also misunderstood in leadership. It was not too long ago when leaders, including principals, were encouraged to develop a strategic vision and then sell it to others in the organization. However, as we will discuss in this section, vision involves a collective process.

A school's vision is not just a dream—it is an ambitious view of the future that administrators, teachers, staff members, and parents can believe in, one that can be realistically attained and offers a future for the school that is better in instruction, curriculum, programs, and activities than what presently exists. In the opening vignette, the vision that Louise had developed of the middle school concept is a good example. After being introduced to the middle school philosophy, she started putting it together in light of her own school. Soon she was able to develop a vision of what Roosevelt Junior High School should be doing. As such, the vision she developed presented an ambitious view of the future that required her to communicate and persuade others to accept and become part of the vision.

Daft (1999) identified five themes common to effective visions:

- *Vision has broad appeal.* The vision cannot be the property of the leader alone.
- *Vision deals with change.* The vision is about action and challenges people to make important changes toward a better future.
- *Vision encourages faith and hope.* A vision helps people believe that they can be effective—that there is a better future they can move to through their commitment and actions.
- *Vision reflects high ideals.* A good vision has power to inspire and energize people only when it points toward an uplifting future.
- *Vision defines the destination and the journey.* A good vision for the future includes specific outcomes that the school wants to achieve.

Many people use the terms *vision* and *mission* interchangeably. Mission is not quite the same thing as vision. A school's mission is its broad purpose and reason for existence.

It often defines the school's core values and reason for being. A mission provides a basis for creating the vision. Likewise, goal statements differ from vision statements. Goals are detailed, specific statements directed at accomplishing the mission and are guided by the vision. Goal statements include the more specific objectives. As we defined it earlier, vision is an ambitious desire for the future, whereas mission is what the school stands for at the present.

Many schools have mission statements that define what they stand for, including their core values and core purpose. Some schools also include the specific vision as a part of their mission statements. It is important to remember that the vision continually grows and changes, whereas the mission endures longer with fewer changes.

Principal Leadership in Vision Building

Principal leadership in vision building involves two levels: the principal's personal vision and the school's collective vision. The effective principal as leader should have a *personal vision* as to the direction the school should be going, especially in the improving teaching and learning for *all* students. This vision concentrates the principal's attention and provides the passion for one activity over another. As Starratt (1993) claimed:

> The leader's vision is what motivates him or her to be a genuine player in the drama and is a call to greatness as well. The leader's vision is also what enables him or her to articulate the major themes of the drama in the role of director. The vision enables the leader/director to see the unity within the various scenes and subplots of the drama, and to call the various actors to express, in their parts, those overarching themes (p. 145).

This perspective involves the principal's own purpose and understanding of the school's mission and provides the passion that motivates the principal's work.

Just as the principal can have a personal vision, likewise other members of the organization, such as assistant principals and teachers, also have personal visions. In fact, at times, someone else's personal vision is the catalyst for the principal's vision. This event was played out in the opening vignette when Louise shared her personal vision with Robert. Obviously, Louise's vision was congruent with Robert's, and thus they were able to pursue a school-wide collective vision.

A school's *collective vision* is what leaders, teachers, staff members, and others in the school community construct regarding the school's future. A school's collective vision is multileveled. Programmatic vision refers to specific kinds of teaching and learning activities, such as a particular reading program (e.g., balanced literacy). Systemic vision focuses on broader organizational directions. A school's reform efforts that reconceptualize roles, relationships, and responsibilities are part of a systemic vision. The middle school philosophy change that Roosevelt Junior High adopted would be an example of a systemic vision because it affects almost all aspects of the school's organization. As Senge (1990) put it, a collective vision changes people's relationship with the organization. It can create a common identity for all participants, connecting them personally and emotionally in the organization. The middle school vision at Roosevelt Junior High became the common thread by connecting the principal, teachers, staff members, and parents.

To develop a collective vision, principals share their personal visions with others and encourage others to express their personal visions. This openness requires that the principal, teachers, and others have both strong communication skills and courage to connect on an emotional level. Good principals give up the idea that vision emanates from only the top and that their personal vision is the only one that can become a collective vision. As Nanus (1992) said, "Often some of the best ideas for new directions float up from the depths of the organization, but only if they are sought and welcomed when they arrive" (p. 38). A principal's ultimate responsibility is to be in touch with the visions that others in the school community have and find common ground that binds these personal visions into a collective vision for the school.

Nanus (1992) suggested four roles that visionary leaders play based on the dimensions of time and environment. These four roles are useful in understanding the principal's responsibility beyond a sole authorship function.

- *Direction-setter.* This role focuses on the future and the external environment. The leader selects and articulates the target in the future external environment toward which the organization should direct its energies.
- *Change agent.* This role emphasizes the future and focuses on the internal environment. The leader is responsible for stimulating changes to make the vision achievable. At times, this role means providing disconfirming information that demonstrates the ineffective ways the school is meeting the needs of students and families.
- *Spokesperson.* This role directs attention to the present and external environment. The leader is both a skilled speaker and a concerned listener. The leader advocates and negotiates the organization's vision with outside constituencies. This role is becoming increasingly important as schools become more competitive and schools of choice become more widespread.
- *Coach.* This is a present function within the internal environment. The leader lives the vision, thereby serving as a mentor and example for others. Principals cheer the school on toward vision achievement. This coaching and cheering function occurs by what the principal pays attention to, rewards, and celebrates.

It is important to understand that as a principal or assistant principal you must provide a visionary leadership role in both external and internal spheres. To ignore one in favor of the other is to abdicate leadership responsibility. Although others in the school may function in these roles at certain times, you, as a school leader, have the critical responsibility to ensure that these roles are enacted effectively.

Further, with the changing demographics of students, the increase in technologies, the rise of accountability movements, and school reform trends by policymakers, you will face a more difficult job in keeping the purpose of schooling clearly in the minds of school constituents. The school's vision cannot remain stagnant. It will need to be reexamined and revised in the dynamic environment that now exists for schools.

Sadly, many past reform and instructional improvement efforts have ignored the consideration of the school's culture and vision. Such efforts can leave the school's organization in disarray and place unpleasant burdens on teachers and staff members. As principal or assistant principal, you need to provide direction to the vision process and content. This is not to suggest that others have no role in constructing the vision but rather that you, as a leader, have a primary responsibility for providing the direction to the process. Likewise, as a school leader you provide the energy for persisting with the process, although it may become uncomfortable and threatening to some in the school. Your commitment and passion to the vision process are critical in finding a direction that improves students' educational experiences and teachers' work lives.

One more area to consider in vision building is that visions can have a dark side. Similar to the dark side of culture, visions can blind leaders and others and cause confusion and chaos in the organization. Fullan (1992) suggested three ways that visions can blind school leaders and others in the organization. First, "the leader who is committed to a particular innovation may pursue it in such a narrow and self-defeating way that teachers resist the idea" (p. 19). Numerous stories from schools tell of principals who became so enamored with their own personal visions with an innovative program that they created confusion and resentment among the faculty and staff. In these situations, it is unlikely that a collective vision was developed, and the personal vision of the principal eventually caused chaos within the organization.

A second way visions can blind is when the leader successfully involves others to use an innovation but does not engage them in other basic changes and alternatives. The dynamic nature of schools requires an ongoing visioning process rather than fixation on one innovation.

Third, visions can blind school leaders and faculties in the case of a "charismatic leader where so much depends on personal strength or pressure but innovation is short-lived" (Fullan, 1992, p. 19). The superhuman image that is used by some principals is not realistic and is not valuable in creating a collective vision. Again, stories from schools abound with charismatic leaders who are able to implement an innovation in a school only to have it die after the leader leaves or moves to another cause.

Challenges of Vision Building

Hoyle (1995) described two challenges for principals in developing a school vision. First, many school leaders give up on the school's vision too soon. Too often school leaders cave in to the opposition. It may come from the external environment, such as community activists, or internally, such as a veteran teaching force. Principals have heard horror stories from colleagues who fell from grace in their communities because of their resistance to some innovative idea such as outcome-based education or whole-language reading. Although Joan of Arc died for her cause, most school leaders do not have the same desire or passion for their cause. Hoyle suggested that a practical way to keep the vision alive is to invite everyone to contribute to the visioning process. As a leader in the school and the community, you should look at the external and internal environments and be sure that constituents from both have opportunities to voice their opinions. Your challenge is to show enough respect to those who will differ from your vision that they will in turn show enough respect for your opinions.

A second challenge that Hoyle (1995) suggested in transforming the vision into reality is the allocation of resources, especially money. "If the foundation to the vision is to be built, the money must be there somewhere" (p. 36). Hoyle's observations of various schools indicated that faculties and communities soon tired of the visioning process if their visions could not be implemented because of finances. Likewise, vision building requires time to plan and reflect. Again, vision-building teams become frustrated easily when they do not have time built into their schedules to accommodate the visioning process. "If you, the leader, desire to transform your team vision into reality, then time and reflection are needed to facilitate careful planning and team building" (p. 37).

Some principals may complain that there is no need to change the school's culture or vision. Perhaps they are right, but consider the number of businesses that have held onto past success only to find that they have not kept up with the new trends and are on the brink of bankruptcy. Schools can be in similar situations. Often school people become blinded by their own perceived successes. As a strong leader wanting to improve teaching and learning in a school, you will want to carefully analyze the school's vision and explore possible future developments. Roosevelt Junior High is moving ahead with the middle school concept because the principal and the faculty realize that although things are going well at Roosevelt, there is always room for improvement. They want to offer the best instruction possible for their students.

Understanding school culture and developing a vision are important, but they may not be enough to influence school reform and improve instruction. As a school leader, you need to communicate the vision to others so that it can be put into action.

Communicating the Vision

To achieve the vision, principals and others must communicate the vision. *Communication* is the process by which information and understanding are transmitted from a sender to a receiver. *Feedback* occurs when the receiver sends a message back to the sender that then enables the sender to determine if the message was interpreted correctly. Errors occur when background, attitudes, and knowledge act as filters and create noise. The processes of sending, receiving, providing feedback, and reducing noise underlie school leadership.

In order to be precise and to help others understand the vision, the first means of communicating is preparing a written vision statement. Written vision statements serve two important purposes. First, being able to write down a vision statement helps make commitment possible. Without a written statement, many participants may misinterpret or misunderstand the school's vision. Likewise, newcomers who were not involved in the initial development of the vision have a written version to read and understand. Second, an organization's ability to write down a vision is an indication of its commitment and understanding of the vision. Visions must be understood to be achieved.

Beyond writing a statement, visions need to be communicated by the actions of those in the school. The principal has a primary leadership role in expressing the school's vision. Sashkin (1988) suggested five ways that the principal expresses the vision:

1. Focusing attention on specific elements of the vision
2. Communicating personally (e.g., active listening, giving feedback effectively, and being specific rather than general)

3. Displaying trustworthiness (i.e., say what you mean and mean what you say)
4. Displaying respect toward one's self and others
5. Taking risks

Only when you as the principal or assistant principal express the vision in your daily activities by what you say and do will you be able to influence others in the school to believe in and commit to the vision.

Using communication as a strategy also involves active listening. Active listening is necessary as a daily, ongoing part of a principal's communication. When principals and assistant principals do not listen, it sends a clear message that others in the school are not important, thus decreasing their commitment and motivation toward fulfilling the school's vision, which in turn affects the school's culture. The connection between personal satisfaction and being listened to applies to everyone in the school. Teachers want to voice opinions and goals, parents want to offer suggestions, and students want to express ideas. Snowden and Gorton (1998) offered an important suggestion for school administrators in listening. They maintained that many administrators' sources of information are limited either because of their position in the organizational hierarchy or because of other people's perception of their availability or receptivity to communication. Although school administrators often proclaim an open-door policy, everyone may not perceive these administrators as open, especially those with a disagreeable message. Consequently, an administrator's contacts may be restricted to only certain kinds of individuals bearing information that is regarded as nonthreatening. Snowden and Gorton suggested that school leaders must be careful to avoid receiving their information from a select group of people who tend to see things in a similar way. School leaders need diversity rather than similarity of opinion. They need to identify and secure ideas and opinions from those students, teachers, parents, and other professional or community people who may hold contrasting sets of values or objectives. It will only be through listening to various opinions that a vision will be an acceptable and collective effort to be implemented.

Dialogue is what you get when active listening spreads throughout the school. As suggested in Chapter 3, a learning community develops among teachers when they can openly speak with each other about teaching and learning. In a profession that has been shrouded in isolation, teacher and principal dialogue is a welcome and important step toward improving the instructional climate in schools.

The principal as a leader also must communicate the school's vision with the people outside the school (external constituents). Again, instead of thinking of communication as a one-way process where principals sell the vision to other members of the school community, principals should see it as a two-way process. Principals need to listen and be sensitive to the concerns of external constituents. A vision cannot be vibrant and dynamic if it only expresses the desires of the faculty and staff. As a principal or assistant principal in contemporary schools, it is imperative that you become involved in the community, be sensitive to the changes in the community, and be aware of the views that the external constituents have about what and how well schools are doing. In the opening vignette, Richard exemplifies the importance of communication. He maintained open communication with the faculty by inviting them to express their ideas at the end of every school year. Consequently, an open culture existed so that Louise talked freely to him about middle schools. His verbal response and nonverbal symbols acted as feedback to her to continue pursuing her idea. The entire school community felt similarly as the middle school concept was presented in a nonthreatening and open communication manner. Further, Richard facilitated leadership so that faculty members took on much of the leadership that was needed.

Principal as Facilitator of Leadership in Others

Although principals are important, their mere presence does not automatically result in the leadership that is needed for school improvement efforts. Effective leadership cannot be centered around one person or one role. Leadership involves an entire organization of leaders and followers who often switch roles. As a principal or assistant principal, leadership will come not only from you but also from those around you, such as teachers, staff, students, and parents. As you practice leadership, you also need to facilitate leadership in others.

A term used with expanding leadership is *empowerment*. Empowerment became a motto of educational reforms in the 1980s and 1990s and continues to be used as a means of getting others in an organization to become more involved in the management and leadership of the organization. Short and Greer (1997) identified two versions of empowerment. The first version draws on the labor-management tradition where power is conceived as a finite commodity within an organization. For example, in a school, teachers become empowered if the principal gives some power to them. Site-based councils that control the school's budget would be an illustration of this version of power. However, a second version of empowerment is a process with a different view in which power becomes an infinite commodity that is available to everyone and produced by many in the organization. To expand the amount of power, the principal involves others in the basic decisions of the school. To illustrate this version of empowerment, Short and Greer used the statement, "The principal gains power by giving it away" (p. 13). Obviously, this version of empowerment is more closely associated with the kind of leadership a principal needs to help others become leaders. However, empowerment does not always come easy, and it usually initiates a learning process on the part of all involved. Learning how to empower and how to be empowered are important elements in leadership.

Certainly the school above other organizations should develop leadership capacity among its members. Compared with other organizations, most notably in the private sector, the majority of the participants in school organizations are educated, ethical, and well-meaning individuals who generally think and act as professionals. As Short and Greer (1997) stated, "They have a wealth of insight into the nature of the learning process and are able to apply such understandings to the problems of the school" (p. 14). Facilitating leadership in others provides principals with the avenue to share these understandings and, in so doing, helps the school improve in teaching and learning.

In this section we discuss the principal's and assistant principal's role in facilitating leadership in others. We will discuss the areas of facilitating leadership in culture and vision building, and then we will turn our attention to facilitating leadership through the tool of collaboration.

Facilitating Others in Understanding and Developing Culture

Earlier we discussed two of Deal and Peterson's (1999) suggested leader roles in understanding a school's culture, historian and anthropological sleuth. Deal and Peterson use six other roles that are connected to the principal's responsibility in helping others understand and develop school culture:

- *Visionary.* Works with other leaders and the community to define a deeply value-focused picture of the future for the school and has a constantly evolving vision.
- *Symbol.* Affirms values through dress, behavior, attention, and routines.
- *Potter.* Shapes and is shaped by the school's heroes, rituals, traditions, ceremonies, and symbols and brings in staff who share core values.
- *Poet.* Uses language to reinforce values and sustains the school's best image of itself.
- *Actor.* Improvises in the school's inevitable dramas, comedies, and tragedies.
- *Healer.* Oversees transitions and change in the life of the school and heals the wounds of conflict and loss (pp. 87–88).

Two roles warrant further discussion in facilitating others to shape the school culture: principal as symbol and as potter. Principals as symbols reflect what they do, attend to, and seem to appreciate. Teachers and community members constantly watch these interests and actions. They signal the values they hold. As Deal and Peterson (2000) suggested, seemingly innocuous actions send signals as to what leaders value. These authors suggested five possibilities that symbolize what principals and assistant principals can do.

- Symbolize core values in the way offices and classrooms are arranged
- Model values through the leader's demeanor and actions
- Use time to communicate what is important, what should be attended to
- Realize that what is appreciated, recognized, and honored signals the key values of what is admirable and achievable
- Recognize that official correspondence is a visible measure of values and reinforces the importance of what is being disseminated (pp. 207–208).

These five aspects of a principal's behavior exemplify the public persona that carries considerable meaning.

Principals as potters symbolize the way they shape elements in the school culture. Deal and Peterson (2000) suggested that principals help shape the culture in four ways:

1. They infuse shared values and beliefs into every aspect of the culture.
2. They anoint heroes and heroines, anointing and recognizing the best role models in the school.
3. They observe rituals as a means of building and maintaining *esprit de corps.*
4. They perpetuate meaningful, value-laden traditions and ceremonies.

We believe that the eight roles play into positive actions that principals can perform that will bind faculty, staff, students, parents, and other community members. There are some differences, however, in how these constituents will help in shaping a school's culture. In this subsection we address the needs of three audiences: internal veterans, internal newcomers, and external constituents.

Internal Veterans.   As mentioned earlier, one of the challenges you face as a new school leader is to view the school through a wider lens than you have previously. However, another equal challenge is for you to help teachers do the same. Since the historic one-room schoolhouses, teachers often have been kept isolated and remote from the total school organization. In fact, they were socialized to view their classroom as the only location where they performed their role. Thus many veteran teachers have had limited responsibility outside the classroom and seldom have become formally involved with the school organization. A common perception among some veteran teachers is that the role of the principal and assistant principal is to take care of the school and that the role of the teacher is to take care of the classroom.

Veteran teachers serve an important role in the cultural leadership of a school. They reinforce the values, beliefs, and behavioral norms of the school's culture to each other and to newcomers. They also check the principal's own susceptibility to being trapped by the culture (Crow, Matthews, and McCleary, 1996). Often they can be the loyal opposition, reminding and prodding the principal and assistant principals to be critical of certain cultural elements. For example, teachers can be helpful to the school's instructional culture by encouraging fewer classroom interruptions that can be distracting.

A major part of veteran teacher involvement in the school's culture is through subcultures. All schools have subcultures because functional differences single out special aspects of the school environment (Deal and Kennedy, 1982). Veteran teachers often form these subcultures around functional areas such as departments, grade levels, extracurricular activities, car pools, and certain causes, for example, the middle school concept in the opening vignette. Subcultures also can develop around socioeconomic and educational backgrounds, educational interests, gender, and out-of-school interests, for example, golf teams, bridge clubs, and religious groups. Each of these subcultures has its own values and beliefs, basic assumptions, and behavioral norms. Subcultures can shape beliefs and determine behaviors of others outside the subculture and can influence the culture as a whole. At times, these subcultures bump into each other and create conflict, which can be both healthy and troubling. These subcultures also can develop into toxic cultures and spread the toxicity into the larger school culture. However, in a healthy school culture, subcultures do not cause serious problems because the overall values and beliefs are strong enough to overcome the subculture's influence. In addition, the differences created by subcultures actually can add to the strength of the entire culture if diversity is welcome and appreciated (Deal and Kennedy, 1982).

To help veterans understand culture and subcultures and the implications that these subcultures play with the total organization, Deal and Kennedy (1982) offered the following suggestions that we have adapted to fit school cultures:

- *Encourage each subculture to enrich and understand its own cultural life.* Rather than be afraid of subcultures, a principal can encourage the positive aspects of the group. For instance, a principal can embrace the English Department's literary student publications and celebrations.

- *Help subcultures understand the problems and needs of other subcultures.* Principals can encourage members from various groups to participate on school-wide teams. Often such participation will help others understand different viewpoints.
- *Help teachers understand that the overall culture is richer because of the strength of subcultures.* Once the learning and sharing of problems of the subcultures are complete, you can help veteran teachers understand how each subculture brings unique strengths and values to the overall culture. Thus subculture conflict can be shown to add to the overall culture of the school.

Another way that principals and assistant principals facilitate veteran teachers in understanding and developing school culture is through routine activities. Saphier and King (1985) suggested that cultures are built through the daily business of school life. "Culture building occurs through the way people use educational, human, and technical skills in handling daily events or establishing regular practices" (p. 72). Deal and Kennedy (1982) also suggested that what people do is determined by what they value. The daily activities that are present in a school are good indicators for veteran teachers to understand what is important in that school. Principals can help teachers reflect on these activities and how they affect the school's culture.

A new principal decided that there would be no traditional Halloween carnival. His decision was based on a belief that the carnival caused the students to be more hyperactive and created unhealthy competition among students as they competed for the best costume awards. He assumed that although students would be disappointed, teachers and parents would understand the rationale behind his action. Surprisingly, the most vocal opponents to his decision were teachers and parents, who argued that the carnival was a long-standing school tradition. There was so much opposition to his decision that he ended up agreeing to retain the carnival. This principal learned the hard way that activities take on symbolic importance for the school culture. In this instance, the importance that teachers and parents gave to this activity made an important statement about what they valued.

Internal Newcomers. The other group of teachers who principals and assistant principals need to address in facilitating cultural leadership is newcomers who arrive on the scene after the culture is well established. New teachers often are forgotten or overlooked as to how they contribute to the school's culture. New teachers can be valuable sources of culture building, especially in helping change a culture.

Newcomers as part of the learning process point out the strengths and weaknesses in a school culture. The assumptions that lay hidden for veterans frequently are brought to the surface by newcomers. This process of exposing the cultural assumptions lays bare both the functional and dysfunctional elements of the culture. The principal can facilitate cultural leadership by recognizing newcomers' perspectives and encouraging veterans to listen to their viewpoints.

External Constituents. External constituents to the school are also a part of cultural leadership. Principals and assistant principals must encourage a dialogue with these constituents regarding the school's values and beliefs. In this regard, communication is not a one-way process in which principals transmit the values and beliefs of the school to parents and the community. Rather, communication needs to flow both ways so that there is an opportunity to listen to, be sensitive to, and address their concerns. School cultures cannot remain vibrant if they only emphasize the values and beliefs of faculty and staff members in the school and ignore the concerns of the community. "Principals must be actively involved in their communities, being sensitive to the ways communities are changing and to the views that external constituents have about what and how well schools are doing" (Crow, Matthews, & McCleary, 1996, p. 66).

Facilitating a Culture Change

Eventually it becomes necessary to facilitate cultural changes. Once it is determined that school culture must change, you can take several actions that will help make the change possible. First, you need to start with yourself. You must become aware of your own assumptions, values, and beliefs. As Schein (1992) suggested, "If . . . [leaders] cannot learn new assumptions themselves, they will not be able to perceive what is possible in their organization" (p. 380). As a school leader, you need to develop the ability to reflect on your own practice and the practice of others. We suggest a simple model: Reflect on what you have done in the past, analyze its impact, reflect on what you could or should have done, and then analyze what you need to do to bridge the gap. In other words, demonstrate double-loop learning (Argyris & Schon, 1974).

Second, as a school leader, you need to exhibit the emotional strength and sensitivity to manage your own and others' anxieties with change. Change creates anxiety. Deal and Peterson (1990) labeled this function of the leader as "healer." The principal as "healer recognizes the pain of transition and arranges events that make the transition a collective experience. Drawing people together to mourn loss and to renew hope is a significant part of the principal's culture-shaping role" (p. 30). Related to this idea is the role that mentors play within schools, as we discussed in Chapter 4. Mentors should be able to help you and others in understanding the anxieties that exist. New teachers especially should receive mentoring to help with the changes that come on top of their own newcomer anxieties.

Third, you can help the culture-changing process by involving others in understanding the social realities of the environment. Teachers and others may not recognize the changing demographics in the community. Likewise, many people may not have had the opportunity to diagnose the culture, or they have only a limited knowledge of the culture.

A fourth way of being involved in cultural change is using subcultures to change basic assumptions, values, beliefs, and behaviors. Subcultures can provide a psychological safety net that is often needed to allow teachers, students, and parents to deal with change. Subcultures also can provide the alternative assumptions that may need to be brought to light for the school to consider change. Rather than getting everyone to conform to the same set of assumptions, principals can take advantage of subcultures. These subcultures can help in changing cultural assumptions in the school. Related to the use of subcultures is the use of the loyal opposition. Block (1987) and Sergiovanni (1987) suggested that a loyal opposition could help leaders understand the reality and practicality of certain changes. As a principal or assistant principal, you will want to embrace those in your school who will offer challenging criticism because they often will help build the stronger ideas.

Facilitating Others in Vision Building

The principal as leader needs to attend to the two areas of process and content in facilitating a collective vision. Typically the content of vision is emphasized, giving the direction toward which the school is heading. Vision, however, also involves a process by which those in the school create the vision. Creating a vision "involves sharing ideas, clarifying and understanding the various points of view reflected in the community as well as the beliefs and assumptions underneath those points of view, negotiating differences and building a consensus" (Starratt, 1996, p. 50). The result of this process should be what Sergiovanni (1996) called "bonding," in which those in the school community become committed to the vision. If no bonding occurs (i.e., no agreement is achieved on the direction the school should take), then the result is a vision that has no commitment and will more than likely die. Many schools and school districts have had experience with visions that have died when they became involved in strategic planning movements. These strategic plans usually had good intentions, but the faculty and principal's commitment often was missing in the process, and consequently, the vision soon died.

The content of the school's vision is not created out of thin air. Visions include elements of the organization's culture that are already valued by most participants in the school. The content of the vision

> . . . should not be construed as a strategic plan that functions like a road map charting the turns needed to reach a specific reality that the leader has in mind. It should, instead, be viewed more as a compass that points the direction to be taken, that inspires enthusiasm, and that allows people to buy into and take part in the shaping of the way that will constitute the school's mission (Sergiovanni, 1995, pp. 163–164).

As we noted earlier in this chapter, the principal's personal vision may serve as a preliminary conception from which the collective vision is developed. Principals "may not possess the total content of the vision—no one does—but they should be willing to lay out a first attempt at articulating the content of a vision" (Starratt, 1996, p. 50). The principal's personal vision, or anyone's, must not become the final version. Preliminary visions may serve as guides to immediate action and places to begin a dialogue, but they should never serve as a sole direction for the future.

Teacher, Student, and Parent Roles in Vision Building.

Followers, that is, teachers, staff members, parents, students, and community members, can play at least three roles in developing visionary leadership: source of vision, sustainer of vision, and critic of vision (Crow, Matthews, & McCleary, 1996). As a source of vision, followers actually may provide the image or picture of the future. "Often some of the best ideas for new directions float up from the depths of the organization, but only if they are sought and welcomed when they arrive" (Nanus, 1992, p. 38). Teachers play an important role in vision building because they are in the position to do so as they perform in the trenches. A principal should never ignore teachers' suggestions as to the direction of the school because they are so close to the work of teaching and learning. Fortunately for Roosevelt Junior High School, Robert paid attention to Louise's ideas for the school's direction. Likewise, parents and students also can play an important role because of their close proximity to the learning process. Parents often can see the strengths and weaknesses of the school's instructional approach and should be encouraged to offer constructive comments. No principal in today's schools should ever ignore the constructive comments that parents can give regarding the school's instructional programs.

Teachers also play an important vision-building role as sustainers of the vision. Because teachers must be committed to the achievement of the vision, their role as sustainers of the collective vision is vital. Principal commitment is not enough to sustain a vision if teachers are not equally as committed. Their belief that a particular vision will work for the school at a particular time is critical to the vision process.

Teachers, students, and parents are also important as critics of visions. Teachers provide leadership by assessing the vision and suggesting ways that it can be redirected. From start to finish in vision building and implementing, principals need to listen carefully and sensitively to what others are saying about the significance and saliency of the school's vision. Listening to a respected teacher's criticism regarding the vision often will stave off serious criticism later and will help in building a stronger commitment to the vision.

Facilitating Teachers in Vision Building.   Earlier in this chapter we identified Nanus' (1992) four roles in vision building. Just as principals and assistant principals take on those four roles, they also encourage teachers, students, and parents to be direction setters, change agents, spokespersons, and coaches. These roles are too critical and too large to be performed by one person in the school. Beyond these four roles, you need to acknowledge the powerful personal visions that teachers bring to the school. Often these personal visions are overlooked as contributions to the school. Teachers' personal visions can be the catalysts for a school-wide vision (e.g., Louise's vision in the opening vignette). Because they perform in the trenches, teachers have sensitivity to what works and does not work. Your role as a facilitator is to encourage teachers to develop personal visions and then to express those visions to others. Robert's example in the opening vignette suggests that his encouragement over a period of years allowed teachers to develop strong personal visions. Robert's conferences with individual teachers prompted their personal vision building and expression. Teachers came to expect that their personal visions counted for something and that they had an opportunity to express their ideas for a school vision. It is not atypical for many teachers to have had ideas about school vision only to have the ideas thwarted by the school's bureaucracy.

Facilitating Others in Collaboration

We established earlier that leadership should come from a variety of sources in the school community. It would be wonderful if all teachers were to develop into leaders. For this to occur, however, a greater emphasis on leadership development needs to take place. Although schools differ, many exist as isolated workplaces where teachers work mostly alone in their rooms and interact with each other in faculty rooms. In these schools, teachers feel separated from one another and seldom engage in professional dialogue, reflection, or sharing. In other schools, teachers engage in professional dialogue with colleagues; share ideas, knowledge, and methods; and participate in problem-solving issues. We propose that in collaborative schools, collegiality is valued and reinforced, and leadership emerges. Principals and assistant principals can facilitate leadership among others through a collaborative culture. Our discussion will focus on five aspects of facilitating a collaborative culture: deciding to collaborate, developing collaboration, collaborative teaming, mediating conflict, and understanding problems that can arise.

Deciding to Collaborate. In the current rhetoric of school reform, principals and assistant principals could come away with the view that collaboration is the panacea to cure all school ills. However, collaboration has its costs (Pounder, 1998), some of which we will address later in this chapter. Here, however, it is important to discuss when collaboration is appropriate for building professional learning communities and promoting success for all students. Based on their review of literature, Hoy and Miskel (1996) identified three tests for determining when to share decision making: relevance, expertise, and commitment. The test of relevance applied to teachers asks whether they have a personal stake in the decisions or the outcomes of the collaboration. For example, collaborating on decisions regarding resurfacing the parking lot is not likely to engender a great deal of enthusiasm for collaboration. The test of expertise asks whether teachers have the expertise to collaborate on foreign-language curricular adoptions and innovations. However, this test must be applied carefully. An administrator may decide that teachers do not have expertise in an area in which they have a personal stake, but the administrator has a responsibility if the other tests apply to determine whether professional development to provide the expertise is warranted. The test of commitment asks if teachers are committed to the mission of the school such that their decisions will be in the best interests of the school. Again, this becomes a major judgment for an administrator. If personal interests are likely to outweigh organizational ones, the administrator may decide that collaboration in a particular area is not in the best interest of the school. However, this decision should be based on ample evidence from multiple sources to ensure that the lack of commitment exists and is not being used by the administrator to avoid opposing views. Collaboration is not a panacea, but when used sensitively and appropriately to enrich the learning community and enhance learning for all students, it is a powerful tool.

One other factor also should be considered in deciding if collaboration is appropriate to solve a particular problem. You need to consider the time that is available before a decision needs to be made. If time is short, then collaboration probably is not the best decision-making approach. However, you must be sure that the decision needs to be made rapidly. Many decisions are made "off the cuff" when they could have been given more deliberation. Decisions that are made in crises, especially those that affect the safety of students, obviously require immediate action.

Developing Collaboration. Moving toward collaborative problem solving and collaborative decision making needs to be developed over time and in consideration of the school's culture. Moving too fast can produce disappointing and wrong decisions. As you consider developing collaboration, several approaches should be considered. Figure 6.1 shows the kinds of decision-making approaches.

The first approach involves unilateral decision making. The principal can make the decision without input from others. In some emergency or urgent situations, this approach would be most appropriate. The second approach is consulting. The principal consults with individuals, gathers the needed information, and decides based on the information received. The third approach is advisory. The principal seeks input and suggestions from the entire team, and the principal makes the decision, which may or may not reflect the team's suggestions. With the fourth approach, the principal shares the problem with the team, and the team offers a recommended decision. The principal considers the decision and decides to accept or reject the team's decision. The fifth approach involves a collaborative team effort with the principal as an equal team member. Consensus is desirable for the final decision, but majority vote may be acceptable. The sixth approach involves the principal offering the problem to the team and then stepping back and allowing the team to collaborate and reach consensus or vote. The seventh approach is placing trust in the team by allowing it to find and determine the problem and then collaborate as to the best decision. This approach shares the governance with the team, and the team actually makes authoritative decisions.

Collaborative Teaming.   An important aspect of collaborative cultures involves professionals working together in teams. Collaborative schools devote considerable time to working in groups on various projects and programs. For example, in a middle school, teams can be used for integrated curriculum planning, advisory class activities, and student problems (Pounder, 1998). The research on teamwork by Maeroff (1993) suggested that teams need skills and knowledge in the following areas:

- Group roles
- Stages of group development
- Leadership in small groups
- Effective communication
- Trust building
- Problem solving, planning, and decision making
- Effective ways to conduct meetings
- Conflict resolution
- Group process evaluation

Without developing team process skills, many teams with great intentions fail to reach conclusive results. Because many school leaders and teachers have had few successful opportunities to collaborate in team settings, it is important that development be offered. In one school several veteran teachers refused to commit time and energy to school teams because of some past team efforts. They had previously committed time to teams that ended in disagreement with no team consensus. It is hard to blame these teachers' reluctance in pursuing new team efforts when their experience had been so negative. In other situations teams are given initial training, but ongoing professional development

Approach 7:
The team functions in problem identification and solving and only involves the principal if necessary.

Approach 6:
The principal shares the problem with the team and allows the team to decide without the principal's participation.

Approach 5:
The principal shares the problem with a team in which he or she is an equal member.

Approach 4:
The principal shares the problem with the team, the team offers suggestions, and the principal decides based on their recommendations.

Approach 3:
The principal shares the problem or issue with a team of teachers to get the team's input, decides, and communicates it to the faculty.

Approach 2:
The principal gathers information from other individuals, decides, and communicates to the faculty.

Approach 1:
The principal makes the decision and communicates it to the faculty.

FIGURE 6.1   Approaches to Decision Making.

is frequently ignored. Research emphasizes that the professional development needs of teams are different at different stages in the teaming process (Crow & Pounder, 2000). As principal or assistant principal, you need to help these teachers with group process skill development that will alleviate some of the team problems.

Mediating Conflict.   Because interaction among people is high in collaborative teams and with school improvement efforts, conflict is inevitable. As we emphasized in Chapter 3, newly defined work roles in contemporary schools also are likely to involve conflict due to greater interaction among roles. *Conflict* refers to the thwarting of goal attainment between and among people. Conflict is not necessarily a sign of weaknesses or destructiveness. However, too much conflict or conflict that is not resolved can interfere with an organization's effectiveness and eventually can cause toxicity in the culture. Although conflict occurs, it may go hidden in some schools for long periods of time. As a principal or assistant principal, one of your greatest responsibilities will be to both identify and mediate conflict effectively.

Identifying the specific sources of conflict in school settings is a complex matter. Organizational variables, interpersonal issues, and personality characteristics influence the conflicts that are experienced by principals, teachers, and others in the school (Welch & Sheridan, 1995). For example, organizational variables such as leadership styles, communication norms, and decision-making practices can trigger conflict among the various stakeholders in the school. Interpersonal factors also contribute to conflict in various ways. Interpersonal conflict can originate from the different expectations that people have toward roles in the school, especially the expectations that teachers may have toward the principal's or assistant principal's role. Finally, personality characteristics such as highly aggressive and competitive behaviors can create conflict among individuals in groups.

Although various writers have speculated as to methods and models for conflict mediation, there does not seem to be one generally accepted method. In fact, leaders dealing with conflict successfully have used various strategies. It also may be necessary for some conflict to go to arbitration. A third party who is not emotionally involved with the situation may give insight into solving the conflict.

Friend and Cook (1992) identified five conflict-management strategies that vary along the dimensions of cooperativeness and assertiveness. They include competitive, avoidance, accommodation, compromise, and collaboration. Each conflict-management strategy has its strengths and its weaknesses. Persons who use a competitive strategy are assertive and opt less to cooperate with others. Winning becomes the most important endeavor regardless if their ideas are good or bad. On the other hand, avoidant strategies of conflict management are characterized as uncooperative and unassertive. These people tend to withdraw in the face of conflict, perceiving both their own goals and relationships as low in importance. In schools or in teams that comprise avoiders, conflict continues because no one is willing to address and resolve it. A person with an accommodating style believes that relationships are more important than personal goals and thus demonstrates cooperativeness but little assertiveness.

Two strategies use a balance of cooperativeness and assertiveness. A compromising style uses both cooperativeness and assertiveness but at a moderate degree. Compromisers sacrifice some of their own ideas and solutions and press others to do the same. The outcome is usually a common ground where issues are addressed and a political solution is chosen so that both conflicting parties make some gains. The collaborative strategy tends to be both highly assertive and highly cooperative. These people may see the conflict as an opportunity to seek out better solutions and achieve a better outcome.

None of these strategies is completely good or completely bad. The use of a particular strategy may be more effective in some situations than in others. For example, faced with an emergency, you may have to employ a competitive style and aggressively tell people to evacuate the building with little concern about how people feel about it. Another example could be that as an assistant principal you avoid a conflict because there are other more important and pressing needs at the time.

Problems with Collaboration.   Fullan and Hargreaves (1996) argued that some kinds of collaboration are best avoided and some are a waste of time. They identified three forms of collaboration that could pose problems in the school: balkanization, comfortable collaboration, and contrived collegiality.

In some schools, teachers associate more closely with some of their colleagues' in-group behaviors at the expense of the school as a whole. Fullan and Hargreaves (1996) identified these kinds of schools as having a balkanized teacher culture—"a culture made up of separate and sometimes competing groups, jockeying for position and supremacy like loosely connected, independent states" (p. 52). They also suggested that balkanized cultures are a familiar feature of junior and senior high schools because of the subject and department structures on which these schools are based. However, elementary schools also can feature balkanization, primarily when teachers separate into various divisions such as early grades or upper grades or within certain wings of the school building. Fullan and Hargreaves also cautioned that "innovation-oriented subgroups such as those found in team teaching or peer coaching" (p. 54) may develop into balkanized groups and actually impede the collaborative culture of the school as a whole.

Collaborative teams can become bounded in the sense that they do not reach down into the principles or ethics of practice. In so doing, they become stuck with the more comfortable business of advice giving, trick trading, and material sharing. Fullan and Hargreaves (1996) suggested that such collaboration does not extend beyond particular units of work or subjects to the wider purpose of what is taught and how it is taught. "It is collaboration that focuses on the immediate, the short-term, and the practical to the exclusion of longer-term planning concerns" (pp. 55–56). As they suggested, collegiality should not stop at congeniality. It is too easy to avoid searching discussions and joint work that might expose disagreements and conflict. "This kind of collaboration is too cozy" (p. 57).

Because collaborative cultures do not evolve quickly, they can be unattractive to educators who want quick implementation. Collaborative teams are also unpredictable, which can be disconcerting to school principals. What collaborative teams develop may not correspond with the principal's preferred purposes or fit into current school board priorities. The unpredictability of collaborative teams can lead administrators toward forms of collegiality that they can control. These more controlled approaches toward collaboration are what Hargreaves and Dawe (1990) called *contrived collegiality*. They defined contrived collegiality as being characterized by a set of formal, specific bureaucratic procedures to increase the attention being given to various forms of collaboration, such as peer coaching, mentoring, and site-based management. These sorts of initiatives are administrative contrivances designed to get collegiality going in schools where little has existed before. They are meant to encourage greater association among teachers and to foster more sharing, learning, and improvement of skills and expertise. So where does the problem lie? Contrived collegiality is double-edged. Fullan and Hargreaves (1996) suggested that at best, contrived collegiality could be a useful preliminary phase in setting up more enduring collaborative relationships among teachers. In fact, some contrivance is necessary in the establishment of virtually all collaborative cultures. Scheduling joint preparation times, releasing teachers to plan together, arranging teacher visits to other classrooms, and allowing a team of teachers to attend a workshop—all these situations can be contrived to create conditions for collaboration.

At its worst, however, contrived collegiality can be reduced to a quick and slick administrative substitute for collaborative teacher cultures. Colleagueships are imposed administratively. For example, a peer coaching relationship that mandates teachers to work together on improving classroom instruction is an imposed collegiality. It may meet certain administrative ambitions but probably makes no lasting cultural changes. As Fullan and Hargreaves (1996) suggested, "Collaborative cultures do not mandate collegial support and partnership: they foster and facilitate it" (p. 59) and "over managing collegiality is something to avoid" (p. 60). When it is used in a facilitative, not a controlling, way, contrived collegiality can provide a starting point for collaborative cultures. However, a strong collaborative culture takes time, patience, and learning.

One other point is worth discussing about collaborative cultures. There is some evidence by researchers (e.g., Shakeshaft, 1987) that women's socialization prepares them better to develop and facilitate collaborative cultures than men's socialization. For example, women more than men tend to mediate conflict to protect relationships and to be less inclined to settle for a win-lose situation. These findings do not mean that women will make better principals or that they will always be more collaborative. Both men and women principals need to learn how to facilitate collaboration in schools. However, as more women move into principalships, our models of understanding effective leadership more than likely will involve facilitating more collaborative cultures in schools.

Conclusion

In this chapter we identified the importance of the leadership role for the principal and assistant principal. After a discussion of what leadership is and does, we identified important areas on which you need to focus your energies: culture, vision, communication, and collaboration. As in the other roles, we also discussed ways that principals and assistant principals facilitate others in developing leadership.

The opening vignette illustrated how a collaborative culture builds leadership and helps develop a learning environment in a school. As the principal, Robert was not the only leader in Roosevelt Junior High School. Many teachers were as committed as he and showed their commitment by their dedication to the school, their teaching, and the students. They were much more valuable in implementing a change such as the middle school concept because of their commitment. When teachers are not committed, they tend to be less valuable to organizational change efforts.

Learning to become a principal or assistant principal who works to develop a learning community and improve instruction also means learning how to manage change. In the next chapter we discuss the important role of principal as manager and explain how this role is related to instructional improvement.

Activities

Self-Reflecting Activities

1. Talk to the custodian and secretary in your school. What are their perceptions of the instructional program in the school? How do they influence leadership in the school?

2. Reflect critically on your own leadership as a teacher. How would you characterize your style and behavior as a leader?
3. What is the vision of your current school? What is its mission?

Peer Reflecting Activities

1. With your colleagues discuss principals with whom you have worked. Analyze their leadership in terms of the proportion of task versus person orientation. How well do these two orientations describe your principals' leadership?
2. Compare and contrast the vision and mission of your schools. To what degree is the vision a collective one or only the principal's personal vision?
3. From your experiences, how do principals facilitate the leadership of parents and community members in their schools?

Course Activities

1. Role-play and discuss a meeting between the principal at Roosevelt Junior High School in the opening vignette and a group of parents. What kinds of issues might parents raise regarding the middle school concept.
2. Discuss Rost's definition of leadership presented in this chapter and in Chapter 1. What are its strengths and weaknesses for defining school leadership?
3. Assign biographies of various well-known leaders, for example, Gandhi, Eleanor Roosevelt, Martin Luther King, Jr., or Mother Teresa. In addition to discussing their traits, discuss what aspects of leadership are not included in the biographies.
4. Have each student conduct a culture audit of his or her current school using the Deal and Peterson questions for understanding school culture presented earlier in this chapter. Discuss the results of the audits in terms of similarities and differences. Identify patterns, such as leaders' characteristics, community type, or school level (elementary/middle/secondary).

Websites

■ *http://www.ucea.org/cases/*
Cases from the Journal of Cases in Educational Leadership
Detert, J., & Detert, N. R. (2001). The family learning center charter school: Leadership and accountability at the crossroads. *Journal of Cases in Educational Leadership 4*(2).
Welch, T., & Rinehart, J. S. (1998). Consensus of the council? *Journal of Cases in Educational Leadership 1*(1).

■ *http://www.nassp.org*
National Association of Secondary School Principals

■ *http://www.naesp.org*
National Association of Elementary School Principals

■ *http://www.nea.org*
National Education Association

■ *http://www.nmsa.org*
National Middle School Association

References

Argyris, C., & Schon, D. (1974). *Theory in Practice: Increasing Professional Effectiveness*. San Francisco: Jossey-Bass.

Barnard, C. (1948). *Organizations and Management*. Cambridge, MA: Harvard University Press.

Barth, R. S. (1990). *Improving Schools from Within: Teachers, Parents, and Principals Can Make the Difference*. San Francisco: Jossey-Bass.

Beck, L. G., & Murphy, J. (1993). *Understanding the Principalship: Metaphorical Themes, 1920s–1990s*. New York: Teachers College Press.

Blackmore, J. (1991). Man the administrator. In *Images of Educational Administration*. Geelong, Australia: Deakin University.

Blake, R. R., & Mouton, J. S. (1978). *The New Managerial Grid*. Houston, TX: Gulf Press.

Blase, J. J. (1989). The micropolitics of the school: The everyday political orientation of teachers toward open school principals. *Educational Administration Quarterly 25*(4), 377–407.

Blase, J. J. (1991). The micropolitical orientation of teachers toward closed school principals. *Education and Urban Society 23*(4), 356–378.

Block, P. (1987). *The Empowered Manager*. San Francisco: Jossey-Bass.

Block, P. (1993). *Stewardship: Choosing Service over Self-Interest*. San Francisco: Berrett-Koehler.

Bower, M. (1996). *Will to Manage*. New York: McGraw-Hill.

Burns, J. M. (1978). *Leadership*. New York: Harper & Row.

Cheng, Y. C. (1993). Profiles of organizational culture and effective schools. *School Effectiveness and School Improvement 4*(2), 85–110.

Crow, G. M., Matthews, L. J., & McCleary, L. E. (1996). *Leadership: A Relevant and Realistic Role for Principals*. Princeton, NJ: Eye on Education.

Crow, G. M., & Pounder, D. G. (2000). Teacher work groups: Context, design, and process. *Educational Administration Quarterly 36*(2), 216–254.

Cuban, L. (1988). Why do some reforms persist? *Educational Administration Quarterly 24*(3), 329–335.

Daft, R. L. (1999). *Leadership Theory and Practice*. Fort Worth, TX: Dryden Press.

Deal, T. E., & Peterson, K. E. (1990). *The Principal's Role in Shaping School Culture*. Washington, DC: U.S. Department of Education.

Deal, T. E., & Kennedy, A. A. (1982). *Corporate Cultures: The Rites and Rituals of Corporate Life*. Reading, MA: Addison-Wesley.

Deal, T. E., & Peterson, K. D. (1999). *Shaping School Culture: The Heart of Leadership*. San Francisco: Jossey-Bass.

Deal, T. E., & Peterson, K. D. (2000). Eight roles of symbolic leaders, *The Jossey-Bass Reader on Educational Leadership* (pp. 202–214). San Francisco: Jossey-Bass.

Fiedler, F. E. (1967). *A Theory of Leadership Effectiveness*. New York: McGraw-Hill.

Fleishman, E. A., & Harris, E. F. (1962). Patterns of leadership behavior related to employee grievances and turnover. *Personnel Psychology 15*, 43–56.

Friend, M., & Cook, C. (1992). *Interactions: Collaboration Skills for School Professionals*. New York: Longman.

French, J. R. P., Jr., & Raven, B. H. (1959). The bases of social power. In D. Cartwright (Ed.), *Studies in Social Power* (pp. 150–167). Ann Arbor: Institute for Social Research, University of Michigan.

Fullan, M. (1999). *Change Forces: The Sequel*. Philadelphia: Falmer Press.

Fullan, M. (1992). Visions that blind. *Educational Leadership 49*(5), 19–20.

Fullan, M. & Hargreaves, A. (1996). *What's Worth Fighting for in Your School?* New York: Teachers College Press.

Greenleaf, R. (1970). *The Servant as Leader*. Indianapolis: The Robert K. Greenleaf Center.

Hargreaves, A. & Dawe, R. (1990). Paths of professional development: Contrived collegiality, collaborative cultures, and the case of peer coaching. *Teaching and Teacher Education, 6*(3), 227–241.

Hersey, P., & Blanchard, K. H. (1977). *Management of Organizational Behavior: Utilizing Human Resources* (3rd ed.). Englewood Cliffs, NJ: Prentice-Hall.

House, R. J. (1974). A path-goal theory of leadership effectiveness. *Administrative Science Quarterly* (Autumn), 81–97.

Hoy, W. K., & Miskel, C. G. (1996). *Educational Administration: Theory, Research, and Practice* (5th ed.). New York: McGraw-Hill.

Hoyle, J. R. (1995). *Leadership and Futuring: Making Visions Happen.* Thousand Oaks, CA: Corwin Press.

Johnson, S. M. (1990). *Teachers at Work: Achieving Success in Our Schools.* New York: Basic Books.

Katz, D., & Kahn, R. L. (1966, 1978). *The Social Psychology of Organizations.* New York: Wiley.

Katz, D., Maccoby, N., & Morse, N. (1950). *Productivity, Supervision, and Morale in an Office Situation.* Ann Arbor, MI: Institute for Social Research.

Kirkpatrick, S. A., & Locke, E. A. (1991). Leadership: Do traits matter? *Academy of Management Executives 5*(2), 48–60.

Lewin, K., & Lippet, R. (1938). An experimental approach to the study of autocracy and democracy: A preliminary note. *Sociometry 1*, 292–300.

Likert, R. (1961). *New Patterns of Management.* New York: McGraw-Hill.

Lortie, D. C. (1975). *Schoolteacher: A Sociological Study.* Chicago: University of Chicago Press.

Louis, K. S., & Murphy, J. (1994). The evolving role of the principal: Some concluding thoughts. In J. Murphy & K. S. Louis (Eds.), *Reshaping the Principalship: Insights from Transformational Reform Efforts.* Thousand Oaks, CA: Corwin Press.

Maeroff, G. I. (1993). *Team Building for School Change: Equipping Teachers for New Roles.* New York: Teachers College Press.

McCreary, J. (2001). Getting clubbed over a club. *Journal of Cases in Educational Leadership 4*(1); retrieved from *www.ucea.org/cases*.

Murphy, J. (1994). Transformational change and the evolving role of the principal: Early empirical evidence. In J. Murphy & K. S. Louis (Eds.), *Reshaping the Principalship: Insights from Transformational Reform Efforts.* Thousand Oakes, CA: Corwin Press.

Nanus, B. (1992). *Visionary Leadership: Creating a Compelling Sense of Direction for Your Organization.* San Francisco: Jossey-Bass.

Newmann, F. M., & Associates (1996). *Authentic Instruction: Restructuring Schools for Intellectual Quality.* San Francisco: Jossey-Bass.

Odden, A. R. (1995). *Educational Leadership for America's Schools.* New York: McGraw-Hill.

Ogawa, R. T., & Bossert, S. T. (1995). Leadership as an organizational quality. *Educational Administration Quarterly 31*(2), 224–243.

Parson, T. (1951). *The Social System.* Glencoe, IL: Free Press.

Peters, T., & Waterman, J. R. H. (1982). *In Search of Excellence: Lessons from America's Best-Run Companies.* New York: Warner Books.

Pfeffer, J. (1978). The micropolitics of organizations. In M. W. Meyer (Ed.), *Environments and Organizations* (pp. 29–50). San Francisco: Jossey-Bass.

Pounder, D. G. (Ed.) (1998). *Restructuring Schools for Collaboration.* Albany, NY: State University of New York Press.

Rost, J. C. (1991). *Leadership in the Twenty-First Century.* New York: Praeger.

Saphier, J., & King, M. (1985). Good seeds grow in strong cultures. *Educational Leadership 42*(6), 67–74.

Sashkin, M. (1988). The visionary leader. In J. Conger & R. Kanungo (Eds.), *Charismatic Leadership: The Elusive Factor in Organizational Effectiveness.* San Francisco: Jossey-Bass.

Schein, E. H. (1992). *Organizational Culture and Leadership* (2d ed.). San Francisco: Jossey-Bass.

Senge, P. (1990). *The Fifth Discipline: The Art and Practice of the Learning Organization.* New York: Doubleday.

Sergiovanni, T. J. (1987). *The Principalship: A Reflective Practice Perspective.* Boston, MA: Allyn and Bacon.

Sergiovanni, T. J. (1992). *Moral Leadership: Getting to the Heart of School Improvement.* San Francisco: Jossey-Bass.

Sergiovanni, T. J. (1995). *The Principalship: A Reflective Practice.* Boston: Allyn and Bacon.

Shakeshaft, C. (1987). *Women in Educational Administration.* Newbury Park, CA: Sage.

Short, P. M., & Greer, J. T. (1997). *Leadership in Empowered Schools: Themes from Innovative Efforts.* Englewood Cliffs, NJ: Prentice-Hall.

Snowden, P. E., & Gorton, R. A. (1998). *School Leadership and Administration: Important Concepts , Case Studies and Simulations* (5th ed.). New York: McGraw-Hill.

Starratt, R. J. (1993). *The Drama of Leadership.* London: Falmer Press.

Starratt, R. J. (1996). *Transforming Educational Administration: Meaning, Community, and Excellence.* New York: McGraw-Hill

Stolp, S. (1994). Leadership for school culture. *ERIC Digest 91*, 1–4.

Tannenbaum, A. S. (1962). Control in organizations: Individual adjustment and organizational performance. *Administrative Science Quarterly 7*, 236–257.

Thompson, J. D. (1967). *Organizations in Action.* New York: McGraw-Hill.

Vroom, V. H., & Jago, A. G. (1988). *The New Leadership: Managing Participation in Organizations.* Englewood Cliffs, NJ: Prentice-Hall.

Watkins, P. (1986). *A Critical View of Leadership Concepts and Research: The Implications for Educational Administration.* Geelong: Deakin University.

Weick, K. E. (1985). The significance of culture. In P. J. Frost, L. F. Moore, M. R. Louis, C. C. Lundberg, & J. Martin (Eds.), *Organizational Culture.* Beverly Hills, CA: Sage Publications.

Welch, M. & Sheridan, S. (1995). *Educational Partnerships: Serving Students at Risk.* Fort Worth, TX: Harcourt Brace.

Yukl, G. A. (1994). *Leadership in Organizations* (5th ed.). Englewood Cliffs, NJ: Prentice Hall.

Principal as Manager

7

Key Terms and Concepts

assessment	shared decision making	systems thinking
evaluation	site-based management	tactical plans
school-based budgeting	strategic plans	

Vignette

Three weeks into his administrative internship, Abe Rosenblatz was still excited each morning as he came into his small office at his assigned middle school. After 14 years as a journalism teacher, he enjoyed the new direction in his career. Although he had enjoyed teaching, he was rejuvenated with his university course work and administrative internship. He was facing his new challenges with enthusiasm and vigor. Although extremely busy with his studies, internship, and family responsibilities, he cherished these opportunities to learn and advance in his career.

Abe was troubled, nevertheless, by one aspect of his internship. In his evening courses on campus he was excited to learn more about leadership, especially instructional leadership. He had recently read Linda Lambert's (1998) book, *Building Leadership Capacity in Schools*. In his internship he was too busy with administrative matters to do much of anything in improving the instruction in the school. His observations of the other three administrators in the school indicated that they too were more involved with day-to-day management activities than they were in leading the school to improve instructional capacity. He had envisioned that the principal and the assistant principals would be visiting classrooms, talking with teachers, meeting with curriculum committees, and planning professional development. Instead, he found none of these activities in the first three weeks of his internship.

As he talked to his mentor about this dilemma, the principal only said, "Welcome to administration. I remember the same classes on leadership. The reality is that we have to hold down the fort here. The teachers expect that of us, and so does the district office. If we did not, we wouldn't be around here very long." After saying these words to Abe, the principal was prompted by his secretary to answer a telephone call, an assistant principal

173

started asking the principal about the afternoon assembly, and a teacher was knocking on the principal's office door wanting to get a purchase order signed. The principal shrugged his shoulders, raised his eyebrows, and gave a little nod to Abe, as if saying, "See what I mean?"

After the conversation, Abe returned to his small office, picked up his daily planner, checked on his next to-do item, and went to work. He tackled each of his assigned tasks with vigor and enthusiasm. It was not that he disliked the daily tasks, but he wanted to work more with teachers and instructional programs. He silently resolved that when he became an assistant principal, he would somehow organize his schedule to allow for more impact with instructional matters.

Introduction

As you have observed principals in action, you invariably have seen managers at work. In fact, many observers see the principal's largest and most time-consuming task as that of managing the affairs of the school. At the same time, however, many teachers, district administrators, and policymakers want more from principals and assistant principals than just managing the schools. Although from its early roots the principal's role was that of managing the building and those who work in it, in recent years the roles of manager and leader often have become conflictual—or at least this has appeared to be so. Principal candidates such as you often have learned that leadership is more important than management and especially that good principals need to be good instructional leaders. You could face the same dilemma as Abe Rosenblatz as you enter administrative practice. You may find the dilemma of what you learned the role is supposed to be and what the realities of the position actually are.

In this chapter we acknowledge the important role that principals and assistant principals play in the management of schools. We heartily endorse the concept that the role of the principal as manager is key in the daily planning, organizing, operating, executing, budgeting, maintaining, and scheduling of numerous processes, activities, and tasks that permit a school to accomplish its goals as a learning community. Above all, the management role includes the routine behaviors and tasks that must take place daily to establish and keep a safe and secure school. However, many of these tasks are school-specific and are not taught easily from a textbook or a course. This does not mean that these tasks are less important because, in fact, they are very important. For instance, safe-school issues are much more emphasized in contemporary schools than they were a decade ago. Principals and assistant principals have the sacred responsibility of protecting children while they are coming, going, and attending school. Learning safe-school strategies is probably best done in the field, learning from your internship and mentor principals. Our attempt in this chapter is to acknowledge the importance of these tasks and to emphasize the management role in the context of building a strong school culture and establishing a shared vision that encompasses school improvement and promotes learning for *all* students.

Too often principals fall into the trap of managing without really improving. We believe that as Speck (1999) described it, effective management helps a school achieve its goals in part by making the school function well enough to allow the leadership roles of the principal, assistant principal, teachers, and others to emerge. Principals and assistant principals do not have to be bogged down in the managerial tasks of the school at the expense of good leadership. Furthermore, school leaders who claim that they do not have time for improving instruction do so because they either do not know how to go about improvement efforts or choose not to take on those improvements because of the assumed risks involved. As a principal or assistant principal, you need to make sure that schedules work, textbooks are ordered, halls and classrooms are swept, and students are safe. However, you should not be fooled into thinking that success as a principal or assistant principal ends with orderly lunchrooms, quiet hallways, or computerized student records. Furthermore, you must not forget that students should be the ultimate beneficiaries of all management actions and that your role as a school leader is to improve their learning in the school.

This chapter begins with a review of the historical perspectives of the scientific management movement that has affected the principal's role. We especially consider the importance of the principal's role in managing school reform and improvement. Because improvement efforts are shifting toward whole-school reform in which the goal is wholesale institutional transformation rather than piecemeal tinkering, we also discuss how principals can facilitate others in building management capacity.

The Principalship and Management Roots

As described in Chapter 2, the role of the principal changed in the early part of the 20th century, and a larger portion of the principal's time was allocated to general management activities. Pierce (1935) noted that by the turn of the century, the principal had become the directing manager rather than the presiding teacher of the school. An initial approach to educational administration was grounded in the scientific management and industrial efficiency tenets of Frederick W. Taylor. This movement grew out of a reform era in which the administrative functions of school districts were being centralized under strong superintendents. The scientific management approach asserted that educational organizations, like commercial establishments, should be business-like and efficient. Tasks and responsibilities should be defined carefully and planned fully to lead to maximized organizational productivity. Organizational scholars such as Henri Fayol and Luther Gulick suggested that organizations should be structured systematically at the top with specialized divisions in a hierarchical model to cause the entire organization to pull together efficiently as a total organic unit. Close coordination and control of subordinate behavior were considered vital to overall efficiency, and an administrator should be careful not to distribute responsibilities among lower-level employees beyond the bounds of what each manager could fully supervise. One culmination of the scientific management effort was Gulick's (1937) master list of things managers do, abbreviated in the acronym POSD-CoRB: planning, organizing, staffing, directing, coordinating, reporting, and budgeting.

Raymond Callahan's (1962) book, *Education and the Cult of Efficiency*, provided an interesting description and critique of the impact of scientific management on the field of education. From the management of classroom instruction through the school system hierarchy, educational organizations were designed for efficiency. Standardized testing, record systems and reports, and score cards for buildings provided a systematic information system for the educational administrator. Studies of cost economics and time usage, even an efficiency index of pupil study habits, were added to the list of what should be considered in judging managerial effectiveness in education. Standards of behavior, qualifications for entry-level jobs, and detailed instructions for job performance were all incorporated into specifications for teachers and administrators.

Gross (1994) labeled the working doctrine of the scientific management era as the "gospel of efficiency" because the dedication of its adherents was of a quasi-religious intensity. It was believed that educational administration could best be improved by the scientific application of managerial expertise. This included carefully planned schedules for work, the instructions for doing it, and the expected standards of performance (Morris et al., 1984).

Many historians believe that the scientific management movement was perfect for its time in education because it indicated the critical importance of organizational management. To the newly developing profession of educational administration, the gospel of efficiency offered a role description similar to managers in other fields, especially in the private sector. This movement added legitimacy to the role and elevated it to the level of other community leaders.

Some critics of education today argue that our schools need to be more tightly managed—a return to the earlier scientific management theories. Other critics argue that our school systems are too tightly managed and often ignore local and individual interests at the expense of the whole system. The debate over principals being managers or leaders has been ongoing for most of a century, and there is little evidence that it will discontinue in the near future. You can be assured that this debate will continue for much of your career. The important matter for you to consider as a new principal or assistant principal is not only understanding these management roots but also assessing your school and its culture as to management expectations. Schools and school districts have different expectations as to management levels and styles. Some schools and districts adhere more closely to the scientific management routines, with a bureaucratic organization in the district. Other schools are experiencing a movement to decentralize, having decision making be more school-based. This movement, often called *site-based management*, places more responsibility and management on the school level rather than on the district level. The site-based management movement does not mean, however, that the principal has more autonomy. Rather, *shared decision making* and *collaborative problem solving* usually refer to the expectations that community members, teachers, and administrators will work together to solve the school's problems and establish a collective vision. Understanding your district's and school's management style is critical for your understanding of the role you will be expected to take and for the boundaries of role making.

In the opening vignette, Abe faced a dilemma that many beginning school leaders encounter. At times it is difficult to be an instructional leader when maintaining an orderly school because managing the school is often so time consuming. However, many principals and assistant principals needlessly get sucked into the drain of maintaining without ever attempting real improvement efforts.

Sergiovanni (1987) provided a perspective on the relationship between the management and leadership roles of the principalship:

> Distinctions between management and leadership are useful for theorists and help to clarify and sort various activities and behaviors of principals. For practical purposes, however, both emphases should be considered as necessary and important aspects of a principal's

administrative style. The choice is not whether a principal is leader or manager but whether the two emphases are in balance, and, indeed, whether they complement each other [p. 16].

Perhaps, the best way to distinguish between managerial and leadership functions is to think of the two not as separate tasks but rather as a combined conceptualized role of the principal. Surely certain tasks will tend to be more managerial than leadership, but the principal's role should be conceptualized as one in which both leadership and management are important. This role is especially necessary for school reform and instructional improvement. It is in these areas that we turn to understand how managing reform is a vital role for school leadership.

Management for School Reform

In Chapter 6 we distinguished ways for principals to provide leadership for school reform, namely, through culture, vision, and communication and collaboration. In this section we discuss the way in which principals and assistant principals manage school reform and improvement efforts in teaching and learning. We suggest four major areas in which management efforts are especially important: supporting, planning, action taking, and evaluating.

Supporting

A not so obvious factor in managing reform efforts is to allow these efforts to take place. Often the school culture prevents reform efforts from getting under way, or if they do get under way, they are soon abandoned. Principals and assistant principals are fundamental in creating a nonthreatening school culture where reform and change are endorsed. Hall (1986) claimed, "Throughout our years of research and experience, we have never seen a situation in which the principal was not a significant factor in the efforts of schools to improve" (p. 1). Principals need to facilitate these improvement efforts by supporting good reform ideas. For example, if teachers propose a peer mentoring program within the school (as outlined in Chapter 4), the principal either supports or obstructs the effort by the support that is given either implicitly or explicitly. The teachers either move the idea forward or are reluctant to continue. Subsequent ideas by the teachers for improvement efforts will be affected if they perceive that their ideas are not supported enthusiastically. In the following subsections we discuss the principal's responsibility in supporting reform through four areas: money, personnel, time, and information.

Money. Too often reform efforts never get started because of an ongoing myth that making any reform is impossible because the budget will never allow it. However, few schools anywhere will ever complain about an overabundance of financial resources, and yet many schools are making changes and improvements. Often schools within the same district that have similar budget allocations are quite different in their approach to creating better instructional programs. Although this is not a chapter on school finance and budgeting, principals need to ask how can some schools operate in an environment of reform and instructional improvement and do so under the same budget restraints as do others.

To answer this question, a school leader should consider three areas pertaining to managing money for school improvement efforts. First, many improvement efforts do not require more money but can survive with support from other areas such as personnel, time, and information—topics we discuss later. Second, many improvement efforts may need only a budget reallocation. Principals often play financial wizardry with their budgets to create ways in which worthy programs are funded. Effective principals find a way. Third, the improvement efforts may be too grand at a particular time and therefore may need to be scaled back. This is a tough position to be in, but the principal may have to be the bearer of bad news or, at the least, steer the improvement efforts into more reasonable directions to reflect the financial resources available.

Principals are also concerned with three acronyms and their application to the budget: ADA, ADM, and FTE. *ADA* refers to students' average daily attendance, and *ADM* refers to the average daily membership. Usually the district office uses either ADA or ADM to determine the school's budget for such items as textbooks and supplies. Full-time equivalency (*FTE*) refers, among other things, to the number of teachers allocated to a building. FTE is determined by the ADA or ADM, depending on the state code. For example, in many districts, one FTE is allocated for a certain number of ADM, such as 20 students. Using this formula, a school of 500 students would have 25 FTEs. Classified staff also can be determined by the ADM or ADA. Managing the ADA, ADM, and FTEs effectively is vitally important to receive correct funding. In fact, problems can occur if a principal reports an ADM that is either higher or lower than the actual numbers. Unfortunately, it is more complicated than what we indicate here because schools can receive variable credit for part-time and special-needs students. You will learn more about your school budget in a finance class and in your internship, but it is important to realize that your management of these formulas will go a long way toward determining your school's budget.

Many schools, especially those in site-based management, can manipulate their FTE numbers for other things than teaching positions. For example, instead of using all 25 FTEs for 25 teachers, a site council could elect to use one of the FTEs for additional monies paid to the faculty for professional development. Such rules and regulations depend totally on the state and local codes.

Policymakers often hesitate at increasing school funding because of various educator opinions on funding priorities. For example, many reformers want money for program development, teacher organizations lobby for salary increases, and administrators often want capital outlay for new buildings or additions. The school community, if divided on school reform efforts, may lose needed financial resources. As a school leader, you will want to manage funding toward the school's shared vision.

One budget area that has caused principals many headaches is the activity and student body funds. These accounts are often problematic because many other people are involved with them. Teachers and coaches often are given responsibility to manage activity budgets without any training or help. A music teacher, for example, is understandably more concerned with teaching than with the accuracy of the music activity budget. Managing budgets is important not only for the principal but also for faculty and staff. As the principal or assistant principal, you have to be aware of teachers' needs so that you can support their programs and their teaching. Often it may be better to have a secretary or another person handle activity budgets to allow teachers time to perform their more important instructional duties.

With any public funding comes accountability. Because schooling is so expensive, the taxpayers' money must be spent legally and equitably. As a principal, you can assume that whatever money flows to your school, a system of accountability also will flow, often in the form of an audit. Although others in the school may be involved in the budget process, when it comes to accountability, the old axiom "the buck stops here" applies directly to the principal. When you know an audit is near, alert all involved so that no one is surprised. Consider the audit as a learning experience, and seek help in understanding how to manage the accounts more efficiently. After all, you do not want the reform efforts to go astray because of accounting problems.

Personnel. The very nature of schools means that different people are involved in their everyday management. If principals only dealt with students and teachers, the role would be complex enough. However, it is not unusual on a daily basis for principals also to interact with unclassified personnel, district office officials, Parent Teacher Association (PTA) and community members, and school board members. Sometimes these interactions take place within a short period. For example, in an hour's time an assistant principal may have talked to a truant student, phoned the student's parents, arranged a field-trip bus with the district transportation director, coordinated the gym schedule with two coaches, transcribed a letter to the secretary, and then chatted with the lunch room director about long lunch lines. These interactions are a big part of managing a school, and yet the vision of improving teaching and learning is still the prime mission. Administrators need to keep in mind that these interactions are necessary, important, and a part of the improvement process.

Supporting school reform for the improvement of teaching and learning and dealing with these various groups are aligned with the development of a learning community (see Chapter 3). All people in a school are learning all the time. The principal's role becomes one of managing the environment so that an optimal learning community can develop and function.

Hargreaves (1997) reported from his studies that a fundamental mismatch exists between the demands of educational reform and the professional development opportunities afforded teachers and administrators. The principal's role in promoting, facilitating, and participating in professional development is integral to developing a school culture where all educators are continual learners. In considering the school vision, the professional development of all educators in the school turns less to the bandwagon and dog-and-pony shows and more to a sustained and developmental approach, one that is linked to school improvement efforts. Past attempts at school reform often have neglected professional development. Reform packages have been implemented with the expectation that everyone is expected to follow along. Even if personnel development was included, often one-day workshops or single inservice classes were all that were offered, having little impact on school improvement efforts. Barth (1990) supported the idea that people in a learning community are not inserviced. Instead, they engage in continuous inquiry: reflecting, discussing, reading, and learning about improving instruction.

Often neglected in professional development are the classified staff members. Administrators mistakenly think that professional development for secretaries means only improving technical skills, such as word processing. It is not uncommon to find school secretaries who have no idea what the vision of the school is, what role they play in this vision, and what other roles in the school are involved with the vision. Yet these secretaries are often the first-line communicators for the school to the rest of the community. Likewise, seldom are custodians, lunch workers, and teacher aides brought into reform efforts and professional development.

Time.   Few beginning principals are more surprised by any other issue than that of managing their schedules. In fact, many principals will admit that their schedules are out-of-control monsters. Time management is quite different for school administrators than it is for business leaders. For one, a school is not an organization in which a chief executive officer can set appointments and assume that everything will take place as planned. Schools, instead, are organizations that are similar to a flock of geese heading south for the winter. The flock is headed in the right direction, but many distractions come along the way to get them off course. Because of unpredictable schedules, it is imperative for school leaders to keep their eyes on the school's shared vision. School improvement does not occur without the principal's and assistant principal's involvement. Time has to be managed, and this requires it to be allocated and scheduled for improvement efforts.

Likewise, school leaders need to support others in the building in their time management, a topic we discuss later in this chapter. Suffice it to say here, however, that the faculty and staff are especially prone to reform burnout because of the many previous unsuccessful reform efforts. Time is as precious as financial resources for busy teachers and staff members (see Figure 7.1).

Information.   Information is usually considered to be something needed in making good decisions. Information is also important in helping others become professionally involved in decision making and the school improvement process. A good example would be in establishing a professional relationship with teachers. If teachers feel that they only get a one-sided report, then they can easily acquire the opinion that they are being manipulated. However, trusting in teachers' good judgment will require giving them all the information so that they can develop their own opinions. As a school leader, you must be careful about withholding information from others—doing so could jeopardize trust in your leadership.

The sharing of information with others in the school community is an opportunity not only to gain support for the school's vision but also to discover resources and potential problems. When school leaders keep others informed, a stronger sense of trust is established. As a general rule, the hotter the issue, the more information and communication are needed.

However, not all information is of equal value. In fact, with the onslaught of the information era, principals can get access to the wrong information. For example, it is entirely possible for anyone to find Web sites that claim that the Holocaust never happened, regardless of the overwhelming evidence. Using the Internet for information is a tremendous source for all educators, but it is also an area that requires caution and discernment.

While there are no simple ways to change principals' daily work, there are several strategies for dealing with it. Principals should

1. *Learn to change gears quickly and smoothly.*
   Like new drivers with stick-shift automobiles, learn to shift from first to second and back without grinding the gears. Principals need to move from task to task with ease.

2. *Learn to go with the flow.*
   It's important to have priorities and "to do" lists, but some days it's not possible to get all the work done. Remember, there's always tomorrow.

3. *Look at the big picture and take a long-term view.*
   Understand how solving immediate problems serves larger purposes. Understand how answering a question about curriculum at 6 P.M. is part of the larger reform effort. Take the long view. See how brief interactions and problem solving with staff build long-term relationships and cement the culture.

4. *Become a historian and anthropologist of the culture* (Deal & Peterson, 1999).
   Hone your skills as a historian by listening to stories of past events, exhuming old planning documents, and reviewing past efforts to understand where the school has come from. However, also develop the skills of an anthropologist by digging into existing norms and values, examining artifacts and symbols, and asking about the deeper meanings of staff traditions and rituals.

5. *Develop a deep understanding of the school's purpose and values.*
   Every school has a deep set of values. In toxic cultures, these values are negative and hostile. In positive cultures, these values hold deep meaning for staff. Learn to identify and interpret what these values are as they relate to curriculum, instruction, approaches to assessment, and learning. See if the current values match the community's and one's own.

6. *Become a bifocal leader.*
   Bifocal leadership means knowing deep down that managerial tasks communicate values and build culture and that symbolic actions help staff and students internalize the actions and routines needed to run schools (Deal & Peterson, 1994). Intuitively, bifocal leaders manage by leading and lead by managing. Every action reinforces core values and purpose. It is harder than it sounds, but it is key to being a successful principal.

7. *Enjoy the rush.*
   A principal's daily work is exciting, surprising, and mysterious. It will never be boring or routine. By celebrating and learning to enjoy the rush of activity through networking, stories, and collegiality, principals will gain new energy to cope with work's challenges.

FIGURE 7.1   *Strategies for Working with the Daily Rush*

Source: Adapted from K. Peterson (2001). The roar of complexity, *Journal of Staff Development* (Winter 2001), 18–21.

You and others can find about anything you want to find on the Internet—whether it is factual, realistic, or practical is another matter.

A common mistake that educators make is to claim that something is "research-based." For example, in supporting a block schedule for high schools, an educator may claim that longer class periods have been shown by research to be more effective for adolescent learners. Often the source is never cited. The study may have limitations as to how generalizable it is to other school settings. Likewise, educators read a lot of literature from journals that is only based on theory and not necessarily researched empirically. As a school leader, you need to understand the existing literature and be able to critique these sources. You also will need to explain to others what good research is and is not.

One of the newest and most important responsibilities of principals and assistant principals in reaching the goals of higher learning achievement for all students is data-driven decision making. Developing your skills at gathering and analyzing information is a critical management skill that has leadership implications. Knowing how to get trust-worthy, timely, and appropriate information and understanding what this informa-tion means for improving teaching and learning is one of the most important things you will do.

As principal, you need to analyze the methods by which you disseminate informa-tion to the faculty and staff. The weekly faculty meeting has been the method of choice for most school principals for many years. Faculty meetings, although important, are not necessarily the best method, especially with the electronic methods now available. Many information-type items can be transmitted electronically through an e-mail listserve to all faculty and staff. Consequently, each faculty and staff member can have the opportunity for individual input. In fact, some schools have established chat rooms for faculty and staff to discuss and share ideas on a particular topic. Not only do these methods ensure more individual involvement, but they also provide a written record.

Planning

To help make improvement efforts actually happen, you, as the school leader, have to plan for success. Nothing is more frustrating to a group that is working diligently on an im-provement effort than to see it fail because of poor planning. Developing an action plan is a necessary step to give the vision a working blueprint for continuation. Action plans iden-tify the what, how, when, who, and how much. Where the shared vision is the direction of improvement efforts, the action plan is the map to follow. However, the action plan is only meant to be a temporary map because it will need to be revised along the journey. The very nature of taking action means that the status quo no longer exists and that change has taken place. This alters how the rest of the plan may have to be implemented. Often ac-tion plans are too rigid in adapting to the changing needs of reform efforts.

Long- and Short-Term Planning.   Long-term plans, sometimes referred to as *strategic plans*, are broad in scope and cover a relatively long time period. Short-term plans, often referred to as *tactical plans*, are used to execute the long-term plans. The key components are outlining the activities that need to be accomplished, determining the resources needed, assigning people who choose to work on the activities, and establishing a rela-tively good time line. Usually each goal of the long-term plan has at least one short-term plan that, when completed, would be replaced with another short-term plan.

Although such strategic and tactical plans have worked in some organizations, they have not always been successful, and principals should use caution in thinking that such planning always will be beneficial. One of the problems with long-range strategic planning is that once the plan is implemented, it may need to change based on what is presently happening with the implementation. As Schlechty (1990) claimed:

> If a plan is effective, its implementation will change the environment in ways that cannot be anticipated in the short term. Since long-term plans must be made in the short term and are based on assessments of present reality, rather than on the reality that is being invented, long-term plans are necessarily based on faulty assumptions (p. xx).

We do not want to suggest that strategic plans do not work in schools. On the contrary, there are many good examples. The point that we would like to make is that developing an action plan is at best short term. Effective planning is dynamic and continuous. It occurs not as a step in the process but as an integral part of the whole process. Once the plan is established, it should be continually improved as it is implemented and results are determined. Talbot (1997) reported that principals, even in reforming schools, found that long-range plans frequently were not helpful because of such events as faculty turnover or legislative and district mandates.

Any worthy action in school improvement needs a written plan as a starting point. The written plan needs to include:

1. What is to be done (the objectives)
2. How it is to be done (activities)
3. When are each of the objectives to be done
4. Who will be responsible for each objective
5. Approximately how much and what kind of resources are needed

The written plan needs to reflect the collaborative efforts of the shared vision. Everyone in the school community should have an opportunity to see the written plan and to shape and reshape the plan as it is implemented.

Instructional improvement requires strong leadership and management from the principal and assistant principal. Often the daily routines of teachers impose too many difficulties in getting the vision into a workable plan. As the principal or assistant principal, you can be involved in the following ways:

1. *Making available correct information to those involved so that planning is meaningful.* For example, in the opening vignette in Chapter 6, research data and the experience of other schools were important in developing a middle school concept.
2. *Providing direction and meaning to the planning process when necessary.* Nothing is more frustrating than to sit through a team meeting when others are spouting off on unrelated topics. At such times you may have to step in and give encouragement for the planning process to remain on its agenda.
3. *Securing the help of others who will be needed in the planning phase.* For example, if the planning takes place during the school day, substitute teachers may need to be hired for teachers who are involved.

Action Taking

Many good reform efforts had great plans that were never implemented. It is often much easier to discuss and plan reform than it is to take action on it. During implementation, the stark realization hits that things are about to change, and although many people could have been involved in the planning stage, the realities of the change could be too threatening. Kimbrough and Burkett (1990) claimed, "During the implementation stage, the principal seems much less of a Prince Charming, but instead seems downright threatening and like an enemy"(p. 149). The implementation stage may be the most trying part of reform for the principal's role.

Although implementation involves everyone and therefore requires the principal to facilitate others in the process, certain aspects of action taking are important for principals and assistant principals to perform. For instance, to implement the plan, the principal and the assistant principals either need to have been involved in the planning and have owner-ship of it or have complete trust in those who were involved in the planning and imple-menting. If the planning was entrusted to others, then the principals must be aware of the progress of the planning. If the plan is not feasible, then the principal needs to help direct replanning and strategizing. This does not mean that the principal acts autocratically but rather cooperatively and collaboratively, suggesting and offering comments as to the plan's implementation.

Being an implementer of school reform also requires individual insight and change. You should constantly evaluate and reflect on your own practices. Certain behaviors, es-pecially those steeped in tradition, may need to be evaluated and possibly changed. You should model change and be willing to transform aspects of your behaviors and activities for the improvement process.

As we discussed in Chapter 6, an important responsibility for school leaders is to understand and communicate the school culture and how that culture will affect the im-plementation of a particular improvement effort. Reform that has been implemented suc-cessfully in one school may not necessarily be implemented with the same success in another school. In fact, it probably cannot. As principal, you must help determine the best way that the improvement plans can be implemented within the context of the school's culture.

Evaluating and Assessing

The main purpose of evaluating and assessing the reform efforts is to gain an under-standing of the progress, direction, and modifications that may be needed. A formal evaluation report also may be necessary for a grant, the district office, or the board of education. Although the two terms *evaluation* and *assessment* often are used inter-changeably, there are some subtle differences. Usually, *evaluation* is the process of col-lecting data to make a decision, for example, to continue or discontinue a program. *Assessment,* on the other hand, often is associated with determining if goals and ob-jectives are being achieved. To understand the process of school improvement efforts, both evaluation and assessment may be necessary. Furthermore, evaluation and assessment are used in both formative and summative ways. *Formative evaluation* can be defined as evaluating a program or process as it is in operation or in progress. *Summative evaluation* is more limiting in that it is an evaluation at the end of a program or process, such as a formal evaluation report.

One of the principal's main tasks in evaluation and assessment is overseeing the collection and analysis of data. Data can be collected by several means, such as observing, testing, questioning, surveying, and anecdotal record keeping. Generating the data actually may be the easy part. Generating the right data and analyzing that data are more complicated, especially in education. For example, a particular instructional program may be judged to be effective by teachers, but student scores may not have increased. The principal may have to help others understand which set of data is more important to consider in the assessment of the program.

As we discussed in Chapter 3, your role as learner permeates all the other roles you will take. Learning is at the essence of evaluation. Goldring and Rallis (1993) suggested that principal leadership, management, and evaluation are tightly linked. Leadership and management may help shape events, but evaluation can change the shape of those events. Evaluation information helps principals learn so that they can understand and shape events. Goldring and Rallis's view of evaluation aims to establish an inquiry ethic. Principals and assistant principals should use assessment results for instructional improvement. This requires that you know how to analyze and interpret school assessment information accurately. As part of your preparation program, you would be wise to pay close attention to the research and statistics courses that will help you to become a better evaluator and assessor.

The Principal as Facilitator of Others in Management

As school leaders build leadership capacity, they also build management capacity among others. As the school culture evolves into a learning community, principals and assistant principals are not only supporting, planning, action taking, and evaluating, but they also are helping others to manage in these areas as well. In this section we discuss how the principal facilitates others in managing the school for instructional improvement.

In an early study on principal responsibility in instructional leadership, Stokes (1984) confirmed that instructional improvement is a shared responsibility and that efforts to evaluate this function by looking only at the activities of the principal were misguided. Stokes concluded that critical functions in improving instruction were shared by many people in the school. One role that can be overlooked but shares in the improvement of instruction is that of the assistant principal. Patton (1987) examined the role of assistant principals and found that their contributions were critical to the instructional quality in effective schools. We have discussed the role of assistant principal throughout this book as a role that needs to be reconceptualized. Perhaps no other area of the assistant principal's responsibility is more important to be reconceptualized than management. Too often assistant principals are slotted into narrow management roles and either neglect or are neglected in instructional reform. The principal's first responsibility in facilitating others in managing instructional improvement is to reconceptualize the assistant principal's role so as to make it an active, involved, and integral part of the reform efforts. Indeed, principals and assistant principals should act as a team in managing all the affairs of the school.

Another role that is often overlooked in school improvement efforts is department or grade-level chairpersons. In a study of secondary schools, Worner and Brown (1993) concluded that principals wanted department chairs to assume more responsibility in improving the instructional climate of the school and, furthermore, that the department chairs were interested in taking on more responsibility. Both the Patton (1987) and the Worner and Brown studies indicated that principals do have opportunities to distribute the management tasks among other leaders in the school to accomplish school improvement efforts. Indeed, more often than not assistant principals and department chairs are not as involved as much as they could and want to be.

Previously we discussed the framework of school reform and instructional improvement and the role of the principal and assistant principal in supporting, planning, action taking, and evaluating. In the next section we continue discussing the framework and how school leaders can facilitate others' actions in these four areas.

Facilitating Support

The principal and assistant principal need to support a nonthreatening environment for reform to take place, and they likewise need to help others be supportive. Risk taking and experimentation by teachers are as easily and as commonly thwarted by peers as they are by administrators. When previous norms have emphasized a status quo mentality, often teachers will perceive others who want to implement reform movements either as threats or as troublemakers. For example, implementing the peer mentoring program, as outlined in Chapter 4, would involve the cooperation of most of the faculty. Some may perceive the program as too costly in both time and money. Others may feel that beginning teachers need to find their own best way of teaching without the interference of others. These types of change efforts are tricky for principals and assistant principals who want to support the effort, want others to support it, but find that doing so polarizes members of the faculty. In this section we discuss how you can help others in the school community be supportive of reform efforts to improve instructional programs. We do this by organizing the support around the four areas mentioned previously, namely, money, personnel, time, and information.

Money.   When resources are thin, and they usually are in schools, money often becomes an issue in terms of who gets how much. Usually the traditional school budget allocates funds for line-item categories that do not reflect a school's goals and needs. Many school districts now allow building principals and site committees to participate in the process of formulating the budget, often known as *school-based budgeting.* One of the principal's roles is that of helping others in the school understand the budgeting process and reflect on the school's priorities. These priorities should be linked to the school's vision that administrators, teachers, and others in the school community share. Individual priorities must be evaluated within the more global view of the school's priorities. The site council has to give special consideration to how the financial resources are allocated to reach the school's collective vision.

Part of the school-based budgeting process involves communication. As Nanus (1992) suggested (see Chapter 6), principals and assistant principals become "spokespersons" for the budget and how it connects to the school's vision. As spokespersons, principals communicate the needs of the school and the vision of the school and how fulfilling the needs will help accomplish the vision. Likewise, as spokespersons, the principal and assistant principals are advocates of the site council's budgeting process and decisions, understanding that everyone in the school should have a voice in the process.

We should not assume, however, that principals are solely responsible for obtaining the money for the school budget. Administrators are not the only source of revenue building. For instance, teachers also can participate in grant writing. In facilitating support, others join in the cause of generating revenue for worthy causes. Because one person cannot possibly do it all, allowing and encouraging others to find sources of funds can help the reform efforts.

Personnel.   Although in recent times educators have paid more attention to their role of facilitating learning through professional development, many of the approaches actually have caused more problems or have added to existing problems. Fullan and Hargreaves (1996) suggested that many professional development strategies have been as fragmented and oblivious to the needs of the teachers and the school as the reform efforts they were meant to supplement. For example, training in teaching methods and strategies often is undertaken separately from the development of peer mentoring programs. Mentoring programs, in turn, often are separated from the supervision model used by principals. Such fragmentation isolates reform efforts into separate initiatives that ignore the wider institutional context. When fragmented, these reform efforts are criticized more easily, especially by those who want to maintain the status quo.

As we discussed in Chapter 3, many professional development initiatives take the form of something that is done to teachers rather than with them. Top-down approaches to professional development embody a deficit view of teachers and teaching—something must be wrong, and it needs to be fixed by experts. If professional development is used as a means of fixing something or somebody, then it only adds to the existing problems. Instead, professional development must be related to the needs of school personnel to fulfill the collective vision. Individual needs must be considered as much—if not more—than institutional needs. Teachers and support staff members differ in their years of experience, gender, stage of career and life, and expertise in certain areas. Teachers can and will support development when they can choose the type of learning that is best for them. Seldom, if ever, should you as a principal or assistant principal enforce professional development programs on others. If it is not voluntary, then little learning will take place.

However, faculty and staff do need to have opportunities in learning and may need some motivation to become involved. You need to assist others to embrace learning opportunities that help them develop personally and that build on the school's vision. As Fullan and Hargreaves (1996) described it, "The greatest problem in teaching is not how to get rid of the 'deadwood,' but how to create, sustain, and motivate good teachers throughout their careers" (p. 63). Fullan and Hargreaves coined the term *interactive professional-*

ism as a solution to this type of development problem. The elements of interactive professionalism are

- Discretionary judgment as the heart of professionalism
- Collaborative work cultures
- Norms of continuous improvement where new ideas are sought inside and outside one's setting
- Reflection in, on, and about practice in which individual and personal development is honored, along with collective development and assessment
- Greater mastery, efficacy, and satisfaction in the profession of teaching (p. 63).

Interactive professionalism will require some needed changes in the way teachers go about their work. Principals need to help facilitate these changes in order for teachers and other personnel to develop an interactive culture. Such a culture requires a change in how we use the element of time.

Time.   Facilitating others to manage reform involves helping others understand the element that time plays in reform efforts. Time has two important functions in effective school reform efforts: (1) the length of time for reform to work and (2) the necessary management of time by those involved.

Many reform efforts have failed before they have been given a chance to succeed. When results are not positive immediately, many reform efforts have been abandoned. Hargreaves and Fullan (1998) claimed, "Most change strategies that make a difference in the classroom take five years or more to yield results" (p. 122). Fullan and Miles (1992) also suggested, "Even in cases where reform eventually succeeds, things often go wrong before they go right" (p. 749). Reform should be considered in the context of longevity. Principals and assistant principals need to play cheerleader—keeping hopes and interest high in the reform efforts and trying to keep discouragement at bay.

The second area that time affects in reform efforts is the management of time by those involved in the process. Teachers can burn out easily and become discouraged if they believe that their efforts are nonefficacious. Most teachers entered the profession wanting to be involved with children and teaching. They often miss seeing the bigger picture because of their isolation in their classrooms. However, effective reform is systemic. "Improvements inside the classroom depend on improvements outside it" (Fullan & Hargreaves, 1996, p. 77). Principals need to support teachers with interactive opportunities and collaborative efforts that are viewed not as add-ons to an already busy schedule but as an integral part of their teaching role. However, a word of caution: Workaholic teachers are not always the most productive teachers. Long hours over long periods of time probably will lead to burnout and other emotional problems. Too often principals ask the same teachers to take on more responsibilities because these teachers have a way of getting things done. As principal, you will want to facilitate all faculty in using time, not only a few of the hard workers.

Information.   Isolated teachers also contribute to another cultural problem—that of information hoarding. When one-room schools were the norm, who else was there for teachers to share and discuss their practice with? Today's schools, although structured differently, still can maintain a one-room school atmosphere in a building with other one-room schools. Often a teacher with a good idea protects that idea with fortified and sacred buttresses. For moral and ethical reasons, information on effective instructional practices should not be hoarded.

Another way for principals and assistant principals to support teachers with information is to ensure that data-driven, decision-making skills are distributed throughout the school. These skills are not the sole possession of the principal or of a few teachers. All teachers must have the skills to base their instructional decisions on accurate, appropriate, clear, and timely information.

Facilitating information dissemination involves providing opportunities for faculty and staff to engage in interactive professionalism (Fullan & Hargreaves, 1996). One example of increasing faculty involvement with information sharing was used by Hillside Elementary School, where small group sessions replaced regular faculty meetings. During these sessions, teachers were invited to join in small groups to discuss various issues. These sessions were voluntary, and scheduling allowed teachers to share ideas with others and explore problems and solutions. These groups later added another learning bonus. As they became more involved with each other, the faculty organized book clubs. This voluntary activity involved a group of teachers reading a book and then sharing ideas about the book in their group meetings. Not only was a collaborative culture established at Hillside, but an increased learning atmosphere also developed.

In this subsection we discussed how you facilitate others to be supportive in managing reform efforts around the areas of money, personnel, time, and information. In this next subsection we continue exploring ways principals and assistant principals facilitate others in management by looking at how they are involved in planning and action taking.

Facilitating Others in Planning and Action Taking

Rarely will school improvement efforts occur by chance. Behind each reform effort are people using time and energy in planning the strategies that are needed to fulfill the col-

---

Professional Dilemma 7.1

In a small, isolated school on an Indian Reservation in Arizona, a heavy turnover of teachers occurred each year. Often young teachers would begin at the school but would leave after the first year or two. The teachers who had stayed at the school had become accustomed to this turnover and were reluctant to share any of their expertise with new teachers. What had developed was a situation in which new teachers felt isolated and removed from the faculty. The principal liked hiring young new teachers because they brought energy and youthfulness to the school. However, good reforms were hard to sustain because of the constant turnover. What should the principal do to help veteran teachers include new teachers into the faculty?

lective vision. As principal or assistant principal, you facilitate others involved in the process to carry out effective planning through at least three areas:

1. Ensuring that information and data are available for everyone in the planning process
2. Arranging for the time and compensation of faculty and staff to be involved
3. Encouraging planning sessions that meet often and regularly before and after implementation

Your role in planning and action taking with reform efforts requires the development of a collaborative culture. As principal, you cannot get bogged down in the details. You must allow others to carry out their responsibilities. This type of leadership and management is more an act of sharing than of delegating. Delegating involves the principal giving someone a task and then following up with that individual. Sharing, on the other hand, involves more of a cooperative, trusting venture in which the principal shares the task with others, accepting a lesser role at times, and trusting that professionals will work through the proper decisions. In a sense, here is where the principal has to let go and trust teachers and others in the school. You cannot be everywhere doing everything.

A study by Short and Greer (1997) found that a principal's trust of teachers resulted from many factors that varied from principal to principal. In one case study of a high school in Murray, Utah, the principal, Richard Tranter, spoke of the shaky decisions that faculty members made. In the end, however, he acknowledged that things had worked out all right and that he had come to believe that the planning and action taken were better than he would have done himself. As the researchers suggested, in Richard's case, even though he had believed for many years that the faculty should be actively involved, it was the actual positive experiences that cemented his belief in the process. Thus, having had success, he was encouraged to use the process again with other reform efforts. His trust in the faculty was strengthened significantly through the experience of letting go and allowing planning and action to take place.

Facilitating Others in Evaluating and Assessing

The principal as facilitator must establish accountability for the progress of students, teachers, and instructional practices through ongoing assessment within the school. However, this is not a one- or two-person responsibility. Evaluating and assessing school improvement are the responsibilities of many stakeholders. It is the principal, however, who must facilitate others to be involved in the effort.

Different stakeholders in education use accountability differently. Policymakers often insist on strict accountability through indications such as student test scores. District office administrators want accountability with budget and resource allocation. Parents are more interested in individual assessments of their children. Recently, several theorists have advocated newer forms of accountability. For example, Stiggins (1994) and Wiggins (1993) argued for "authentic" or performance-based testing—testing not only for what students know but also for what they can do. Regardless of the accountability measures that exist within a district or a school, the principal must facilitate the process. Most important, however, is facilitating the correct approach that will yield the information needed for continual improvement. As your school becomes involved in improvement efforts, you need to select those assessment measures that will render the results of the improvement. For example, standardized testing, although required by the state, will not evaluate new teacher morale as to their professional development. Therefore, as a principal, you need to match an appropriate assessment for the new teacher development plan.

A caution for principals is to be careful about giving mixed messages, especially with pet projects. Often schools can have goals for instructional programs and then another set of goals for assessment of learning. For example, a school goal could be to improve instruction of reading by implementing a reading one-on-one program. Another goal could be to raise aggregate reading scores by one grade level. The principal's and teachers' goal may involve more interest in the one-on-one reading program than on its results, thus giving the mixed message that the success of a particular program is more important than is the learning goal. Programs may be successful with teachers but not successful for student learning.

One area of evaluation and assessment that principals should emphasize with other educators is reflection on practice. Continual reflection on practice by teachers involves both individual inquiry and meaningful dialogue with others, especially teachers, parents, and students. Principals can facilitate this process by providing time and encouraging reflective practice. As colleagues, teachers and principals should discuss questions about the why, what, and how of curriculum, instruction, and assessment.

A school community needs to be accountable for student learning and assessment practices. Principals and assistant principals must lead and facilitate discussion among others about assessment practices so that the school focuses on working toward the collective vision and achieving the school goals.

Institutionalizing School Reform

For any reform to become institutionalized, it is necessary for it to become part of the school's culture. School culture exists at a very deep level and has resulted from the values, norms, and beliefs of those involved with the school over a number of years. Changing anything in that culture requires considerable effort over a period of time. Many scholars (e.g., Schein, 1992) believe that it is impossible to operate directly on culture. Rather, culture changes gradually as the people in the organization change in the way they go about doing their work and relating to others in their work. Given enough time, reform efforts can become part of the school culture and therefore institutionalized.

Because reform is holistic, every aspect of the school has the potential to be affected. This underscores the importance of systems thinking; that is, changes in one part of the system have an impact on others. For example, implementing a professional development program on cooperative learning affects everyone in the building, not just teachers and students. Custodians may have to help with classroom seating arrangements, secretaries could be asked to schedule team meetings, an assistant principal may communicate the teaching method to parents, and teaching aides may have to work with small groups rather than with individual students. A cooperative learning program also can affect other elements in the system, such as instructional time. Because cooperative teaching may take longer, certain curricula may have to be changed to accommodate the new approach. Likewise, other professional development activities may have to be postponed while cooperative teaching is being learned. Thus the change in one instructional approach usually has an impact on other elements in the school.

Based on the work of Senge (1990) and Senge and colleagues (2000), we have adapted several features of systems thinking that are critical in facilitating reform efforts. First, seeing interrelationships and processes is necessary. Instead of viewing school improvement as a series of change projects, viewing it as integration of changes is critical. Instead of understanding school reform efforts from a snapshot perspective, it is important to understand them as an ongoing system-wide process involving different people, tasks, times, places, and ideas.

Second, principals and assistant principals need to influence others to move beyond blame. Instead of accusing others of preventing or hindering school improvement, look at system-wide structures and processes that discourage attitudes of change. Furthermore, "avoid symptomatic solutions" (Senge et al., 2000, p. 15). The urgency of schooling sometimes encourages individuals to shortcut inquiry and focus on the symptoms rather than on the problems and opportunities of school improvement. Engaging in problem finding and problem solving is critical in creating an environment that supports substantive, transformative change in schools.

Third, principals need to develop in themselves and others the skill of focusing on areas of high leverage. Rather than attempt to change all areas of instructional practice, the principal as facilitator should influence school constituents to focus on those areas where change is most possible and where change will make the most difference for school improvement. This will vary with each school. Nevertheless, it is the principal's responsibility to know the system and to communicate and develop that understanding with followers so that decisions can have the most effect.

Institutionalizing a school reform effort involves understanding the existing culture, establishing systems thinking, and creating a cooperative and collaborative culture that works toward the collective vision. We suggest the axiom that you should consider when you want school reform to be institutionalized: Think big, start small, and go slow.

Conclusion

In this chapter we discussed the role that principals and assistant principals play in the management of schools. The role of the principal as manager is key in the daily planning, organizing, operating, executing, budgeting, maintaining, and scheduling of numerous processes, activities, and tasks that permit a school to accomplish its goals as a learning community. However, the manager role also should emphasize building a strong school culture and establishing a shared vision that encompasses school improvement and promotes learning for *all* students.

Abe Rosenblatz was disillusioned in the heavy managerial aspects of his administrative internship in the introductory vignette. However, these managerial responsibilities are important for developing a culture and vision that support improvement in teaching and learning. However, knowing how politics affects the role will determine a great deal of how you will practice being a principal or assistant principal. In the next chapter we discuss the important role of principal as politician. In this chapter we move into the role conceptions that focus on the external context of the principalship.

Activities

Self-Reflecting Activities

1. If you are not an intern, talk to someone who is an intern about his or her experiences in the management area. If you are an intern, critically reflect on your own experiences. Does the intern/your experience match Abe's in the opening vignette?
2. Get a copy of your school's budget. What are the obvious and subtle things that are being emphasized in the budget?

Peer-Reflecting Activities

1. With a colleague, reflect on your experiences of how current and former principals balanced management and leadership.
2. Critically reflect on a recent school change initiative. What management tasks were critical for the principal or assistant principal to perform? In what ways were these administrators effective and ineffective in performing these tasks?

Course Activities

1. If school-based budgeting is used in your area, invite a principal to class to discuss how this affects the role and how it affects school improvement efforts.
2. Invite a principal or assistant principal to discuss pupil scheduling. How does the administrator relate this task to student learning and school improvement?
3. Analyze a school improvement plan.

Websites

■ *http://www.ucea.org/cases/*
   Cases from the Journal of Cases in Educational Leadership
   Hassenpflug, A. (1998). All in a day's work. *Journal of Cases in Educational Leadership 1*(2).

■ *http://www.oise.utoronto.ca/~vsvede*
   School Leadership: A Profile Document. This site allows you to compare your present leadership practice to the ideal practice towards which you strive

References

Barth, R. S. (1990). *Improving Schools from Within: Teachers, Parents, and Principals Can Make the Difference*. San Francisco: Jossey-Bass.

Callahan, R. (1962). *Education and the Cult of Efficiency*. Chicago: University of Chicago Press.

Deal, T., & Peterson, K. (1994). *The Leadership Paradox: Balancing Logic and Artistry in Schools*. San Francisco: Jossey-Bass.

Deal, T., & Peterson, K. (1999). *Shaping School Culture: The Heart of Leadership*. San Francisco: Jossey-Bass.

Fullan, M., & Hargreaves, A. (1996). *What's Worth Fighting for in Your School*. New York: Teachers College Press.

Fullan, M., & Miles, M. B. (1992). Getting reform right: What works and what doesn't. *Phi Delta Kappan 73*, 745–752.

Goldring, E. B., & Rallis, S. F. (1993). *Principals of Dynamic Schools: Taking Charge of Change*. Newbury Park, CA: Corwin Press.

Gross, B. (1994). The scientific approach to administration. In D. E. Griffiths (Ed.). *Behavioral Science and Educational Administration*, 63rd yearbook of the National Society for the Study of Education. Chicago: University of Chicago Press.

Gulick, L. (1937). Notes on the theory of organization. In L. Gulick &. L. Urwick (Eds.), *Papers on the Science of Administration* (pp. 1–45). New York: Institute of Public Administration, Columbia University.

Hall, D. T. (1986). Breaking career routines: Midcareer Choice and Identity Development, *Career development in organizations* (pp. 120–159). San Francisco: Jossey-Bass.

Hargreaves, A. (1997). *Rethinking Educational Change with Heart and Mind*. Alexandria, VA.: Association for Supervision and Curriculum Development.

Hargreaves, A., & Fullan, M. (1998). *What's Worth Fighting for Out There*. New York: Teachers College Press.

Kimbrough, R. B., & Burkett, C. W. (1990). *The Principalship: Concepts and Practices*. Boston: Allyn and Bacon.

Lambert, L. (1998). *Building Leadership Capacity in Schools*. Alexandria, VA: Association for Supervision and Curriculum Development.

Morris, V. C., Crowson, R. L., Porter-Gehrie, C., & Hurwitz, J., E. (1984). *Principals in Action: The Reality of Managing Schools*. Columbus, OH: Charles E. Merrill.

Nanus, B. (1992). *Visionary Leadership: Creating a Compelling Sense of Direction for Your Organization*. San Francisco: Jossey-Bass.

Patton, J. (1987). *The Role and Function of Assistant Principals in Virginia's Public Schools*. Blacksburg, VA: Virginia Tech.

Peterson, K. (2001). The roar of complexity. *Journal of Staff Development* (Winter), 18-21.

Pierce, P. R. (1935). *The Origin and Development of the Public School Principalship*. Chicago: University of Chicago Press.

Schein, E. H. (1992). *Organizational Culture and Leadership* (2nd ed.). San Francisco: Jossey-Bass.

Schlechty, P. C. (1990). *Schools for the 21st Century: Leadership Imperatives for Educational Reform*. San Francisco: Jossey-Bass.

Senge, P. (1990). *The Fifth Discipline: The Art and Practice of the Learning Organization*. New York: Doubleday.

Senge, P., Cambron-McCabe, N., Lucas, T., Smith, B., Dutton, J., & Kleiner, A. (2000). *Schools That Learn*. New York: Doubleday.

Sergiovanni, T. J. (1987). *The Principalship: A Reflective Practice Perspective*. Boston: Allyn and Bacon.

Short, P. M., & Greer, J. T. (1997). *Leadership in Empowered Schools: Themes from Innovative Efforts*. Englewood Cliffs, NJ: Prentice-Hall.

Speck, M. (1999). *The Principalship: Building a Learning Community*. Englewood Cliffs, NJ: Prentice-Hall.

Stiggins, R. J. (1994). *Student-Centered Classroom Assessment*. Englewood Cliffs, NJ: Merrill/Prentice-Hall.

Stokes, R. L. (1984). *Instructional Leadership Activities in Senior High Schools in Virginia*. Blacksburg, VA: Virginia Tech.

Talbot, D. (1997). Looking for tomorrow through yesterday's eyes: A study of training, experience, and role conceptions of principals in restructuring schools. Unpublished doctoral dissertation, University of Utah, Salt Lake City, UT.

Wiggins, G. (1993). *Assessing Student Performance*. San Francisco: Jossey-Bass.

Worner, W., & Brown, G. (1993). The instructional leadership team: A new role for the department head. *NASSP Bulletin 77*(553), 37–45.

Principal
as Politician

8

Key Terms and Concepts

bargaining	buffering	micropolitics
boundary spanning	coalitions	power
bridging	conflict	social capital

Vignette

The day had been relatively calm, and Carl Patterson, principal of Jefferson High School, always appreciated the calm days. Jefferson was not a tough school relative to other high schools in the city, but it had a vocal and demanding parent group that sometimes made the principal's job tough, trying to respond to multiple and conflicting pressures. The larger community in which Jefferson was located was in the Bible belt of the country and prided itself on maintaining conservative values.

As Carl sat in his office at the end of the day relishing the calm, Susan Cantor and Joe Martin asked to see him. Both students were on the honor roll and seldom created disciplinary problems for Carl and the other administrators. Susan and Joe told Carl that they represented a group of gay and lesbian students as well as straight students who wanted to form a school club. They said the club could provide a support group for gay and lesbian students at Jefferson who, they said, frequently experienced verbal attacks from other students and insensitive remarks from teachers. They believed that the club was permissible under the Equal Access Act and that it could help teach tolerance to students and teachers. Carl was impressed that the students had done their homework on legal issues regarding clubs and recognized that there had been occasions of verbal and even physical attacks on gay and lesbian students at Jefferson. He also knew, though, that this was a hot-button issue in this very conservative community.

Before giving the students an answer, Carl called the district office to speak with the area superintendent. His immediate supervisor was cautious but agreed that the students had the same rights as students in other noncurricular clubs. She left the decision to Carl but suggested that he try to keep things quiet. Carl met with Susan and Joe again and approved the Gay, Lesbian, and Straight Students' Club of Jefferson High.

As Carl recalled later, the next two months were a blur. The club became anything but quiet. As other students and parents found out about the club, Carl was bombarded with angry phone calls at work and at home. Some parents accused him of immoral conduct and of encouraging students to experiment with alternative lifestyles. As the conflict progressed, Carl felt the district office backing off of its support of him. One district administrator confidentially told him that he could lose his job over this.

Several parents went to their school board members asking that the board "outlaw this horrible club." The school board and district administrators sought the help of their attorney and were told that federal law prohibited discriminating against one type of club as long as other noncurricular clubs were recognized. The law had been written in part to protect the rights of students who wanted to create religious clubs. It seemed to many parents that the school misused the law by allowing the gay and lesbian club.

As the board considered what action to take and Carl continued to experience hate mail and verbal threats, the state legislature, which was in session during this time, weighed in on the debate. The highly conservative legislators who were in control of the legislature held a closed-door session with the state school superintendent and other education officials, reprimanding them for allowing this immoral action to occur. The media condemnation of the illegal closed-door session seemed only to fuel the legislators' anger over the incident, and eventually they passed a resolution condemning the school's actions in regard to the club and encouraging all district boards in the state to prohibit gay clubs.

The school board decided that its only alternative for squelching the uproar was to ban all noncurricular clubs. If the school board members thought this would calm the storm, they were very wrong. The ban created even more turmoil as students and parents who were undecided about the gay and lesbian club became irate that all noncurricular clubs were banned.

The students at Jefferson High staged a walkout that was widely reported by the media. The only thing that kept the walkout from turning ugly was Carl's calming presence with the students and his public acknowledgment of their democratic right to protest what they considered injustices. Carl convinced the students to return to class and make their views known to the appropriate elected officials.

Although many parents supported Carl's position and the media applauded his efforts, other powerfully connected parents continued to pressure the school board. Carl eventually was transferred to another school in the district.

The Gay, Lesbian, and Straight Students' Club of Jefferson High continued to meet with support from various national gay and lesbian organizations who paid the fee to rent space at Jefferson High after school. The American Civil Liberties Union sued the legislature for an illegal closed-door meeting, and several parents joined a lawsuit against the school board for banning noncurricular clubs. (To read about a similar case, see McCreary, 2001).

Introduction

Carl's experience with the gay and lesbian club incident illustrates the political nature of the principal's role. Public schools are societal institutions that are influenced by the larger society and community in which they exist. Their funding, governance, curricula, and administration cannot escape the pressures and demands of these larger societal and community structures.

The principal's role fits into this larger system. We take the position in this chapter that this political role is not only necessary because schools are public institutions but also can be valuable in understanding and promoting learning for all students. The learning conception of the principal's role, which we discussed in Chapters 3, 4, and 5, exists in a political arena. If schools are to be learning organizations, principals must acknowledge and respond to the political qualities and nature of schools both internally and in their community contexts. Furthermore, the culture- and vision-building elements of the leadership conception and the supportive functions of the managerial conception exist in a highly political context. Values and resources, for example, those related to teaching and learning, are two areas where conflict is frequent and intense in schools. These conflicts are clearly political and demand a political role of the principal and assistant principal.

The traditional political view of the role of the school principal has tended to emphasize three approaches. In one approach, principals are expected to be apolitical or even nonpolitical. One era of the history of education could be described as an attempt to rid education of politics. The move away from the ward politics of urban areas, such as New York and Chicago, during the 1920s to separately elected boards of education with nonpartisan members was an attempt to avoid the political maneuvering in which schools and administrative positions were used as paybacks for political contributions (Tyack and Hansot, 1982). To avoid this type of political role, educators historically have been cautioned to stay out of politics. They have been encouraged to take no stands that might be opposed by some political constituency. This conception has encouraged the notion—typically among new administrators—that they should take no politically controversial positions. More recently, this fear of politics in the schools may have subsided. Crowson (1998) suggested that "memories of machine politics run amuck have faded, as today's new realization is that the public schools may be too important to the city's welfare not to be politicized" (p. 57). This memory has faded to such a degree that in several urban areas, for example, Chicago and New York City, the mayor now has a direct and close involvement in the management of schools.

The second approach conceives of the principal's political role as based on politics as manipulation. In this conception, principals gain political clout among powerful constituencies in order to manipulate resources, including people, to satisfy their own self-interests. Traditionally, this takes the form of paternalistic principals who encourage dependency relationships and perpetuate the principal's power in ways unrelated to the school's shared vision. At others times, principals become Machiavellian. Whatever tactics are necessary to maintain the principal's power and achieve the principal's vision of success are considered appropriate. This conception reflects what McClelland (1975) referred to as the negative face of power as exploitation rather than the positive means for creating change.

Third, a subtler traditional political role of the principalship is one that emphasizes buffering the school from parents and the community. Veteran principals frequently advise this conception of the role to new administrators, and this view is taught in some educational administration courses. Although at times the principal needs to buffer school faculty and staff from interruptions and inappropriate pressures, if buffering becomes the primary political role of the principal, the school loses the rich contributions of diverse constituencies that may contribute to the learning organization. Bridging is a more appropriate political role for contemporary principals than buffering.

The principal has a critical role to play as politician that is more appropriate and valuable to schools than these three traditional conceptions. Before moving to the specifics of the principal's role as politician, we first identify elements of a political perspective.

Thinking Politically

In developing a conception of the principal's and assistant principal's roles that take seriously the political dimension, several elements of a political perspective are important to consider. Bolman and Deal (1991) identified five propositions that constitute a political perspective:

1. Organizations are *coalitions* composed of varied individuals and interest groups (e.g., hierarchical levels, departments, professional groups, gender and ethnic subgroups).
2. There are *enduring differences* among individuals and groups in their values, preferences, beliefs, information, and perceptions of reality. Such differences change slowly, if at all.
3. Most of the important decisions in organizations involve the *allocation of scarce resources*; they are decisions about who gets what.
4. Because of scarce resources and enduring differences, *conflict* is central to organizational dynamics, and *power* is the most important resource.
5. Organizational goals and decisions emerge from bargaining, negotiation, and jockeying for position among members of different coalitions (p. 186).

Carl's experience, described at the beginning of this chapter, illustrates these ideas and the importance of thinking politically. Jefferson High School and its community were composed of a variety of *coalitions* of individuals and groups. Some, like Susan and Joe, represented a group asking for resources, that is, school sponsorship and facilities. Others, such as the angry parents and legislators who opposed the club, formed coalitions that were at odds with those who wanted to grant these resources to the students on the basis of their values, beliefs, and preferences. When Carl responded positively to the students,

Professional Dilemma 8.1

At a Rotary Club meeting, a leading businessman approaches you. He mentions to you that his sister's son, who is a seventh grader in your school, is bored by his history teacher. You have observed frequently in this teacher's classroom and find the teacher's lessons to be well organized and relevant to seventh graders. Do you tell the teacher what the businessman told you?

he was caught between competing and enduring interests and differences, that is, a conflict of values.

The coalitions that developed after formation of the club and after the school board's decision to ban all noncurricular clubs used various types of power to persuade decision makers to agree with their point of view and restrict or provide resources (e.g., club sponsorship). Sanctions, lawsuits, and other political tools were used to bargain and negotiate positions and resources with decision makers. Carl's skill in avoiding escalating conflict among students during the walkout also was a powerful tool used in settling disputes.

Two factors previously identified are central for thinking politically: *conflict* and *power*. We typically think of conflict as something to avoid. Yet conflict in a political system is a necessary process to allow individual interests to be heard. Diverse interests and groups are becoming an increasingly apparent feature of contemporary schools. This diversity is not only racial and ethnic but also ideological. The principal who sees conflict as something always to avoid runs the risk of trying (ultimately unsuccessfully) to silence groups whose voices traditionally have not been heard but whose perspective is important. Conflict can be beneficial in developing alternative ways to address differences of values and scarcity of resources (see discussion on mediating conflict in Chapter 6).

> A tranquil, harmonious organization may very well be an apathetic, uncreative, stagnant, inflexible, and unresponsive organization. Conflict challenges the status quo and stimulates interest and curiosity. It is the root of personal and social change, creativity, and innovation. Conflict encourages new ideas and approaches to problems, stimulating innovation (Heffron, 1989, as cited in Bolman and Deal, 1991, p. 185).

In postindustrial society, where diversity is a central feature of work, principals and assistant principals must be able to acknowledge not only the inevitability of conflict but also its value.

Power is also central to thinking politically. Traditionally, we think of power in negative terms, for example, coercing or forcing people to do what we want them to do. Yet power is more diverse. French and Raven (1959) identified five types of power:

- Reward (based on the ability to provide rewards)
- Coercive (based on the ability to punish or remove rewards)
- Legitimate (based on a legitimate right to prescribe behavior, e.g., position or authority)
- Referent (based on an identification or relationship with the person with power)
- Expertise (based on special knowledge)

Leaders and followers use rewards to influence other individuals to do something. Administrators use their position of authority to influence decisions. In the opening vignette, Carl used referent power to convince the students to return to class after the walkout. In the Chapter 3 vignette, Nancy Lowenstein used expert power concerning professional learning communities. Educators also can use teaching expertise to influence decisions. Bolman and Deal (1991), based on their review of the literature, identified three other forms of power: alliances and networks, access to and control of agendas, and control of meaning and symbols (pp. 196–197). Thinking politically means recognizing the multiple forms of power and when they are appropriate. Principals who confine their power to position (authority) will rapidly discover the limited potency of this form of power. Teachers, parents, students, and community members also possess power that frequently is stronger than the principal's authority for making changes and negotiating conflict. Kotter (1985) used the term *power gap* to describe this discrepancy between the authority of the manager and the power necessary to get things done or make changes. Most veteran principals will tell you that relying on your own authority as a principal will not suffice to make changes, mediate conflicts, or influence others to improve instruction. Thinking politically means expanding your understanding not only of the power you have but also of the power that others have.

Thinking politically also means recognizing the spheres in which political activity occurs. Traditionally, school administrators have been trained to concentrate attention only on what is occurring within the school. In political terms, this means addressing the conflict among teachers, students, administrators, and possibly parents. Parsons (1951) identified two problems that all organizations, and thus their administrators, must address: internal integration (e.g., morale) and external adaptation (e.g., responding to environmental demands). Principals must think politically not only in terms of how conflict within the school is negotiated and power is used but also in terms of the environmental spheres in which schools exist and within which principals are politicians. Bolman and Deal (1991) referred to organizations like schools as both political arenas and political tools. Schools are nested within districts, communities, and the larger society, and thus these spheres influence the political nature of schools.

In the remainder of this chapter we address the principal's political role in terms of societal, community, district, and school contexts. As we address the principal's role as politician and as facilitator of other politicians, we acknowledge a broader role than the one traditionally identified as existing only within the school. We maintain that you as principal have a political role to play in the larger society, community, and district, as well as in the school, that promotes the learning of *all* students.

Principal as Politician

In the Society

As we have mentioned, educators tend to see the principal's political role as limited to the internal context of the school. Yet we argue that the principal plays a political role that is influenced by and occurs within the society. We base our understanding of the principal as politician in the society on an understanding of schools as political institutions.

Slater and Boyd (1999) identified three ways that schools can be considered polities, or political institutions: political systems, civil societies, and the rule of the many in the interest of the whole, or democratic institutions. We will use these distinctions to organize both our understanding of schools as political institutions in the society and our understanding of the principal's and assistant principal's roles.

Schools as Political Systems.   Understanding schools as political systems seems to emphasize the internal political nature of schools, that is, how schools act as political systems using power to respond to conflicts about scarce resources. However, schools also can be seen as political systems that occur within the larger political environment of the society. One way to understand this larger political environment that influences the school as a political system is in terms of ideological differences and how individuals and groups holding these differences address social and economic changes.

Various ideological perspectives confront schools and principals with different demands and approaches to addressing the social and economic changes that contemporary schools now face. Cibulka (1999) identified three major societal changes confronting schools that are addressed by various ideological perspectives. First, there is a decreasing faith in institutions such as schools. Cibulka used the annual Gallop Poll data to illustrate this. Public support for education, as evidenced in the Gallop Poll, has declined 20% from 1970, from 58 to 38%. Second, we are seeing the mobilization of powerful interest groups and movements that in some instances are opposed to public schools and administrators. Among the most potent movements influencing schools are, according to Cibulka, business activism, growth of the religious right, and elected public officials, such as governors and mayors, who take a more active role in school reforms. Third, the transformation of the American economy to a globalized and nonindustrial economy is another change that influences schools and the ideological pressures being placed on schools and principals.

> All these changes made less probable and even obsolete the traditional ideology of school administration as an autonomous, apolitical, professional, technically neutral enterprise. Indeed the greater demographic diversity of the country has merely reinforced the trend toward more overt "politicization" of school affairs (Cibulka, 1999, p. 170).

These societal changes confront principals with often conflicting demands and pressures.

> Conservatives see the performance decline in public schools as the predictable result of liberal philosophies and dominance by liberal special interests (elites). Liberal analyses accept that there is a legitimate basis for public concern and seek programs and policies to restore confidence, while at the same time seeking to protect the institution against the mobilization of the political right (but not necessarily business interests). Radical interpretations, by contrast, stress that the performance problems of public schools are rooted in the structural inequities of the larger social and economic order (Cibulka, 1999, p. 177).

Principals, such as Carl in the opening vignette, frequently face conflict among two or more ideological perspectives. The growth of the conservative religious right and the demands of those seeking radical reform of the inequalities they experience put the principal in the middle where compromise is not obvious. Schools and their principals exist in a political system where conflicts over values, beliefs, and resources are increasing.

Schools as Civil Societies.   Slater and Boyd (1999) identified a second way in which schools are polities that have implications for the principal's political role: schools as civil societies. In this way, schools are not only influenced by the political system but also can contribute to the larger society by helping to create a civil society. Slater and Boyd described the characteristics of a civil society based on Lasswell's earlier work. These characteristics include "(1) an open ego, by which he [Lasswell] meant a warm and inclusive attitude toward other human beings; (2) a capacity for sharing values with others; (3) a multi-valued rather than a single-valued orientation; (4) trust and confidence in the human environment; (5) relative freedom from anxiety" (p. 328).

The contemporary emphasis in school reform on student performance, defined by standardized achievement test scores, fails to recognize a fundamental quality that historically we have expected schools to engender in students, that is, the willingness to contribute to society. Writers have noted recently the American emphasis on individuality and the growing disregard for community. Bellah and colleagues (1985) identified this historical tendency toward individualism in American society, recorded as far back as de Tocqueville, and the need for developing an understanding and sensitivity to community. Putnam (1995), in a work with the provocative title "Bowling Alone," demonstrated evidence that individual efforts are increasing and communal efforts decreasing.

Schools are one of the first and primary institutions where students encounter non-family members and confront the need to learn how to live, work, and play with others. Yet, as Slater and Boyd (1999) argued, the traditional curriculum and forms of instruction in schools reinforce individualism rather than community; two exceptions to this are character education and service learning. Principals play a critical political role in helping to make schools into civil societies that prepare students to contribute to their communities.

Schools as Democratic Institutions.   The third form of schools as polities involves the school as a democratic institution (Slater & Boyd, 1999). The view that schools have the responsibility to teach democracy is not new. Thomas Jefferson viewed education as a key determinant for the success of a democracy. In the 1940s during World War II, schools were seen as a critical social institution for perpetuating democracy. More recently, several reforms encourage not only teaching democracy but also modeling democracy in the school. We might argue that reforms such as decentralization and site-based management could be attempts to make schools more democratic. More radical reformers have argued that schools must do a better job of modeling democracy in ways that not only respect faculty members but also value students' voices.

Maxcy (1995) identified three democratic values that contemporary schools not only must acknowledge but also must base their educational practice on:

1. A dedicated belief in the worth of the individual and the importance of the individual in participation and discussion regarding school life
2. A belief in freedom, intelligence, and inquiry
3. A conviction that projected designs, plans, and solutions be results of individuals pooling their intelligent efforts within communities (p. 73).

Maxcy argued that

> School restructuring is failing, not because it is inefficient or lacks proper means for accounting for "school effects"; the problem is deeper than this. We must refocus and turn

away from modernist assumptions regarding the way organizations and persons flourish. Postmodern schools as new forms of educational space should be built on the twin values of democracy and educational value (p. 180).

Apple and Beane (1995), in a discussion of democratic schools, identified several conditions on which a democracy depends:

1. The open flow of ideas, regardless of their popularity, that enables people to be as fully informed as possible
2. Faith in the individual and collective capacity of people to create possibilities for resolving problems
3. The use of critical reflection and analysis to evaluate ideas, problems, and policies
4. Concern for the welfare of others and the "common good"
5. Concern for the dignity and rights of individuals and minorities
6. An understanding that democracy is not so much an "ideal" to be pursued as an "idealized" set of values that we must live and that must guide our life as a people
7. The organization of social institutions to promote and extend the democratic way of life (pp. 6–7).

According to these authors, democratic schools have two major characteristics: democratic structures and processes and democratic curriculum. Among the democratic structures is the widespread participation in governance and decision making. School decisions are not just made by administrators, but teachers, students, and parents also contribute to the problem solving and decision making. In democratic schools, diversity is valued because all voices need to be heard, and the diversity of these voices adds richness to the decision making and practice of the schools. Also, in democratic schools, adults and students see themselves as part of a larger community. "Democratic educators seek not simply to lessen the harshness of social inequities in school, but to change the conditions that create them. For this reason, they tie their understanding of undemocratic practices inside the school to larger conditions on the outside" (Apple & Beane, 1995, pp. 11–12).

Apple and Beane (1995) also found that curricula in democratic schools are distinctive. Students are provided access to a wider range of information and a right to hear those with varied opinions. Instead of the "official knowledge" present in many schools, democratic schools reach beyond the traditional and bring in the voices of those typically silenced. Democratic curricula also encourage students and adults to be critical readers of their society. The authors provided an illustration of a class discussion of media reports of "natural events." Their teacher led them to consider whose definition of *natural* was being used. One example of a natural event reported in the media was of massive mudslides in South America. As the students thought more critically about the example, they discovered that the wealthy individuals lived in the fertile valleys, whereas the poor could only find housing on the hillsides where floods caused mudslides. "A democratic curriculum invites young people to shed the passive role of knowledge consumers and assume the active role of 'meaning makers.' It recognizes that people acquire knowledge by both studying external sources and engaging in complex activities that require them to construct their own knowledge" (Apple & Beane, 1995, p. 16).

Historically, we have expected schools to prepare students to live, work, and contribute to a democracy. "Surely it is an obligation of education in a democracy to empower the young to become members of the public, to participate, and play articulate roles in the public space" (Greene, 1985, p. 4). Principals, in their role as politician, must lead schools to fulfill this purpose.

Role of Principal as Politician in Society.   These three views of schools as political systems, civil societies, and democratic institutions lead to three conceptions of the political role of principals and assistant principals. First, principals must understand the current ideologies that influence school reform and practice. To ignore the fact that ideologies play a role in reform is to run the risk of being blindsided by controversy. Whether you agree with a particular ideology or not, individuals deserve a voice. Principals must be sensitive to those voices that are not being heard as well as those voices that gain media attention. Although not all the problems you face can be solved by giving people a listening ear, refusing to hear or ignoring individuals and groups that want to be heard is likely to aggravate the situation and intensify the negative aspects of the conflict. As an illustration, several years ago a rural high school received a substantial donation of concrete from the local Red Devil Cement Company for construction of curbing around the football field. In appreciation for the donation, the principal convinced the student council to adopt the mascot of Red Devils. Now, many evangelical religious groups want the name changed because of its satanic reference. The principal ignored the vocal group's request until the group went to the media, which escalated the conflict.

In responding to these ideological differences, as principal you must acknowledge the changes that these differences are addressing, for example, demographic differences. Some of the criticism of public schools has been aimed at the ways some schools ignore problems and needs until ideological sides have developed around them. During the early 1970s, the public school's lack of response to students with disabilities spurred the development of political lobbying groups that forced schools and districts to take decisive action. Perhaps an earlier, more proactive response to an obvious problem would have resulted in more intentional strategies and less governmental and judicial involvement.

Second, as principals and assistant principals, you have a critical role to play in encouraging and fostering the development of schools as civil societies. An obvious basis for the deadly violence experienced in schools in the last few years has been the bullying behavior that ostracized and humiliated some students. Creating a more civil society can go a long way toward addressing the causes of school violence. Programs such as character education and service programs are ways principals can encourage schools to be civil societies. These types of programs encourage students to develop skills in contributing to a society instead of merely pursing their self-interests.

As a principal, you will have the opportunity to influence a vision of the school. The priorities that you encourage will contribute to that vision. What you pay attention to will be noticed by others. Given this critical political role of fostering schools as civil societies, it seems clear that those priorities should include sensitivity and respect for differences.

Third, principals and assistant principals can play a critical political role in developing schools as democratic institutions. Crow and Slater (1996) described the type of school leadership necessary for educating democracy as systemic leadership. This leadership occurs at classroom, school, and community levels. Principals can play a political role in fostering schools as democratic institutions in three ways: articulating purpose, striking balances, and educating for democracy. First, principals can articulate purpose by empowering individuals to be learners. We will return to this idea in the last section of this chapter on facilitating others as politicians. At this point, however, we should say that the role for principals identified here involves including representatives from all school constituencies in conversations and decisions, facilitating group discussions in such a way that all voices are heard, and emphasizing individual growth in and through a professional learning community.

Second, principals foster schools as democratic institutions by striking balances (Crow & Slater, 1996). New principals in particular have to learn to strike a balance between extremes. Encouraging traditionally silenced groups to voice their views does not mean putting the school up for the highest—loudest—bidder. Principals can play a critical role in helping constituents understand each other's perspectives and keep the focus on students and their needs within the larger society.

Third, principals play a critical role in educating teachers, students, parents, and the community about the value and processes of democracy. One of the best ways to do this is to help the school be a model of democracy in the way voices are heard and decisions are made. Also, principals can be key to providing training in consensus building, living with conflict, team building, and other areas of education that are critical to individuals knowing how to be part of a democracy. "In a democracy and democratic organizations, leadership is, ultimately, everyone's business and everyone has a moral obligation to exercise it" (Crow & Slater, 1996, p. 5).

In the Community

In addition to the larger societal contexts in which principals enact their roles, principals also have a political role to play in their local communities. Not long ago it was assumed that only superintendents played a community role. However, now principals clearly have a community role to play. Several political issues create the need for principals to think politically in the context of their communities. First, the homogeneity of interests once reflected in school communities has given way to diverse interests based on racial, ethnic, and ideological differences. Post (1992) described a California suburban community that changed from a homogeneous population with similar liberal interests to a community torn apart after more conservative elements moved in. These conservative parents left larger urban areas in an attempt to escape liberal and multicultural perspectives and approaches to education. The political conflict resulted in long-time school board members being voted out of office and a climate of turmoil that involved principals and teachers. Principals, in communities like this, daily face the political dilemmas created by diverse interests that seek resources for their particular values and beliefs.

Second, although parents typically rate their community schools higher than schools in general (according to the Gallop Poll), a strong distrust of public education and its professionals creates political conflicts in schools. Principals encounter parents and other community members who reject what they see as the public education monopoly and the professional expertise of teachers in making decisions regarding what is best educationally for their children. In this case, principals are required to build coalitions of support for their schools.

Third, at times media portrayals of schools reinforce negative and insensitive images of schools and educators. These images frequently support attempts to privatize education and diminish the influence and power of educators. As you gain experience in the principalship, you will find it necessary to develop relationships with the local media to diminish the effects of the negative images.

Fourth, although school funding is typically a district-wide effort, principals frequently are pulled into this political arena to highlight school successes that would influence citizens to support tax increases and bonding measures. These often pit principals and district administrators against other community groups who see these funding decisions as attempts to reduce resources for other community needs. In addition, these funding initiatives may pit administrators against those who want to decrease taxes.

In conceiving the principal's role as politician, we base our understanding on two views of school-community relationships that reflect political concerns. Driscoll and Kerchner (1999) identified two perspectives of schools. The first perspective views schools as beneficiaries of community support. This is the view principals and other educators use most frequently in discussing the school-community relationship. This perspective identifies the human and financial resources that community members make to support the schools. The two most obvious are parental involvement in providing services to schools and business partnerships. These relationships, in many cases, provide needed volunteer and financial services that would be difficult to obtain otherwise. The example of parents who accompany teachers on field trips with third-graders illustrates how this affects the teaching and learning core of the school. In addition, business partnerships provide technology that would be impossible for some schools to buy on their own.

However, these relationships are not without their political costs. For example, businesses are not wholly altruistic in their contributions to schools. Along with their gifts come expectations and demands that schools will respond to their needs, for example, high-school graduates trained in particular technologies that decrease the company's cost in training new employees. In addition, some businesses expect schools to display their logos on school property. These business and community interests sometimes conflict with other school responsibilities, for example, developing critical thinking skills and more open and diverse skills that prepare students for larger citizenship roles. New principals, while seeking these needed resources, need to be acutely aware of the potential political costs.

The second perspective that Driscoll and Kerchner (1999) identified views schools as agents of *social capital*. This perspective, although not new, has received more recent attention. These authors argued that "education in a democracy is supported in part because schools help to create a public good from which the whole society benefits" (p. 385). Instead of schools only being recipients of what the community offers, this perspective maintains that schools need to emphasize what they contribute to the community.

> It is our contention that although schools benefit from the social capital that results from extra-organizational ties among students and their families, they need not be merely passive receptacles of or thoroughfares for the accrued social capital of their student and fam-

Professional Dilemma 8.2

A middle-school principal found herself in the middle between a group of students who espoused vegan policies and a fast-food chain that provided tutoring and computers to the school.

The fast-food chain requested that the school fly a flag with the company's logo. When the flag was raised, the vegan student group protested. What should this principal do?

ily constituencies. Schools can also play an important role in building the social capital of the community at large and have a vital part in creating and maintaining social capital in modern cities (pp. 385–386).

This perspective could be useful to you in your political role. Principals can demonstrate the contribution that schools make that increases the quality of life in their communities.

Crowson (1998) clarified this perspective of schools as agents of social capital by identifying two ways that schools have or can contribute. The first way is to reach out "to families and the community with assistance and supports designed to strengthen the learning and development (and thereby the opportunities) of children" (p. 59). This approach primarily has involved interagency collaborations or school-linked integrated services in which schools work with, for example, social and mental health agencies to provide holistic services to children and their families (Smrekar & Mawhinney, 1999). The second approach is to reach out in ways "to strengthen the self help capacities of individual families and their children (through empowerment) by simultaneously developing and strengthening local supports and institutions" (p. 59). This empowerment approach views schools as contributing to the capacity of communities to meet the needs of their citizens, especially in ways that reverse urban degeneration (Crowson, 2001). Crowson argued that to date, schools have been less inclined to be involved in these empowerment attempts. He suggested that this is due to school professionals' distrust of a market orientation and their fear that their power as professionals would be weakened.

These two approaches create political issues, especially for new principals. Both service and empowerment approaches link educators with other community professionals and citizens. In so doing, they create the possibility of conflict between diverse expectations and approaches. As we mentioned in Chapter 3, the nature of work in postindustrial society involves more frequent and intense interactions with other roles, thus creating the likelihood of increased conflict. Principals must help educators and their partners negotiate these role conflicts in ways that not only sustain the school's interests but also maintain productive and effective relationships with other community individuals and groups.

These interactions and partnerships with community organizations likely will increase in the future. These approaches make sense in terms of providing more realistic and effective services to students and their families and acknowledging the embedded nature of schools in their communities. Although these relationships are valuable, they will necessitate that principals develop greater political sensitivity and expertise.

Role of Principal as Politician in the Community.   The most obvious feature of the principal's political role in the community is that principals have to interact not only with the internal school setting but also with the community in which the school exists. Various writers have described this role as one of *boundary spanner*. The principal as politician in the community is situated between school and community boundaries. This necessitates political expertise in addressing the conflicts inherent in the interests of the school and the community.

Goldring and Rallis (1993), in their study of "principals in charge," suggested that this *boundary-spanning* responsibility involves several different roles:

> They [principals] take on the roles of negotiator and communicator, explicitly explaining and publicizing the school's mission and relevant programs to community constituencies while developing and nourishing external support. . . . They build bridges between the school and the surrounding worlds and then bear the school's flag across those bridges. They transmit what the school stands for, and they maneuver for strength, independence, and resources in a competitive world (p. 72).

Negotiator, communicator, flag-bearer, and bridger are political roles. They involve many of the political elements identified earlier in this chapter in the work of Bolman and Deal (1991). These roles involve building coalitions; responding to diverse interests in values, preferences, and beliefs; allocating scarce resources; and addressing conflict.

Earlier we mentioned that the political role of the principal typically has involved *buffering* teachers and the larger school setting from community pressures and demands. We acknowledge that there are times when principals and assistant principals must buffer. For example, pressures that disrupt the core technology of teaching and learning need to be diminished and buffered. However, buffering is inherently a distancing and isolating strategy. The valuable and appropriate voices and resources that could enrich the teaching and learning of schools and classrooms are lost when buffering is the sole political strategy.

Instead of buffering, principals need to bridge the school and community. *Bridging* involves acknowledging valuable voices and resources and encouraging those who can contribute to teaching and learning. Obviously, there is some selection that will occur in terms of what the principal and the school community believe contributes to their collective vision. But bridging also involves developing that collective vision with the community so that community organizations and individuals feel a sense of ownership of what the school is doing. Such bridging diminishes the likelihood that these community members will make undue demands on the school. As an illustration of the importance of bridging, one new principal learned how important the local newspaper reporter was to the school. The previous principal had strong public and media relations, and thus school personnel, students, and activities often were published in the paper. When the new principal arrived, she did not immediately see this bridge to the community through the reporter. Instead of positive media reports, the newspaper reporter, feeling somewhat slighted by the new principal, began writing articles on the problems at the school. Although the problems had existed prior to the new principal's arrival, the relationship between the previous principal and the reporter had kept the newspaper articles positive. Goldring and Rallis (1993) identified two major types of strategies that principals use in this political role of bridging. These authors claimed that principals respond to the environment and manage the relationship with the environment. First, in responding to the environment, principals lead the school to restructure in ways that address environmental contingencies or broaden the mission of the school to address new elements of the community environment. Responding to the changing demographics of the community by providing bilingual education programs is one example of this type of strategy.

Principals' roles also involve managing the relationship with the community. Goldring and Rallis (1993) identified two strategies used by principals in managing this relationship: reducing the environment's influence on the school and cooperative strategies. Reducing the community's influence on the school includes such actions as buffering, which, as we mentioned earlier, involves trying to isolate the school from the community. This type of strategy also involves public relations as well. Working with the media and with parents to develop a community image of the school communicates what the school stands for and the successes of the school. This builds coalitions of support that can reduce undue pressure and influence on the school. A principal who inherited bad public relations when she entered the school began to cultivate positive relationships with the media. She invited journalists to special events that celebrated the school's successes, and when crises arose, she openly provided the school's perspective rather than trying to block journalists' access to the school.

Managing the relationship with the community also can involve cooperative strategies aimed at joint action between the school and its community. The reforms mentioned earlier that included integrated services and community empowerment are good examples of this. Goldring and Hausman (2001) argued for the importance of the principal's role in helping the school build civic capacity.

> As decades of research on effective schools and school reform has [*sic*] indicated, it is unlikely that substantial change can occur in the nature of school-community partnerships unless school principals embrace a more community-oriented perspective, that is, unless school principals view the development of civic capacity and community building as part of their roles (p. 10).

This role can include such actions as engaging government systems, building local institutions, investing in outreach, involving the corporate sector, and developing new structures. However, these two authors found that urban principals spend very little time in this type of political role.

> The infrequency with which these principals work with social/community agencies and businesses and the lack of importance attributed to this role are alarming given the high number of students at risk in this urban sample, the low level of resources characteristic of so many schools today, and the lack of community building activities in the neighborhood at large (pp. 18–19).

The principal has an increasingly significant political role to play in communities. Ignoring the role of principal as politician in the community harms the school's ability to respond to student and family needs in a changing context.

In the District

In the United States, public schools are embedded in districts or similar political arrangements. This unique historical arrangement produces numerous political issues for assistant principals and principals. This occurs because principals are hired and evaluated by the district, most of the human and financial resources that principals acquire come through the district, and district administrators are often the medium through which community demands and concerns are transmitted to the school.

In most situations, principals are hired and evaluated by district administrators and board members. Because of this, these groups have influence especially over new principals and assistant principals. Peterson (1984) identified several mechanisms that districts use to control principals, including supervision, input control (e.g., resources), behavior control (e.g., policies and procedures), output control (e.g., monitoring and evaluation of performance), selection-socialization, and environmental control (e.g., public reaction). These mechanisms may create conflicts between the principal's emphasis on the school context and the district administrators' emphasis on the larger district context.

District administrators also affect principals' political role in terms of the resources they provide or withhold. Gamoran and Dreeben (1986) emphasized the role that the district can play in the instructional decisions made in schools. For example, the way district administrators draw attendance boundaries has significant effects on schools. Attendance areas can affect the types of programs, the types of disciplinary problems teachers confront, and a host of other issues. The resources that principals have to enable the work of teachers can have an influence on the principal's political relationship with teachers (Crow, 1990). The allocation of scarce resources is the source of a great deal of political conflict between the principal and the district office.

District administrators also influence schools and the political role of principals when they transmit community concerns and demands to the school. District officials also can buffer schools and principals. However, owing to the politically vulnerable nature of superintendents and boards, new principals should not be surprised to find district administrators less willing to buffer or support them when the principals are involved in politically sensitive situations. In the opening vignette, Carl's experience with the request for a controversial club is a good example.

Role of Principal as Politician in the District.   The political role of principals is defined in part by the traditional middle-management nature of the job. "Principals, as middle managers, must simultaneously manage at least four sets of relationships: upward with their superiors, downward with subordinates, laterally with other principals, and externally with parents and other community and business groups" (Goldring, 1993, p. 95). The specific relationship we are emphasizing in this section is the principal's relationship with administrative superiors in the district, but it is important to understand, as we will emphasize later, that this middle-management relationship interacts with other relationships.

Being in a middle-management relationship with the district creates various political demands on the principal. However, there are multiple ways of responding to these political demands. Crow (1990) found that principals tend to conceive of these roles in relation to the district office in one of two ways: as agents of the central office or as school leaders. Principals who conceive of their role as agents of central office emphasize their responsibility for enforcing district policies and procedures. In contrast, principals who see themselves as school leaders emphasize their relationship with the district as one of advocate for the school. Obviously, as middle managers, principals are involved in both types of responsibilities. However, what principals emphasize in their role influences behaviors and political relationships with other groups, for example, parents and teachers. We will discuss the relationships with teachers in the next section.

District administrators influence the political role that principals play with parents. Goldring (1993) found that administrative superiors influence principals' response to involving parents in school policies, and this influence tends to be affected by district socioeconomic status (SES). In high-SES districts, principals were more likely to involve parents in policymaking if administrative superiors used parental involvement as a criterion for evaluating the principal. This was not true for principals in low-SES districts.

The district presents another political arena for principals and assistant principals. Resources are negotiated, coalitions with parents are formed, and conflicts regarding school-district differences are encountered. Principals may enact their political role in the district by emphasizing their district role or their school role, but regardless, they play a political role that influences their practice and the teaching and learning in the schools.

In the School

Schools are political arenas. Everyday life in schools involves conflicts among teachers, between teachers and students, and between teachers and administrators. These conflicts involve differences in values, beliefs, and preferences. Students, teachers, and administrators struggle over scarce resources. In the opening vignette, Carl was faced with one group of students who wanted the resource of school sponsorship and space; other students wanted their clubs as well. The decision regarding resources for the gay and lesbian students resulted in conflicts with other students focusing on the resource of extracurricular clubs that was denied in protest to the gay and lesbian club.

In order to accomplish their aims and garner scarce resources, teachers, students, and administrators form alliances and coalitions. The gay and lesbian students in the vignette formed their organization to secure the types of resources they could not obtain on their own.

Although schools are more than political arenas, to ignore the political qualities of the school is to be blindsided by the politics that can affect teaching and learning as well as the everyday work life of students, teachers, and administrators. The politics of the society, community, and district, while real, do not have the immediacy and closeness that politics within the school have. Various writers have referred to this level of politics as *micropolitics*. Blase (1991) maintained that micropolitics involves the "strategic use of power in organizations for two purposes, influence and protection" (p. 356). School constituents attempt to persuade others that their preferences, values, and beliefs are appropriate and should be supported, and they try to protect their interests against those who wish to deny them resources or devalue their beliefs.

Role of Principal as Politician in the School.   In examining the principal's political role in the school, we will focus on the two primary groups: teachers and students. Principals and teachers form an implicit political partnership in schools that influence their professional lives together. Although this partnership is more than political, as we have demonstrated throughout this book thus far, the political nature of the partnership is evident and critical to acknowledge. In the traditional perspective, this political partnership involves an exchange relationship in which principals agree to leave teachers alone and to respect their autonomy, and teachers agree to keep students under control and diminish any embarrassment to the principal and the school at large. Such a political arrangement has existed in some schools for years and negatively affects the ability of the school to change and the culture of the school to foster innovation and experimentation in teaching and learning. A more innovative partnership between principals and teachers involves the principal providing resources, encouragement, and mentoring and the teachers contributing their expertise, commitment, and willingness to improve teaching and learning. The principal's political role in these two perspectives is very different.

Blase (1991), in a significant study of the micropolitics of schools, investigated the style of effective and ineffective principals and the political tactics used by teachers with these two types of principals. He found that ineffective principals, which he called "closed" principals, tended to promote "the development of relatively closed political orientations in teachers, orientations characterized by the use of protection, reactive, and indirect (covert) strategies" (p.359). The exchange relationships between teachers and closed principals "were characterized by a strong concern on the teachers' part with minimizing costs—achieving protective goals" (p. 361).

The closed principals in Blase's (1991) study tended to be characterized as authoritarian, inaccessible, unsupportive, inequitable, inflexible, and inconsistent and were known to avoid conflict. In response, teachers used the following political strategies that emphasized protection:

- Avoidance
- Rationality
- Ingratiation
- Confrontation
- Coalitions
- Intermediaries
- Noncompliance
- Documentation

We have maintained that the principal's political role affects the other role conceptions presented earlier in this book. Blase (1991) argued that "a leadership orientation characterized by control and/or distance tends to limit significantly the possibility of developing collaborative and mutually supportive working relationships with teachers" (p. 373).

In contrast, effective, or "open," principals have different characteristics, and the teachers who work with these principals use different sets of political strategies. Blase (1989) found that teachers perceived open principals as having high expectations, being honest and nonmanipulative, being communicative, using participation in their decision making, and being collegial, informal, supportive, and accessible. In response, teachers used such political strategies as the following:

- Diplomacy
- Conformity
- Extra work
- Visibility
- Avoidance
- Ingratiation

Although some strategies were the same with the two groups, the major strategies were different: diplomacy, conformity, and extra work for teachers with open principals and avoidance, rationality, ingratiation, and confrontation for teachers with closed principals. Moreover, teachers "engaged in more two-way (i.e., bilateral influence) and more complex interaction with open versus closed principals" (Blase, 1989, p. 398).

The principal's political relationship with teachers is also influenced by the district office. Crow (1990) found that district administrators influenced principals' relationships with teachers by refusing to consider the school as unique, by placing principals in untenable positions, by creating chaos with district decisions, and by reducing principal's autonomy. Although the opening vignette did not delve into this influence, we should not be surprised if Carl believed that the district's and state's decisions regarding controversial clubs influenced his political role by creating chaos, limiting his autonomy as principal, and placing him in an untenable position. Obviously, districts also can contribute to a principal's relationship with teachers by providing resources, encouraging and supporting the school's shared vision, and treating the school as a unique professional learning environment.

Bolman and Deal (1991) identified three political skills of leaders that may be useful to you as a principal or assistant principal in your political role with teachers. First, these authors maintained that leaders need to be able to set an agenda. Agenda setting involves working with teachers in developing a vision and the strategies for achieving that vision. We have discussed in Chapter 6 the importance of vision for the principal's role as leader. Having a vision that is developed collectively is a powerful political strategy as well. Its effect on influencing change and persuading others to commit their efforts is an effective political tool.

Second, Bolman and Deal (1991) suggested networking and coalition building as effective political tools. This involves first finding out who needs to have ownership in the decision, plan, or vision and which interests of these individuals or groups are important to them. The principal plays a critical role in developing networks among teachers, parents, and other community groups that support learning for *all* students.

Third, these authors suggested bargaining and negotiation skills that are critical to leaders. *Bargaining*, or "horse trading," involves first of all knowing what is important to the teacher or group of teachers that must be acknowledged in reaching consensus or developing commitment to an idea. Negotiating is a routine part of the principal's political role. Bolman and Deal (1991) suggested that a major problem with negotiating is that many leaders engage in "positional bargaining." This involves staking out a position and then making concessions to reach agreement. These authors recommend a different strategy involving "principled bargaining," based on the work of Fisher and Ury (1981). Fisher and Ury identified four strategies in principled bargaining:

1. Separate the people from the problem (pp. 3–4).
2. Focus on interests, not positions (p. 11).
3. Invent alternatives that are mutually advantageous.
4. Insist on objective criteria.

In addition to teachers, students are primary constituents within the school political arena. Because there is an implicit political partnership among teachers and principals, there is an arrangement among teachers, administrators, and students. The traditional arrangement is based on control, where teachers and administrators provide a certain degree of autonomy to student groups, and students agree to respond to the control of teachers and administrators, especially in classroom environments. When this implicit exchange relationship breaks down, chaos ensues. Carl was able to prevent chaos among students by using his referent power—as someone the students trusted. In more innovative political partnerships, this relationship with students takes on more than control and autonomy and invites the participation of students in their own learning experiences.

Principals play a political role with students not just in exercising reward and coercive power to control student behavior. They also play a political role in encouraging and supporting the contribution of students in their own learning. Opotow (1991) suggested that one of the places that this learning can take place is in students' learning to deal with political conflict among themselves. "With adult control diminishing, adolescents actively explore interpersonal influence, deal with threat, negotiate power balances, and learn to cope with social success and disappointment. Their conflict experiences constitute a compelling moral education that absorbs much of their attention" (p. 417). She argued that the typical way administrators respond to student peer conflict is by overreacting, for example, suspensions, or underreacting, for example, "privatizing the conflict." Instead, she suggested that school administrators and teachers should help students learn to deal with their conflict by bringing it out in the open as a learning experience. The principal and assistant principal play an important political role by helping students become successful political actors in their peer struggles.

Assistant Principals as Politicians

Although much of what we have said applies to assistant principals as well as principals, the assistant principalship is situated in a frequently difficult and unique political position. Based on interviews with assistant principals, Marshall and Mitchell (1991) identified the features of the "assumptive world" or political culture in which assistant principals work.

In the cognitive map of the administrative culture, there are roles, statuses, tasks, loyalties, appropriate values, appropriate risk taking, and uses of power. If assistant principals violate these expectations, they can suffer sanctions that are understood by all members of that culture. Some result in a mere smack on the hand with no wider implications, and some challenges result in harm to their careers (p. 410).

According to these authors, assistant principals work in a political environment that constrains initiative and values. Assistant principals learn that while they can initiate policy, they must limit their policymaking to areas that are approved by the district and by the principal. They also learn that "their personal and professional ethics and morality must be modified to conform to the dominant values in the culture of school administration" (p. 411).

Marshall and Mitchell (1991) identified several rules of the political arena of the school that assistant principals learn:

Rule 1: Limit risk taking
Rule 2: Remake policy quietly.
Rule 3: Avoid moral dilemmas.
Rule 4: Don't display divergent values.
Rule 5: Commitment is required.
Rule 6: Don't get labeled a troublemaker.
Rule 7: Keep disputes private.
Rule 8: Cover all your bases.
Rule 9: Build administrator team trust.
Rule 10: Align your turf.

The rules and descriptions of assistant principals' political world depict a traditional role for these individuals. We provide this as an excellent example of political life for assistant principals as it currently exists in many schools. However, both principals and assistant principals in effective schools need to conceive of the political role of the assistant principal in ways that are not protective and reactive but innovative and proactive. Assistant principals need to develop a political role that, like that of the principals, is conducive to facilitating the work of teaching and learning in the school. There is a legitimate political role for you as an assistant principals to play, and it contributes to an inviting and innovative professional learning community.

Professional Dilemma 8.3

An assistant principal observes a security guard deliberately provoking a student who the assistant principal had been counseling and who had improved in behavior. When the guard reported the incident as an assault, the assistant principal explained what had happened to the principal and told him that she was going to write a negative report on the guard. Her principal, a friend of the guard and a believer in military-style discipline, responded that if she wrote such a report, he would write a negative evaluation of her. What should she do? (This is based on an actual case in Marshall and Mitchell, 1991.)

The Principal as Facilitator of Others as Politicians

Principals and assistant principals not only play a direct political role; they also facilitate the political role played by others. We view schools, districts, communities, and societies as in part political entities. Within these various levels, principals and assistant principals are not the only politicians. Others are playing political roles as well. Some of these have a negative impact on the school as individuals and groups attempt to promote their own self-interest without consideration of the larger purpose of learning for all students. Others have a positive impact on the school toward some collective purpose that involves individual student growth in and for the learning community (Crow & Slater, 1996).

As a principal or assistant principal, you can play a significant role in facilitating the political role of others. This role, which can be described as "systemic leadership" (Crow & Slater, 1996), helps to empower others in their political contributions toward a learning community. As we did in the preceding section, we will organize our discussion of the principal's facilitative, or systemic leadership, role in terms of the four levels of society, community, district, and school.

In the Society

We have indicated that the principal plays a profound role beyond the school in the larger society. Principals can play an even more significant role by encouraging and supporting teachers, students, and parents to play a political role in the society. This facilitative role can involve viewing schools in the three ways we identified before: as political systems, as civil societies, and as democratic institutions.

Facilitating the political role of teachers, parents, and students in society involves helping them understand schools as political systems. As we mentioned earlier, this involves understanding the political ideologies that influence schools and the societal transitions that are changing schools. In order to make positive contributions to schools in our society, teachers, parents, and students need to understand how various ideologies view schools and what the practical consequences of these ideologies are for the purposes of schools. The principal can expose teachers, parents, and even students to these ideologies and guide them in a critical reflection of what these ideologies mean for school practices. The principal also can help others understand the social and economic changes that are occurring in our society and how these changes affect schools. Sometimes parents and teachers try to deny the reality of demographic and technological changes. Such a denial not only can make schools inflexible to change, but it ultimately also weakens the political contribution of those who deny these societal changes.

Principals also can facilitate the political role of others in the society by encouraging them to view schools as civil societies. This may be one of the most profound political actions principals can take as they help teachers, parents, and students to examine the inequities and understand how the school can act as a learning community. The indictment of Bellah and colleagues (1985) of the extreme individualism that pervades our society calls for all those involved in educating to work to develop ways to make schools civil. Our children learn to be uncivil to each other by watching the lack of civility of their teachers, parents, peers, legislators, and other political leaders. Principals can remind these constituents that schools can and should become civil societies that support individual growth in and for a learning community.

Finally, principals can facilitate the political role of others by helping teachers, students, and parents to model democracy. Both the content of the curriculum and the structure of the school can empower others to help build the school as a democratic institution. Supporting the open flow of information about the curriculum and how schools are organized and providing time and resources for teachers and students to critically reflect on this information empowers others politically.

These activities may seem monumental as you enter your first administrative position. However, viewing your role beyond the internal school context will allow you ultimately to make a powerful political impact that affects the lives of students and their families.

In the Community

The principal also has a role to play in facilitating the political role of teachers, students, and parents in the community. This facilitative role has at least two parts. First, principals can help to sensitize others in the school to the politics of the community. This sensitizing may begin by helping teachers understand that teaching and learning take place in a community with various political agendas and potential conflicts. This is most obvious in the case of community beliefs and values regarding curriculum. The case of Joshua Gap, discussed earlier and found in Post's (1992) article, centered around the use of a multicultural curriculum that some parents found offensive. Frequent community battles over sex education are another case of this type of political conflict. Often principals try to shield teachers from these political conflicts by either handling them "out of sight" or by demanding that teachers not use certain objectional curriculum. However, facilitating the political role of teachers involves sensitizing them to these power conflicts over beliefs and values. A paternalistic orientation aimed at shielding teachers does not enable the kind of systemic leadership necessary to make teachers stakeholders in the political process. Frequently, principals have relied on the teachers' union to be the only political vehicle for teachers. However, the public frequently views the union as having a vested interest in maintaining membership. Teachers need to become strong political constituents in their own right.

Second, principals can help educate teachers to be active political partners. Understanding and developing skills at networking, building coalitions, and negotiating are necessary political skills for teachers working in communities. In school-community partnerships, such as interagency collaboration and community development (Crowson, 2001; Smrekar & Mawhinney, 1999), teachers discover quickly that they need the skills to be strong political partners with other community agencies. Many of these agency personnel already have these political skills that strengthen their bargaining positions. Principals can provide professional development to help build these types of skills for teachers in working with community groups.

By sensitizing teachers to community politics and by supporting the development of political skills, principals help teachers to be part of the bridging process. Instead of principals orienting their approach to teachers and community conflict solely in terms of buffering, principals can help teachers to become bridges that will strengthen school-community partnerships in ways that support teaching and learning.

In the District

Teachers are becoming increasingly more a part of the political process in districts. They serve on district committees with parents and other community members. They serve as interpreters of the district agenda. At the beginning of a two hundred million dollar bond campaign, district administrators educated the teachers to become strong interpreters of district needs and the details of the campaign. The teachers' efforts resulted in one of the largest successful bond elections in the country.

Principals can facilitate the political role of teachers in the district by encouraging teachers to take on committee assignments and by finding substitutes for them to attend meetings. Principals also can facilitate this political role for both teachers and parents by helping them understand the resource-allocation process in districts. Although this is not without risk, for example, with district administrators, ultimately it provides teachers and administrators with more educated partners in the political process. When teachers and parents do not have the necessary budgetary and legal information to be active political partners, they are more inclined toward distrust and opposition.

In the School

Many of the most recent educational reforms at the school level involve political processes. Strategies such as site-based management, shared decision making, and professional learning communities typically have been described in morale and instructional terms. Yet they involve political processes that frequently are ignored. Site-based management and shared decision making depend on teachers, parents, students, and administrators being able to build consensus and work as teams. These processes involve political skills such as agenda setting, networking, coalition building, and negotiating. Yet few teachers are taught these skills in their preservice education, and many do not receive additional professional development in these areas. Professional learning communities assume that teachers have the skills to resolve value conflicts in an environment where diversity is welcomed. Although diversity among faculty can contribute to richness in the school context, it also invariably leads to conflict as teachers with different ideologies of teaching, understandings of learning, and approaches to classroom conduct come together.

Principals can facilitate the development of the political skills necessary to make these reforms successful by providing professional development and helping teachers and parents to recognize the political process inherent in these strategies. Providing professional development in such areas as conflict mediation, consensus building, the positive use of power, agenda setting, networking, coalition building, and effective negotiation is a powerful tool for principals to give to teachers.

In addition, principals can facilitate the political role of teachers and parents by the principal's own political style. As Blase's work (1989, 1991) attests, the principal's orientation—whether closed or open—influences the types of political tactics that teachers use. Principals with closed and ineffective orientations tend to influence teachers to use protective, reactive, and covert strategies, whereas principals with more open orientations influence teachers to use more collegial political tactics. One of the strongest ways principals can facilitate teachers as politicians is by modeling orientations that emphasize more effective, open, and collegial approaches.

In addition to teachers and parents, principals and assistant principals can facilitate the political role of students. Helping students understand conflict as a democratic process teaches a powerful lesson about living in a democratic society. As Opotow (1991) suggested, principals, by bringing conflict to the surface instead of underreacting or overreacting to it, can help students develop the necessary skills to function effectively in a democratic society. Assistant principals, who frequently carry the majority of responsibility for resolving student conflict, can help students understand the positive side of conflict. They also can teach students political skills, such as negotiating, compromising, and diplomacy, that encourage open and productive forms of response to conflict. Such skills will help to provide a profound understanding of how to contribute productively to a civil society.

Principals play a crucial role for teachers, parents, and students in facilitating their political role. Instead of ignoring or trying to diminish the importance of the political role, principals can help others develop critical political skills that contribute to a civil society and to schools as democratic institutions. By understanding teaching and learning as occurring in a political context, principals can make a profound contribution at societal, community, district, and school levels.

Conclusion

Politics may not be a four-letter word, but it certainly is a topic many principals wish to avoid. However, as Carl Patterson, the principal of Jefferson High School in the opening vignette, found, it cannot be ignored. We have chosen to include the principal as politician as a major innovative role conception because we believe that politics is not only necessary but also valuable for the leadership of learning. Your political role, as a principal or assistant principal, takes place at all four levels of society, community, district, and school. Understanding and communicating how these levels affect the learning of all students is a necessary part of creating learning communities. Rather than being a necessary evil, politics can become a valuable tool for focusing your attention and the attention of others on learning as power.

In Chapter 9 we move to another external role of principals that uses power for leadership in learning—the principal as advocate. Understanding the needs of students who face challenging circumstances because of their race, culture, language, social class, gender or sexuality, disabilities, or at-risk conditions; being an advocate for these students; and facilitating the advocacy of others are critical for building a school where *all* students learn.

Activities

Self-Reflecting Activities

1. Reflect on the political conception of the role of a principal you have known. Of the three approaches to the political role presented early in this chapter, which most represents how this principal conceived his or her role? What have been the consequences?

2. Reflect on the professional dilemma presented in this chapter of the principal faced with a student vegan group protest over the involvement of a fast-food chain in the school. What would you do as the principal?

3. Talk to a retired principal regarding her or his relationship with the district office. How did district administrators affect the principal's relationships with teachers and parents? How did this principal respond to district influence?

Peer-Reflecting Activities

1. Discuss with your colleagues the first professional dilemma in the chapter regarding whether to give community criticism to a teacher. Role play how you would respond to the businessman.

2. Brainstorm ideas for how a principal as supervisor and learner could help teachers critically reflect on whether the class and school curriculum is democratic.

3. Reflect with a colleague on the political strategies you both use in relating to your principal. Analyze your reflections in terms of Blase's findings regarding teachers' political strategies with open and closed principals.

Course Activities

1. Have each student develop a case that focuses on some specific political incident or issue at a local school or district. Use Bolman and Deal's (1991) five propositions of a political perspective to analyze the politics of the case. Also use French and Raven's (1959) five types of power to identify the kinds of power used in this situation.

2. Invite a panel of community members, including businesspeople, journalists, and government officials, to discuss their view of the schools and their expectations. At another time invite a local principal to discuss the nature of school-community relations.

Websites

- *http://www.ucea.org/cases/*
  Cases from the Journal of Cases in Educational Leadership
  Strader, D. L. (2001). Keep kids off drugs. *Journal of Cases in Educational Leadership* 4(3).
  McCreary, J. (2001). Getting clubbed over a club. *Journal of Cases in Educational Leadership* 4(1).

DiPaola, M. F. (1999). Scandal at Placido High: Coincidence or conspiracy? *Journal of Cases in Educational Leadership 2*(3).

Brown, R. S., Penn, J. L., & Claudet, J. (1999). Equal access: Community values and student rights. *Journal of Cases in Educational Leadership 2*(2).

Lundt, J. C. (1999). Facing community pressure: When emotion overrules logic. *Journal of Cases in Educational Leadership 2*(1).

Lyons, J. E. (1998). Leadership, authority, and community: Control at Southwood High School. *Journal of Cases in Educational Leadership 1*(1).

■ *http://www.aft.org/*
American Federation of Teachers. The American Federation of Teachers "represents one million teachers, school support staff, higher education faculty and staff, health care professionals, and state and municipal employees"

■ *http://www.ecs.org*
Education Commission of the State. The mission of the ECS "is to help state leaders identify, develop and implement public policy for education that addresses current and future needs of a learning society"

References

Apple, M. W., & Beane, J. A. (Eds.) (1995). *Democratic Schools.* Alexandria, VA: Association for Supervision and Curriculum Development.

Bellah, R. N., Madsen, R., Sullivan, W., Swidler, A., & Tipton, S. (1985). *Habits of the Heart: Individualism and Commitment in America.* New York: Harper & Row.

Blase, J. J. (1989). The micropolitics of the school: The everyday political orientation of teachers toward open school principals. *Educational Administration Quarterly 25*(4), 377–407.

Blase, J. J. (1991). The micropolitical orientation of teachers toward closed school principals. *Education and Urban Society 23*(4), 356–378.

Bolman, L. G., & Deal, T. E. (1991). *Reframing Organizations.* San Francisco: Jossey-Bass.

Cibulka, J. G. (1999). Ideological lenses for interpreting political and economic changes affecting schooling. In J. Murphy & K. S. Louis (Eds.), *Handbook of Research on Educational Administration* (2d ed., pp. 163–182). San Francisco: Jossey-Bass.

Crow, G. M. (1990). Central office influence on the principal's relationships with teachers. *Administrators Notebook 34*(1), 1–4.

Crow, G. M., & Slater, R. O. (1996). *Educating Democracy: The Role of Systemic Leadership.* Fairfax, VA: National Policy Board for Educational Administration.

Crowson, R. L. (1998). Community empowerment and the public schools: Can educational professionalism survive? *Peabody Journal of Education 73*(1), 56–68.

Crowson, R. L. (Ed.) (2001). *Community Development and School Reform.* Oxford, England: Elsevier.

Driscoll, M. E., & Kerchner, C. T. (1999). The implications of social capital for schools, communities, and cities: Educational administration as if a sense of place mattered. In J. Murphy & K. S. Louis (Eds.), *Handbook of Research in Educational Administration* (pp. 385–404). San Francisco: Jossey-Bass.

Fisher, R., & Ury, W. (1981). *Getting to Yes.* Boston: Houghton Mifflin.

French, J. R. P. J., & Raven, B. (1959). The bases of social power. In D. Cartwright (Ed.), *Studies in Social Power.* Ann Arbor, MI: Research Center for Group Dynamics, Institute for Social Research, University of Michigan.

Gamoran, A., & Dreeben, R. (1986). Coupling and control in educational organizations. *Administrative Science Quarterly 31*(4), 612–632.

Goldring, E. B. (1993). Principals, parents, and administrative superiors. *Educational Administration Quarterly 29*(1), 93–117.

Goldring, E. B., & Hausman, C. (2001). Civic capacity and school principals: The missing links for community development. In R. Crowson (Ed.), *Community Development and School Reform.* Oxford, England: Elsevier.

Goldring, E. B., & Rallis, S. F. (1993). *Principals of Dynamic Schools.* Thousand Oaks, CA: Corwin Press.

Greene, M. (1985). The role of education in democracy. *Educational Horizons 63*(Special Issue), 3–9.

Heffron, F. (1989). *Organization Theory and Public Organizations: The Political Connection.* Englewood Cliffs, NJ: Prentice-Hall.

Kotter, J. P. (1985). *Power and Influence: Beyond Formal Authority.* New York: Free Press.

Marshall, C., & Mitchell, B. A. (1991). The assumptive worlds of fledgling administrators. *Education and Urban Society 23*(4), 396–415.

Maxcy, S. J. (1995). *Democracy, Chaos, and the New School Order.* Thousand Oaks, CA: Corwin Press.

McClelland, D. C. (1975). *Power: The Inner Experience.* New York: Irvington.

McCreary, J. (2001). Getting clubbed over a club. *Journal of Cases in Education Leadership 4*(1); retrieved from *http://www.ucea.org/cases.*

Opotow, S. (1991). Adolescent peer conflicts: Implications for students and for schools. *Education and Urban Society 23*(4), 416–441.

Parsons, T. (1951). *The Social System.* Glencoe, IL: Free Press.

Peterson, K. D. (1984). Mechanisms of administrative control over managers in educational organizations. *Administrative Science Quarterly 29*, 573–597.

Post, D. (1992). Through Joshua Gap: Curricular control and the constructed community. *Teachers College Record 93*(4), 673–696.

Putnam, R. (1995). Bowling alone. *Journal of Democracy 6*, 65–78.

Slater, R. O., & Boyd, W. L. (1999). School as polities. In J. Murphy & K. S. Louis (Eds.), *Handbook of Research on Educational Administration* (2nd ed., pp. 323–335). San Francisco: Jossey-Bass.

Smrekar, C. E., & Mawhinney, H. B. (1999). Integrated services: Challenges in linking schools, families, and communities. In J. Murphy & K. S. Louis (Eds.), *Handbook of Research on Educational Administration* (2d ed., pp. 443–462). San Francisco: Jossey-Bass.

Tyack, D. & Hansot, E. (1982). *Managers of Virtue: Public School Leadership in America, 1820–1980.* Boston: Basic Books.

Principal as Advocate

9

Key Terms and Concepts

advocacy
at-risk
bilingual education
Brown v. *Board of Education*
Education for All Handicapped Children Act (EAHC)

English as a second language (ESL)
ethnocentrism
gifted and talented (GT)
inclusion
Individuals with Disabilities Education Act (IDEA)

limited English proficient (LEP)
mainstreaming
multicultural education
social reconstruction
Title I

Vignette

As the only assistant principal at Salt Creek High School, Curtis Erickson was facing more challenges than he ever had before becoming an administrator. Curtis had grown up and attended schools in this rural Rocky Mountain valley. After his graduation from Salt Creek High School, Curtis went to a Christian church–sponsored college in the Midwest. There he met and married a woman from Nebraska. Both he and his wife were offered teaching positions in his hometown, and after teaching for five years, Curtis took extension courses in administration from the state land grant university. He was the first assistant principal at the high school since its opening seventy-five years ago. The school had been small and only needed one administrator. However, in the twelve years since Curtis's own graduation, Salt Creek High School had grown considerably. Another small high school on the other end of the valley had been consolidated into Salt Creek, with students either being bused or driven into town. The Bureau of Indian Affairs had closed a nearby reservation school, and the Native American students were now being bused into Salt Creek High School. A large California electrical power company constructed and opened a new plant nearby. The mountain coal mines surrounding the valley had expanded and increased production to supply the power plant. Larger ranching firms were buying out the small ranches. These changes had increased the population of the entire valley, and the new families moving in were quite different from the families that had settled the valley originally.

Curtis's own family had moved to the valley in the late 1890s and had started a cattle ranch. All six of his brothers and sisters continued to live in the valley, and an older brother worked the ranch, although it had long lost its profitability. Most of Curtis's friends from school also were still hanging around the valley, working at various jobs, and supporting fairly large families. Curtis was known throughout the valley, and his family was well respected, with both his father and his grandfather having served in various leadership positions, including the local school board. Because his wife was from a rural Nebraska town, she was quite content living and working in Salt Creek Valley.

Now Curtis was looking out over the assembly of high school students. It was almost as if he were noticing for the first time how different they were from his own high school student body. The students represented several ethnic groups besides the Anglo whites. The next largest population was Latino, most of whom had migrated to the valley from southwestern states. Some had emigrated from Mexico. A few were in the United States illegally. The Native Americans mostly were indigenous to the area, and most lived on the reservation. Other groups, such as Pacific Islanders, Asian Americans, and a few African Americans, had migrated to Salt Creek Valley for employment reasons. The valley ranches and grain farms attracted some seasonal migrant families who mostly came from Central and South America. There also was some religious diversity among the newcomers. The Protestant and Catholic congregations had had to make room for other religious groups. Some of the families, especially among the Asian population, were not Christian. Two of the black families were Muslim. Many Native Americans practiced a traditional worship.

The assembly today was the annual Winter Music and Drama Festival. The school choir, band, orchestra, and drama departments had put the assembly together for the student body and then for the community in the evening. In the past, the assembly was known as the Christmas Pageant. This year, however, Curtis convinced the student council to rename the assembly because of pressure from some individuals who did not think it appropriate to call it a Christmas Pageant.

Changing the name was not as easy as he had anticipated. The student council was receptive and immediately voted to change the name. A few days later, however, three parents and a minister entered his office demanding to know the reasons for taking Christ out of the schools. The three parents were long-time members of the community who had strongly influenced the valley and school politics. They expressed concern about changing the assembly name. One parent commented that it was bad enough not to be able to have prayer in school, but now even Christ had been kicked out. She told Curtis that his father and grandfather would have been appalled at the change. The group demanded that the school administration immediately change the name back to Christmas Pageant. Curtis had a hard time responding and knew that he was unprepared to defend the change adequately.

The name change was only part of the controversy. The day before the festival, the choir teacher approached Curtis and told him that one of her students was protesting the singing of the traditional Christmas carols. She told Curtis that she had never even thought about the music being offensive to anyone, and it was definitely too late to change the songs for the next day's festival. Curtis later met with the student and found out that her family was Jewish. He had no idea that the community or the high school had any Jewish members. He did not know what to do about the situation and added it to the long list of items he needed to talk to the principal about.

However, the meeting never occurred that day. After school, a fight broke out in the bus pickup area between two groups of students. One group was known as the "Cowboys" because they often came from the ranch families and wore cowboy boots and other western regalia. The other group was a Latino group. Evidently, the Latino group of students had been waiting for the bus to go home. A few members of the Cowboy group had lobbed snowballs over the crowd and hit several of the Latino students. In the beginning it was only a snowball fight, but tempers flared, and soon several students were in fisticuffs with each other. Fortunately, Curtis was not far away and was able to get to the scene before anyone was seriously hurt. However, he had to take the main instigators into his office and suspend them. By the time he had finished, it was after 6:00 P.M. and he was exhausted. The principal was supervising the basketball games in the gymnasium. Curtis left his office and walked down to the game.

On his way to the gym, Curtis saw some members of the Latino group huddling in the corner. When they saw him, one of them came up to him and asked him why they had been suspended when they had not started the fight. Curtis reminded them that the "Safe School Policy" strictly prohibited fighting of any kind. He then told them that they had been suspended from school and needed to leave the building. One of the group members told him that they would be back to settle the matter.

By the next afternoon, Curtis and the principal still had not had time to discuss these pressing issues, and the assembly was underway. Curtis was tense during the entire program. He was concerned about the decisions he had made recently. He found it hard to concentrate on the assembly because of all the issues surrounding the school. He knew that if he was to remain in school administration, he had a lot more learning to do. He had felt confident at the time he was appointed to be the new assistant principal. Now, however, he was not so sure. He was uncertain about his own values and beliefs concerning the changes in the school and community. He recognized his own weaknesses in handling differences among the students. He wondered if Salt Creek would ever be the community it was when he was growing up. As his thoughts swirled with inadequacies, the principal came and sat next to him. His words brought some comfort when he whispered to Curtis, "I can tell you're troubled. Remember, we are here for *all* the kids. After the assembly, let's go to my office and talk about some of these issues."

Introduction

Introduction Throughout this book we have emphasized the important role of the principal as a learner. In this chapter we discuss how learning also involves advocacy. Similar to Salt Creek High, school populations everywhere have become increasingly heterogeneous, and learning must involve all students and all educators. Driven by social justice, access to knowledge, statutory regulations, and legal decisions, the school communities have had to adapt to the diversity of race and ethnicity, disabilities, language acquisition, gender, sexuality issues, and socioeconomic status. Some of these issues have resulted in the creation of new programs that have to be administered. Some issues have caused increased tensions and stresses on principals, teachers, students, and parents. As a principal or assistant principal, you will be expected to serve as an advocate for all children and to help other educators perform advocacy roles. You will be expected to act equitably and promote social justice and access to education for all children. As early as 1923, Cubberley suggested in describing the principal's responsibility: "No other person in the community can so immediately mould [sic] its life and shape its ideals" (p. 36). Although being an advocate for children is not a new role for principals, it has been emphasized as school populations have become more diversified.

The last two decades of the 20th century saw school leaders turn more attention toward educating all children, no matter their socioeconomic status or their academic abilities. Principals became part of a *social reconstruction* of communities, where every person deserved an education with dignity and respect. At times, this type of leadership put principals at odds with fundamentally conservative subcultures of their communities. Consequently, being a strong school leader also required the principal to be a strong moral leader in the community and to take positions that were morally right rather than what were popular or what had been done in the past. As Beck and Murphy (1993) suggested, in the 1990s, "there . . . [were] serious efforts developing to transform the principalship into an instrument of social justice" (p. 194).

As we discussed in earlier chapters, emphasizing learning for *all* children leads to conceiving of schools as learning organizations and communities. Learning is not just an individual event but rather occurs within a social context—within a community. Although it may be possible to generate a product with individuals performing separate and isolated activities, it is not possible to learn outside a social context. When we discuss the principal as advocate, we do so with the understanding that this role conception is focused on advocating for individual students as learners and each student's right to learn within the school community.

In this chapter we organize the discussion of the principal's role as advocate in three ways. First, we discuss the meaning of advocacy—what it is, who is involved, and why it is important. Second, we describe the principal as advocate and identify practical ways you as a principal or assistant principal can develop advocacy. Third, we discuss special programs and the administration of these programs. In the fourth section of this chapter we focus on the principal as facilitator of advocacy, helping create advocacy among others, especially teachers.

Defining Advocacy

In this chapter we use the term *advocacy* in the sense of supporting, maintaining, and defending moral, legal, and thoughtful educational principles and practices for children and youth. In supporting moral, legal, and thoughtful principles and practices, the principal actively promotes these principles and practices through specific behaviors such as speech, nonverbal messages, behaviors, and activities. For example, principals can support inclusion of students with disabilities in regular education classes by talking to interested teachers and sharing the philosophy of inclusion, providing resources for their attendance at inclusion workshops, and allowing the teachers to visit other inclusive classrooms. In this way, principals support a moral educational practice such as inclusion by supporting teachers to become involved in the practice. The three criteria for advocacy are moral, legal, and thoughtful.

Moral. The first criterion for being an advocate is maintaining what is morally right. The principal is an advocate by sustaining and upholding the principles and practices that have proven successful and that are needed for their continuance. For example, maintaining a safe school is necessary for all children to learn.

An advocate defends moral causes when internal or external forces threaten those causes. Internal forces such as a teacher subculture can be destructive to good causes. For example, a principal may need to defend a girls' soccer team's right to have the same access to the playing field as the boys' soccer team. External forces, such as the parents and minister in the opening vignette, also threaten moral causes, in that case the attempt by Curtis to create a more sensitive name for the winter assembly. In some communities, fundamentalist religious groups and individuals have sought to ban the Harry Potter and Goosebumps books because they are perceived to promote the occult and mystical powers. Although the principal has to be sensitive to these concerns, allowing subgroups in a society to censure reading materials can be quite dangerous.

If principals are to be advocates for moral, legal, and thoughtful causes, then it is important to understand what constitutes a moral cause. We advance the concept that education is inherently a moral enterprise. Because parents entrust their children to the school, educators have a moral responsibility to protect and educate those children. Also, schools act as a major source of moral instruction for the young to be socialized into the larger society. Youth learn citizenship, language, laws and mores, and the inherent responsibilities that are needed to live in and contribute to a community.

Sirotnik (1990) identified five moral responsibilities of educators: (1) inquiry, (2) knowledge, (3) competence, (4) caring, and (5) freedom, well-being, and social justice. In the following subsections, we will discuss each of these moral responsibilities.

Inquiry. Sirotnik (1990) suggested that the first principle of moral commitment, and its ethical root, is inquiry. A matter of increasing concern to many is what appears to be a decline in thoughtfulness, in reflective habit, in the value placed on inquiry itself—especially in a culture that is amusing itself to death. As Sirotnik put it, "Too often we have heard educators say something to the effect, 'Well, that's interesting, but it's just philosophical; let's get back to what we can do in the real world.' Thinking appears to have become increasingly alienated from 'doing'" (p. 299).

As principal or assistant principal, you need to acknowledge explicitly the moral commitment to inquiry. As we discussed in Chapter 3, the demands of a postindustrial society will require you to be a learner who reflects in such a way that your assumptions are questioned and information from a wide variety of new sources is used. This reflectivity is not a luxury of professors but a necessity for practitioners. In the opening vignette, Curtis realized that he had to learn more about the students in the school and their differences. He reflected on his own learning and realized that he had a lot more learning to do. Similarly, you also need to be constantly reflecting on your own learning and on ways to continue your learning.

As you practice inquiry, you also must promote inquiry and reflectivity among teachers and students. At times, practicing and promoting inquiry may put you at odds with policymakers and others who may champion standardized measurements without understanding their limitations. As Arendt (1958) said, "The highest and perhaps purest activity of which men are capable is the activity of thinking" (p. 5). This concept is not always understood or practiced by many policymakers and educators.

Knowledge.   Sirotnik (1990) suggested that inquiry without knowledge is fraudulent and that knowledge without inquiry is impossible. The question has to be asked, however: What kind of knowledge is a moral commitment? Is knowledge being viewed as bits and pieces of information that can be deposited and withdrawn as a series of facts in a bank? Knowledge is far more encompassing and dynamic than a body of accumulated information. As Sirotnik argued, as important as the facts are, taken separately or together they do not constitute knowledge. Knowledge is what we make of the facts and what we learn through explanation, interpretation, and understanding. In short, knowledge is what we gain through inquiry; moreover, inquiry is stimulated and sustained by what we know. This is accomplished through active and intellectual engagement with information in the context of being human.

Competence.   In describing competence and incompetence, Sirotnik (1990) suggested that competence is a natural aspiration for humans. He suggested that we as humans aim to reward success and not failure. We also reward excellence and not mediocrity. Because we are more interested in success and excellence, being competent is something that humans aspire to. An "ethic of competence," or a moral commitment to doing and learning to do things well, seems to be an important moral ingredient in working in a society and a community. As Sirotnik suggested, when we focus on justice and human interrelationships, we do so under the assumption that people will serve each other well, not poorly.

Caring.   The fourth moral principle outlined by Sirotnik (1990) is based on the premise that the relationships among people are basic to the human condition. He used caring to refer to "deep relationships among people based on mutuality, respect, relatedness, receptivity, and trust" (p. 302). In Nel Noddings' (1984) words:

> Apprehending the other's reality, feeling what he feels as nearly as possible, is the essential part of caring from the view of the one-caring. For if I take on the other's reality as possibility and begin to feel its reality, I feel, also, that I must act accordingly; that is, I am impelled to act as though in my own behalf, but in behalf of the other (p. 16).

Because we care about each other and ourselves, we need to watch out for each other. However, we would argue that you must be somewhat prudent and wise in your caregiving. Educators can and do burn out because of their caretaking of others. We suggest that you first take care of your own basic needs, such as nutrition, exercise, and other good health habits. We then suggest that you take care of your family and loved ones. If you do not care for your own and your loved ones' needs, you may find that your energy for caring for others will be greatly diminished and you may approach burnout.

Freedom, Well-Being, and Social Justice.   James Madison (1788) observed, "If men were angels, no government would be necessary" (p. 262). Freedom and well-being are essential features of the human condition, and we are duty-bound to preserve and protect these features. When preserving and protecting freedom and well-being cannot be adequately accomplished by individuals, then society, usually through government, has to become involved. Americans have placed a great deal of faith in the nation's schools (most of which are an arm of the government) to socialize and acculturate youth into the society. However, socializing our youth does not mean accepting the way things are but helping youth to be willing to change things to the way they ought to be. It is here that schools can be more than a mechanism for transmitting social values but also a way of reconstructing values for a just society.

Legal.   You also must consider the second criterion for advancing educational principles and practices—of being legal. Everyone should receive equal access under the law. If a government provides a school system, everyone should have equal access to the educational system and the curricular and extracurricular programs.

The Fourteenth Amendment to the United States Constitution provides for equality under the law by stating: "No State shall . . . deny to any person within its jurisdiction the equal protection of the laws." Although, by today's standards, "equal protection of the laws" is interpreted as everyone having equal access, in 1895, the U.S. Supreme Court stated that equality under the law also could mean "separate but equal." One of the results of the *Plessy* v. *Ferguson* ruling was that segregated education based on race could be legal under the Fourteenth Amendment. This ruling, of course, was overturned in 1954 when the Supreme Court ruled in *Brown* v. *Board of Education of Topeka* that segregated education was inherently unequal. This ruling meant that if school facilities, teachers, equipment, and all other physical conditions were equal among racially segregated schools, the schools would still be unequal because of racial segregation.

Thoughtfulness.   The third criterion for defining educational principles and practices to advocate is thoughtfulness. Perhaps one of the problems today is the demand for instant decision and comment. For example, no sooner does the President of the United States give a press conference than newscasters are following with commentaries. When a critical incident occurs at a school, principals find microphones in their faces asking for an immediate decision or comment. There is little tolerance for uncertainty and doubt. However, in advocating the moral and legal principles and practices, we also must be thoughtful as to the consequences of the principles and practices. For example, suspending a first-grade boy for kissing a playmate on the cheek because it is a violation of sexual harassment rules may be following a policy, but it also is a mindless act. As a principal or assistant principal, you must learn not to be afraid of withholding judgment, of challenging the assertions of others, and of having your own ideas challenged in return. Thoughtfulness often takes time, and it flourishes as more questions are asked. In the opening vignette, perhaps Curtis could have taken more time to solve the problems thoughtfully.

Some people have argued that government has no place in socialization efforts for moral, ethical, and thoughtful principles and practices. They have argued that family, churches, businesses, and other private organizations, such as scouting, can be better socialization agents for youth than can government organizations such as schools. Perhaps

they can, or at least perhaps they have the potential. However, if we relied on these organizations entirely, then some of our children and youth who do not have access to family, church, or scouting would be left out of the socialization process. Schools are the only
available means that have the potential of reaching all youth and instilling accepted moral
commitments.

As a principal and assistant principal, you become a major player in this charge. Any
practice that perpetuates social and economic inequities should be targets of your advocacy. Schooling in America has a long history of attempting to balance equity and excellence, and at times, schools have excluded populations in an attempt to achieve excellence.
It is important to understand that equity and excellence do not have to be mutually exclu-
sive in schools. Sirotnik (1994) offered definitions for *equity* and *excellence,* indicating
that both could be attainable:

> Excellence is indicated by conditions, practices, and outcomes in schools that are associ-
> ated with high levels of learning for most students in all valued goal areas of the common
> curriculum. Equity is indicated when there are not systematic differences in distributions
> of these conditions, practices and outcomes based upon race, ethnicity, sex, economic sta-
> tus, or any other irrelevant group characteristic (p. 168).

In the past, the debate over equity or excellence tended to polarize educators and
policymakers. It often came down to either having one or the other. As a principal, however, you can go beyond this rhetoric and choose to advance both equity and excellence.
In fact, Sirotnik (1994) claimed that there could be no educational excellence without educational equity.

As an advocate, you can be a leader of a school that not only serves the best interests of all students but also provides a valuable educational lesson by modeling the *just*
society. Kerr (1987) summarized the purpose of moral commitments of schooling:

> This cultural conception of education is fundamental to social justice, to cultural commu-
> nity, to democracy, and to our ability to interpret what we see—to structure experience. It
> is this broad and basic conception of education that justifies the institution of schooling
> generally. . . . The central task of schooling is education as an initiation into the ways of
> understanding and inquiring. Education so conceived cannot be improved by courses in
> critical thinking, for it is itself an initiation into the disciplines of critical thinking. It can-
> not be passed over in favor of "basic education," for there is no education that is more basic
> (p. 25).

Throughout this book we have proposed the concept of learning as being part of
community. In the larger sense of community, consider America as a collection of multiple communities defined by different interests, races, ethnicities, regions, economic strat-
ifications, religions, and so on. Celebrating these differences is part of what makes the
nation great (Sirotnik, 1990).

In the remainder of this chapter we address the principal's and assistant principal's
roles as advocate and as facilitator of others to be advocates. However, we acknowledge a
broader role of advocacy than the one traditionally identified as existing only within the

school. Similar to the political role that we discussed in Chapter 8, we maintain that principals have an advocacy role to play in the larger society.

Principal as Advocate

Understanding Differences

We begin our discussion of principal as advocate by first exploring the nature of differences that exist within society and schools. We then discuss six factors that can affect education and schooling: race, ethnicity, and culture; language; poverty and social class; gender and sexual orientation; students with special needs; and at-risk students.

Because our culture is so much a part of what we are and what we do, we often view other cultures as being inferior. *Ethnocentrism,* the belief in the superiority of our own culture, can lead us to judge others in terms of our culture and to conclude that those who do not conform to the norms of our culture are in some ways inferior or irresponsible. When the dominant group in a society adopts the posture that its own set of values constitutes the only idealized norm in that society, the practices or traits of minority cultures are likely to be seen as deficient and must be corrected either by education or coercion. As Pai and Adler (2001) put it, the dominant culture tends to treat minority cultures as sick forms of the normal culture and to define differences as deficits. In Chapter 5 we introduced the concept of deficit view, which assumes that something is wrong and needs to be fixed. Although in Chapter 5 we discussed the deficit view regarding supervision and mentoring of teachers, the deficit view can target many groups and behaviors in the schools, such as racial and ethnic groups, language usage, students with disabilities, gender and sexual orientation, and those living in poverty. Too many times in America's history educators and policymakers have segregated groups of students because of their differences from mainstream students. As a principal or assistant principal, your role as advocate should be to oppose the deficit view among teachers, staff members, students, policymakers, and members of the community.

The notion that a difference is not a deficit is also useful in exposing ethnocentric assumptions underlying various school curricular and extracurricular programs. Access to all school programs has not been available to all groups. For instance, some schools have *ability groups* and *tracking programs* to differentiate among student interests and abilities. Poor and minority students often have been left at the bottom of the system (Burnett, 1995). Ability grouping is still common in schools because teachers often believe that it is easier to teach a group of students with similar abilities. Groupings usually are based on reading and math levels, but the grouping designations often transfer into other subject areas, especially if standardized testing is used to determine the groupings. Ability grouping usually begins in elementary school and continues through high school as students are tracked into curricular paths. For example, the college-preparatory track has had fewer representatives from poor and minority students. Unfortunately, too often placement in school programs correlates directly with the child's background, language tests, appearance, and socioeconomic variables (Oaks, 1986). Because teachers and counselors often recommend students for placement into programs, some of these educators may hold a deficit view of various students. Even more troubling is the fact that these placements tend to be fairly stable over time. Students placed in low-ability groups find it more difficult to catch up with high-ability groups over the years.

In an early classic study, Rosenthal and Jacobsen (1968) tested the effects of teacher expectations on interactions, achievement levels, and student intelligence. Their conclusion that once a child is labeled by the teacher and others, a "self-fulfilling prophecy" operates. The teacher expects certain behaviors from the child, and the child responds to the expectations. More recent studies (e.g., Banks, 1999) have shown that teacher expectations play a significant role in determining how much and how well students learn. Teacher expectations are influenced by various factors, including records of a student's previous work and test scores; the student's dress, name, physical appearance, attractiveness, race, gender, language, and accent; the parents' occupations; single-parent and motherhood status; and the way the student responds to the teacher.

Ethnocentric assumptions also can affect extracurricular programs. For instance, certain athletic programs have become known as "country club" sports because of the nature of those who participate. To compete with others and qualify to participate in certain sports, students have had to have considerable experience in playing in year-round sport clubs or access to expensive golf courses and ski resorts. Because of these high-cost activities, many students and their families simply cannot afford to participate and thus are viewed as being deficient because their talents are not as visible as those who can participate. Likewise, instrumental music also can pose a barrier to participation for students who cannot afford to rent or purchase musical instruments. Often schools have to charge extra fees for the musical and athletic activities, preventing some students from access to the programs. Eliminating ethnocentric assumptions that lead to discriminatory practices is a target of the principal's advocacy role.

In the next subsection we discuss how ethnocentrism can affect our view of differences among students, schools, and community members. Some of these basic assumptions about different cultures have lead to unsound educational practices. In your role as advocate, you need to be aware of these practices, help to eliminate them, and support others' awareness and actions against the practices.

Racial, Ethnicity, and Cultural Diversity

The late 19th and early 20th centuries were a time of massive immigration to the United States. However, the immigrants who reached American shores after 1870 were different from their predecessors (Pai and Adler, 2001). The new immigrants came from southern and eastern Europe, Asia, and South America and did not have the Anglo-Saxon heritage. Thus they had more difficulty adjusting to the English language and the Protestant orthodoxy that dominated the public schools. Rather than establishing schools as a multicultural microcosm of society, educators reaffirmed their belief that being an American meant conforming to the Anglo-Saxon, Protestant view. The educational historian, Elwood Cubberley (1909), who was introduced in Chapter 2, remarked:

Our task is to break up these groups or settlements, to assimilate and amalgamate these people as a part of our American race, and to implant in their children, so far as can be done, the Anglo-Saxon conception of righteousness, law and order, and popular government, and to awaken in them a reverence for our democratic institutions and for those things in our national life which we as a people hold to be abiding worth (pp. 15–16).

It soon became apparent to native-born Americans and the new immigrants that simple Anglo conformity was not reasonable. Hence what immerged was the idea of a *melting-pot ideal*. Pai and Adler (2001) reported that according to this view, ethnic differences that were melted into a single pot would produce a synthesis—a new homogeneous culture that was not Anglo-Saxon, Jewish, Italian, or Asian. However, the melting-pot ideal never materialized. "In reality, what happened in the melting pot . . . was that all varieties of ethnicities were melted into one pot, but the brew turned out to be Anglo-Saxon again. The ingredients of this melting pot were, in fact, to be assimilated to an idealized Anglo-Saxon model" (p. 63). Most people realize now that using the melting pot metaphor to describe the United States was never accurate.

In the 1960s, many educators and minority leaders pointed out that America's schools were ethnocentric in curriculum and instructional practices despite the 1954 *Brown* v. *Board of Education* ruling that pronounced "separate is not equal" in schools. They proposed that schools failed to provide equal educational opportunity to poor and minority children. What followed was a confusion of meanings for *multicultural education*. Several kinds of curricular and instructional practices came under the guise of being multicultural, although they did little in promoting better understanding of cultural differences. Banks (1999) suggested four approaches or levels in developing multicultural curriculum: (1) the contribution approach, (2) the additive approach, (3) the transformative approach, and (4) the social action approach.

The first two levels, the contribution approach and the additive approach, are most common. Using the contribution approach, the curriculum includes content about holidays and celebrations of various ethnic groups. Because of this approach, educators started celebrating Black History Month, Cinco de Mayo, and Pacific Islanders Week. The second level, additive approach, uses the curriculum to add content about minorities without changing the basic goals and structure of the curriculum. An example of the additive approach would be including Langston Hughes' writings in a literature course.

Banks (1999) advocated that schools should move to the levels of the transformative and the social action approaches. The transformative approach changes the basic assumptions of the curriculum and enables students to view concepts, issues, themes, and problems from different perspectives. Curriculum is aimed at helping students understand events from the perspective of different ethnic groups. For example, Columbus's discovery of America is seen differently from the Anglo-Saxon perspective than it is from the Native American perspective. Students would be expected to study events and institutions from various points of view and to reach their own conclusions based on their study. This is a type of constructivist learning, as discussed in Chapter 3.

The social action approach suggests that once students have studied an issue and drawn their own conclusions, they should be able to take personal, social, or civic action.

For example, a class of students could investigate literature anthologies as to the reasons publishers do not include more pieces by people of color. The students then could create their own anthology or write to publishing companies urging a more balanced approach.

As Beyer and colleagues (1997) reported, in the United States, an individual's race and ethnicity are socially not scientifically defined. On most government forms, including those used by schools, people are asked to identify their race. In some countries, a person's ethnicity is defined by an individual's ancestry. In other countries, religion or language distinguish the major ethnic groups. For example, race and ethnic definitions overlap because Latino/as may be of any race. The overlap confuses many Latino/as who do not identify with any of the race categories that are often on government forms. Furthermore, individuals of mixed racial parentage are also confused as to the category to which they belong. For example, professional golfer Tiger Woods has a mixed racial parentage. Because race is self-reported, individuals are free to choose the racial category with which they most closely identify.

Cultural differences also apply to religious diversity. It is important to note that religious diversity does not relate solely to immigrant or minority children. Catholic and Jewish families who have been in America for generations often have felt discrimination in the public school system.

Some school and classroom practices have conflicted with religious beliefs. For example, consider the following situations:

1. Muslim elementary school students having to go to the cafeteria during lunch even though they were fasting during Ramadan
2. Sikh children assigned to play angels in the Christmas pageant
3. Hindu children having to participate in Easter egg painting and hunting
4. Seventh-Day Adventist students scheduled to play athletic events on Saturdays
5. Evangelical Christian students asked to participate in the Halloween costume parade

Although most educators understand the concept of separation of church and state, especially regarding prayer and Bible study, the issues are more confusing when it comes to other classroom practices, such as those just listed. A holiday party may be considered an example of how a school as a state agency does not always remain neutral in some of its practices. Although some of these activities may be long-time traditions in the school, what is frequently absent is a recognition that some children are isolated by the activities. Often these children are left to decide if they will participate or remove themselves from the activity and their peers, which further emphasizes their differences and alienates them from other students.

In 1963, the Supreme Court ruled in *School District of Abington Township* v. *Schempp* and *Murry* v. *Curlett*, with regard to support of religion, the "State is firmly committed to a position of neutrality." This ruling, however, does not prevent educators from including religious thought and practices in the curriculum to reflect a multicultural society. Indeed, to completely remove religion from the curriculum is to limit student understanding in such areas as history, music, and literature in other cultures. Often culture is manifested through religious practices.

Misunderstanding of the court rulings also has led to wrongful practices. Consider the following:

1. A teacher confiscates a Bible from a student during free reading time and states, "This is against the law!"
2. Students were told that they could no longer assemble for a morning prayer circle in the commons area.
3. A student is told not to offer a silent prayer before eating lunch.
4. A teacher was told by her principal to remove classroom posters that had sayings by Moses, Jesus, Buddha, Mohammed, and Gandhi.

This kind of misinformation can lead to discriminatory practices as much as promoting one kind of religious or cultural activity. As an advocate for moral, legal, and thoughtful principles and practices, you have a responsibility to protect all students from discrimination and feelings of isolation. One helpful hint may be to evaluate activities in the school as to their intended purpose. If the purpose is not to promote knowledge or reflection of other cultures, then the activity may exist only because of tradition and could alienate some students and parents.

Language Diversity

One area of concern for educators that is often linked to racial and cultural diversity is language differences. The challenges with language diversity are usually with immigrants and native-born students who are raised in a non-English-speaking environment. The National Center for Education Statistics (1996) predicted an increase of 5 percent in elementary school enrollments from 1994 through the year 2006 due to a combination of immigration and rising birth rates that started in 1977. The anticipated growth of *limited English proficient (LEP)* children poses a challenge for teachers and principals.

Native-born students also can experience language barriers. Most notably is the use of what is considered nonstandard English among African Americans (often called *Ebonics*), Native Americans, and Latino/as. Many principals and teachers regard standard English as the only correct form of English and treat other language patterns as broken English. Often these children's language diversity is viewed as a serious learning obstacle to their cognitive development and classroom success. We do not suggest that children from ethnic communities should not be taught to use standard English. However, as Pai and Adler (2001) suggested, standard English should be learned as a second language similarly as non-English-speaking students learn English as a second language. Generally, these students want and need to learn standard English to be successful in the American culture, but their native language usage should not be viewed as a deficit. As principal or assistant principal, your respect and advocacy for students and their language diversity will indicate to others the importance you place on their ethnicity and culture. When a school community is likely to have a community of language diversity for a period, then you also might consider acquiring that language. You can provide professional development programs for teachers to acquire the language. Such programs have been successful in areas such as the America Southwest with educators in Latino and Native American communities.

Another challenge regarding LEP students involves their parents, who may not be as involved with their children's school because of the language barrier. The school building may be an uncomfortable place for parents who cannot speak English fluently. Likewise, written school communications that are sent home, for example, notices of parent meetings and conferences, may not be understood. Each school will have its own community culture that will require special consideration in bridging communication gaps.

Zepeda and Langenbach (1999) offered three personal qualities that social workers and psychologists have used in building relationships with those who speak a language different from the mainstream culture. These three qualities are warmth, empathy, and genuineness. Warmth can be communicated to students and parents both verbally and nonverbally. Warmth promotes a sense of comfort and well-being and can put students and parents at ease. Empathy involves being in tune with how the students and parents feel. Empathy requires the educator to convey that the student's and parents' situations are understood. In the context of LEP student relationships, the teacher may convey in both verbal and nonverbal ways an understanding of how the student and parents may feel torn between what is being taught in school and what is taught at home. As Zepeda and Lagenbach suggested, empathy is a skill that involves visualizing how it must be to walk in that person's shoes. The third quality is genuineness, or the ability to be authentic or real. Genuineness involves the sharing of self by relating in a natural, sincere, spontaneous, and open manner.

Poverty and Social Class

Educational researchers have indicated for several years that a statistically significant relationship exists between poverty and academic achievement. For example, Wolf (1977) reported that a poor child is almost twice as likely to be a low academic achiever as a child who is not living in poverty. However, the factors that explain the variation in student achievement are not necessarily linked to the parental income levels or socioeconomic status. Rather, measures of home atmosphere such as parental aspirations for their children, the amount of reading material in the home, and family attitudes toward education are more indicative of student achievement. Two conditions of poverty affect student achievement. Some children are from families that are impoverished temporarily because of such things as illness, job loss, marital breakup, or unexpected expenses. Other children may be living in families in later-term poverty that is due to a lack of occupational skills, disabilities, or living in a high-impact unemployment area. A student's home atmosphere and expected academic performance differ among children residing in households experiencing different types of poverty (Orland, 1994).

Another research finding by Wolf (1977) showed a statistical relationship between poverty and achievement at the school-building level. From this study, researchers and educators have been able to predict with considerable accuracy a school's academic performance by knowing its overall rate of poverty. In fact, the school's rate of poverty has been a stronger predictor of student achievement than an individual student's poverty level. A nonpoor student in a poor school is actually more likely to be a low achiever than is a poor student in a wealthier school. There appear to be several factors of the school environment that may contribute to student achievement. Examples of such factors include the influence of peers, the resources available, the quality of the teachers, the presence of school characteristics such as a shared vision, the expectations of teachers for student performance, and parent involvement (Orland, 1994).

There is also an association between the length of time students are poor and the likelihood that they will be behind their expected grade level. For each age cohort and among each ethnic group, the proportion of students behind grade level increases with the number of years in poverty. The length of time a child is likely to be poor is related to several demographic conditions, the most important of which is probably race. For example, among black sixteen-year-olds, about one in six is behind the expected grade level. This likelihood doubles to about one in three for those who have spent eight or more years living in poverty (Orland, 1994).

These findings should not be construed to suggest that increased time in poverty causes lower student achievement. Other factors in combination with the length of time in poverty play into children falling behind in school. For example, more boys are behind than girls. Also, a mother's education level increases the likelihood of her children's lower achievement. More than likely, the length of time in poverty is strongly associated with many other features of the home and school environment (Orland, 1994).

Poor children and children attending a school with high poverty concentrations have a greater likelihood of performing poorly in school. We suggest that as a school leader, your efforts in school reform will be more effective in serving these students than in blaming the students' or the community's impoverished conditions. As a principal, you can be an advocate by reducing some of the barriers at the building level that prevent high student achievement. As suggested in Chapter 8, principals can use school-community initiatives such as interagency collaborations to attack the effects of poverty.

Gender and Sexual Orientation

Gender differences and issues in education are not new. Most early European and American schools discouraged girls from attending. Evidence indicates that both subtle and blatant differences in the treatment of girls and boys still occur at all levels of the school system. Sadker and Sadker (1994) summarized research on discrimination against girls in

Professional Dilemma 9.1

In a school district that recently changed its boundaries and added neighborhoods with lower socioeconomic families, several veteran teachers were troubled with the makeup of their classes. Not having had much experience with the populations they were now teaching, many of the best teachers were asking for transfers. The principal knew that if the veteran teachers left, the best of the faculty would be gone. At the same time, the principal wanted to honor their requests for transfers because of their loyalty in the past. What should the principal do?

their book, *Failing at Fairness: How America's Schools Cheat Girls.* One result of their research was that girls were equal to or ahead of boys in most measures of academic achievement and psychological health during the early years of schooling, but by the end of high school, girls had fallen behind boys. On entrance examinations to college, girls scored lower than boys, particularly in science and mathematics. The Sadkers suggested several contributing factors to this gap; namely, teachers interact differently with boys than with girls, women are represented less in textbooks, and standardized tests have discriminatory content.

The Sadker and Sadker (1994) book is important because it has focused attention on gender differences in education. However, factors other than education play into gender differences. Parental support and involvement also influence attitudes among girls and boys in their curricular choices (Tocci & Engelhard, 1991). Parents with higher socioeconomic status are more likely to be active in their daughters' course selections (Muller, 1998). Societal factors also influence gender differences. Boys tend to receive more toys that are science-related, such as chemistry sets, doctor kits, telescopes, and microscopes (Richmond-Abbott, 1992). Popular video games, television shows, and movies also often portray gender-role stereotypes.

In some subjects in school, girls are doing better than boys, and this has caused disagreement among researchers and educators as to which gender is actually doing better. In her book, *The War Against Boys,* Sommers's (2000) cited research that showed boys, not girls, on the weak side of an educational gender gap. Sommers cited several National Center for Education Statistics (NCES) reports to support her claims (Tables 9-1 through 9-3). Her reports indicated that boys, on average, are a year and a half behind girls in reading and writing; they are less committed to school and less likely to go to college; girls get better grades; girls have higher educational aspirations; and girls follow a more rigorous academic program and participate more in advanced placement (AP) courses. Sommers concluded, however, that "none of that has affected the 'official' view that our schools are 'failing at fairness' to girls" (p. 14).

Many young people experience other forms of sexual discrimination in school. In one study of students in grades eight through eleven, 85 percent of girls and 76 percent of boys experienced some form of sexual harassment, with sexual jokes, gestures, and com-

TABLE 9.1   Number of Students Who Took AP Examinations (per 1,000 Twelfth-Graders), by Sex

	1984	1985	1986	1987	1988	1989	1990	1991	1992	1993	1994	1995	1996
Total	50	59	64	66	81	88	100	103	109	117	115	125	131
Male	50	61	65	68	76	86	101	96	102	108	101	111	117
Female	50	58	63	65	85	90	98	101	117	127	129	140	144

Source: U.S. Department of Education, National Center for Education Statistics, *The Condition of Education 1998* (p. 90). Washington, D.C.: U.S. Government Printing Office, May 1999.

TABLE 9.2 Percentage of 1994 High School Graduates Taking Selected Math and Science Courses, by Sex

	Males	*Females*
Mathematics		
Algebra I	64.7	68.1
Geometry	68.3	72.4
Algebra II	55.4	61.6
Trigonometry	16.6	17.8
Analysis—Precalculus	16.3	18.2
Statistics/probability	2.0	2.1
Calculus	9.4	9.1
AP calculus	7.2	6.8
Science		
Biology	92.3	94.7
AP/honors biology	4.0	5.1
Chemistry	53.2	58.7
AP/honors chemistry	4.1	3.7
Physics	26.9	22.0
AP/honors physics	3.0	1.8
Engineering	0.4	0.2
Astronomy	2.0	1.5
Geology/earth science	22.8	23.2

Source: U.S. Department of Education Statistics, National Center for Education Statitics, Digest of Educational Statistics 1998 (Table 138, p. 152). Washington, D.C.: U.S. Government Printing Office, May 1999.

ments most common, followed by touching or grabbing in a sexual way. Most of the harassment came from the students' own peers.

The implication for you as the principal or assistant principal is in developing your own awareness as to how gender affects student learning and how you advocate for improving learning for all students as you mentor and supervise all students. In addition, as advocate, you must develop a nonthreatening culture where sexual jokes, gestures, and other forms of harassment have no place.

Another form of discrimination exists with sexual orientation among students and among their parents. Being an advocate for children includes affirming the worth and dignity of *all* children regardless of their sexual identity. Being sexually different in a society of sexual sameness can create a heavy psychological toll on students. Struggling to cope with their sexual identity, these students are more likely than other youth to attempt suicide, to abuse drugs or alcohol, and to experience academic problems (Zera, 1992). The American School Health Association issued a policy statement regarding gay and lesbian youth in schools that stated:

**TABLE 9.3   Percentage of High School Seniors Participating in
Extracurricular Activities in 1992, by Sex**

	Male	*Female*
Interscholastic team sports	41.2	19.7
Academic clubs	22.9	27.4
Honorary societies	14.4	22.7
Student government	13.1	17.7
Newspaper or yearbook	14.0	23.5
School service clubs	10.3	17.4
School play or musical	14.1	16.7

Source: U.S. Department of Education, National Center for Education Statistics, *Digest
f Education Statistics 1998* (Table 144, p. 155). Washington, D.C.: U.S. Government
Printing Office, May 1999.

School personnel should discourage any sexually oriented, deprecating, harassing, and
prejudicial statements injurious to students' self-esteem. Every school district should provide access to professional counseling, by specially trained personnel for students who
may be concerned about sexual orientation.

Likewise, children coming from homes that have gay, lesbian, or bisexual parents
also need advocates. The most commonly experienced problem or fear confronting children, most notably adolescents, from lesbian or gay households is rejection or harassment
from their peers (Bigner & Bozett, 1990).

Students with Special Needs

From the beginning of American education, the needs of students with disabilities often
were neglected. The political movement for legislation to aid students with special needs
followed a path similar to other civil rights movements. After efforts to change local and
state governments regarding the education of students with disabilities, organized parent
groups turned to the federal government. In 1975, Congress passed Public Law 94-142,
the *Education for All Handicapped Children Act (EAHC),* requiring that all handicapped
children between the ages of three and twenty-one have access to a free, appropriate public education in the least restrictive environment. The law also required public agencies to
ensure that children with disabilities are educated with children without disabilities to the
maximum extent possible. The law was renamed in 1990 as the *Individuals with Disabilities Education Act (IDEA).* IDEA changed terminology from *handicapped children* to
children with disabilities, shifting emphasis from the handicap or disability to the child.
Under these laws, each student classified with a disability has to have an *individual education plan (IEP).* The law requires that the *local education agency (LEA)*—the school—
and the child's parents or guardians jointly develop the IEP. Thus the law gives parents the
right to negotiate with the school the type of services to be delivered.

The number of children identified with disabilities has risen since 1977. Currently, approximately 13% of all children from birth to twenty-one years of age qualify for special education services. Of these students, the largest number has learning disabilities, followed by speech and language impairments, mental retardation, and serious emotional disturbances. If student disabilities are a new area for you, take time to become familiar with all types of disabilities and the programs that will benefit children with such disabilities.

A major concern regarding the education of children with special needs has been their isolation from other students and the lack of access to the educational opportunities of a regular classroom. Under the original act, Public Law 94-142, the requirement of "least restrictive environment" resulted in the practice of *mainstreaming*. The basic idea of mainstreaming was that students with disabilities should spend part of the day in regular classrooms. However, many parents and educators felt that mainstreaming did not go far enough to provide a least restrictive environment. The concept of full *inclusion* was introduced that allowed special-needs students to spend all or most of their time in a regular classroom. The isolation of children with special needs often deprived them of contact with other students and denied them access to facilities and equipment found in regular classrooms. However, all educators and parents of children with disabilities do not support the idea of inclusion. Some believe that separate education classrooms have provided benefits for children that inclusion would not have provided. Further, some surveys find that most teachers object to including students with special needs in their classrooms (Spring, 2002). This does not mean that inclusion does not work. As an advocate of children and those practices that help children, you need to help others understand the concept of inclusion and how best to serve all children regardless of their disabilities. Your advocacy role also involves removing the structures and obstacles that discourage teachers from creating inclusive classroom environments.

Gifted and Talented Students

The U.S. Department of Education estimates that about 2 to 3% of students are considered gifted. Marland (1972) identified gifted children as those who generally exhibit high performance or capability in one or more of the following ability areas, singly or in combination:

1. General education ability
2. Specific academic aptitude
3. Creative or productive thinking
4. Leadership ability
5. Visual and performing arts
6. Psychomotor ability

Gifted and talented (GT) education has been a hotly debated topic. Those who promote gifted programs claim that gifted children need instruction at a level, pace, and conceptual complexity commensurate with their levels of ability and achievement. Those who oppose GT programs claim that they are a neoconservative reaction to the funding for special-education students or that they are a subtle way to avoid integration. GT program opponents often indicate that privileged backgrounds contribute to the classification of being gifted and talented. They also claim that by creating GT programs, the schools create an elitist group among students.

Regardless of how you feel about GT programs, the fact is that some students do have characteristics that may be defined as gifted. Again, as an advocate for *all* children, you will want to provide the best educational programs for those who have exceptional abilities. Whether you promote a pullout program or an in-class enhancement program, a GT program should be something you consider.

Students at Risk

The term *at-risk* has been used in various ways in education. Some people have used the term to describe students who are at risk because of conditions out of their control, such as disabilities, ethnicity, and poverty. The term also has been used to describe behaviors that students engage in that affect their education, such as alcohol and drug abuse, sexual experimentation, or suicidal tendencies. The term also has been used to describe students who are at risk of dropping out of school or being expelled from school. For the purposes of this chapter, we use the term *at-risk* to describe students who, for one reason or another, are not succeeding academically and are unlikely to finish their schooling unless interventions occur. Regardless of the reasons or conditions, at-risk students should be of major concern to principals and assistant principals.

Several researchers (e.g., Sagor, 1993; Beyer et al., 1997) have outlined behaviors that identify at-risk students:

1. At-risk students usually exhibit low self-esteem, a lack of self-confidence in themselves and their work, and a lack of self-worth. They regard themselves as being in a state of helplessness and feel powerless in most situations.
2. At-risk students often avoid school, and they avoid contact or confrontation with other students and adults. They find it easier and often more enjoyable to skip classes rather than to face the reality that they are behind and do not know what is going on. School is seen as threatening to them because it is not responsive to their needs.
3. Usually, at-risk students distrust adults and the adult world in general. They often view adults as the cause of the unfairness they are experiencing. Adults are deemed unresponsive to their needs and are even seen as being abusive by some students.
4. At-risk students tend to live in the present and have a very limited view of what the future will bring them. They are responsive to their own short-term successes but do not do well with long-term projects or planning. The future to them does not hold a positive place in their lives. Because of their viewpoint, they experience a detachment from the school setting.
5. At-risk students often feel that the adults they know in general have given up on them by the time they reach their teen years. They are usually behind academically by this time because they lack skills in reading, writing, and math and think that others view them as being dumb rather than unskilled. This leads them to feel hopeless about their situation at school and implants the idea that they cannot learn.

6. At-risk students generally do not do very well in regular classroom settings, where the norm is a routine with long periods of sitting and listening with little variety. They are usually impatient with this type of environment and often are viewed as being disruptive because of their impatience.

7. At-risk students often can apply what is being taught in a very practical manner if this type of behavior is encouraged or even allowed. They do well with experiential-type learning situations and usually can verbalize what takes place better than they can write about it.

8. At-risk students have a hard time forming a link between the effort something takes and the achievement gained. Instead, they view success as just luck, or they talk about how easy the task was to begin with. They see everything as happening to them, and they believe that they have little control over what goes on in their lives. When a task is not done or when it is done poorly, it is because the task was too hard to begin with, or they could not get the help they needed to complete the task. At-risk students generally do not assume personal responsibility and seldom learn anything from the mistakes they make.

As an advocate for children and for moral, legal, and thoughtful educational principles and practices, you will need to further your knowledge and understanding of these six issues that can affect students, their access to education, and their success in schooling. In response to these issues, policymakers at local, state, and national levels, educators, parents, and commercial organizations have created various programs—some successful, others questionable. We will discuss some of these programs and the principal's and assistant principal's roles in administering these programs. Again, as an advocate, you must ensure that *all* students are taught in such a way that they benefit academically and socially from the school experience.

Educational Programs

Special programs have been designed and developed to meet the academic and social needs of students, especially in preventing at-risk behaviors and conditions and compensating for differences in individuals. No one program can in and of itself be either preventive or compensatory. The total schooling experience that involves educators, parents, and community has to be considered for *all* children.

Multicultural Education Programs

Multicultural programs have developed over a period of time. To understand the development of multicultural education programs, Banks (1999) identified four phases: monoethnic courses, multiethnic studies courses, multiethnic education, and multicultural education.

Originally, multicultural education was linked to concerns about racism in schools and the lack of representatives in nonwhite cultures in school curricula such as history, music, and literature. In phase one, monoethnic courses focused on ethnic courses for a particular race and culture. For example, black studies were needed for African American students and Native American studies for Native American students. Phase two multiethnic courses broadened curricula offerings to be more inclusive of the whole school. Phase two focused on several ethnic histories and cultures often from a comparative point of view. School curricula offered such courses as multiethnic history, minority literature, and ethnic music. Banks (1999) concluded that phase two did not bring about educational reform toward equality. In phase three, multiethnic education developed an educational reform that included the entire school environment. Phase three developed a pluralistic approach that tried to address all racial and ethnic minority groups. However, it excluded numerous subcultures within mainstream culture. For example, Native American tribes usually were considered as one group, Appalachian whites were not considered as a culture, and certain religious groups were included only within ethnic groups. Because of these omissions, a broader reform movement began that attempted to focus on a wider range of groups. Currently, phase four refers to education that relates to race, ethnicity, religion, and social class. However, multicultural education also considers gender, disabilities, and regions and how these factors interrelate. For example, we often now refer to black women, young and impoverished Latinos, and second-generation Asian Americans (Banks, 1994).

The current view of *multicultural education* considers more of a process or philosophy than a program. It is a movement built on the ideals of freedom, justice, equality, and equity. Multicultural education involves all academic disciplines and extracurricular programs. Its intent is to help all students develop positive self-concepts and understand the strength of human diversity. Multicultural education involves curriculum and instruction that includes the contributions, perspectives, and experiences of various groups that are a part of society. As Banks (1992) suggested:

> Rather than excluding Western civilization from the curriculum, multiculturalists want a more truthful, complex, and diverse version of the West taught in the schools. They want the curriculum to describe the ways in which African, Asian, and indigenous American cultures have influenced and interacted with Western civilization. They also want schools to discuss not only the diversity and democratic ideals of Western civilization, but also its failures, tensions, dilemmas, and the struggles by various groups in Western societies to realize their dreams against great odds (p. 34).

Bilingual Education

Schools across America are enrolling greater numbers of children who are of limited English proficiency (LEP). The Bilingual Education Act was first legislated by Congress in 1968. The act is also known as Title VII of the Elementary and Secondary Education Act. The optional programs under this act called for instruction for LEP students that was well organized and encompassed part of the regular school curriculum. Due to slow program implementation, stronger legislation was required, and the act was again amended in 1974, making *bilingual education* mandatory in all schools receiving federal funds. The purpose of the act was to educate LEP children and youth to meet the same rigorous standards for academic performance expected of all children and youth. The act was amended again in 1978, 1988, and 1994, clarifying that the goal was to help develop the English-language skills of students who were deficient in these skills while simultaneously providing instruction in their native language (Beyer et al., 1997). However, most existing bilingual education programs are designed to be "transitional" as opposed to "maintenance." The goal is for children to learn English and move into regular classrooms as soon as possible (Zepeda & Langenback, 1999).

English as a second language (ESL) programs emerged as a way to teach LEP students in the secondary schools. ESL programs typically are pullout programs that teach English based on the principles of foreign-language teaching. Literacy in the first language is necessary for learning a second language. Usually in ESL programs, students receive English instruction one or two periods per day and continue to participate in the regular classroom for the rest of the time.

Discussions about the effectiveness of bilingual education have continued since the first congressional act in 1968. The controversy often has focused on identifying the types of programs that work best in helping LEP students. The debate is frequently around which approach is better: teaching children in their native language or teaching them in English. The research on these methods of instruction has not proven conclusive.

As an advocate for LEP children, you should provide the direction and administration of bilingual programs. The following recommendations are adapted from Beyer and colleagues (1997). As a principal or assistant principal, you should

1. Implement family education programs and parent outreach and training activities designed to assist parents to become active participants in the education of their children.
2. Improve the instructional program for LEP students by identifying, acquiring, and upgrading curriculum, instructional materials, educational software, and assessment procedures and, if appropriate, applying educational technology.
3. Compensate personnel, including teacher aides who have been specifically trained or are being trained to provide services to children and youth of limited English proficiency.
4. Enrich instruction and other related activities such as counseling and academic and career guidance.

Special Education

The development of special-education programs for students with disabilities has been long, hard, and problematic for parents, students, teachers, and administrators. This subsection offers an overview of special education; however, it should not replace your own investigation and personal study.

With the enactment of Public Law 94-142 in 1975 and the subsequent legislation since then, most notably IDEA, special and regular educators began developing programs that would better help meet the needs of special needs students. The first programs and services were pullout programs. Typically, students who were identified as having a special need were pulled out of the regular classroom to receive services. Depending on the degree of the disability, some students were excluded from the regular classroom and placed in what is still referred to as a *self-contained classroom*. Pullout programs were and still are questioned as to their effectiveness. More inclusive services began to emerge in the form of mainstreaming and inclusion. However, with inclusion came tension between regular education and special education teachers, parents and teachers, and teachers and administrators and among students.

Approximately one in ten students in public education qualify for and receive services under special education (Terman et al., 1996). Administering the correct educational programs is one of the biggest challenges for special educators and principals. However, this is an area in which no one person in the school can or should make all the decisions. Special education teachers, regular education teachers, district office personnel (if necessary), parents, and sometimes the students themselves help determine what services are needed and provided by the school.

IDEA mandates that students with disabilities receive their education with nondisabled peers to the maximum extent appropriate. To meet this requirement, federal regulations require schools to develop a continuum of placements ranging from general classrooms with support services to homebound and hospital programs. Determining the "least restrictive environment" will be the challenge. The intent of each individual's plan would be to transition to the next environment. For example, if the student is presently in a self-contained classroom, the challenge will be to develop a plan to transition the child to only partial self-contained classroom and partial resource room or a regular classroom.

As principal, a major challenge that you will face in special education is hiring the right people. Selecting qualified special education teachers has always been a challenge because special-education teacher candidates have been among the scarcest of all teaching candidates. Some districts have collaborated successfully with universities to provide certification and masters' programs for existing teachers. These programs often are paid for in part or in full by the district if the teacher is willing to become a special-education teacher in that district.

However, selecting special education teachers is only part of the challenge. As principal, you also want to select regular education teachers who are willing and able to work with special needs students in the regular classroom. In your selection process, it is important for you to determine their beliefs, interest, and qualifications in such areas as inclusion, knowledge of disabilities, learning styles, and teaching methods.

As principal, you also will want to coordinate professional development activities for existing teachers in working with special needs students. Regular education teachers hardly can be expected to perform well in inclusive classrooms without training in teaching students with disabilities. Usually teachers will have to consider changing their instructional methods to provide for children with special needs. This may include both a philosophical and an instructional change. You also will need to allow time for shared planning and collaboration among special education teachers and regular education teachers so that they can coordinate their services and provide the best education.

Your challenge is to rise above the rhetoric that surrounds special education issues and provide the services, programs, and opportunities that are needed for students with disabilities. If inclusion in regular classes of students with special needs is in their best interests, then you can help reduce the barriers that prevent inclusion and work toward its implementation. Students are most likely to achieve their potential by learning in the company of their peers.

Gifted and Talented Programs

Although controversial, GT programs are a reality in many schools. Your knowledge and leadership will be expected. The program options for GT students vary from limited to extensive adaptations of the regular instructional programs. The following types of GT programs are listed from the least to the most adaptation:

Enrichment in the regular classroom.
Enrichment in the classroom means accommodating the wide range of abilities and interests that are present in any group of students. Enrichment in the regular classroom is the easiest to provide from the administrative point of view because there is no need for special teachers, extra classrooms, or special scheduling. It may be the most challenging for teachers because of the extra preparation in creating instructional activities for the individuals identified as gifted and talented. The critics of GT programs often contend that enrichment activities are the most fair for all students (Zepeda & Langenbach, 1999).

Enrichment pullout programs.
Pullout programs necessitate GT students leaving the regular classroom for part of the day or week. Pullout programs are more common at the elementary school level. In secondary schools, GT students more likely would be assigned to honors or AP classes.

Acceleration.
Acceleration at the elementary school level could mean an early entry into school, for example, beginning first grade at age five. It also could mean skipping grades along the way. Acceleration may make sense when GT students are seen as being more like older students than their agemates. Acceleration at the secondary school level usually takes the form of advanced classes or AP classes for college credit. Many high schools have adopted early-graduation policies, where students may accelerate their studies by taking more credits or testing out of some classes and may graduate a year or a semester earlier than their classmates.

Curriculum compacting.
Curriculum compacting is a means by which GT students can pass through the content without spending as much time as is usually allocated for it. It is different from enrichment in that it is not horizontal exploration of content but rather vertical pro-

---

Professional Dilemma 9.2

Many college preparatory and advanced placement courses in high schools have high admissions criteria based on testing, teacher interviews, and previous experience. Often these criteria eliminate many students of color and those of diverse cultural backgrounds. Should these honors courses be open to any student who wishes to take the course if they are committed to do the work, or should the courses be restricted by admissions criteria?

gression through the curriculum in an accelerated manner (Zepeda & Langenbach, 1999).

Extraschool activities.

After school, Saturday, or summer programs can be opportunities to offer educational experiences that may not be available during the school day and year. Special courses or activities are offered for GT students that extend beyond the regular curriculum. Some of these programs are offered by universities that sponsor summer programs in math, sciences, technology, and the arts (Zepeda & Langenbach, 1999).

Magnet schools.

Magnet schools specialize in a field such as math and science or performing arts. Parents and students elect to apply for admission to a magnet school where typically there are high admission criteria. For example, students may have to audition, provide a portfolio of previous work, or have high marks on a test in the fields the school emphasizes. Some magnet schools are housed in regular schools, making them "schools within a school" (Zepeda & Langenbach, 1999).

Regardless of the program that your school uses or the ones you want to develop, as an administrator and leader, you do need to be aware of the following:

- Use various instruments in the selection process rather than rely on one measure (Zepeda & Langenbach, 1999).
- Be aware that performance on intelligence and achievement tests is often influenced by the child's socioeconomic status, racial and cultural background, and previous educational experience (Sapon-Shevin, 1994).
- Increase learning opportunities for disadvantaged and minority children with outstanding talents.
- Emphasize teacher development. Teachers must receive better training in how to teach high-level curricula (Beyer et al., 1997).
- Work with parents and community members in providing opportunities for students with special talents.

Title I

As part of President Lyndon Johnson's Great Society and War on Poverty, Congress enacted the Elementary and Secondary Education Act (ESEA) in 1965. *Title I* of this act provided for supplementary academic assistance and compensatory services for economically disadvantaged children. These services were meant for all children of poverty, including children from Native American families living on or near reservations, migrant families, homeless families, and urban and rural families. The purpose of Title I was to provide supplementary services in the basic skill areas of reading and mathematics. In 1994, Congress reauthorized the ESEA and renamed the Title I section "Helping Disadvantaged Children Meet High Standards." Part of Title I addressed prevention and intervention programs for children and youth who are neglected, delinquent, or at risk of dropping out.

Not all schools or districts qualify to receive Title I funding. School districts may identify as eligible any school in which at least 35% of the children are from low-income families. The following criteria are used by districts as a measure of poverty to determine student eligibility for Title I services:

1. The number of children ages five to seventeen in poverty as counted in the most recent census data
2. The number of children eligible to receive free or reduced-priced lunches
3. The number of children in families receiving assistance under Aid to Families with Dependent Children
4. The number of children eligible to receive medical assistance under the Medicaid program
   (ESEA was reauthorized in January 2002. Check Website for up-to-date criteria. www.ed.gov/offices/OESE/esea).

These criteria are important to the school principal because it is at the individual school level that total student count must be determined. The number of students in the school eligible for "free and reduced-priced lunches" is often used as a baseline for low-income student count. The accuracy of this student head count may mean the difference between a school receiving Title I funds or not (Beyer et al., 1997).

Originally, Title I was a pullout program, in which identified students were taken out of their regularly assigned classrooms to receive supplemental instruction in reading and mathematics. Subsequently, send-in programs were implemented, in which services were provided within students' own classrooms. Other programs have used extended-day services, where students meet before or after school.

Professional development is an important element of Title I programs. The legislation requires the schools or districts to describe the strategy they will use to provide professional development. Because of this opportunity, principals can help teachers and aides in collaborative planning, integrated instruction, and teaming.

Your role as principal is critical in administering Title I programs. If economically disadvantaged students are to be served, your role as advocate is to become familiar with the program requirements and new legislation that affects Title I. You also need to be aware of the funding opportunities and the formula that your district or state uses for eligibility.

Alternative Education Programs

Most alternative programs are established to help at-risk students to achieve academic success in a smaller, more personable environment that will lead to their graduation with a high school diploma. Some contemporary alternative programs are not designed solely for at-risk students. For example, earlier in this section we discussed magnet schools for GT students. Magnet schools are a type of alternative program. However, most alternative programs are meant to serve adolescents who do not fit in traditional school settings. Kelly (1993) reported that these kinds of alternative schools represent a dual response to (1) students' need for flexibility and personalization and (2) conventional high schools' need for mechanisms to isolate students who pose discipline and other problems.

Alternative programs are housed in both traditional schools as "schools within schools" and in separate school buildings. Both kinds of schools usually provide a structure in which students can be mentored by adults who care about their personal, academic, and social success. Alternative school programs were created, in part, to face the emergence of large and impersonalized school systems in which high numbers of students were dropping out. A typical school within a school has a small group of teachers and counselors that provides individual assistance to students. Testerman's (1996) study of alternative schools indicated positive effects for students, such as improved grades, better attendance, increased studying, and more dedication to schoolwork. As Zepeda and Langenbach (1999) reported, changing the structure of the day and encouraging more meaningful interactions between students and teachers can yield positive results.

Raywid (1994) suggested that features that made alternative educational programs effective were their small size, their being designed by those who were going to operate them, and their relative freedom from district interference. Kellmayer (1995) believed that as much as possible, participation in the alternative program should be voluntary for both students and teachers. Teachers should volunteer for the program rather than being assigned by an administrator to teach in the program. If they are interested in working with these youth, usually they will have more success if they have the training and experience in working with at-risk behaviors and are willing to accept the challenges of developing caring relationships with their students.

Although these educational programs were created to attend to the special needs of children and youth, as a principal, you should not limit your advocacy to only these formal programs. Some students still get left out. Some programs are ineffective. Some students need more service than a program offers. Your advocacy means more than just administering educational programs. It means a total awareness of the needs of all students all the time.

Principal as Facilitator of Advocacy

You not only play a direct advocacy role as a principal, but you also must facilitate others to be advocates. To be effective, advocacy needs to be both a personal and a collaborative effort. As an individual, you can and should advocate for children and for moral, lawful, and thoughtful principles and practices that help to serve *all* children. However, alone this can be a daunting task. As an advocate for children, you must help others be advocates as well. For example, to be an inclusive school requires the efforts of nearly all members of the school community.

Facilitating advocacy among others requires the playing out of all the previous roles that were discussed in this book. In this section we will discuss how each of the seven roles that have been discussed previously is part of facilitating the advocacy role.

As learner and facilitator of learning, you help define the direction of the learning community. One way that you can do this is in creating professional development and parent education programs that promote equity for students. The definition of learning that was used in Chapter 3 is based on constructivism and emphasized the active capacity of *all* learners to construct new knowledge, the need of a community for the development of learning, and the importance of critical reflection in this learning process.

Mentoring is also an act of advocacy. You have the opportunity to mentor new and veteran teachers, parents, and other community members. In particular, the support and development of a new teacher are highly moral acts of leadership that you need to take seriously. Unfortunately, principals too often neglect or abdicate these responsibilities. The reality is that new teachers do not emerge from their preparation program as fully developed professionals. They vary widely in the skills and life experiences that they bring to the classroom. Many have had no or only limited experience with teaching children of color or children with disabilities. New teachers need administrative support and help with these types of assignments. Likewise, carefully and thoughtfully assigning a supporting peer mentor to a new teacher also can promote advocacy. However, peer mentoring runs the risk of perpetuating the status quo. If peer mentors have not developed their own moral, legal, and thoughtful practices, then it is unlikely that they will advocate such attributes. Never forget that as a leader and facilitator of advocacy, you are the most important part of the new teacher's induction.

Mentoring veteran teachers as advocates can be a daunting task. Some veteran teachers have fallen into the endurance game, wherein they are simply trying to outlast the latest education reform, and they are not interested in changing the curriculum or their practice to respond to changing student characteristics. Some have remained in the same school for most of their careers and have found a sense of pride in being part of the school history and culture. A few of these teachers find it difficult to change their teaching styles and want schools and students to remain the way they think they were in the past. This is especially difficult when the demographics of a school have changed and the community is experiencing new populations with different cultures. Many veteran teachers have not been trained or have not had any experience working with students with disabilities, students with limited English proficiency, or students with disadvantages. As a facilitator of advocacy, your task in mentoring veteran teachers to become advocates for all children requires considerable patience and understanding. However daunting, your advocacy and your mentoring of teachers in advocacy for all children and youth are the right things to be doing.

As principal, your influence on students can be tremendous. School is the place where students begin to learn how to behave in groups outside their families. Students learn a lot about social relationships from their teachers and principals. As principal or assistant principal playing out the role of advocacy, you can help influence students in their relationship with other students, teachers, and parents.

Facilitating advocacy also involves the role of supervision, especially in building instructional capacity in the school. The main component of your supervisory role is the learning that occurs with *all* teachers and *all* students. Recruiting and selecting capable and committed teachers who are diverse and are passionate about diversity enriches the instructional capacity in schools.

Your role as leader and manager may seem somewhat obvious as you facilitate advocacy among others, but certain aspects of these roles are especially important. We suggested earlier that the leader and manager roles mainly involve improving instruction and curriculum. In the leader role, one way that you can perform advocacy is by understanding, creating, maintaining, and changing culture. A way of being involved in cultural change is using subcultures to transform basic assumptions, values, beliefs, and behaviors. Subcultures can provide alternative assumptions that may need to be brought forward.

These subcultures can help in changing assumptions about race, ethnicity, religion, cultures, disabilities, poverty, and at-risk behaviors that affect children in school.

In the manager role, we also suggested four major areas in which management efforts are especially important: supporting, planning, action taking, and evaluating. These four areas are also important in facilitating advocacy. For example, your support in money, time, and other resources will greatly improve the chances that teachers will be advocates of multicultural education. Likewise, your help in planning the implementation of inclusion will greatly improve the chances for inclusion to work. Taking action and implementing the changes that are proposed also help teachers understand that there is something that emerges from the rhetoric. And finally, managing the evaluation and assessment of the effort will allow others the opportunity for critical input.

Perhaps one of the most important roles that you can take as facilitator of advocacy is the political role. A traditional political role of the principalship has been one that often buffered the school from parents and community. Although at times the principal needs to buffer teachers from interruptions and inappropriate pressures, if buffering becomes the primary political role of the principal, the school loses the rich contributions of diverse constituencies. Bridging is a more appropriate political role for contemporary principals than buffering. Bridging involves developing a shared vision with the community so that community organizations and individuals understand and work toward creating a learning environment for all children and youth.

In Chapter 8 we discussed the principal's role as politician based on two views of school-community relationships (Driscoll & Kerchner, 1999). The first perspective views schools as beneficiaries of community support. This perspective could help in advocacy by identifying the human and financial resources that community members could supply. For example, parents of children of color can help in the classroom with all activities as well as multicultural activities. The second perspective views schools as agents of social capital. Education in a democracy is important because schools can help create a public good from which the whole society benefits. Instead of schools only being recipients of what the community offers, this perspective suggests that schools need to stress what they contribute to the community.

One of the most thoughtful political actions you can take as you help others become advocates of children and children's causes is to help them examine existing inequities and to help them understand how the school can act as a civil community. Children often learn to be civil to each other by watching the civility of their teachers and parents. You can help teachers and parents to see that schools can and should become civil societies that support individual growth in and for community. Likewise, you can facilitate advocacy by helping teachers, students, and parents to model democracy in the school.

Conclusion

In the opening vignette, Curtis is an assistant principal in a school that has seen dramatic changes in its community. Because of some of these changes, Curtis has had to learn to be an advocate to promote learning for all students. Advocacy involves supporting, maintaining, and defending moral, legal, and thoughtful educational principles and practices. In contemporary school settings, being an advocate and facilitating advocacy of others involve understanding racial, ethnic, and cultural diversity; language diversity; poverty and social class; gender and sexual orientation; and students with special needs. The principal's advocacy role is the last of the seven role conceptions that we propose to be an innovative principal. We now move to a discussion of how you will learn these innovative role conceptions.

Activities

Self Reflecting Activities

1. Using the definition of advocacy, think of ways that you have supported, maintained, and defended educational principles and practices for children in the schools in which you have served.
2. Reflect on the reasons principals and assistant principals must become familiar with federal, state, and local policies regarding special needs children.

Peer Reflecting Activities

1. Reflect on Salt Creek High School. What ways have schools in your area changed because of demographic changes?
2. Brainstorm ways that schools can involve more parents in the programs offered for special needs children.

Course Activities

1. Invite special education, at-risk, and gifted and talented directors to present to the class the scope of their roles and the services they provide for principals and schools.
2. As a class, discuss ways that could have prevented the incidents at Salt Creek High School. Discuss how the principal could have helped Curtis.
3. Investigate schools in your area. How has inclusion been implemented? What constraints exist in these schools to be inclusive?
4. Visit an alternative school in the area. Reflect on the school's successes and failures.

Websites

■ *http://www.ucea.org/cases/*
  Cases from the Journal of Cases in Educational Leadership
  Howley, A. (2002). *When everyone's vulnerable.* Journal of Cases in Educational Leadership 5(1).
  Livingston, M. & Bruner, D. (2001). Zero tolerance: One size fits all. *Journal of Cases in Educational Leadership 4*(3).

Swicord, B. (2001). Making the most of your chances. *Journal of Cases in Educational Leadership 4*(3).

White, G. P., & Mayes, T. A. (2001). Making an appropriate special education placement: Conflict abounds. *Journal of Cases in Educational Leadership 4*(2).

Davis, S. (2000). Accusations of discrimination. *Journal of Cases in Educational Leadership 3*(3).

Enomoto, E. K. (2000). Insubordination or otherwise. *Journal of Cases in Educational Leadership 3*(1).

Ashby, D. (1998). Does inclusion include the right to die at school? *Journal of Cases in Educational Leadership 1*(2).

■ *http://www.ri.net/gifted_talented/character.html*
Characteristics and Behaviors of the Gifted

■ *http://www.nfgcc.org/*
The National Foundation for Gifted and Creative Children

■ *http://www.niss.ac.uk/admin/sp-needs.html*
National Information Services and Systems

■ *http://wwwcsteep.bc.edu/ctestweb/special/special.html*
Testing Students with Disabilities

■ *http://www.ed.gov/offices/OESE/esea*

References

Arendt, H. (1958). *The Human Condition*. Chicago: University of Chicago Press.

Banks, J. A. (1992). Multicultural education: For freedom's sake. *Educational Leadership 49*(4), 32–36.

Banks, J. A. (1994). *Multiethnic Education* (3d ed.). Boston: Allyn & Bacon.

Banks, J. A. (1999). *An Introduction to Multicultural Education* (2d ed.). Boston: Allyn & Bacon.

Beck, L. G., & Murphy, J. (1993). *Understanding the Principalship: Metaphorical Themes, 1920s–1990s*. New York: Teachers College Press.

Beyer, B., Engelking, J. & Boshee, M. (1997). *Special and Compensatory Programs: The Administrator's Role*. Lancaster, MI: Technomic Publishing Co.

Bigner, J., & Bozett, F. (1990). Parenting by gay fathers. In F. Bozett & M. Sussman (Eds.), *Homosexuality and Family Relations*. New York: Haworth Press.

Burnett, G. (1995). Alternatives to ability grouping: Still unanswered questions. *ERIC Clearinghouse on Urban Education ED390947* (111).

Cubberley, E. P. (1909). *Changing Conceptions of Education*. Boston: Houghton Mifflin.

Cubberley, E. P. (1923). *The Principal and His School*. Boston: Houghton Mifflin.

Driscoll, M. E., & Kerchner, C. T. (1999). The implications of social capital for schools, communities, and cities: Educational administration as if a sense of place mattered. In J. Murphy & K. S. Louis (Eds.), *Handbook of Research in Educational Administration* (pp. 385–404). San Francisco: Jossey-Bass.

Kellmayer, J. (1995). *How to Establish an Alternative School*. Thousand Oaks, CA: Corwin Press.

Kelly, D. M. (1993). *Last Chance High School: How Girls and Boys Drop In and Out of Alternative Schools*. New Haven: Yale University Press.

Kerr, D. H. (1987). Authority and responsibility in public schooling. In J. I. Goodlad (Ed.), *The Ecology of School Renewal, 86th Yearbook (Part I) of the National Society for the Study of Education*. Chicago: University of Chicago Press.

Madison, J. (1788). The Federalist no. 51. In G. Wills (Ed.), *The Federalist Papers*. New York: Bantam Books.

Marland, S. (1972). *Education of the Gifted and Talented: Report to Congress.* Washington, D.C.: U.S. Government Printing Office.

Muller, C. (1998). Gender differences in parental involvement and adolescents' mathematics achievement. *Sociology of Education 71*(4), 336–356.

National Center for Education Statistics. (1996). *Projects of Education Statistics to 2006* (25th ed., pp. 96–661). Washington: U.S. Department of Education, Office of Educational Research and Improvement.

Noddings, N. (1984). *Caring: A Feminine Approach to Ethics and Moral Education.* Berkeley: University of California Press.

Oaks, J. (1986). Tracking, inequality, and the rhetoric of reform: Why schools don't change. *Journal of Education 168*(1), 60–80.

Orland, M. E. (1994). Demographics of disadvantage: Intensity of childhood poverty and its relationship to educational achievement. In J. I. Goodlad & P. Keating (Eds.), *Access to Knowledge.* New York: College Entrance Examination Board.

Pai, Y., & Adler, S. A. (2001). *Cultural Foundations of Education* (3d ed.). Upper Saddle River, NJ: Merrill, Prentice-Hall.

Raywid, M. A. (1994). Alternative schools: The state of the art. *Educational Leadership 52*(1), 26–31.

Richmond-Abbott, M. (1992). *Masculine and Feminine: Gender Roles over the Life Cycle* (2d ed.). New York: McGraw-Hill.

Rosenthal, R., & Jacobsen, L. (1968). *Pygmalion in the Classroom.* New York: Holt, Rinehart, and Winston.

Sadker, M., & Sadker, D. (1994). *Failing at Fairness: How America's Schools Cheat Girls.* New York: Scribners.

Sagor, R. (1993). *At-Risk Students: Reaching and Teaching Them.* Swampscott, MA: Watersun Publishing.

Sapon-Shevin, M. (1994). *Playing Favorites: Gifted Education and the Disruption of Community.* Albany, NY: State University of New York Press.

Sirotnik, K. A. (1990). Society, schooling, teaching, and preparing to teach. In J. I. Goodlad, R. Soder, & K. A. Sirotnik (Eds.), *The Moral Dimensions of Teaching.* San Francisco: Jossey-Bass.

Sirotnik, K. A. (1994). Equal access to quality in public schooling: Issues in the assessment of equity and excellence. In J. I. Goodlad & P. Keating (Eds.), *Access to Knowledge* (pp. 159–185). New York: College Entrance Examination Board.

Sommers, C. H. (2000). *The War Against Boys: How Misguided Feminism Is Harming Our Young Men.* New York: Simon & Schuster.

Spring, J. (2002). *American Education* (10th ed.). New York: McGraw-Hill.

Terman, D. L., Larner, M. B., Stevenson, C. S., & Behrman, R. E. (1996). Special education for students with disabilities: Analysis and recommendations. In R. E. Behrman (Ed.), *The Future of Children.* Los Altos, CA: Center for the Future of Children and The David and Lucile Packard Foundation.

Testerman, J. (1996). Holding at-risk students: The secret is one-to one. *Phi Delta Kappan 77*(5), 364–365.

Tocci, C. M., & Engelhard, G. E., Jr. (1991). Achievement, parental support, and gender differences in attitudes toward mathematics. *Journal of Educational Research 84*(5), 280.

Wolf, A. (1977). *Poverty and Achievement.* Washington, D.C.: National Institute of Education.

Zepeda, S. J. & Langenbach, M. (1999). *Special Programs in Regular Schools: Historical Foundations, Standards, and Contemporary Issues.* Boston: Allyn & Bacon.

Zera, D. (1992). Coming of age in a heterosexist world: The development of gay and lesbian adolescents. *Adolescence 27*(108), 849–854.

Becoming an Innovative Principal

10

Key Terms and Concepts

adjustment socialization
    stage
anticipatory socialization
    stage

creative individualism
encounter socialization
    stage
organizational socialization

personal socialization
professional socialization
socialization

Vignette

The waitress appeared for the fifth time asking if there was anything she could get Beth and Debbie. Obviously, she was wondering why they were still there after two hours. Beth ordered another cup of coffee, her third. Beth and Debbie met each Wednesday morning for breakfast in part so that Beth could ask Debbie, her mentor, for help. Gradually, Debbie had also used Beth as a sounding board for some reforms she was considering. This Wednesday morning was during winter holiday break, and they both had more time to talk. This gave Beth time to reflect on her first few months in the job as principal of Brookside High School.

Debbie had been a mentor to Beth for several years, beginning when Beth interned with Debbie at another high school in the district. The two remained close during Beth's assistant principalship and especially now that they were the only female high school principals in the district. Debbie had been a high school principal for ten years and had a great reputation with the district and with her school faculty and parents. She had been able to turn her high school around from having the worst reputation to being one of the best.

Beth had completed the administrator preparation program at State University and had received strong letters of endorsement from her professors and from Debbie, her internship supervisor. The program had a full-time internship program with a great deal of collaboration between the university and the school. Debbie had provided ongoing feedback to Beth but also had gradually given her more responsibility. Beth felt that her internship experience had prepared her well for administration. Her course work also had helped her develop extensive knowledge and skills related to best practices and reform strategies.

However, nothing could have prepared her for her first administrative position as an assistant principal. The principal with whom she worked found it difficult to turn loose of responsibilities, except the uncomfortable ones. Primarily, he gave Beth student management assignments, which were extensive. The school had no school-wide discipline policy, and the principal encouraged the teachers to send their problems to Beth. By the third day of school, Beth always had a line of students outside her office by 9:30 A.M. Gradually, she worked with the teachers to develop some alternative classroom methods that were successful and earned her the respect of most faculty. However, she received little praise or support from the principal. If it had not been for Debbie, Beth was not sure that she could have made it through that first year.

Beth had been appointed to Brookside during the summer only a month before the school year began. She had the strong support of the superintendent, who was impressed with how she had turned around the disciplinary referrals. However, a large group of parents and some of the older teachers in the school preferred another person and were disappointed when Beth was appointed.

As Beth reflected with Debbie about her last four months as a principal, she identified two major problems that she figured would follow her during the remainder of the school year: a coach with poor teaching skills and a group of parents who were working behind the scenes to undermine her. The football coach was a veteran of the school who had support from the parents of the football players. However, other parents whose children were in his history classes were not so impressed. Before school started, Beth had heard from a committee of irate parents who wanted their kids removed from his class. As Beth observed in his classroom, she found his teaching methods archaic and his classroom management methods dictatorial. However, the coach let her know very quickly that he did not respect her and that as a woman she knew nothing about football, which was all that counted.

Beth's second problem involved a group of vocal and powerful parents who had preferred the other candidate for the principalship at Brookside. The leader of this group was the sister of a board member. She let Beth know from the beginning that she had preferred the other candidate. As the semester progressed, Beth was getting calls from the district office about rumors that Beth was convinced were started by this parent.

Debbie asked Beth how her relationship with teachers was going and whether any of these problems had influenced that relationship. Beth felt that she was beginning to establish a good rapport with the teachers. She smiled when she recalled how some of the teachers had tested her in the first month by creating little "nonproblems" and then waiting to see how she would respond, for example, teacher dress code and student referrals. Beth felt that she had won these teachers over with humor and humility. However, she knew that most teachers were waiting to see how she handled the problem with the football coach. She felt that it might be the defining moment for clarifying for the faculty and staff her vision for the school.

As Debbie shared some memories of her first year as a principal, Beth thought how much she had learned already this first year. But there were still five months to go.

Introduction

As Beth learned, becoming a principal is not a simple or easy transition. Even with adequate university preparation, a successful internship, and extensive prior administrative experience, becoming a principal involves surprises and frustrations. As we demonstrated in Chapter 3, the principal must be a learner, and this learning occurs throughout the career.

In previous chapters we identified seven conceptions of the principal and assistant principal roles that involve innovative ways to view these roles. In this chapter we focus on how an individual learns to enact these role conceptions. Like the view of learning we espoused in Chapter 3, this type of learning is an active process by the individual involved. In other words, becoming an innovative principal or assistant principal is not a passive process in which others are solely in charge of your learning. Rather, it is a process in which you contribute significantly to your own learning. Another way of describing this learning process is that you and the organizations in which you will work will coconstruct innovative images of the principalship. Part of the process of coconstructing involves understanding how learning to become a principal or assistant principal happens. This chapter will help you understand the learning process of becoming an innovative principal.

In order to help you understand this learning process, we begin with a general introduction to socialization—how learning a new role occurs. We identify and discuss the sources, methods, stages, and outcomes of this learning and apply it to school leadership. After this general introduction to socialization, we discuss the specific process of learning to become a new innovative assistant principal. Although the two roles of principal and assistant principal have many similarities as school leadership roles, there are unique features of both that relate to the seven innovative role conceptions we have identified. Thus, becoming an innovative assistant principal has certain unique characteristics that are worth exploring.

Following our discussion of the socialization of assistant principals, we turn to how to become an innovative principal. Again, we focus on the distinctive elements of principal socialization and how to learn the seven role conceptions. We end the chapter with a discussion of how principals at midcareer become innovative. Although this book has been written primarily from the point of view of a new principal, many of the issues surrounding instructional improvement and innovative role conceptions are pertinent to someone who has been in the principalship for several years but is confronting change—either in position or in role conception. Many of the reform initiatives of the last several years, for example, site-based management and shared decision making, challenge veteran principals with dramatic changes in the role.

Socialization: Learning a New Role

Any time someone enters a new stage of life or accepts a new position, learning is necessary. When you entered kindergarten, you had to learn how to act in a group of strangers, how to find your way around a new building, and how to follow directions from someone who was not your parent. As you enter school administration, learning is also necessary. Much of this learning will be second nature to you because of your long experience as a student and teacher. However, some of the learning will involve a new way of seeing things that you have been experiencing for years. For example, as a teacher, you saw the principal conducting faculty meetings, observing in your classroom, disciplining students, and monitoring the hall. However, as a principal or assistant principal, these responsibilities will have deeper meanings as you learn how district administrators, parents, and government entities affect these responsibilities and how a vision of the school guides how, when, and why you enact your role.

Nature of Socialization

The typical way of describing and understanding how someone learns a new role emphasizes what the organization—usually through the supervisor—does *to* the novice. This passive process may include formal training or subtler manipulations to get the novice to do and believe what the organization and the supervisor want. Research on learning and socialization suggests that the novice is not a blank tablet waiting to be instructed but an active participant who brings experience, values, and tools for learning (Wentworth, 1980). Rather than a pawn in the organization's hands, you are a partner in this learning process.

Being a learning partner means that you are involved in two types of socialization—role taking and role making (Hart, 1993), which we discussed in Chapter 1. Role taking, which is a more passive process, involves accepting the responsibilities and mission of a role that are defined primarily by the way things have been done in the past. As an administrative intern, you are learning how principals, teachers, district supervisors, and even students define the role and how you are expected to enact it. Role making, in contrast, is a more active process that emphasizes molding the job to fit your perspectives, values, and expectations, as well as the school's needs. Beth's experience as an assistant principal demonstrates that rather than simply taking the role as the principal defined it for her in terms of student management, she molded the role in a more proactive way. Role taking and role making are seldom completely discrete activities. Both are usually present in learning any new role. As a new principal or assistant principal, you will need to learn the expectations that others have of you. However, you also will have the opportunity to develop your own vision based on your values and perspectives of the role. In becoming an innovative principal or assistant principal, your socialization "not only presents a world, it constructs one" (Wentworth, 1980).

Role taking and role making draw attention to two perspectives for understanding socialization, which are important for you to consider. First, socialization can be understood from the school or the district's perspective as "mechanisms through which members learn the values, norms, knowledge, beliefs, and interpersonal and other skills that facilitate role performance and further group goals" (Mortimer & Simmons, 1978, p.422). The faculty, staff, students, and parents in your first school, as well as your district supervisors, will greet you with expectations about how they expect you to enact the role of principal or assistant principal. Your predecessor in the role, years of tradition at the school, or recent crises that generate the need for change may influence these expectations. These groups will use various tools—some formal and some subtle—to influence you to enact your role in ways that meet these expectations.

A second perspective emphasizes an individual way of understanding socialization. "From the perspective of the individual, socialization is a process of learning to participate in social life" (Mortimer & Simmons, 1978, p. 422). As you enter this first school, you bring with you previous experiences as student and teacher, perspectives from your university preparation, experience from your internship, your own values and beliefs about how schools should be learning environments, and other personal goals and needs. These elements create your own expectations for the role. You also bring to this socialization process learning tools that have worked for you in the past. For example, Beth used her experience with her mentor, Debbie, as a way to reflect on her experiences and to learn how to enact the role. Your own learning style and your previous experience with learning will affect the tools you use to learn the job.

We define *socialization* as "a reciprocal process in which both organization and individual are active participants in professional learning" (Crow & Matthews, 1998, p. 19). To maximize your learning to become an innovative school leader, you must acknowledge this reciprocal process that involves not only your influence but also the influence of those around you. Understanding the perspective and tools that the organization uses to influence your enactment of the role is as important as understanding your own perspective and learning tools.

Learning to become an innovative school leader involves three elements (Feldman, 1976). First, you must develop the work knowledge and skills to be an innovative principal or assistant principal. This includes everything from the simplest skills necessary to negotiate a contract with a soft drink company to maintaining or changing a school culture. Some of these you have learned in your university preparation. Others are more specific to the school context. For example, while there are common elements to budgeting, districts use different models, and your district supervisors will expect you to learn and use the preferred one. Likewise, maintaining or changing a school culture is very context-specific.

Second, learning to become an innovative school leader necessitates adjusting to the work environment. Many administrators believe that this aspect of socialization is much more difficult to learn than developing technical skills. In the opening vignette, Beth had developed excellent skills, for example, in student management, but when she became a principal, she had to learn how things are done in a new environment. She may have developed excellent interpersonal skills in earlier settings, but she had to endure new testing in a different environment. Learning to adjust to a new work environment includes understanding personalities, relationships, and subcultures present in this new setting. Failure to learn this aspect of socialization can thwart attempts to be an innovative school leader by demonstrating insensitivity to the traditions and culture of the new school. Being innovative does not mean being callous to the current values and norms of the setting. In fact, being innovative depends in part on a recognition and sensitivity to these cultural elements.

Third, learning to become an innovative principal or assistant principal involves learning new values. Some of these values arise from the study and reflection in which you are currently engaged or from subsequent mentors. However, these values also may include new values that arise in your first school. Some new administrators make the critical mistake of assuming that nothing innovative or of value can come from their new context. Such cavalier behavior results in numerous conflicts and misguided attempts to change behavior that ultimately delay or thwart school effectiveness. Openness to new values from numerous sources can result in dynamic learning experiences that benefit the new school leader as well as the school.

Sources of Socialization

Learning to become an innovative school leader also involves recognizing that there are multiple sources of socialization. In this subsection we will identify three types of sources: professional, organizational, and personal.

Professional Socialization.   Becoming a principal or assistant principal is influenced by the expectations that the larger society in general and university training in particular communicate regarding how to enact the role. These influences emphasize the patterns of values, beliefs, and assumptions that have grown up around a role. They help the individual develop an administrative perspective—a way of thinking that includes relationships with teachers, the community, and supervisors and the development of sensitivity to school-wide issues and organizational stability (Greenfield, 1985a).

The society holds certain views of what any principal should be and do. As Chapter 2 details, these societal views frequently have been influenced by business conceptions of the role that emphasize efficiency (Callahan, 1962). With the move to a postindustrial society, all work roles, including those of principal or assistant principal, emphasize more complexity (Bell, 1973; Hage & Powers, 1992). Society, as a source of socialization, presents ways of viewing the role that may conflict with expectations of the role from other sources, for example, university or district.

University training is another source of professional socialization and frequently is referred to as the "first wave" of socialization. This source includes course work and internship experiences that present certain conceptions of the role. Frequently, new administrators question the relevance of their university training in terms of specific work tasks that must be learned after they arrive in their first assignment. Others have pointed out that what effective university training has done for them is to provide the big picture and the innovative conceptions that sometimes get lost in the harried rhythm of the new administrator's work. Your socialization from this source hopefully will provide the important generic skills for problem solving and decision making that are fundamental to leadership for learning. For example, developing your ability to reflect on your and others' actions has become essential for effective school leadership (Osterman & Kottkamp, 1993).

Another aspect of an effective university training program and excellent source of socialization is a sustained, supervised, and quality internship experience. This experience provides a hands-on way of learning the tasks of administration and the pace and rhythm of the administrator's day—the brevity, variety, and fragmentation of the job (Peterson, 1977–1978). In addition to learning the specific tasks and rhythm of the role, effective internship experiences help interns to learn the specific culture of the school in which they are placed. This provides an opportunity to develop skills for understanding and adjusting to the work environment that will be crucial in their first regular administrative assignment. Probably the most important thing that an effective internship with a trained mentor helps the intern to learn is how to reflect on what the intern sees and does. This socialization content emphasizes skills for learning to learn. As Chapter 3 emphasized, the principal as learner is a critical role conception essential for school leaders in an increasingly complex school and societal environment.

Organizational Socialization.   Becoming an innovative school leader is also influenced by sources that occur when you enter your first school as an assistant principal or principal. At this stage, the more generic skills and administrative perspective learned during university training are reinforced, modified, and expanded as principals and assistant principals learn how things are done here. Several sources play a major role in the socialization of new school leaders, including, teachers, students, parents, other school administrators, and district administrators.

Within the school, teachers, students, and parents hold strong expectations about how the roles of principal and assistant principal should be enacted. Teachers are the primary source of influence on new principals (Duke et al., 1984). Teachers not only have expectations about what tasks new administrators should do, but they also influence the type of information to which principals and assistant principals can gain access in order to make decisions (Long, 1988). A typical early mistake of new administrators is to view teachers as a unitary group, when in fact there are frequently various subcultures and groups of teachers that sometimes hold conflicting expectations for the principal.

Students influence the socialization of new principals and assistant principals by reinforcing certain images of the role. As we will discuss later, this influence is especially potent for assistant principals in a student management role (Reed & Himmler, 1985). New administrators sometimes surprisingly forget that students have an incredible influence on the culture and climate of the school and thus can strongly influence the learning of new school leaders.

Parents also have strong expectations of what administrators are to do and how they are to act. In recent reform strategies, such as site-based management and shared decision making, parents play a critical role not only in school governance but also in the socialization of new principals and assistant principals. Parents, like teachers and students, are also not always a homogeneous group but frequently present the new administrator with contrasting and conflicting expectations and demands.

Other administrators, both inside and outside the school, influence the process of becoming a new innovative principal or assistant principal. As we will discuss, principals are a critical source of socialization for new assistant principals through the tasks they assign and the images they portray. Administrators outside the school are also major sources of influence on new administrators' learning. Networks of fellow administrators can provide valuable support and encouragement for new principals and assistant principals, but they also can reinforce status quo images of the role.

District superiors are a major source of socialization for new principals and assistant principals. This socialization can occur through the selection process, evaluation, and supervision (Peterson, 1984). These superiors have clear expectations about the role conception they expect principals and assistant principals to hold. In the opening vignette, Beth's superintendent supported her image of the assistant principal's role that went beyond viewing student management as removing students from the classroom. In so doing, this superintendent influenced Beth's socialization by promoting an innovative role conception that encouraged Beth's inventive spirit. A contrasting superintendent could have reinforced a status quo image that would have discouraged experimentation and learning of more innovative role images.

Personal Socialization.   In addition to the professional and organizational socialization sources that we have identified, friends and families influence new principals and assistant principals. Although these groups may be less influential in helping the new school leader learn the technical skills or how to adjust to the work environment, they can be extremely powerful socialization agents for supporting images of the role. Family members and friends can be critical sources of support for encouraging role conceptions that involve more innovative images. Sometimes these images require more risk taking or more time that may be viewed as interfering with family obligations. If family members or friends view these images as inappropriate or in conflict with family concerns, they may put pressure on new principals and assistant principals to reconsider these role conceptions.

Stages of Socialization

Becoming an innovative principal or assistant principal does not occur overnight. It will not and should not occur simply when you get your master's degree or state administrative license. Rather, this learning or socialization process is an evolutionary process.

One way to view this evolution emphasizes information processing and the different types and sources of information that are available to new school leaders at different stages. "Newcomers' ability to acquire information is affected by the type of organization and/or occupation entered, previous organizational experience, channels available for acquiring information, and availability of peers" (Stout, 2000, p. 23). As you will discover, learning the skills, adjusting to the work environment, and acquiring values all involve information. Moreover, becoming an innovative school leader who is a learner, mentor, supervisor, leader, manager, politician, and advocate requires obtaining information.

Socialization has been conceptualized as occurring in three stages with different names for the stages. One of the most frequently used schemes includes anticipatory, encounter, and adjustment stages (Hart, 1993). Typically, in the *anticipatory socialization stage*, the individual is a stranger to the occupation. However, aspiring school administrators like you are not total strangers to the occupation. You have witnessed the work of principals and assistant principals since the time you were a kindergartner. However, this experience provided a limited, "on stage" view of the role. As we mentioned before, even as a teacher there were aspects of the role that were not evident to you. Moreover, depending on your experience, the innovative role conceptions we have explored in this book may be strange and unusual to you. During the anticipatory stage, you are meeting new administrators or new sources of socialization that may have different views of the role than what you have experienced thus far. At this stage you are acquiring information about how the larger society, your university professors, and your internship mentors view the role.

As you move into your first administrative assignment as a principal or assistant principal, you enter the *encounter socialization stage*. You move from being a stranger to becoming a newcomer. As you acquire new information about the school and the expectations of its constituencies, you are likely to experience "reality shock" as the expectations you developed earlier during teaching and the internship conflict with the expectations you encounter in this first school (Hughes, 1959). Even if you had an exceptionally good and relevant internship experience, you are likely to encounter surprise as a newcomer. This does not mean that the information you acquired during the anticipatory stage was bad information but rather that expectations are likely to vary in different settings. You may have expected as an assistant principal to be given wide latitude in working with teachers on instructional leadership. However, you may encounter administrators, teachers, and parents who expect you to focus totally on student discipline issues. Your internship experience, far from providing inaccurate information, provided a way to view the role that is worth considering rather than abandoning.

The information you acquire to respond to the surprises you encounter will depend on your previous experiences, your personality characteristics, and the availability of others around you (Louis, 1980a). Acquiring information about the school and using the interpretations of others constitute an appropriate socialization strategy for you to use during this stage. However, you should be cautious in blindly accepting others' interpretations of the expectations and norms of this new environment. First, it is very likely that school faculty members' interpretations will vary. Thus you will be faced with the question of which interpretation to choose. Second, interpretations from some school veterans may or may not help you to develop an innovative role conception. Some of these veterans may have an interest in convincing you to perpetuate the status quo even if change is needed.

The third stage, the *adjustment socialization stage*, involves acquiring the information to move from newcomer to insider. Frequently this is "privileged information" that only a few people in the organization possess but which permits learning the tasks, interpersonal relationships, and values of the new setting. In this stage, the principal or assistant principal resolves the issues of the encounter stage and becomes an inside member of the organization.

Frequently, new principals find that they never really are considered insiders by the veteran power block of the school. Sometimes a group of veterans conceals privileged information in order to protect their turf and maintain dysfunctional organizational stability. New principals or assistant principals are deprived of this information until they can be trusted not to rock the boat. This may inhibit change and discourage more innovative role conceptions.

New school leaders also may encounter an environment in which a former administrator hoarded the privileged information and even veterans in the organization never became real insiders. What constitutes insider and outsider status in an organization is a fundamental quality of the culture of the school and can have amazing influence on innovation. Role making, in part, involves working with others in the organization to redefine and expand the "insider" status so that all organization members can experience the privileges. This is the political role we discussed in Chapter 8 and that the new principal or assistant principal may need to develop early in the socialization process.

Methods of Socialization

Learning to be an innovative principal or assistant principal involves a variety of methods. Some of the methods are obvious, such as coursework or mentoring. Other methods are subtler, such as teacher testing. The methods themselves communicate the content and goals of socialization. Some, for example, maintain the status quo of the role, whereas others encourage innovation and change.

Both the organization and the individual influence the methods of learning how to become an innovative school leader. Organizational methods reflect the cultural values and norms of the school or university. For example, schools that value risk taking are more likely to use socialization methods that celebrate and reward innovation. However, you as a new principal or assistant principal also have socialization methods at your disposal that can encourage innovation or maintain the status quo. We will discuss many of these individual methods later in this chapter when we discuss the unique socialization processes for assistant principals, principals, or veteran principals. In this subsection we will identify two types of socialization methods: organizational methods and individual influences.

Organizational Methods.   Often schools are not aware of the methods they use to socialize newcomers, including assistant principals and principals. It is critical, however, for you as a newcomer to be sensitive to the socialization methods that school veterans use. These methods can contribute to your conception of the role in innovative ways, or they can encourage you to maintain the status quo when change is needed.

Van Maanen and Schein (1979), two researchers at the Massachusetts Institute of Technology who explored how individuals learn to become organizational members, developed the classic identification of organizational socialization methods. Their scheme involved identifying methods by posing opposites:

- Collective versus individual
- Formal versus informal
- Sequential versus random
- Fixed versus variable
- Serial versus disjunctive
- Investiture versus divestiture

Collective versus individual refers to whether the socialization occurs in a group or alone. If you were part of a cohort in your university training, you were part of a collective socialization method. When you become a principal or assistant principal, much of your socialization will be individual; that is, you probably will be learning the role by yourself instead of with a group of new administrators.

Formal versus informal methods relate to whether your socialization involves being segregated from the work setting or not. Although much of your university training is formal, little of your organization socialization will be formal. Some districts provide regular, formal professional development for new administrators, but most of the training is informal.

Sequential versus random refers to whether there is a sequence of steps leading to the role. For example, learning to be a doctor involves medical courses, internship, and residency. Learning to be a principal, however, involves courses, usually an internship, and immersion in the actual role. As veterans and newcomers will tell you, you will get all the responsibilities when you are first appointed. There is no gradual induction.

Fixed versus variable involves whether or not the learning process is defined in terms of a fixed timetable. Although courses and internship come before the actual role appointment, after you become a principal or assistant principal, no other timetable is apparent. Some administrators have suggested that there are informal district timetables such that if you have not been appointed to a principalship after a certain period of time since you received your license, you are unlikely to be appointed.

The final two methods that Van Maanen and Schein (1979) identified are especially critical to learning to become an innovative school leader. *Serial versus disjunctive* refers to whether or not veteran administrators are available to prepare newcomers. Superintendents, for example, rarely have incumbents still around to train them in the role; thus, their socialization is more disjunctive. Principals, however, may have veteran administrator mentors who help them learn the tasks, relationships, and values of the role. Mentors can be very effective in learning the role. However, they also can perpetuate a status-quo image of the role. Serial socialization methods, such as mentoring, tend to discourage innovative role conceptions. However, there are ways you can identify mentors and work with veterans in ways that encourage rather than discourage innovation.

Divestiture versus investiture refers to the ways organizations use the prior experiences, values, and characteristics of newcomers in helping them to learn the role. If new principals or administrators are encouraged by districts to devalue their teaching experiences and skills, divestiture is being used. In contrast, if district administrators value the use of administrators' prior teaching experience in becoming instructional leaders in their schools, they are using investiture. Depending on the quality, type, and conception of the prior experience, this type of socialization method can encourage or discourage innovation.

In addition to these methods, other authors focus on learning cultural values, norms, and beliefs. Trice (1993) discussed socialization methods that influence the passage through occupational roles. He suggested that rites, ceremonies, rituals, and stories can be powerful tools for learning the norms and values of a role. For example, when veteran teachers tell new principals stories about former principals, they are doing more than simply presenting interesting tales; they are also emphasizing administrator characteristics that are valued or condemned. These stories can be useful to you not only as ways the school uses to help you learn acceptable norms and values, but they also can be useful sources of information for you to use in understanding the school and its values as you develop an innovative conception of your role.

Crow and Pounder (1996) found various socialization methods that schools used to socialize administrative interns to the values and norms of the role. These methods included cultural forms such as artifacts (e.g., keys to the building, office space), rituals (e.g., early bombardment of responsibilities and shadowing), rites (e.g., selection process and testing by faculty), and ceremonies (e.g., introduction to faculty).

Individual Influences.   In addition to the socialization methods that schools and districts use to shape the way you learn the administrative role, you use various methods to influence the role. Some of these methods are described more accurately as characteristics that influence the socialization process rather than methods you choose.

Your own personal characteristics, such as gender, may influence the learning or socialization process. Men and women may approach learning the job and attaching to individuals in the organization in different ways (Hall, 1987). In addition to your characteristics, your values, attitudes, and vision affect how you learn the job. Various attitudes, such as desire for control, tolerance for organizational influence, and sense of self-efficacy, can influence the socialization process (Nicholson, 1984; Schein& Ott 1962; Jones, 1986).

Previous experience also influences the socialization process. The ways or styles you developed in learning previous roles or expectations can create "cultures of orientation" that influence the ways you learn to become an innovative school leader (Van Maanen, 1984). As we discussed in Chapter 3, the constructivist view of learning involves in part the use of previous experiences and learning to serve as scaffolding for new learning. In addition, if your previous experience is aligned with the school's expectations or orientations, the types of socialization tactics used by the school are likely to emphasize investiture. In contrast, if your previous experience is out of alignment with the school's values, a "destructive or unfreezing phase" of socialization may be used (Schein, 1988).

A more specific socialization method used by aspiring administrators has been identified by Greenfield (1977a) as *GASing*, that is, "getting the attention of superiors." GASing is a socialization method that interns use to promote their candidacy and to learn the administrative perspective. Greenfield found that more assertive interns, that is, those who tested the limits and exploited resources, tended to develop broader administrative perspectives, that is, involving the whole school, than their more complacent counterparts. These findings suggest that rather than being a passive recipient of the socialization process, you have the opportunity to actively participate in your own learning to become an innovative school leader.

Outcomes of Socialization

Socialization obviously involves some outcome. In your case, the outcome of learning this new role should result in an innovative role orientation. The major portion of this book has emphasized the nature of this outcome in terms of seven role conceptions of the principalship. However, this role is complex; it involves maintaining organizational stability as well as improving teaching and learning. The balance in the role depends on the district, the community, the school, and you. The process of learning the role that we have thus far described in this chapter leads toward different ways to balance the role and different outcomes.

Focus of Socialization Outcomes.   We tend to think of professional learning as what happens to the individual during the socialization process. However, socialization can focus on two other areas that typically are ignored but are critical for change: role and organization. The outcome of socialization for you as a school principal or assistant involves learning new knowledge and skills, developing new values and norms, and relating to a new environment. As we described earlier, you will encounter a variety of expectations that district administrators, parents, teachers, and students have for you involving what you do, whom you listen to, what you believe, and what you value. The outcomes of socialization from an individual point of view focus on these knowledge, skills, values, and beliefs. As we will discuss later, this does not mean that you have been socialized successfully when you acquire everyone else's skills, beliefs, and values. The socialization outcomes for you involve the reciprocal process we discussed earlier.

Socialization also involves changes in the role. In earlier chapters we identified seven innovative role conceptions or different ways to imagine the roles of principal and assistant principal. Socialization to these role conceptions does not only mean that you should enact your role in these different ways but also that you should influence the way others see the role. Roles can change in terms of the knowledge base that informs practice, the strategies typically used to enact the role, and the purpose or mission of the role (Van Maanen & Schein, 1979). Roles change because of societal pressures, your style in comparison with your predecessor's, and deliberate attempts by such groups as universities, professional associations, and national accrediting bodies. Thus the socialization process of learning to become an innovative principal or assistant principal can result not only in changing your beliefs but also in influencing the way others view the role.

Socialization also involves changes in the organization. Anyone who has witnessed the arrival of a large group of newcomers to a school understands how these types of groups can change the organizational culture and climate. "Educational organizations make room for newcomers they value by adding new structures (e.g., courses or course levels), adapting procedures (e.g., giving reduced teaching loads to newcomers), and adjusting reward systems (e.g., giving extracurricular assignments to adjust the pay of newcomers)" (Crow & Matthews, 1998, p. 28). Without dismissing the powerful influence that the school will have on your learning, you have significant influence on the organization. As a new principal or assistant principal, if you are sensitive to the school's culture, you can have a powerful influence during this socialization process on the image that others have of the role.

Types of Outcomes.   Because this chapter is concerned primarily with how the innovative role conceptions we discussed earlier in this book are learned, we will concentrate on two types of socialization outcomes: individual adaptation and role adaptation. These are closely aligned with role taking and role making. In terms of individual adaptation, several outcomes are possible as you take on the role of principal or assistant principal and as you respond to the expectations that others have of you. A useful scheme for identifying these is Schein's (1988) three types of responses that depend on whether you accept or reject the pivotal, relevant, and peripheral values and norms of the organization. Conformity involves the acceptance of all organizational or professional values regardless of whether they are pivotal, relevant, or peripheral. Rebellion, in contrast, involves the rejection of all these values. A *creative individualism* response to socialization involves the acceptance only of the pivotal values and norms and rejection of the others. An assistant principal who accepts the importance of student discipline but rejects the necessity of an autocratic approach has assumed a creative individualist response to socialization. Obviously, some values, norms, and expectations in your first school setting are worth conforming to and, in fact, must be accepted in order for you to fulfill your responsibilities, for example, being a good steward of the public's money. However, to assume that all values must be accepted uncritically is to contradict your role as a change agent. There is a place for conformity, a place for rebellion, and certainly a place for creative individualism in your response to the socialization process.

Learning to become an innovative principal or assistant principal also results in role adaptation. Again, there are three possible role orientations: custodianship, content inno-

vation, and role innovation (Schein, 1971). A custodial orientation to the role involves accepting the current knowledge base, strategy, and mission of the role as practiced by most
principals or assistant principals. This orientation is what we have described in earlier sections as the traditional conception of the role. For example, a custodial orientation of the
principal's supervisory responsibility assumes a deficit model of the teacher, a top-down
"snoopervision" strategy, and the centrality of a control mission.

The second role orientation that is a possible outcome of socialization is content
innovation. This orientation would be reflected in an assistant principal who accepts
the student management mission of the role but rejects the knowledge and strategies
typically used in enacting this mission. An assistant principal who is molding the role
in a content-innovative orientation would acknowledge the new understanding, for example, of early adolescent development and search for strategies that engender self-
discipline.

A third orientation is role innovation, which is a more radical response to socialization. This orientation involves the rejection not only of the customary strategies for enacting the role but also of the traditional mission or purpose of the role. A principal who
conceives the mission of the role in terms of mentor rejects the traditional control mission.
Likewise, a principal who conceives the political role as contributing to a civil society has
responded to socialization by rejecting an apolitical purpose or a manipulative mission of
the role.

As with the preceding three responses to individual adaptation, these role orientations are more complex than simply opting for a role-innovation perspective. As a school
leader, some of your response to the role will necessitate a custodial orientation when it is
important to maintain organizational stability and integrity. At other times, a more innovative orientation will be necessary to move the school toward a shared vision.

The traditional perspective on socialization outcomes identifies underconformity as
a central problem when newcomers do not acquire the skills, values, and beliefs required
by their organizations. Several researchers, however, have suggested that overconformity
may be a much bigger problem (Feldman, 1981; Fisher, 1986; Long, 1988). Although
conformity may be desirable in some occupational roles or organizational settings, for example, bank tellers and members of marching bands, it can be dysfunctional for other
roles and organizations. We have argued in this book that for principals and assistant principals to be leaders of leaders and leaders of learners, they must imagine innovative role
conceptions. In this instance, conformity is likely to be dysfunctional for schools to become learning communities for all students.

Becoming a principal or assistant principal involves a variety of socialization methods, some of which encourage outcomes that are custodial, whereas others emphasize
more innovative conceptions of the role. Some researchers have found that some methods,
for example, collective, formal, fixed, sequential, serial, and investiture methods, are negatively related to innovative role orientations (Jones, 1986). For example, mentoring—a
serial method because it involves incumbents training newcomers—can lead to outcomes
that encourage maintaining the status quo.

However, other researchers (Baker, 1990) have found that individual differences, for
example, tolerance for organizational influence, may moderate this relationship. Your influence in the socialization process can help to question the value of certain methods and

the balance of custodial or innovative orientations. The type of principal or assistant principal you become is not a determined outcome. Although others have expectations of you and their influence is significant in becoming a school leader, you can make a significant difference in the outcome of your own professional learning process.

In the remainder of this chapter we will examine the unique socialization features of becoming an assistant principal and principal and those features of changing role conceptions at midcareer. In each instance we will identify some socialization methods that can contribute to your becoming an innovative school leader in each of the seven role conceptions identified earlier in this book.

Becoming a New Assistant Principal

In the opening vignette, Beth's experience as an assistant principal was a shock from what she had expected in her administrative preparation and internship experiences. She encountered a principal and a group of teachers whose image of the role of assistant principal was one of student controller. Beth's experience is not unusual for many new assistant principals. The role of assistant principal is ambiguous, limited, and stressful in many settings. Yet, as an assistant principal, you can make a significant contribution to the instructional program of the school. Learning to become an innovative assistant principal who contributes to instructional improvement, however, takes place in a context of socialization that is important for you to know. In this section we will identify the distinctive features of the socialization of assistant principals. Some of these features reinforce traditional roles. We describe them in order for you to understand the socialization processes and methods that some individuals may use to encourage you to maintain the status quo. However, also woven into our discussion will be suggestions to help you in your socialization as an innovative assistant principal in terms of the seven role conceptions we discussed previously in this book.

Distinctive Features of the Socialization of Assistant Principals

The role of assistant principal is undergoing a change in contemporary schools that creates role confusion and ambiguity. Catherine Marshall (1985) described this confusion.

> For the assistant principal—whose daily tasks and roles are ambiguous, whose function is ill-defined, who is caught between students and teachers, school and community, teachers and higher administrators, who are [*sic*] expected to implement change policies whether or not there are adequate resources—the stress must be multiplied [p. 56].

Numerous images of the assistant principal's role can be found, including hatchet man, activity coordinator, handy man, and fire fighter (Reed & Himmler, 1985). Such ambiguity and confusion create difficulty for socialization. Several distinctive features of the assistant principal's socialization can be identified and should be helpful to you as you move into this significant leadership position.

Content of Socialization.   Becoming a new assistant principal will involve two images of the role. One image is a limited vision of the role that emphasizes primarily student management and maintenance of order (Austin & Brown, 1970; Greenfield, Marshall, & Reed, 1986). The tasks involved in this view of the role include monitoring, supporting, and remediating (Reed & Himmler, 1985). Learning to be an assistant principal in this view involves both technical and cultural content. The technical content of socialization includes developing the skills to assess unstable situations and remedy them. Knowing how to monitor and to acquire the information necessary to prevent disorder or to uncover problems is a critical component of the assistant principal's socialization. You may have developed some of these skills as a teacher, but it is unlikely that you experienced the extensive and school-wide nature of the stability issue in your prior experience.

In addition to the technical skills to monitor, support, and remedy unstable situations, you will have to learn cultural sensitivity to community values and standards regarding disorder and discipline. In some schools, issues such as noise in the classroom, wearing caps, or congregating in the hall are considered inappropriate and are dealt with harshly by some administrators. In other schools, these are not issues at all, and noise in the classroom is considered important to instructional engagement. Your ability to discover these community values, which may be contradictory to your previous teaching or internship experiences, is critical.

The second image of the assistant principal's role is a more expanded one in which the role is enlarged to support instruction for all students (Greenfield, 1985a; Spady, 1985). This image does not ignore the student management role but views it in the larger school context of instructional support. Learning to be an assistant principal in this image necessitates developing skills to work with teachers in improving instructional effectiveness and to contribute to a professional learning community that encourages inquiry and collaboration. This includes technical, interpersonal, and cultural skills, such as observation, collaboration, active listening, and conferencing. Many of these you bring with you from your previous experience as a teacher or from your preparation. Some of these skills you will learn as you become an assistant principal in a specific setting with values, norms, and beliefs similar to or different from your experience.

Sources of Socialization.   Although your socialization as an assistant principal involves some of the same sources as for principals, three are specifically distinctive for you as a new assistant principal. One of these distinctive elements is the influence of the principal as a source of socialization. Beth's experience in the opening vignette demonstrates the significance of the principal's influence as a source of socialization for new assistant principals. Your principal will influence your socialization in three major ways: assigning tasks, creating role images, and providing support. The principal almost certainly will determine the tasks that you are assigned. Some assistant principals have found that principals often take the more interesting tasks for themselves and assign the remainder to the assistant principal (Hess, 1985).

Principals also influence the assistant principal's socialization in a more subtle but profound way—by creating role images. These images include what receives attention in the school environment; the nature of the relationships with teachers, students, and parents; issues of control and authority; and what gets rewarded and punished. For some principals, the image of the role of administrator involves an autocratic and distant relationship with teachers and students. For others, school administrators are facilitators and learners rather than autocrats and controllers. New assistant principals "learn very quickly that to be successful in the organization, they must buy into the system, learn the rules, and think like their boss" (Long, 1988, pp. 113–114).

Your principal also can influence your socialization as a new assistant principal by providing support, encouragement, and advice. In many instances, the principal becomes a mentor to the new assistant principal. Whether a mentoring relationship occurs, other principals can be influential in your socialization by what they praise and encourage about your performance and by their support and sponsorship of your future career.

A second major source of influence for assistant principals is teachers. The relationship with teachers can be both a positive influence and a perplexing dilemma. Teachers can reinforce or balance the role images presented by the principal. They can respond positively or negatively to an expanded view of the assistant principal's role. The relationship with teachers also presents a dilemma for new administrators. In some conceptions of the role, assistant principals are expected to divest themselves of the teacher role and develop distancing relationships with teachers. Marshall (1985) called this one of the critical tasks in the enculturation of assistant principals: "separating from and defining relationships with teachers" (p. 45). It is not unusual for new assistant principals, especially if they are assigned to the same school where they taught, to realize that they are no longer welcomed in the faculty lounge. Some find that previous friends stop talking with them or inviting them out. The distancing that occurs is influenced not only by administrators themselves but also by teachers who regard the new assistant principal as a member of the "them" group.

Some new assistant principals fall into a trap by assuming that this distancing relationship is necessary. In fact, the folklore of school administration frequently supports the view. However, such a view is contradictory to more innovative and expanded images of the role in which you contribute to the professional learning community. This is not to say that if you choose these more innovative images, you will not experience teachers who want to distance themselves from you. Nor do we suggest that choosing this image will shield you from making hard decisions or conducting evaluations that may alienate some teachers. However, becoming an innovative assistant principal does not require you to purposely distance yourself from teachers.

A rarely acknowledged source of socialization for assistant principals is students. Although much of the job has focused traditionally on relationships with students, the literature seldom acknowledges the powerful socializing role played by students. Assistant principals are expected by teachers, parents, and principals to develop an image with students that emphasizes authority. This image can be one of drill sergeant, mother superior, or bully (Reed & Himmler, 1985). Students influence assistant principals' socialization by reinforcing the images of authority. This reinforcement may be influenced by the image held by predecessors. Some new assistant principals who try to develop a role image with students that is different from that of their predecessors are dismayed to discover that the students reject the image.

Assistant principals are also sources of their own socialization in terms of their personal characteristics and previous experience. Your gender, for example, may encourage certain images of the role. "Perhaps women's socialization and the organizational expectations regarding women's roles enable them to [more easily than men] infuse an element of caring, nonaggression, and support into the task of maintaining control in schools" (Marshall, 1985, p. 53). The typically longer teaching experience of women also contributes to more instructional expertise and images of the role that encourage instructional effectiveness (Shakeshaft, 1987).

In addition, your previous experience, especially as a teacher, influences the socialization process. The level of teaching, the social class of students and parents, and the administrative setting can influence the kinds of skills and sensitivities you bring or need to acquire as a new assistant principal. Moving from teaching middle-class suburban students to an assistant principalship in an inner city can require you to develop many new skills that will especially aid you in being an advocate and facilitating others' advocacy.

Stages of Socialization.   Becoming a new assistant principal involves three critical issues of time. First, the assistant principalship is a period of testing. "As they separate from the old reference group, seek entry and pass through career and organizational boundaries, they undergo a period of testing while the new group checks to see whether the aspirant can conform and adhere to their norms and meet performance expectations" (Marshall, 1985, p. 30). Administrators, teachers, parents, and students conduct this testing to determine the assistant principal's competence, loyalty, authority, and support. "Administrators evaluate the assistant principal's competency and loyalty. Teachers evaluate the assistant principal's competency, authority, and support. Students and parents assess authority and relationships" (Crow & Matthews, 1998, p. 75).

Another temporal element is what we have referred to as the *encounter stage,* where the expectations of the assistant principal meet the reality of the school context. The "reality shock" (Hughes, 1959) that occurs when expectations and reality are incongruent can be a difficult experience for the new assistant principal. Beth's reality shock (in the opening vignette) occurred when she encountered a principal who discouraged her more expanded view of the assistant principalship role. Early in the process of becoming an assistant principal, you will encounter different expectations and demands. Part of the response to these reality shocks is to acknowledge what others expect of you and decide what is important to you in terms of the image of the assistant principalship you want to mold.

A third distinctive temporal element in becoming an assistant principal is experiencing a sense of loss. "The first year administrators seemed to experience a sense of loss regarding their old roles and their previous close relationship with peers" (Akerlund, 1988, p. 181). Although not all new assistant principals experience loss, those who do talk about how they miss the intensive instructional contact with students and the social relationships with fellow teachers. Recent school reforms, such as professional learning communities, suggest that this loss may be more dysfunctional than originally thought. As we discussed earlier, there may be some discomfort in the evaluative role that administrators play in the school, but there is no necessity of intentionally creating hierarchical distancing that hinders professional community to support learning.

Methods of Socialization.   Becoming an assistant principal involves a variety of methods. Some are tools used by principals, teachers, district administrators, parents, and students to shape the new recruit and reinforce values, norms, and beliefs held by the organization. We maintain that there are other methods that assistant principals can use not only to respond to the expectations of school constituents but also to help shape an image of the role that is innovative and expanded.

Although school organizations use many methods in socializing the new assistant principal, three seem especially distinctive to this role. First, learning to become a new assistant principal is typically a trial-and-error process. This means that instead of the formal, collective, and fixed process that you probably encountered in the internship, your new learning is informal, individual, and variable. Although some districts are moving toward more formal arrangements that involve assigning veterans to new administrators, the large majority of new assistant principals find that they are on their own. The trial-and-error process, however, does not mean that the organization is not aware of your actions, successes, and failures. This process tends to be influenced by such things as the style of your predecessor and the criticality of specific needs, such as student management.

Second, as we have noted, administrators, teachers, parents, and students routinely test the new assistant principal to determine competence, loyalty, authority, and support. Although some testing may have occurred during the internship, the stakes are higher for assistant principals. The testing is often subtle, and the individual assistant principal is only aware after the fact. A former graduate student described a less subtle testing that occurred in her first assistant principal position. Her previous teaching experience had been in suburban schools, but her first administrative position was in an inner-city school. One of the teachers asked her to proctor an exam for second graders while the teacher made a call to a parent. The students responded to the "new" teacher by cheating and other disruptive behaviors. When the teacher returned, the new assistant principal acknowledged that she had lost control of the class. However, she asked if she could return in a week and "try again." The teacher agreed, and when the assistant principal returned to teach the class during the next week, a line of teachers was standing in the back of the room to witness her "second try." Her humility and humor—and success at the second try—won her respect from the teachers. She passed the test!

A third distinctive method used by organizations to socialize new assistant principals is divestiture. Divestiture processes regarding movement toward the assistant principal role appear to be gradual and subtle. As the candidate begins to do some of the organizational scut work (that many teachers may refuse to do) associated with monitoring children—helping to "set up" for parent and other meetings, being a "go-for," and helping the administrator with an endless stream of minor (and sometimes major) projects—the "teacher" self is gradually shed and the "administrator" self evolves (Greenfield, 1985b, pp. 22–23). Both teachers and administrators use divestiture to establish certain norms regarding what is expected of new assistant principals. Teachers, in order to maintain the teacher subculture, try to keep the division of authority and lines of communication clear. Administrators, sometimes in response to this subculture, attempt to close ranks and create an "us and them" perspective in new assistant principals.

As we have argued before, this insider/outsider perspective does not foster a professional learning community. Thus divestiture is dysfunctional for socializing new assistant principals to an innovative image of the role that views both teachers and administrators as learners and leaders.

We have maintained throughout this chapter that socialization involves both role taking and role making and that the individual is an active partner in the learning process.

Thus there are methods that you can use as a new assistant principal to learn this role and help to mold the role in terms of the seven conceptions we discussed earlier in this book. First, you can use a variety of methods to enhance your role as a learner. In addition to the obvious methods, such as reading books and journals, attending professional conferences, and continuing conversations with university faculty and administrative mentors, you also can form associations with other assistant principals that you believe have adopted more expanded and innovative conceptions of the role. Visiting each other's schools, forming book clubs, and other forms of networking can help reinforce more innovative conceptions of the role of assistant principal as learner.

In terms of a mentoring role, you can develop your own mentoring relationship with students and teachers and reflect on this experience to determine how it works. Reflecting on your own experience as a mentor also opens your experience as a protégé. Peer mentoring arrangements with other former interns and veteran assistant principals can reinforce more innovative images.

Learning to be a supervisor can be difficult in situations where teachers and administrators emphasize only student management as your role. Although it may take a while to convince veteran teachers of your contribution in this area, you might start with new teachers as you reinforce the idea of student management as an instructional rather than control role. In developing your skills in this area, you can invite veteran administrators or district office specialists who have reputations as excellent instructional coaches to witness your observations or conferences and give you feedback. You also might use your networking group of former university classmates to discuss frustrations, ideas, successes, and failures.

Becoming an innovative assistant principal, we have argued, involves a more expanded role than student management. Identifying and communicating with assistant principals or principals who view the assistant principal's role in this way can help reinforce the image. Another tool to use in this regard is to become part of a school-university partnership that conducts action research. Not only does this reinforce your image as a learner, but it also helps emphasize your instructional role as you work with teachers on instructional problems.

Frequently the assistant principal's role is restricted in terms of learning managerial tasks that will be necessary if the individual becomes a principal. Restricting the assistant principal to student management roles ignores the need to learn such critical managerial tasks as budgeting and facilities management. Getting to know the custodian and the cafeteria workers has multiple benefits including learning how the building and the lunch program function. By asking these staff members to give you a tour of the facilities, not only will you impress them with your interest in their areas, but you also probably will see more of the building than you saw on your formal introduction to the facility.

Becoming an assistant principal involves learning the micropolitics of the school and district. Developing and using your sensitivity to the conflicts that different school groups have over resources and values are important learning issues. Becoming an innovative assistant principal also involves getting to know the larger political system and structure that influences community, district, and school decisions. Attending school board and city council meetings can give you enormous information about who wields power over what resources in your community.

Learning to become an innovative assistant principal involves the critical area of learning to be an advocate in order to respond to the diverse needs of students and families in your school community. Even in situations where new assistant principals are constrained to a more limited student management role, learning about the diversity of your school community can have a powerful influence on your effectiveness. Getting to know district special education, English as a second language (ESL), and bilingual administrators can help you develop an understanding of needs, programs, and procedures to respond to diversity. Attending events sponsored by ethnic communities in your area will provide valuable information regarding the concerns and values of diverse groups in your school and help you to develop the sensitivity, skills, and understanding to become an innovative school leader who advocates for diverse students and their families.

Outcomes of Socialization.   There are two ways to think about the socialization outcomes for assistant principals. First, we can identify the career outcomes of socialization. The assistant principalship traditionally has been viewed as an apprenticeship position for the purpose of grooming new principals. However, more recently, the role has become focused on student management. There is some concern that this more limited role has decreased the qualifications of assistant principals to become principals (Pounder & Merrill, 2000). and thus contributed to perceptions of a shortage in qualified candidates for the principalship.

As Beth in the opening vignette found, becoming an innovative assistant principal contributed toward her visibility in the district and her eventual move to the principalship. One of the socialization outcomes of the assistant principalship is the successful move to a principal position.

Another career outcome may be developing an innovative conception of the assistant principal's role and remaining in that role. Some assistant principals find that they prefer this position because it allows them to stay closer to students. Do not assume that remaining in the assistant principal position is a failure of socialization. As we have argued in this book, the assistant principalship is a critical leadership role in the school and deserves innovative leaders.

The second way to view socialization outcomes is in terms of role image. Earlier we identified three outcomes: conformity, rebellion, and creative individualism (Schein, 1988). In terms of becoming an assistant principal, enacting the limited view of the role as student management is clearly a more conformist outcome. However, new assistant principals must respond to the expectations of those around them as well as try to mold the role in a more instructionally focused way. In the beginning, it is not unusual for new assistant principals to focus on conforming to this limited role. However, in order to provide the type of innovative role as learner, mentor, supervisor, leader, manager, politician, and advocate that is needed to make schools dynamic learning environments, you should keep in mind how the role of assistant principal can be changed. Creative individualism provides the opportunity to both understand and respond to the role as given and mold the role in more innovative ways.

The assistant principalship is a critical leadership role that can help change schools. We encourage you to imagine your role as assistant principal in innovative ways. Schools can be more effective learning environments for all students if more innovative images can be fostered and mentored.

> Examining the interaction of district preferences, assessment, sponsorship, and support and selection systems may show that people with strong ideals and strong personalities are filtered out of the administrative ranks unless they have continuous mentoring to disguise this tendency; so that they have a defender against those who see them as unpredictable and untrustworthy (Marshall, 1985, p. 54).

Becoming a New Principal

Many, if not most, elementary school principals enter the role without assistant principal experience. Secondary school principals are more likely to have had this prior administrative experience. If you are a new principal who has never been an assistant principal, you may want to read the preceding section on becoming an assistant principal. Many of the features are similar between a new assistant principal and a new principal who has not had prior administrative experience. In this section we identify those elements of socialization that are distinctive to a new principal. As we did with assistant principals, some of our discussion focuses on traditional socialization processes that encourage maintaining the status quo. We describe this traditional socialization so that you know what methods others may be using to influence you. However, we also identify more innovative strategies that you can use to learn and implement the seven role conceptions.

Content of Socialization

One of the most distinctive elements of the principal's socialization is the importance of tasks involving external constituents, including district administrators and the community. Assistant principals are obviously involved to some degree with these external groups, but the role of principal could be described as balancing internal and external demands. The role complexity described in Chapter 3 that has become so apparent in the work of principals in contemporary society can be thought of as having both internal and external parts (Crow, Hausman, & Scribner, 2002). We will discuss the content of socialization in terms of internal, external, and personal spheres.

Internal Sphere.   Learning to become a new principal clearly includes learning the tasks, work environment, and culture of the school. The tasks have been described in the earlier chapters of this book in terms of the different role conceptions of the principalship. Learning the work environment is probably more complex as you learn the names, job responsibilities, sources of information, and personalities of the individuals with whom you work. When you enter your new school, you will encounter a large amount of chaotic, equivocal information from which you will develop "cause maps" that allow you to predict behavior (Weick, 1979). Learning what information you need, which sources of information to trust, and what to do with the information you receive is an extremely important part of your learning as a new principal.

Learning to become a new principal also involves learning the norms, values, and beliefs of the school culture. Whether or not you have had prior administrative experience, you will need to learn the unique culture of this school. Learning the culture—how things are done here—is critical to becoming an innovative principal in the seven areas we identified earlier. For example, you cannot be a change agent if you are insensitive to the norms and values of the context. Another part of this cultural learning is recognizing that the culture has been there much longer than you and that cultural values and norms are much harder to change than you might assume (Schein, 1992).

External Sphere. The complexity of the principalship has increased recently primarily because of external demands, such as accountability, markets, and civic capacity requirements or trends (Crow, Hausman, & Scribner, 2002). Schools are embedded in their social settings, and principals' roles are likewise embedded.

Learning to become a new principal involves confronting new tasks, political relationships and dilemmas, and a culture that may have values in conflict with the school's vision. Your first day on the job will no doubt include district reports, responses, and requests. Whether you imagine your role as a leader of the school or agent of central office (Crow, 1987), you still must respond to district administrators who hired you, will evaluate you, and from whom many of your resources come.

In addition to the new sets of tasks involving the district office, you must learn the cultural norms and values of the district and the larger community. These groups have their own sets of cultural values and mores that may conflict with yours or the school's. Principals discover, sometimes very early, that the values of the community are not necessarily the values of the teachers and administrators of the school (Post, 1992). Frequently, these value differences occur over curriculum and student management styles. Learning what these value differences are will not resolve them, but you cannot work to resolve them unless you are aware of what areas of conflict exist.

One of the major types of learning that new principals face and which is frequently ignored in preparation programs is political skill (Bolman & Deal, 1991). We advocated in Chapter 8 that the political role is not simply a necessary evil but rather a valuable conception of the principal's role. Learning to negotiate, compromise, and bargain is a necessary and critical part of the role. Although these skills do not develop overnight, they are as critical as learning how to change culture to your becoming an innovative principal in a learning community.

Personal Sphere. In addition to learning the technical and cultural components of the internal and external parts of the job, new principals are developing personal learning. As you begin your experience in a new job and new context, you will develop a self-image as a principal. Discovering new strengths and talents of which you were unaware and learning new skills not held previously will contribute toward seeing yourself in new ways. This new self-image can be a powerful area for socialization. It can provide confidence and encouragement to take on initiatives and resolve old conflicts. However, it also can raise new conflicts among work, family, and other significant elements of your life. Reflecting on how your self-image is changing and using a mentor to help with this reflection can be a powerful learning tool.

Sources of Socialization

In the same way that the content of your socialization involves internal and external spheres, so there are internal and external sources of your socialization. In addition, you are also a source of your own socialization.

Internal Sources.   Your learning as a new principal will include two distinctive internal sources: teachers and your predecessor. Although teachers certainly influence assistant principals, they are the primary source of socialization for new principals (Duke et al., 1984). Teachers hold expectations for the new principal that influence the learning that occurs. They assume certain tasks that the principal will do. A traditional view of this assumption is that teachers expect principals to keep things running smoothly and buffer them from interruptions and irate parents. However, they also expect to have a voice in those decisions that they care about (Ortiz, 1982). The role conception we have encouraged in Chapter 8, which involves bridging rather than buffering teachers from parents, may run head on into expectations that some teachers have of you when you first arrive. Understanding the norms and values that teachers hold will help you understand what you face.

Teachers also influence the learning of new principals in terms of the information they provide. Identifying credible and trustworthy sources of information will be a major learning in your early days as a principal.

The second internal source of socialization is your predecessor as principal. A large body of literature emphasizes the importance of the predecessor for a new leader's socialization (Hart, 1993; Weindling, 1992; Weindling & Earley, 1987). In her study of new principals' socialization, Shackelford (1992) found that "when a new principal arrives on the scene, the school culture responds to everything about that person that is different from the predecessor" (p. 142). As Shackelford found, this can include gender, race, world view, and leadership style.

Your predecessor may be another principal in the same district or a neighboring district, in which case you may have the opportunity to discuss norms, values, personalities, and change attempts. Regardless of whether your predecessor is close or has moved far away, the predecessor's influence can be great. The expectations that teachers, parents, and students have of your leadership style, the tasks you do, the norms and values you hold, and the degree of interest in change will be affected by this person. Even if the faculty and staff disliked your predecessor, this person will be a major influence on expectations of you in your new role.

External Sources.   Learning to become a principal is also influenced by individuals outside the school, including district administrators, other principals, and the community. Because the external sphere of the principal's work has become so critical, these individuals become powerful sources of socialization.

District administrators are a major source of socialization for new principals in part because they hire, evaluate, and provide resources. The relationship between principals and district administrators is typically close but not necessarily positive. Districts have a stake in how new principals learn their jobs. Not only have they invested time and money in the selection process, but their own political vulnerability in the community is also affected strongly by the successes and failures of principals. District administrators use a variety of methods including selection, evaluation, and supervision to influence principals to learn to enact their roles in ways that protect district interests and maintain smooth and "silent" operations of the school (Peterson, 1984).

District administrators also influence new principals in two other ways: the autonomy they allow new principals to have and the ways they influence principals' relationships with teachers. Principals need autonomy to be able to respond to the unique circumstances of their schools. In addition, district administrators can affect the principal's relationship with teachers by ignoring the school's uniqueness, pitting the principal against the faculty, enacting unpopular policies, and limiting the principal's autonomy (Crow, 1990).

A second source of new principal socialization is the influence of other principals (Akerlund, 1988). New principals turn to veteran principals for information about district-school issues when they feel uncomfortable displaying their ignorance about policies or when information is not available from the district office. Other principals use humor and oral tradition to teach new principals. Using stories about principals who succeeded and those who failed provides powerful socializing messages to new principals.

Because the principal is a "boundary spanner" (Goldring & Rallis, 1993) between the school and the external community, powerful parents and community leaders have a strong socializing force on the new principal. These individuals bring expectations regarding appropriate role images, values, norms, and beliefs that are communicated to the principal overtly and covertly in terms of support for the principal's initiatives.

Individual Principal. Shackelford (1992) cautioned new principals, "Principals should take control of the socialization process, set their vision, refine their reflective skills, and develop the strategic sense needed to dodge the bullets and when to brace for support" (p. 163). Part of taking control of the socialization process is to acknowledge your individual characteristics that have an impact on the socialization experience. The literature suggests several individual sources of socialization, including gender, ethnicity, and prior experience.

Your gender affects socialization in a variety of ways. Crow and Pounders (1995) found that new female urban principals tended to be placed in larger schools. Such an initial context can affect the types of tasks, expectations, and resources you encounter and thus the kinds of learning necessary and available. Gender also affects role image. There is significant evidence that women, because of their longer teaching experience, tend to emphasize instructional leadership more than men "Women, then, have been found to view the job of principal or superintendent more as that of a master-teacher or educational leader, whereas men often view the job from a managerial perspective" (Shakeshaft, 1987, p. 173).

Ethnicity also can affect socialization in terms of the types of settings of the first appointment. Several researchers have found that principals of color tend to be placed in "troubled schools" (Crow & Pounders, 1995; Ortiz, 1982). Crow and Pounders found that African American principals tended to be initially appointed to schools with high Title I populations, high student poverty, high teacher absences, low student attendance, low teacher salaries, and fewer certified teachers. This type of initial appointment presents challenges, resources, and expectations from districts and the community that strongly affect the content and methods of socialization for new principals.

Ethnicity also may affect role image. For example, several researchers have pointed to the community involvement and leadership that African American principals emphasize (Lomotey, 1989; Monteiro, 1977). Ortiz (1982) suggested a subtler but negative socialization vignette. Because principals of color are placed in troubled schools, they are expected "to contain the student unrest and community complaints, but are not readily allowed to make changes regarding the physical plant, personnel, or curriculum" (p. 104).

This discussion of individual characteristics is not intended to suggest that if you are a woman or principal of color your role conception will be determined because of these socialization sources. Rather, if, as Shackelford urged (1992), new principals need to control their socialization, it is important for you to recognize how others may perceive you and how you can use these perceptions and these characteristics as ways to create more innovative role images.

Stages of Socialization

When you become a new principal, you do not suddenly move from being a total novice to being an all-knowing expert in the job. Research suggests that learning to become a principal is a gradual and evolving process that began before you were appointed and lasts for several years (Parkay & Hall, 1992). In fact, your learning to become an innovative principal does not end even after several years as a veteran principal.

There are several underlying assumptions about your development as a principal that are important to recognize. First, the influences on your learning begin before you are appointed. Your professional socialization during the administrative preparation program and your previous experience as a student and teacher both influence your learning. Another more subtle but powerful influence on your learning is the "shadows of principals past" (Weindling, 1992, p. 334). Weindling used this provocative phrase to emphasize that you enter the principalship with the previous principal's style and relationship with teachers influencing the expectations that others have of you. He quoted a new British headteacher (principal) who described this influence of the previous administrator: "One of the biggest problems for a new head is not what you do or do not do, but rather something which is out of your hands, namely, what sort of relationship existed between your predecessor and the faculty. It's annoying because there is nothing that you can do about it" (p. 335).

Four other assumptions underlie the stages of your socialization as a new principal (Parkay & Hall, 1992):

- Principals begin their careers at different stages of development.
- Principals develop within their careers at different rates.
- No single factor determines a principal's stage of development.
- Principals may operate at more than one stage simultaneously (pp. 354–355).

These assumptions emphasize that the stages of your socialization may be similar to others but that there are unique features to each new principal's socialization timeline.

Two factors that can influence the uniqueness of the development are previous administrative experience and prior organizational location. Previous experience, especially as a school administrator, can affect the school where you are appointed and may affect individual factors. Crow and Pounders (1995) found that new urban principals' first appointments tended to be affected by whether or not they had had assistant principal experience. Those with previous administrative experience tended to be placed in schools with lower teacher absences and fewer Title I and special-education students. These organizational characteristics may present different socialization experiences for new principals. Previous administrative experience may provide opportunities for new principals to have more realistic expectations, gain experience in identifying credible sources of information for decision making, and develop skills for responding to uncertainties in the school environment.

Prior organizational location also affects the unique character of the socialization process. Various researchers have found that whether a new administrator comes from outside or inside the school or district can affect socialization (Carlson, 1972; Crow & Pounder, 1994). Crow and Pounder found that principals who come from inside the district tend to focus on maintaining smooth operation and seek support from internal school constituents. Outsiders, in contrast, seek support from individuals outside the school, such as the superintendent. Where a principal finds support is likely to influence sources of socialization.

Research on socialization stages of new principals suggests three features of development: learning and uncertainty, gradual adjustment during which outcomes emerge, and stabilization (Hart, 1993). These features are translated into three stages. First, new principals begin with encounter, anticipation, and confrontation. This first stage involves confronting the differences between what you expected the principalship to be and reality. The degree of difference depends on the amount of change between the old and the new—contrast and surprise. In response to these differences, new principals engage in sense making (Louis, 1980a), that is, using past experiences and others' interpretations to understand and respond to these differences between expectations and reality. For some new principals, this stage can be difficult if these differences are extreme. Some principals come with a "Mr. Chips" conception of the role, assuming that they will become "head teachers" inspiring and mentoring their teacher protégés to excellent instruction. When they encounter the managerial complexities and demands of the role, these principals are shocked that this instructional image seems impossible. The response may be one of giving up the ideal conception and assuming a managerial role conception that emphasizes maintaining the status quo. Such a response is neither necessary nor effective for building communities where all students and educators can learn.

The second stage for a new principal emphasizes adjustment to "the work role, the people with whom [he or] she interacts and the culture of the new school" (Hart, 1993, p. 29). At this stage, the shock that confronted the principal at the first stage of socialization subsides, and the new administrator develops ways to respond to these demands. However, sometimes these responses are inappropriate or misunderstood by school constituencies. "The new principal is like a high school freshman at the first prom—ignorant of etiquette and at times a step or two behind the band" (Cabrera & Stout, 1989, quoted in Shackelford, 1992, p. 23). This second stage is the point at which various outcomes emerge. As our example at the end of the preceding paragraph suggests, these outcomes may emphasize the status quo or role conceptions that are not conducive to instructional improvement.

The third stage of socialization emphasizes stabilization, where the new principal fits into the role. This period involves the negotiation between two spheres: internally with students, faculty, and staff and externally with superiors and the community (Hart, 1993; Duke et al., 1984). However, this stage is not the end of development. In fact, Nicholson and West (1988) suggested that this is likely to be preparation for the next cycle of change and development. Because of the change inherent in work, the cycle of socialization does not end. As we emphasized in Chapter 3, work in postindustrial schools involves rapid change in response to more complex environments and technological advances. This type of change means that principals and other educators must be constantly redefining and thus relearning their roles.

Other researchers have provided more detail to the socialization stages of new principals. In a major study of principals, Parkay and Hall (1992) identified five stages: survival, control, stability, educational leadership, and professional actualization. Instead of ending with stability, these authors suggested ongoing learning and growth. In the fourth stage, educational leadership, the focus is on curriculum and instruction, and the fifth stage emphasizes creating a culture for empowerment, growth, and authenticity. With the current emphasis on learning for *all* students, the focus on instruction may occur earlier.

Another way to understand new principal socialization emphasizes how these new administrators learn to "take charge" and respond to the need for change. Weindling and Earley (1987) conducted an informative study related to socialization and change with British headteachers (principals). These researchers identified six stages that cover the first eight years of a new administrator's career:

Stage 0: Preparation prior to appointment.

Stage 1: Entry and encounter (first months). The new administrator "attempts to develop a cognitive map of the complexities of the situation, the people, the problems, and the school culture" (Weindling, 1992, p. 12).

Stage 2: Taking hold (approximately 3 to 12 months). The new administrator begins to challenge the taken-for-granted nature of the school and introduces some organizational changes. There is frequently a "honeymoon period" in which faculty are more open to change.

Stage 3: Reshaping (second year). Having gone through a full cycle of the school year, the administrator is ready to take on major changes. Faculty and staff members are also more aware of the administrator's strengths and weaknesses.

Stage 4: Refinement (third to fourth years). Administrators feel that they are "hitting their stride" by refining previous innovations and introducing other curriculum changes.

Stage 5: Consolidation (fifth to seventh years). Because changes are firmly in place, administrators begin to consolidate. New legislative and external changes result in the need to reexamine some changes.

Stage 6: Plateau (eighth year and onward). If they stay in the same school, administrators begin to feel disenchantment.

These authors found that the types of changes these new administrators learned to make were different for various stages of the career. For example, organizational changes, involving communication, consultation, and positive school image, were made in the first year. In contrast, curricular changes began in the second year. These kinds of changes entail different socialization methods and sources.

In addition to the types of changes that are related to the socialization process, new principals face a variety of critical events that create learning opportunities and designate changes in the principal's insider/outsider status. Events such as first public event, first crisis, and first performance appraisal signal that the new principal has moved from outsider to insider and from encounter stage to stabilization or adjustment (O'Brien, 1988).

Methods of Socialization

The methods or tactics that the organization and you will use in your development as a new principal are varied and individual. "New principals essentially design their own socialization process with specifics unique to each principal" (Crow & Matthews, 1998, p. 106). Although district administrators and school faculty and staff contribute to your socialization, the tactics they use are seldom formal. Although some districts have recently established mentoring programs for new principals, you have the primary responsibility for your learning.

In addition to being individual and informal, your socialization tends to be serial and include both divestiture and investiture (Van Maanen & Schein, 1979). Your primary socialization sources other than yourself are those currently or formerly in the role—school and district administrators. As we noted earlier, the subtle tactics of serial socialization encourage the maintenance of the status quo. In addition to serial socialization tactics, new principals' socialization involves both divestiture and investiture. District administrators and other principals may expect you to abandon your identity as a teacher and may even encourage an "us or them" type of view. At the same time, your previous experience may be valued in terms of becoming an instructional leader, as it was with Beth in the opening vignette. This conflict between divestiture and investiture may present dilemmas for you in learning to become an innovative principal.

In addition to the general socialization tactics described earlier, you can use specific methods to help you learn to be an innovative principal with the seven role conceptions we introduced earlier in this book. Because all these role conceptions are based on the importance of instructional improvement, your learning should be focused on making schools more effective learning organizations for all students.

Becoming a principal who is a learner is probably the most important thing you can do as a new principal. Using methods that help you to become a learner not only benefits you but also facilitates others' learning. Storytelling is a common method used by principals in their socialization. Shackelford (1992) described four types of stories she experienced in her own socialization as a new principal: historical, organizational, humorous, and inspirational. Historical stories provided information about the school before the new principal arrived. Organizational stories described the traditions and norms of the school. Humorous stories were therapeutic in responding to the differences between expectations and reality. Inspirational stories were sources of information and support. Although storytelling is not a new method, it can be useful to you in developing your learning about this new school and its history. What are the past school improvement efforts? Are they viewed as successful? Seeking out stories also communicates to teachers, students, and parents that you care about what has happened in the school and that learning is an important part of your leadership style.

Becoming a principal who is a mentor involves similar methods as we described with assistant principals, for example, identifying and seeking the help of a mentor and reflecting on your own mentoring. As a new principal, you probably will have more experience being mentored and thus more variety of mentoring styles on which to reflect. You also will have more experience mentoring others, for example, assistant principals. Reflecting on what worked and did not work will help you refine your skills. In addition, mentoring workshops through universities, districts, and professional associations can help you refine your skills.

In learning to become a principal as supervisor, you need to understand the norms and history of the school regarding supervision. Is supervision seen as "snoopervision"? Is there widespread mistrust of the principal as supervisor? Listening to stories, watching reactions from teachers when you visit classrooms, and having conversations with teachers about teaching and learning will help you learn the context in which you will be developing your supervisory style. Furthermore, asking a veteran administrator whom you trust to observe classrooms with you and give you feedback on your conferencing behaviors will help you to learn to refine your skills and knowledge as an innovative supervisor.

Becoming an innovative leader also involves socialization methods you can use. One method is to conduct your own school culture diagnosis, for example, the culture inventory described in Chapter 6 (Deal & Peterson, 1999). In specific, look for the cultural artifacts of the school, for example, celebrations, rituals, stories, and language that convey the existing culture of the school. Understanding the cultural context in which you lead is a critical first step in learning to be an innovative leader. Remember that changing culture is very difficult, especially for the new principal. Before you can lead others to change, you must take the time to understand the context in which change might occur. In addition, you can conduct a vision audit (Nanus, 1992) of your school. Doing this audit with teachers, staff, and parents also provides an opportunity for you to learn their vision of the school and to facilitate a collective vision.

Learning to be an innovative manager is critical for the new principal. Although we have emphasized the importance of being a leader, if you do not develop managerial skills, your leadership will be handicapped. Your first few months as a new principal will no doubt focus primarily on learning the managerial aspects of the job. You can use a variety of methods to help you learn these managerial skills while at the same time acknowledging the importance of leadership. For example, touring the building with custodians, lunchroom staff, counselors, librarians, and teachers will give you a sense of the physical environment and how it fosters or hinders learning. An added benefit of touring with custodians and other staff is that you communicate to these essential school constituents that creating a learning environment for all students is important to you and that their work is critical in developing this environment. Walking the building with an older student or with a parent may stimulate your thinking about issues that need to be confronted and new ways to think about solving old managerial dilemmas.

Learning to be a principal who is a politician involves understanding and developing coalitions in both internal and external spheres. O'Brien (1988) found that new principals discovered the interpersonal and political features of their jobs in conversations, school district literature, and nonverbal feedback. Conversations with various individuals both inside and outside the school, for example, at the local Kiwanis, Rotary, or Lions Clubs, not only provides you with information about how the school is viewed by the community but also initiates dialogue that eventually can result in bridges between community and school. The role of principal in building civic capacity (Goldring & Hausman, 2001), which we described in Chapter 8, can be learned through your conversations with community leaders. Visiting a local café early in the morning may provide a wealth of information in learning your political role, and it certainly does not hurt the public image of the school.

Finally, learning to be an innovative principal who as an advocate cares about and promotes the value of diversity in the school also involves methods you can use. Taking the time to meet ethnic leaders in the community and attending local churches in minority areas of the school community provide opportunities for you to learn the issues and concerns of diverse constituents. Although making these visits has public relations values to the school, the primary reason is for you to develop your own sensitivity to community diversity. In addition, meeting with district special education, ESL, and bilingual teachers and staff and visiting with parents of at-risk students are other learning opportunities for developing your skills and attitudes regarding diverse populations in the school.

Outcomes of Socialization

In addition to the three types of socialization outcomes we discussed in the assistant principal section—conformist, rebellion, and creative individualism (Schein, 1988)—new principals' socialization may result in both personal and role development (Nicholson, 1984). Personal development involves changes in professional identity. Role development, in contrast, involves changing the conception of the job itself. Both of these are possible as you move into the principalship.

Nicholson (1984) identified four possible outcomes that result from various socialization methods. First, replication results when neither your self image nor the role change. Second, absorption occurs when your self image changes but the role does not change. Both of these are custodial outcomes. Third, determination occurs when you as a new principal change very little, but the role changes extensively. Fourth, exploration occurs when both personal and role development occur. As Hart (1993) pointed out, any of these four outcomes can be functional or dysfunctional. For example, changing the role but not your image of your professional identity may stifle your learning.

One of the most important points in the previous discussion is the importance of affective development—your personal identity. Hart (1993) pointed out that typically socialization for new principals emphasizes the technical aspects of the job, for example, learning how to develop a budget; however, affective and emotional growth is just as important and possibly more important. Learning to become an innovative principal involves more than learning how to do the tasks of the job. The learning we encourage in this book involves your identity as a learner, mentor, supervisor, leader, manager, politician, and advocate. Such learning involves the values, attitudes, and self image you develop that enable you to move beyond the traditional to more innovative role conceptions that affect schools as learning environments for all students.

> If job change has the power to effect changes in identity as well as in organizational performance, then how the transition process is managed has a vital bearing on the well-being and effectiveness of organizations. It would appear that few organizations recognize this (Nicholson & West, 1988, p. 212).

Not only should organizations realize the importance of how learning influences their effectiveness, but new principals also must recognize that how they learn the job influences the role conceptions they develop.

Becoming an Innovative Mid-Career Principal

Although this book focuses on being and becoming a new assistant principal or principal, learning to be an innovative school leader is a continuing process. Thus we end this chapter by examining socialization at mid-career. Because learning to be innovative will be an ongoing process in your career, it is important for you to understand how your socialization continues after you are established in the position. The pattern of learning you develop now is likely to be the pattern you rely on later in your career.

Focusing on socialization at mid-career is also important because, as we discussed in Chapter 3, work in postindustrial society requires you to constantly redefine work roles and conceptions. Due to the complexity created by changing demographics and technology, work roles in schools, like other occupational contexts, will require you and the school to constantly reexamine and redefine how work in a professional learning community is organized, conducted, and learned.

Mid-career is a confusing concept because it does not necessarily mean the same as midlife. A more useful definition of mid-career is the period occurring "during one's work in an occupational (career) role after one feels established and has achieved perceived mastery and prior to the commencement of the disengagement process" (Hall, 1986, p. 127). For principals, this can occur any time after the major tasks of the role are mastered; there is no set time (Parkay & Hall, 1992). Weindling (1992) found that between the third and fourth years, new British headteachers were "hitting their stride," ready to redefine their work in school change.

Mid-career also involves a variety of different types of changes. One way to categorize these changes is in terms of inter-role and intra-role career transitions (Louis, 1980b). Inter-role transitions involve such changes as entry/reentry to a job or organization or department, movement to a new profession, or exit. Intra-role transitions include changes in role conception by remaining in the same role, expanding to additional roles, and responding to changes in role, career, and life stage. The most obvious midcareer inter-role transitions for principals involve changing schools or districts (inter-role transitions). The most obvious intra-role transitions involve changing role conceptions, adding an additional role (e.g., officer in a professional organization), or moving to a new stage of career or life (e.g., empty-nest stage). The transition that is most pertinent to us in this book involves changes in role conception, where the individual and/or the organization are redefining the role.

Unique Features of Mid-Career Socialization

Instead of discussing the content, sources, stages, methods, and outcomes of socialization, as we have done in the discussions of assistant principal and principal socialization, we will identify several unique features of mid-career socialization before discussing methods that mid-career principals can use in becoming innovative principals in a learning community. These features are identified in the literature on mid-career socialization, most notably in the work of Hall (1980, 1986).

First, mid-career socialization tends to have fewer institutionalized status passages. Instead of university graduation and administrative licensure as formal events that recognize the passage to a new role, mid-career socialization involves more subtle changes. For example, recognition by the principal of gradual demographic changes in the school may initiate a different way of conceptualizing the principal's role in integrating diverse populations in the school and creating an environment where all students learn. No formal ceremony is likely to acknowledge this change. However, the change is no less important.

Second, the socialization process at mid-career tends to emphasize individual rather than collective methods. Although the district may provide formal training in new methods for mid-career principals, for example, ESL training, it is more likely that role conception changes will occur by the individual principal's efforts to learn more about linguistic differences. This does not mean that districts have no role to play in mid-career socialization to more innovative role conceptions. Rather, individual efforts tend to be more likely at this stage. Veteran principals who strive to be innovative use peer mentoring; conversations with colleagues, university faculty, and teachers; and a variety of other individual methods.

Third, the sources of socialization tend to be different at mid-career than at the beginning of the career. Peers, family, and friends take on a more pronounced role in influencing mid-career changes. Rather than more experienced principals being the source of socialization, peers at similar career stages may be more influential. Furthermore, because family and life stages become more important, family members have an increasing influence on the socialization process to new role conceptions. This can work toward either custodial or innovative outcomes. If family members believe that the redefined role conception takes away from family obligations, they may try to discourage the change. However, if family members see the principal as frustrated in the role, they may encourage innovations that would bring excitement and challenge to the role.

Fourth, mid-career socialization involves a heightened awareness of longer-term dimensions of career effectiveness. Various models of adult and teacher development point to the move from concerns with survival and mastery to concerns of effectiveness and impact (Fuller, 1969). In mid-career, after the tasks of the role are mastered, principals should focus more on effectiveness. Questions of whether or not they are having an impact on the lives of students and the work of teachers should become more critical. Thus the outcomes of mid-career socialization are not just redefining the role but doing so in a way that enables the principal to have an impact on learning for students, families, teachers, and the larger community.

Fifth, mid-career socialization may involve more of the process of undoing earlier career socialization and separating from an old role. Frequently, mid-career principals who are committed to innovation realize that the images they developed earlier in their careers must be abandoned in order to view their roles differently. For example, the traditional image of the role of teacher as deficient that many principals acquired early in their careers must be undone in order to think about a conception of supervisor that affirms teachers' voice and expertise. Abandoning a safe image of the role is, in many respects, much more difficult than acquiring a new image at the beginning of the career because it means moving from an image of oneself as master to one of novice.

Sixth, one of the major methods of mid-career socialization is exploration (Hall, 1986). Exploration is necessary to identify what options are available to redefine a role. Sometimes this means trying on new images of the role to determine whether or not they fit the context and the individual. Exploration does not mean abandoning everything that one has learned, but rather it frequently involves a more incremental process of determining whether a new image fits with a previous image.

Learning to Be an Innovative Principal at Mid-Career

We have emphasized that much of the socialization at mid-career is individual rather than collective. You can use a variety of methods to become an innovative principal at mid-career who develops the kinds of role conceptions we discussed earlier in this book.

In order to become an innovative principal who emphasizes learning, it is important to recognize that your learning does not end with mastery of the tasks of the principalship. The context in which your school is located, the technology of teaching and learning, and a host of other factors require constant learning. Finding ways to keep abreast of the latest research on instructional improvement, on changes in your school and community, and on leadership will help you to become the kind of principal that not only is a learner but also facilitates the learning of others. As we have mentioned several times, your example as a learner encourages teachers, students, parents, and others to view themselves as learners and to see the school as a learning community.

Becoming an innovative principal as mentor at mid-career can involve a new resource—peer mentoring. Although new principals certainly can use their peers as a method of socialization, peer mentoring is an invaluable resource for mid-career colleagues who have developed a wealth of expertise. In exploring more innovative role conceptions, veteran principals can use conversations and reflections with peers. Sharing, reflecting, and collaborating regarding the change and learning processes are important elements of peer mentoring (Crow & Matthews, 1998). This peer mentoring experience can be an excellent source for developing new conceptions of mentoring that contribute to the improvement of teaching and learning in the school.

Redefining the role of principal as supervisor can occur as the veteran principal engages in discussions with university professors, administrative colleagues, and teachers on the latest research on teaching and learning and on new innovative strategies for working with teachers to improve instruction for all students. More and more universities are expanding their roles beyond preservice to assist administrators and teachers in improving teaching and learning. The veteran principal's concern for long-term effectiveness allows the principal to move beyond simple mastery to work with teachers in ways that facilitate peer supervision.

As demographic and technological changes continue to occur, veteran principals will need to think in new ways about how leadership is enacted and how leaders influence changing cultures within the school. New research on distributed leadership (Elmore, 2000), encourages the need for veteran principals to conceive of their roles in new ways. Keeping up with the new leadership literature and having conversations with colleagues on new ways to conceive of the leadership role are excellent methods for learning to be an innovative veteran school leader. Also, as environmental changes occur, it will be necessary for veteran principals to help faculty and parents rethink the school's cultural norms and beliefs. Inviting a colleague either inside education or outside to help inventory the school culture can be a valuable socialization method for learning and redefining this critical leadership role.

At mid-career, most principals have mastered managerial tasks. However, rather than use the same old, tried and true managerial methods, an innovative school leader needs to watch for more efficient managerial techniques that will permit more time for leadership activities. Conversations with managers in other fields may provide information regarding these new techniques.

With more complex environmental settings and demands, the veteran principal must redefine the political role. Finding mentors and other administrators who are sensitive to these societal changes can provide socialization methods for learning this redefinition. Mentors that work outside school or district organizations, for example, doctors with interns, ministers, and directors of nonprofit agencies, can be valuable resources in learning innovative ways to respond to external communities.

Other mentors can be useful in helping to learn new ways to conceive of the role of principal as advocate that recognizes the value of diversity. Changing demographics and more heterogeneous communities require veteran principals to learn new ways to respond to diversity. Mentoring by ethnic community leaders, conversations with ministers from ethnic churches, travel, and reading literature that describes the experiences of diverse populations broaden the veteran principal's sense of the nature and value of diversity.

Conclusion

In this chapter we moved from a discussion of *being* an innovative principal, which involved the seven role conceptions, to *becoming* an innovative principal. The importance of learning has been foundational throughout this book, and your own learning to become an innovative principal is not something to leave to chance. Beth, the principal in the opening vignette, found that her relationship with her mentor, Debbie, was a valuable tool to help her intentionally reflect on her learning. Hopefully, you are already developing resources in your university program and your relationships with peers that will serve as tools for your own development as an innovative principal.

To aid you in this development, we have described the nature, sources, stages, methods, and outcomes of socialization for new principals and assistant principals. These are presented in this book to help you intentionally reflect on and enrich your own development.

We also have emphasized that learning to become an innovative principal or assistant principal is not a one-time event but a career-long endeavor. In Chapter 3 we stressed that one of the features of work roles in postindustrial society is the ongoing redefining of the role. In the final chapter we present some considerations for the future of the role. Just as the principalship is changing to meet postindustrial realities, you can expect that new realities will confront you as you continue in the role. Becoming a lifelong learner who can proactively respond to these future realities is essential to creating and maintaining learning environments for *all* students.

Activities

Self-Reflecting Activity

Reflect on your prior work experience. In what ways does it influence your current learning to be a principal or assistant principal. For example, what are you likely to emphasize? What tools or styles of learning are you likely to use? How do your family and friends influence your socialization?

Peer-Reflecting Activities

1. With a colleague, interview an assistant principal in her or his second year. What were the sources of socialization in this assistant principal's school? Who influenced her or his learning, and what methods were used?

2. Consider principals with whom you have worked. How would you characterize the outcome of their socialization using Schein's (1971) three orientations of custodial, content innovation, and role innovation. What is your evidence for this characterization?

Course Activities

1. Invite a panel of new principals to class. Interview them in terms of what they had to learn in their first few days/weeks on the job. How did they learn these things? Organize your questions and analysis in terms of the three areas of work knowledge/skills, adjustment to the work environment, and learning values.

2. Collect job descriptions for a variety of principal vacancies. Analyze the job content. What kinds of learning would be necessary? Brainstorm methods for learning these things.

Websites

http://www.ucea.org/cases/
> *Cases from the Journal of Cases in Educational Leadership*
> Talbot, D. (2000). Out with the old, in with the new: Principal succession at Liberty High. *Journal of Cases in Educational Leadership 3*(1).
> Hackman, D. (1999). Interviewing for the principalship. *Journal of Cases in Educational Leadership 2*(2).

References

Akerlund, P. M. (1988). The socialization of first-year principals and vice-principals. Unpublished doctoral dissertation, Seattle University.

Austin, B. D., & Brown, H. L. (1970). *Report of the Assistant Principalship.* Washington: National Association of Secondary School Principals.

Baker, R. Z. (1990). A control perspective of organizational socialization: Tactics, tolerance for organizational influence, and outcomes for new entrants. Unpublished doctoral dissertation, University of California at Los Angeles.

Bell, D. (1973). *The Coming of Post-Industrial Society.* New York: Basic Books.

Bolman, L. G., & Deal, T. E. (1991). *Reframing Organizations.* San Francisco: Jossey-Bass.

Cabrera, R., & Stout, K. (1989). Helpful hints for first-year principals. *Principal 68*, 22–24.

Callahan, R. E. (1962). *Education and the Cult of Efficiency: A Study of the Social Forces That Have Shaped the Administration of Public Schools.* Chicago: University of Chicago Press.

Carlson, R. O. (1972). *School Superintendents: Careers and Performance.* Columbus, OH: Charles E. Merrill.

Crow, G. M. (1987). Career mobility of elementary school principals and conflict with the central office. *Urban Review 19*(3), 139–150.

Crow, G. M. (1990). Central office influence on the principal's relationship with teachers. *Administrators Notebook 34*(1), 1–4.

Crow, G. M., Hausman, C. S., & Scribner, J. P. (2002). Reshaping the role of the school principal. In J. Murphy (Ed.), *The Educational Leadership Challenge: Redefining Leadership for the 21st Century.* Chicago: National Society for the Study of Education.

Crow, G. M., & Matthews, L. J. (1998). *Finding One's Way. How Mentoring Can Lead to Dynamic Leadership.* Thousand Oaks, CA: Corwin Press.

Crow, G. M., & Pounders, M. L. (1994, October). *The symbolic nature of the administrative internship: Building a sense of occupational community.* Paper presented at the University Council for Educational Administration, Philadelphia.

Crow, G. M., & Pounders, M. L. (1995). *Organizational socialization of new urban principals: Variations of race and gender.* Paper presented at the American Educational Research Association, San Francisco.

Crow, G. M., & Pounders, M. L. (1996, April). *The administrative internship: "Learning the ropes" of an occupational culture.* Paper presented at the American Educational Research Association, New York.

Deal, T. E., & Peterson, K. D. (1999). *Shaping School Culture: The Heart of Leadership.* San Francisco: Jossey-Bass.

Duke, D. L., Isaacson, N. S., Sagor, R., & Schmuck, P. A. (1984). *Transition to Leadership: An Investigation of the First Year of the Principal* (Transition to Leadership Project). Portland, OR: Lewis and Clark College.

Elmore, R. (2000). *Building a New Structure for School Leadership.* Albert Shanker Institute.

Feldman, D. C. (1976). A contingency theory of socialization. *Administrative Science Quarterly 21*, 433–452.

Feldman, D. C. (1981). The multiple socialization of organization members. *Academy of Management Review 6*, 309-318.

Fisher, C. (1986). Organizational socialization: An integrative review. *Research in Personnel and Human Resources Management 4*, 101–145.

Fuller, F. F. (1969). Concerns of teachers: A developmental conceptualization. *American Educational Research Journal 6*(2), 207–266.

Goldring, E. B., & Rallis, S. F. (1993). *Principals of Dynamic Schools*. Newbury Park, CA: Corwin Press.

Greenfield, W. D. (1977a). Administrative candidacy: A process of new role learning, part I. *Journal of Educational Administration 15*(1), 30–48.

Greenfield, W. D. (1985a, April). *Being and becoming a principal: Responses to work contexts and socialization processes*. Paper presented at the American Educational Research Association, Chicago.

Greenfield, W. D. (1985b). Studies of the assistant principalship: Toward new avenues of inquiry. *Education and Urban Society 18*(1), 7–27.

Greenfield, W. D., Marshall, C., & Reed, D. B. (1986). Experience in the vice principalship: Preparation for leading schools. *Journal of Educational Administration 24*(1), 107–121.

Hage, J. & Powers, C. (1992). *Post-industrial Lives. Roles and Relationships in the 21st Century*. Newbury Park, CA: Sage.

Hall, D. T. (1980). Socialization processes in later career years: Can there be growth at terminal level? In C. B. Derr (Ed.), *Work, Family, and the Career* (pp. 219–236). New York: Praeger.

Hall, D. T. (1986). Breaking career routines: Mid-career choice and identity development. In D. T. Hall (ed.), *Career Development in Organizations* (pp. 120–159). San Francisco: Jossey-Bass.

Hall, D. T. (1987). Careers and socialization. *Journal of Management 13*(2), 302–321.

Hart, A. W. (1993). *Principal Succession: Establishing Leadership in Schools*. Albany, NY: State University of New York Press.

Hess, F. (1985). The socialization of the assistant principal: From the perspective of the local school district. *Education and Urban Society 18*(1), 93–106.

Hughes, E. C. (1959). The study of occupations. In R. K. Merton, L. Broom, & L. Cottrell (Eds.), *Sociology Today* (pp. 442–458). New York: Basic Books.

Jones, G. R. (1986). Socialization tactics, self-efficacy, and newcomers' adjustments to organizations. *Academy of Management Journal 29*(2), 262–279.

Lomotey, K. (1989). *African-American Principals: School Leadership and Success*. New York: Greenwood.

Long, D. H. (1988). *A study of the socialization process of beginning public school administrators*. Unpublished doctoral dissertation, Vanderbilt University, Nashville, TN.

Louis, M. R. (1980a). Surprise and sensemaking: What newcomers experience in entering unfamiliar organizational settings. *Administrative Science Quarterly 25*(2), 226–251.

Louis, M. R. (1980b). Toward an understanding of career transitions. In C. B. Derr (Ed.), *Work, Family, and the Career* (pp. 200–218). New York: Praeger.

Marshall, C. (1985). Professional shock: The enculturation of the assistant principal. *Education and Urban Society 18*(1), 28–58.

Monteiro, T. (1977). Ethnicity and the perceptions of principals. *Integrated Education 15*(3), 15–16.

Mortimer, J. T., & Simmons, R. G. (1978). Adult socialization. *Annual Review of Sociology 4*, 421–454.

Nanus, B. (1992). *Visionary Leadership: Creating a Compelling Sense of Direction for Your Organization*. San Francisco: Jossey-Bass.

Nicholson, N. (1984). A theory of work role transitions. *Administrative Science Quarterly 29*(2), 172–191.

Nicholson, N., & West, M. A. (1988). *Managerial Job Change: Men and Women in Transition*. Cambridge, England: Cambridge University Press.

O'Brien, D. E. (1988). Taking the role of principal: A qualitative investigation of the socialization during the first year. Unpublished doctoral dissertation, Kent State University.

Ortiz, F. I. (1982). *Career Patterns in Education: Women, Men, and Minorities*. New York: Praeger.

Osterman, K. F., & Kottkamp, R. B. (1993). *Reflective Practice for Educators. Improving Schooling Through Professional Development.* Newbury Park, CA: Corwin Press.

Parkay, F. W., & Hall, G. E. (1992). *Becoming a Principal. The Challenges of Beginning Leadership.* Boston: Allyn & Bacon.

Peterson, K. D. (1977-78). The principal's tasks. *Administrator's Notebook 26,* 1–4.

Peterson, K. D. (1984). Mechanisms of administrative control over managers in educational organizations. *Administrative Science Quarterly 29,* 573–597.

Post, D. (1992). Through Joshua Gap: Curricular control and the constructed community. *Teachers College Record 93*(4), 673–696.

Reed, D. B., & Himmler, A. H. (1985). The work of the secondary assistant principal. *Education and Urban Society 18*(1), 59–84.

Schein, E. H. (1971). Occupational socialization in the professions: The case of the role innovator. *Journal of Psychiatric Research 8,* 521–530.

Schein, E. H. (1988). Organizational socialization and the profession of management. *Sloan Management Review,* February, 53–65.

Schein, E. H. (1992). *Organizational Culture and Leadership* (2nd ed.). San Francisco: Jossey-Bass.

Schein, E. H. & Ott, J. S. (1962). The legitimacy of organizational influence. *American Journal of Sociology 67,* 682–689.

Shackelford, J. A. (1992). *An uphill battle: Socialization of a novice female elementary principal.* Unpublished doctoral dissertation, Oklahoma State University, Stillwater, OK.

Shakeshaft, C. (1987). *Women in Educational Administration.* Newbury Park, CA: Sage.

Spady, W. G. (1985). The vice-principal as an agent of instructional reform. *Education and Urban Society 18*(1), 107–120.

Stout, K. R. (2000). The re-conceptualization of organizational socialization: The multiple levels of inclusion and exclusion in sorority membership. Unpublished doctoral dissertation, University of Utah, Salt Lake City, UT.

Trice, H. M. (1993). *Occupational Subcultures in the Workplace.* Ithaca, NY: ILR Press.

Van Maanen, J. (1984). Doing new things in old ways: The chains of socialization. In J. L. Bess (Ed.), *College and University Organization* (pp. 211–247). New York: New York University Press.

Van Maanen, J., & Schein, E. H. (1979). Toward a theory of organizational socialization. In B. M. Staw & L. L. Cummings (Eds.), *Research in Organizational Behavior* (Vol. 1, pp. 209–264). Greenwich, CT: JAI Press.

Weick, K. E. (1979). *The Social Psychology of Organizing* (2nd ed.). Reading, MA: Addison-Wesley.

Weindling, D. (1992). New heads for old: Beginning principals in the United Kingdom. In F. W. Parkay & G. E. Hall (Eds.), *Becoming a Principal: The Challenges of Beginning Leadership* (pp. 329–348). Boston: Allyn & Bacon.

Weindling, D., & Earley, P. l. (1987). *Secondary Headship: The First Years.* Philadelphia: NFER-Nelson.

Wentworth, W. M. (1980). *Context and Understanding: An Inquiry into Socialization Theory.* New York: Elsevier.

Looking to the Future as a Principal 11

Vignette

Angela sat at her office desk as the new principal of Truman Middle School. The teachers and students would arrive in one week. She was excited and terrified! She felt good about her university training and the assistant principal experience she had had. Elaine, her mentor and the principal of the school where she had served as assistant principal, had given her many opportunities to develop skills in working with students, teachers, parents, and the larger community. The superintendent had expressed enormous support for her and obviously had great expectations.

Truman was a new middle school formed after the district decided to focus on middle-level education. Although the building was not new, Angela had had some say in the remodeling of the building and the selection of faculty and staff. She knew that the teachers, board members, and community would be looking over her shoulder to see if this middle-level education concept really worked and whether this new principal could succeed.

One of Angela's major concerns was how to instill a sense of professional learning community in the school and a strong school-community connection. The community was made up primarily of professionals working at the new computer software company that had just been built in the area. Angela knew that these young professionals had high expectations for the school that centered around preparing their young adolescents for challenging but uncertain futures.

During the school board debates over middle-level education and her appointment as principal of the school, some board members wondered out loud if the principalship was still a viable role in the school or if they should create a new school led by a committee of teachers. Others had more traditional views but still questioned whether a newcomer could fill this role adequately.

As Angela pondered the year that lay ahead, she considered what skills she would need to define her role in ways, perhaps, that were very different from what her mentor or others who had prepared her had assumed. A year from now, how would she define her role as principal?

I **ntroduction**   In this book we have identified seven role conceptions of the principalship. Our attempt has been to identify innovative ways to imagine the principalship. One of our arguments throughout this book has been the importance of understanding and redefining the role. Any attempt to identify the role conceptions of the principalship suffers from one major difficulty. The society in which schools exist and the schools themselves are in a state of constant change. It is not surprising, then, that the role of principals also must change. In this concluding chapter we speculate about how the principalship may change in the coming years. Your experience as an assistant principal or principal also will change as you progress through your career.

In this chapter we will identify several possible scenarios for the future of the principalship. We do not claim that the scenarios are accurate descriptions of the future. We hope, however, that these scenarios provide an opportunity to reflect on your future as an assistant principal or principal.

Before identifying possible scenarios for the future of the principalship, we identify ten societal trends that will affect schools and principals and assistant principals who serve them (Marx, 2000). The societal trends include

1. For the first time in history, the old will outnumber the young.
2. The country will become a nation of minorities.
3. Social and intellectual capital will become the primary economic values in society.
4. Education will shift from averages to individuals.
5. The millennial generation will insist on solutions to accumulated problems and injustices.
6. Continuous improvement and collaboration will replace quick fixes and defense of the status quo.
7. Technology will increase the speed of communication and the pace of advancement or decline.
8. Knowledge creation and breakthrough thinking will stir a new era of enlightenment.
9. Scientific discoveries and societal realities will force widespread ethical choices.
10. Competition will increase as industries and professions intensify their efforts to attract and keep talented people.

These societal trends suggest several changes that will affect schools, principals, and assistant principals. It is obvious from these trends that schools and their leaders will experience changing demographics. The students of the schools of the future will not be like the students of the 1950s or even the 1990s, which were the times when much of the current curricula were developed and buildings were built. Principals, assistant principals, and teachers must recognize that many of the programs that were established to meet the needs of former students no longer work to meet the changing demographics and technological needs of future students.

These societal trends also suggest that education will be even more important in the future. Knowledge will be the coin of the realm (Marx, 2000). But education in the future may take forms that are very different from what we expect now. Instead of the school building being the only or even primary place for creating knowledge, the Internet and other technologies will enable students and adults to access information, act on the information, and solve problems that did not exist several years ago.

Social justice, instead of being a minor interest of the school, will be a major focus. The changing demographics, the gap between the rich and the poor, and the millennial generation's concern with solving problems of injustice will influence responsibilities for educators. Instead of the insulated form of schools of the past, schools now and in the future must become intimately connected with their neighborhoods and with the larger societies in which injustices thrive.

The societal trends and the current concern with accountability will demand that schools demonstrate improvement rather than simply assume their continued existence. Although there is much to criticize in the current emphasis on accountability and standardization, the societal interest that schools improve and that they demonstrate this improvement is not likely to disappear in the future.

Only someone who has lived on a desert island for the last twenty years would ignore the role of technology in our society and education. Technology will become an even more important resource for schools to use in improving learning and opening access to all students. For this to occur, the digital gap between the rich and the poor must be bridged. Schools are one of the more likely places for this to occur.

Contemporary and future schools must see their role as knowledge creation, not just information acquisition. This means that principals and teachers must create learning communities that build understanding and learning capacity.

The societal trends also suggest major ethical choices for students and the schools that serve them in the future. Access to technology, medical advances, income disparities, disenfranchisement of large segments of the population, and the disillusionment of segments of the society present major ethical dilemmas from which schools are not immune.

The importance of education, especially from an economic point of view, increases the competition for controlling and providing that education. Business organizations in particular are developing alternative methods for delivering education. Schools no longer have a monopoly on providing education. Even within school districts, the emergence of charter schools and other alternative choices has increased competition among schools, especially in recruiting and retaining teachers and students.

The societal trends we have identified have critical implications for the changing role of principals and assistant principals. First, these trends suggest the importance of the internal environment in which principals and assistant principals do their jobs. The major implication of these trends for this internal role is the importance of building a professional learning community that promotes the learning of all students. As we suggested in earlier chapters, the principal's role as learner is fundamental for creating innovative leadership for the future. The principal's roles as learner, mentor, and supervisor are critical in creating an environment where knowledge is created, where both adults and students have access, and where the expertise for teaching and learning is distributed.

Second, the role of principals and assistant principals has external implications. No longer can these administrative roles be focused solely on what happens inside the walls of the school. Principals and assistant principals have fundamental responsibilities for communicating the importance of social justice, implementing programs and structures that give voice to the disenfranchised, and monitoring school activities to make sure that social justice initiatives become reality. However, these school leaders have an even more fundamental responsibility to facilitate the sensitivity and commitment of school constituencies toward these social justice initiatives. This external role of principals and assistant principals also necessitates that bridges with external communities be built in the years to come. The day of buffering as the primary strategy for dealing with external communities is over.

Third, the societal trends require a new kind of leadership. This leadership, rather than being based on the positional authority of one person, resides in the distributed leadership of the whole school. Facilitating the leadership of both internal and external communities becomes critical to responding to the societal trends. In addition, this leadership is an ever-evolving and dynamic role. In postindustrial society, leadership roles as well as all other roles must be redefined constantly based on changing environments. Finding a comfortable style and sticking with it for your career are neither effective nor possible in schools of tomorrow.

We suggest four possible scenarios for the future of the principalship. Our purpose is not to see how accurately we can forecast the future but rather to identify possible directions for your consideration as you define and ultimately redefine your role as a principal or assistant principal.

The first scenario is one in which the traditional role of the principalship remains. Leadership is defined in this scenario as the influence and actions of one person. The focus would be on maintaining the status quo in schools. A managerial orientation would consume the attention of principals and assistant principals. Obviously, from the perspective taken in this book, we do not believe that this is likely to be a viable alternative. Maintaining the status quo in the face of the societal trends we have identified is neither likely nor effective.

The second scenario involves the elimination of the roles of principal and assistant principal. This scenario has been considered for several years. The argument is that the principal's responsibilities are too numerous for instructional leadership to be emphasized. When principals have been shadowed in their job, instructional activities are found to be the least frequent. Those who argue for this scenario suggest that teachers or parent-community representatives would be better school leaders than bureaucratic principals. Obviously, the perspective of this book is that the roles of principal and assistant principal should be enriched and emphasized rather than eliminated.

Professional Dilemma 11.1

In a large school district that included both inner-city and suburban schools, the assistant principals of color traditionally were placed in the most ethnically diverse schools. As role models for many students of color, these assistant principals served well in the urban schools. However, the suburban schools often had no administrators of color, limiting their perspective to mostly Caucasian models. Should the ethnicity of administrators be considered in their placement at schools?

The third scenario involves moving the principal's role to a business-manager role, with teachers being responsible for instructional leadership. The concept of the principal's role would be similar to that of a hospital administrator. In most hospitals, a medical director oversees the medical functions of the organization, whereas a nonmedical administrator handles the business and managerial responsibilities. Many writers suggest that focusing the principal's attention on the business-management functions of the school makes the role more realistic and follows historical patterns that emphasize the efficiency role of school administrators. There have been attempts to implement this type of role change; however, the typical difficulty has involved freeing teachers for instructional leadership responsibilities. Nevertheless, this bi-leadership scenario is being seriously considered and practiced in some locations.

The final scenario involves a much more complex role for the principal and assistant principal. The tasks of this role are varied, dynamic, and evolving. This scenario could take shape in at least three ways. First, several writers argue for distributed leadership in schools (Hallinger & Richardson, 1988; Elmore, 2000; Spillane, Halverson, & Diamond, 2001). Rather than seeing the principal as the only leader, this approach argues for multiple leadership roles that can be fulfilled by a variety of individuals. Second, this scenario could be seen as balancing internal and external complexities (Crow, Hausman, & Scribner, 2002). Principals would be responsible internally for facilitating the development of a professional learning community committed to the learning of all students. Externally, principals' primary role would involve building bridges for accountability, markets, and civic capacity. In this view, principals are also not seen as the sole leaders but rather as the facilitators of leadership that balance external and internal complexity. Schools of the future, like schools of the present, involve the balance of continuity and change. Thomas Friedman (1999), in his work on globalization entitled, *The Lexus and the Olive Tree*, suggested that we live in an age of continuity and change. This is an age in which modern technology has changed our patterns of living and interacting. However, it is also an age where we yearn for stability, continuity, and home. The school traditionally has been the center of the community. In postindustrial society, the question of whether the school can be both a place of technological advancement and a community center is certainly an important issue for debate. However, the reality for principals and assistant principals of balancing continuity and change is more than a topic for debate; it is a fundamental dilemma of the role.

This final scenario involving a more complex role for the principal also can be seen in terms of three metaphors. Murphy (2002) identified these three metaphors as moral steward, educator, and community builder. The moral-steward metaphor suggests that the role of principal should be focused on values and value judgments. Principals and assistant principals, as we have argued, have a social-justice role to play. This moral-steward role involves a concern with defining purpose and vision. However, in this role conception, vision is a means not an end. The metaphor of educator means that the principal's role will be based in the culture of teaching. As we discussed in Chapter 2, teaching is the historical basis for the principal role. In Murphy's formulation, the principalship would return to its roots. The principal as educator would move from leadership as management to leadership as learning. Finally, the metaphor of community building focuses the principal role on facilitating access and voice for parents and community members. In addition, this metaphor calls attention to the need for principals to build communities of learning and personalized learning environments for *all* students.

Conclusion

Just as Angela, the new principal at Truman Middle School in the opening vignette, contemplated the future, you are standing at that threshold now. This is an exciting time to become an assistant principal or principal. The societal trends and possible scenarios previously identified make it clear that things will not be as they have been for school leaders. Over the next several years you will see fundamental changes in the way schooling is provided, in the way teaching is enacted, in the way learning occurs, and in the way school leadership is conceived.

Rather than being a passive spectator watching these changes occur around you, you can and should play an active role in helping to shape the way schools and school leaders respond to the societal trends. Learning to be an innovative principal or assistant principal for the next generation requires you to be an active participant in this process. Principals and assistant principals must not play the same roles they have played in the past. The future of our students—and the larger global society—depends on your active participation.

Activities

Self-Reflecting Activities

1. Visualize a school without a principal. What would it look like in terms of leadership?
2. Reflect on each of the three forms of the final scenario. Which appeals to you and why?

Peer-Reflecting Activities

1. Consider the ten societal trends. How are these affecting your current educator role?
2. Reflect on the issues regarding balancing continuity and change in schools. What does the principal's role become in the balancing process?

Course Activities

1. Debate two of the three forms of the final scenario.
2. Divide the class into three groups. Assign each group one of Murphy's (2002) three metaphors: moral steward, educator, and community builder. Have each group elaborate on what these might mean for how principals enact their roles.

References

Crow, G. M., Hausman, C. S., & Scribner, J. P. (2002). Reshaping the role of the school principal. In J. Murphy (Ed.), *The Leadership Challenge: Redefining Leadership for the 21st Century* (pp. 189–210). Chicago: National Society for the Study of Education.

Elmore, R. (2000). *Building a New Structure for School Leadership*. Albert Shanker Institute.

Friedman, T. L. (1999). *The Lexus and the Olive Tree*. New York: Farrar Straus Grioux.

Hallinger, P., & Richardson, D. (1988). Models of shared leadership: Evolving structures and relationships. *The Urban Review 20*(4), 229–245.

Marx, G. (2000). *Ten Trends: Educating Children for a Profoundly Different Future*. Arlington, VA: Educational Research Service.

Murphy, J. (2002). Reculturing the profession of educational leadership: New blueprints. In J. Murphy (Ed.), *The Educational Leadership Challenge: Redefining Leadership for the 21st Century*. Chicago: National Society for the Study of Education.

Spillane, J. P., Halverson, R., & Diamond, J. B. (2001). Investigating school leadership practice: A distributed perspective. *Educational Researcher 30*(3), 23–28.

Index